OUR NEW PUBLIC,
A CHANGING CLIENTELE

Cleveland State University Library Lounge, partial view with closed caption television

OUR NEW PUBLIC, A CHANGING CLIENTELE

Bewildering Issues or New Challenges for Managing Libraries?

Edited by James R. Kennedy, Lisa Vardaman, and Gerard B. McCabe

Foreword by Henry Stewart

Preface by Bernadette Roberts Storck

LIBRARIES UNLIMITED LIBRARY MANAGEMENT COLLECTION

A Member of the Greenwood Publishing Group

Westport, Connecticut • London

Library of Congress Cataloging-in-Publication Data

Our new public, a changing clientele : bewildering issues or new challenges
for managing libraries? / edited by James R. Kennedy, Lisa Vardaman,
and Gerard B. McCabe.
    p. cm. — (Libraries Unlimited library management collection,
ISSN 1557–0320)
  Includes bibliographical references and index.
  ISBN 978–1–59158–407–0 (alk. paper)
 1. Library administration.   2. Academic libraries—Administration.   3. Library
users—Effect of technological innovations on.   4. Libraries and students.
5. Generation Y—Attitudes. I. Kennedy, James R. (James Robert),
1943– II. Vardaman, Lisa. III. McCabe, Gerard B.
  Z678.O92   2008
  025.1—dc22   2007035907

British Library Cataloguing in Publication Data is available.

Library of Congress Catalog Card Number: 2007035907
ISBN: 978–1–59158–407–0
ISSN: 1557–0320

First published in 2008

Libraries Unlimited, 88 Post Road West, Westport, CT 06881
A Member of the Greenwood Publishing Group, Inc.
www.lu.com

Printed in the United States of America

The paper used in this book complies with the
Permanent Paper Standard issued by the National
Information Standards Organization (Z39.48–1984).

10 9 8 7 6 5 4 3 2 1

CONTENTS

CONTENTS

Part VII. Hope for the Future

Part VIII. Bibliographic Essays

FOREWORD

When reviewing the history of libraries, one finds that the earliest libraries were really more archives collections than libraries, and they included records of commercial transactions that would be of limited interest, except for those in need of business records. Libraries changed over the centuries with the development of different means to store and record information. There was change from clay tablets to parchment and papyrus scrolls, the development of the codex in the early Middle Ages, then paper and the famous Gutenberg printing press that truly enabled the spread of information in the Middle Ages and beyond. Through all of these changes libraries collected the different formats of information, and they continue to do so in the modern electronic age of information.

As time passed in the invention and development of different formats of information, the users of libraries changed as well from those who wanted archival type information to those who wanted other forms of information including the scholarly or fact and those who wanted fiction or entertaining material. These individuals and groups have changed into modern information seekers who want information immediately and at their fingertips.

During the past 30 to 40 years, there have been amazing changes in information accessibility and storage. Who knew what changes would be wrought by Steve Jobs and Steve Wozniak's 1976 homemade microprocessor computer board that became the Apple II, which may be the first personal computer. Shortly afterward in the early 1980s, the U.S. National Science Foundation created the first TCP/IP-wide area network, which developed into what is now known as the Internet. Some 10 or so years later the Mosaic Web browser was released. By the mid 1990s, the word "Internet" had become a commonly used term.

Developments in technology, which have made lightening strides in the last 15 to 20 years, have enabled an extreme decentralization of information and data. Library users, especially those born after 1985, have developed a need for almost immediate satisfaction of their information and data needs. These users "want it all and they want it now" as described by Ms. Boon in her chapter "'I Want It All and I Want It Now!': The Changing Face of School Libraries." Today's users are often impatient for their information and to some extent do not seem to be as discriminating as earlier generations. They are also not very willing to be contemplative once they get the information. Users are far more demanding than in the past (even 25 years ago). These are the millennials (also referred to as generation Y), and a large proportion of this book is devoted to them, as they are a predominant portion of current library users.

The millennials are the children of the baby boomers, and they have seen the results of the strikingly quick technology developments that have placed personal computers in many homes (the development of Instant Messaging) and almost all libraries (many thanks to the Gates Foundation); the rise in popularity of laptop computers; the almost ubiquitous cell phone with text messaging, iPods, Tivo, flash drives, BlueTooth, hands-free communication devices, and whatever new communications device tomorrow brings.

Anne-Marie Deiterling presents a fascinating discussion in "Reflection and Thinking and All of that Stuff" of the millennials, which she refers to as the net generation. She discusses how librarians need to develop libraries to serve this generation and the requirements for educators to get them to become engaged learners. She describes this need as being necessary from K-12 through college. There is a definite disconnect between the teachers and librarians, regardless of level, and the net generation. They expect to be entertained; they assume the use of technology; they have high expectations; they multitask at warp speed, but they often do not want to put any real effort into the learning and critical thinking that baby boomer teachers and librarians might expect.

Carol C. M. Toris, Ashlee B. Clevenger, and Katina Strauch, in "Information Literacy and the Modern University Library," discuss the definition of information literacy developed and published by the Association of College and Research Libraries and the need for librarians and faculty to partner in advancing the development of information literacy among university students. They discuss the changing nature of information in the library and the use of information by the latest of the millennials, describing them as true digital natives who have "never known a world without personal computers and URLs."

"Enhancing Library Instruction," by Mark Horan, Suhasini L. Kumar, and John Napp, is a very good review of various current models of library instruction from a number of different universities that are aimed at trying to reach the millennials. The authors use these approaches to guide them in developing a comprehensive online library instruction program for their institution that perhaps others may use as well. They note that, like the library's users, the library and its resources are constantly changing. This means that there cannot be a static library instruction program. It must be constantly changed and revised to keep it "up to date and authentic."

Librarians must keep their educational programs for users current and they must also keep their buildings up to date and modern. This is difficult to do when administrators are concerned about the costs associated with maintaining and remodeling older buildings, as well as the costs associated with new buildings. A relatively recent concept is the Information Commons or the Learning Commons, which may be succinctly described as a way of integrating information, technology, and writing services together with talented staff to create an educational environment that is more complete, comprehensive, collaborative, and much more exciting. John C. Phillips and Brian Hickam, in "Planning an Information Commons," go into extensive detail about the planning stages for their Information Commons. They discuss the role of the dean in getting acceptance of the idea by higher level administrators and then the many decisions made in the preconstruction phase. There is some excellent discussion of the involvement of the Information Technology Department, which is an integral part of the concept. Others envisioning their own Information Commons may wish to visit the University of Toledo's Carlson Library to see how it is working.

Rachel Applegate and David Lewis, in "Renewing the Tech-Forward Library," discuss the development of the Indiana University-Purdue University Indianapolis Library, which opened in 1993, when Mosaic was released, as a technology-rich library environment. They discuss many things that went right with the library, as well as some problems with the initial layout. Some of the problems were the result of changes in technology, as well as changes in the use of technology by the millennials. Additional changes were to some extent the result of changes in teaching techniques. From the opening in 1993 to the present, there has been a great increase in the amount of collaborative work encouraged by instructors. Students engage in many more group projects that have demanded physical changes in libraries to meet the needs of users. Many more areas for group study are required while still maintaining the need for privacy and quiet contemplation on the part of other students. Flexibility in the use of space has become much more common. The authors have provided a good overview of how the original open floor design concept has worked well over time.

Bethany Latham and Jodi Poe, in "Evaluation and Selection of New Format Materials: Electronic Resources," provide an excellent view of the evaluation and selection criteria that may be used in acquiring, or providing for student use, Web sites, electronic books, electronic journals, and electronic databases. They explain how libraries have always adapted and adopted new materials and resources for library users. Libraries collect information in any and all formats that may be useful to their users. The evaluation and selection criteria that they describe for materials have been in use for many years. They have suggested the addition of new criteria in the selection of electronic material that are thoughtful and seem fairly comprehensive.

I have not attempted to provide a description of all of the chapters in this book, nor to be comprehensive in the chapters I have mentioned. These comments provide a taste of what readers can and should discover for themselves. There is good reading and good information ahead. Bon appetite!

Henry Stewart
Troy, Alabama

PREFACE

Those readers who believe that libraries are living, evolving organisms may well find something in this book to support that viewpoint. Using the framework of a new generation of users, the millennials—the various writers have described how they develop ideas and plans to keep their libraries vital and valuable in the ever changing information environment. Colleges and universities are rearranging their interiors to accommodate the Information Commons. They are reconfiguring entire buildings, purchasing new furniture and equipment, redistributing collections, reassigning staff, and in general creating a whole new concept for their individual libraries.

The young people who are the main audience for all of this discussion are seen as totally connected electronically to their world. They are described as communicating on a constant basis in real time using every gadget and tool available to them. That connectivity crosses barriers between classrooms, libraries, and the outside world via wireless devices as well as more conventional tools. To ensure that all parties affecting these young people are involved, several writers have discussed the need to bring in other members of the college or university hierarchy for the buy-in necessary to make their schemes work. These partnerships bring with them the intellectual input necessary between departments to secure support for change, both by the agreement that such change will benefit their students and the agreement that the funding will be well spent. Acknowledgment that people in general look to other areas such as online access points for their information and that, in fact, sometimes that information may not be adequate has given rise to a renewed dedication to broadening staff development via cross-training and assignment. Librarians are the first among faculty to develop such training programs. Not only are they looking to their own backgrounds but to those areas from among their institutions that prepare students to deal with society from other fields.

The bulk of this book is concerned with academic libraries and the demands placed on them for change if they are to remain relevant to their users; however, public libraries are not immune to the need for change. They, too, see that their clientele is looking beyond the traditional reference services and book stacks and into a future where the interlibrary loan takes place with the click of the mouse, where the answer to a reference question comes with free access to a broad database paid for by their tax money and available to anyone with a library card, where their children's homework help comes online from an invisible librarian who may or may not even be in their local library.

These libraries are refurbishing and rearranging to accommodate new demands from various governmental entities that refer clients to their local libraries for a wide variety of services—tax forms, voter registration, food stamp applications, immigration forms and information, etc. These requests often come without financial support from the agency that is actually responsible for such services to libraries that do not have staff trained in social work or in the variety of languages needed to serve various areas. The *raison d'être* for the public library continues to be to serve all people—and that is a challenge. Learners of all ages, from all walks of life, wishing to learn all kinds of things come to the public library.

There is also an interesting chapter on school libraries. Those librarians recognize that their charges are the new millennials and that the experiences they have in middle and high school will lead them to certain expectations when they move on to community college or university life. School librarians work in a more restrictive environment, but they, too, are looking to prepare their faculty counterparts for a new view of the role of the library or media center as an integral part of the curriculum.

Communities where librarians from all types of libraries communicate with each other benefit from the exchange of viewpoints, experiences, and ideas. Each of these chapters offers practical experience and advice, and, regardless of type of library, each may be seen as adaptable to place and role as determined by the community and the society served. The end product is after all an individual who is prepared to meet his or her own life goals and challenges and who knows where to find the tools and information needed to guide that life successfully.

Bernadette Roberts Storck
Tampa, Florida

INTRODUCTION

In recent years a new generation of young people has begun to appear in our libraries. As their numbers have increased, librarians have sensed the need for changing and adapting to a new set of expectations from these new users. Social scientists have dubbed these people the "millennials," and they are entering our libraries as part of the general public, as new corporate employees, and as students, steeped in technology and impatient to grow personally and professionally.

As editors committed to produce books with helpful information for librarians practicing our profession, we wondered just what librarians were and are doing for this new clientele. How is library service affected by providing for these "millennials," maintaining order for our older and more established clientele, and sustaining progress? We decided to ask librarians to discuss themes of change and issues common among all libraries because these young people are expecting services and results when using libraries while older generations in the library environment continue to expect high quality services of longstanding custom.

We broadcast our request for authors mostly through the Internet and the 18 chapters in this book are the result of this effort. The chapters are arranged topically and are followed by a bibliography. Our authors speak directly to their readers and we make no effort at interpretation. Our preface and foreword authors address their own observations and comment freely.

Working in libraries has been exciting and challenging for generations; somehow these "millennials" have "raised the bar." Please enjoy reading our authors' work; adapt and borrow their ideas however you prefer.

James R. Kennedy, Lisa Vardaman, and Gerard B. McCabe

I

WHERE ARE WE?

1 THE LIBRARY AS PLACE IN THE NEW MILLENNIUM: DOMESTICATING SPACE AND ADAPTING LEARNING SPACES

Delmus E. Williams

Early in my career as an academic librarian, I came to believe that there were three physical facilities that would always stand at the center of any college campus: the administration building representing the organizational center of the campus, the student union as the center of social life, and the library as the intellectual heart of the enterprise. But times have changed. Twenty years ago, those of us who pioneered OhioLINK sought to address space problems by developing an electronic library designed to take the library to the scholar's worksite, and that tactic has now become standard in the field. But this move toward providing every scholar with a library on his/her desktop has profoundly changed how libraries work and how they are viewed on campus. The availability of electronic resources, chat references, electronic reserves, the Web, ubiquitous computing on and off campus, laptops, wireless communications, among other things have made it possible for students and faculty to use our resources and others any time and any place they choose.

As a result, the primacy of the library as a place is less assured than it once was, and the kind of space that is needed to support library services and information resources has irrevocably changed. Although it has become clear that libraries are not likely to fade from the scene, we are now being asked to reconsider how we use the space we have and how we reenvision reallocated space to meet the needs of users. As noted by Steven Foote, Partner, Perry Dean Rogers Architects in Boston in private correspondence, "It's now commonly accepted that libraries are partners with conventional academic departments in the educational enterprise. This concept acknowledges that knowledge is actually created in the library as well as stored there in the form of collections and accessed via staff skill."[1] It is now generally understood that, as Geoffrey Freeman noted, "the library must reflect the values, mission and goals of the institution of which it is a

3

part while also accommodating myriad new information and learning technologies, including collaborative and interactive learning modalities" (2005, 2) to earn its place on campus. Operationalizing that understanding means that library buildings must adapt to the changing needs of the campus and its students.

In the last few years, the literature has offered us a number of show-and-tell examples of new libraries that offer a clean slate on which to develop the library of tomorrow. But, for both political and economic reasons, it is the rare library leader today that has the opportunity to help create a new library designed specifically to support today's new learning paradigm. Articles like Lynn Sutton's "Imagining Learning Spaces at Wayne State University's New David Adamany Undergraduate Library" (2000, 139–146) are instructive in offering suggestions as to how library design can address the challenges presented by technically savvy students and faculty. But they do not address the needs of libraries that must adapt to changing times without the resource base that allowed a library of this quality to be built, and to some extent mask the fact that even a new library, built to serve a campus for 25 years, will have to change constantly to address the needs of our users and the reality that the technologies we use now change every five years. The need to reconfigure—indeed, to repurpose—older academic libraries to support collaborative learning models is becoming a constant as we continuously adapt to modify the learning spaces we oversee to meet the demands of a changing environment.

THE CHALLENGE OF THE OLDER LIBRARY

Redesigning older buildings is one of the most difficult and interesting challenges now confronting the architect and the librarian. In 1925, it was noted that "Institutions are usually blessed with some old buildings located in the most important positions on the campus and often constituting an obstacle to future growth. Such facilities, built at various times of need and under pressure of economy, have seldom anything in common, having been built in various styles of architecture and of different materials. They are not readily adaptable to modern uses, yet have associations that endear them to the alumni. Moreover, because of the present cost of building, it is not advisable to destroy any usable educational space" (Perkins, Fellows & Hamilton Architects 1925, 66).

Remember, this was said in 1925—more than 80 years ago—but it is no less true today. In developing new concepts for library building usage on college campuses with older original library buildings, one finds that there is seldom much interest on the part of campus planners to start from scratch with a new facility, either because there is not enough money available to construct such a facility or because other priorities on campus must be addressed first. Campus leaders also know that donors and funding agencies that underwrite construction projects have become tired of funding ever larger storage facilities, particularly when they read of technological advances that have consistently promised to make the library obsolete. And, of course, there is always the rationale that: "Perhaps we should wait a few more years and make do with what we have; after all no one *really* knows where libraries are headed, right?" Make do, buy time. But collections continue to grow to the point where libraries become shackled to the image of a "book warehouse."

Two things have become clear in recent years. First, the need for libraries will persist for many years to come. Second, the character of that need has changed for ever. As Geoffrey Freeman, the architect for Illinois Wesleyan's library, put it, the library is increasingly viewed as a critical center, the breakout space of the classroom. "You turn in one direction and see a book; turn in another and see a terminal. They are both there, designed in scale and detail supportive of their role as central to the university's academic center" (Morris 2002, 32). Whether our clients come to the library for books or for computer access or even just as a place to study between classes, the classic role of the library as the academic heart of the campus must be filled. "The central idea of the learning library is that of integration...Rather than an external 'add on' to the educational experience, the library, as information resource and gateway, is a primary catalyst for cognitive, behavioral, and affective changes in students—as they interact with information resources as directed by faculty, as they complete assignments and study with peers, as they extend their knowledge at multiple levels, seeking connections and making meaning in more self-directed ways. The learning library, rather than being a repository of materials or a study hall, is therefore an agency of change in students' lives" (Simons, Young, and Gibson 2000, 124).

STUDENTS AS CLIENTS

College and university students have choices. They are attracted to institutions with modern residences, including private baths and cooking facilities. They also want parking garages and wireless data networks in common areas and close access to Club Med-like recreational facilities. These students are also more diverse and very different from those who came to our campuses 25 years ago. New students come with diverse college readiness levels and include many different ethnic groups who find that physical handicaps are not viewed as an impediment to their future. Students often work in teams and seem to genuinely enjoy working together in collaborative projects and are not always comfortable in environments like the traditional library that encourages quiet solitude. Indeed, it is rare that we see students using even a few of the hundreds of carrels we have placed in the library. Students expect to have easy access to electronic networks, printers, and media ranging from films to photographic images to books. Although they take for granted the fact that these things will be in their environment, they come to college with a wide range of skill sets, with some who are more adept at getting what they want from the university than their teachers and some who are technologically naïve. But no matter their level of competence, these students want to do things on their own, be actively involved in creating new knowledge and learning from fellow students as well as from teachers, and are wary of systems where they are expected to defer to "experts." Malcolm Brown (2005) contends that these students have a number of traits that should be accommodated when designing learning spaces. In his views, our current student users are:

- Oriented toward group activity and like to work collaboratively in a supportive environment, requiring small-group work spaces.
- Goal and achievement oriented, requiring that they have easy access to tutors consultants and faculty, either in person or electronically.
- Multitaskers who require table space for a variety of tools and resources.
- Experimental, trial-and-error learners who need integrated lablike facilities.
- Heavily reliant on network access requiring computer connectivity in their workspace.
- Pragmatic and inductive, requiring easy access to equipment and primary resources.
- Diverse, requiring accessible facilities and online resources.
- Visual, requiring shared screens and the availability of printing.
- Interactive, requiring space that will facilitate work groups and provide access to experts. (30)

To meet the needs of these students, colleges and universities are expected to address the sensitivities of our users, offer an array of places where students can study, ranging from comfortable chairs to quiet carrels where people can retreat from the hubbub of campus to small rooms, and flat tables where people can meet to discuss their work. As a result, building facilities that will help us compete for students and satisfying them once they are on campus is a highly competitive industry that has spurred construction and renovation projects for all kinds of facilities. Too often, libraries are considered places where authority controls the environment and where students are expected to defer to that authority. As we move to a situation where basic resources can be had without entering the library physically, however, the library, in the words of Scott Bennett, needs to be "domesticated" to mimic the attractions of other comfortable spaces that students may choose as places to work and study. It must produce spaces that are shared by people who know each other and how they use the space, have little within them that are alien to its community of users, offer few threats to a student's ability to complete the tasks at hand, offer a chance for spontaneous and responsive learning, and celebrate the occupants' identities and activities (Bennett 2005). In short, it should be a comfortable, inviting place with resources that are of value, an atmosphere that is supportive, and staff who are available to help without being intrusive.

THE LIBRARY'S COMPETITION FOR THE ATTENTION OF STUDENTS

Until recently, students and faculty were compelled to come to the library to get the resources they needed. Paper resources required to support coursework were either stored in the library or could be acquired only with the help of librarians.

The librarians were the experts who made the rules, and users were obliged to follow those rules, enforcing quiet and making every effort to discourage "inappropriate activities" to include socialization, courtship, food and drink, and even, in some cases, studying personal materials other than those housed in the library. These efforts were generally unsuccessful, but they left an impression that libraries were generally sterile places to be avoided, and, to this day, many potential users associate the library only with books. But, even with this level of control, usage of most libraries remained relatively low, and a fair percentage of undergraduates could boast (and often did) that they finished their degrees without visiting the library.

Times have changed. We talk often of the competition Google and other search engines pose to the library, but the truth of the matter is that, on large campuses and small, libraries have created their own competition by enriching the resource base of the Web with electronic collections that can be accessed anywhere. Students can shop around for the services they need, accessing free electronic resources, data that the library pays for, course reserves, streaming video, art images, and much more anywhere that they can access the Internet. And, with wireless connections in classrooms, student centers, and even the local Borders bookstore and high speed Internet in homes, offices, and almost everywhere else, students can shop among the offerings of various libraries on and off campus, among information sources on the Internet, and for services like chat references and course reserves whenever and wherever they want. If students want to find a group study room, they may come to the library or they may go to a technology center on campus, the local public library, the student center, or even to Borders or Barnes & Noble bookstores. If they want a quiet place, there are many of those around. And, if they want a cup of coffee while they work, it is not that hard to find a wired cybercafé or a Starbucks cafe.

If libraries want to maintain their role as the intellectual center of the campus and as an attractive place where serious students gather, where faculty come to meet one another and to interact with students, they must compete based on their desire to meet the needs of users as the users define them, and that may mean developing cafes in the library, varying work space to fit the desires of students, identifying places where people can work together without disruption, and quiet places that meet the needs of students who work best in that environment. To meet the demand, libraries and those who work in them must adapt to new expectations for service and step out of their role as "experts" and become facilitators. As Thomas Findley, library architect with Leo A. Daly, Architects, noted recently with an associate of the author, "the library is becoming more and more of a campus community social interaction center and gathering space, with coffee shops, bookstores, art exhibits, and many differently sized collaborative learning spaces planned within." But to maintain this reputation requires a rethinking of our purpose. "The central idea of the learning library is that of integration...Rather than an external 'add on' to the educational experience, the library, as information resource and gateway, is a primary catalyst for cognitive, behavioral, and affective changes in students—as they interact with information resources as directed by faculty, as they complete assignments and study with peers, as they extend their knowledge at multiple levels, seeking connections and making meaning in more self-directed ways. The learning library, rather than a repository of materials or a study hall, is therefore an agency of change in students' lives" (Simons, Young, and Gibson 2000, 124).

At the same time, the library must establish itself as part of an interlocking environment and become a "Third Place," a public place for social interaction that is supportive and is neither a place to live nor a place to work (Carlson 2005). Technology has blurred the lines between many campus learning support operations and has encouraged new alliances with campus and community partners that were previously dismissed out of hand. "For the library to be a true convergent point in the information landscape, we need to develop an environment from which users can intuit that they are in a hub where an abundance of intellectual and informational resources, from a wide variety of disciplines, schools of thought, times, geographic locations, ethnic voices, production formats, and so on, are coming together. It is in this desire to be a place of convergence that we set ourselves apart from other information providers" (Baker 2000, 87). Students should think of the library as a place that stimulates to be better than they are but in an atmosphere that is supportive and inviting.

To accomplish this goal, it is important that expert assistance be available at predictable places in the library. People at the reference desk or at locations that are close by and obvious to the user must be able to help with technical problems with their computers as well as content issues, and it is valuable for people working with or in writing centers to be able to have ready access to staff who can help with both the style and substance of what is being written. Centers for the improvement of teaching draw from libraries and computer centers, and, as users integrate graphs, media, and other resources into their projects, they need access in a single place to people who can help them with all of the elements of their work. Some users will still prefer to work in their bedrooms, in residence hall lounges, in classroom buildings, and in offices, but we as librarians must find more reasons for them to explore options in the library building and be provided with ample and appropriate space to accommodate their work.

TYPICAL SOLUTIONS

We know that the opening of new libraries tends to expand usage. Students like attractive new surroundings that offer support for their activities. As noted earlier, however, few campuses are building new libraries, and, without them, many colleges and universities today are opting for a combination of a reconfiguration of stack space and perhaps a small building addition that might both create an inviting new entrance to the building and afford immediate exposure to the information commons or learning commons. We believe that any repurposing objectives should consider the following goals:

- Strive for maximum flexibility so that the building can grow and change to accommodate changes in technology and the campus environment.

- Develop a point of entry that opens onto an inviting atmosphere that implies that the user is entering a cultural center that will enrich them, emphasizing library materials along with attractive art and other accoutrements that evidence a warm, inviting, and invigorating place.
- Focus on the first floor—all or most user services should be there.
- Provide easy access to the staff that assists with both technical and content problems as users enter the library.
- Offer signage that quickly orients users as they enter the building.
- Provide easy and sufficient access to electricity and telecommunications and campus networks throughout the building.
- Offer lots of computing equipment using both wired and wireless communications.
- Offer equipment and human support for the development of multimedia presentations, combining both traditional technologies like lamination machines, and more sophisticated support for accessing streaming video, high resolution images, and a wide array of other media.
- Provide shelf-lined signature reading room that can be reconfigured easily for public events.
- Use high density shelving whenever possible so that stack space can be converted to space for collaborative learning.
- Address access and security issues that the repurposed library will bring forth.
- Develop small library-learning commons areas as part of new residence halls and learning/living communities.
- Sponsor lectures, exhibits, and informed dialogue to nurture a sense of academic community and make the library the academic center of the campus.
- Think "from the inside out" and reenvision the landscaping around or near the entrance to the library, considering patios and outdoor conversation and gathering areas that entice users to wander in and out of the library.

A more radical solution, and often the more challenging one, is exemplified by the University of Massachusetts Amherst "Learning Commons" (http://www.umass.edu/provost/initiatives/learningcommons/). UMass's library has partnered with other units on campus to address the new learning paradigm. The concept that emerged from this process of reinvention of its service program includes a vibrant open studio environment encompassing most of the main floor of the library. Its seamless, coordinated resources and services use state-of-the-art technology for research and coursework; provide intimate spaces for faculty and fellow student collaboration; offer inviting breakout rooms; and provide ready access to experts in research, technology, writing, and the various disciplines. The Learning Commons is intended to encourage engagement with information in its various forms, reinforce the value of collaborative inquiry, and create new opportunities for community interaction.

A learning commons should be built around the social dimensions of learning and activities, and modes of interaction within them should be managed by students themselves for purposes that may vary greatly and change frequently. As Scott Bennett (2003) has observed, the core activity of a learning commons evolves from efforts to manipulate and master information as expected in an information commons, but extends to include others that support collaborative learning through which students turn information into knowledge.

Today's students are often invited by campus planners and architects to participate in the creation of new learning environments in expectation that this close collaboration will help them become comfortable with their new learning environments. The challenge, it seems, is how to make a place of social interaction and learning that is not the home or the office or classroom. Whatever is done to make the library one of the preferred places to be on campus—if not the best place to be—will require an image rebranding that is forcefully and consistently driven by senior academic leaders and reinforced by deans and faculty opinion-leaders. Nothing less will do.

ADDING VALUE TO THE CAMPUS EXPERIENCE

In her chapter titled "Net Generation Students and Libraries," in *Educating the Net Generation*, Joan K. Lippincott argues that a disconnect exists between the present culture of the academic library and that of Net Gen students. To date, most of what we have done under the cover of transformation is really little more than cosmetic, for example, the creation of information commons, rearranging furniture into pleasant more intimate groupings, opening up stack floors by sending lesser used books and bound journals to remote or compact storage, and marketing campaigns to "sell" the library to students who have decided that the library is not relevant to their studies. That strategy needs to change. We as librarians and as those who invest in libraries need to ask students and faculty what they need from us and then use their advice to reinsert the library into the mainstream of academic life.

It is comfortable for librarians to argue that they must be the drivers of student use of the library, but we do this at our peril. We must never forget the role of faculty in this effort. Recently a school of education faculty member noted that instructors' assignments are, in fact, driving the nature of student library usage at his institution in several significant ways. First, the use of that library's breakout rooms reflects a significant amount of students' collaborative learning at strategic points in the semester. And reference librarians have told our colleague that it is not unusual for three or four students from one of these groups to approach the reference desk together to ask a question and share the response. In his opinion, the incidence of collaborative learning in this colleague's library clearly mirrors his university's commitment to the philosophy of a community of learners coupled with extensive staff support operating in cross-functional teams. Enthused, this anonymous professor noted that the library design, library acquisitions, and student use are heavily driven by professors' instructional goals and assignments, together with the culture of the campus. As a profession, we as librarians have known this to be true since the 1960s, but what is old has become new again. This culture of collaboration between librarians and faculty has to be intentionally orchestrated and sustained by all campus constituents, and must be supported by the educational hierarchy working under the chief academic officer. Perhaps it is time to revisit Louis Shores's vision from the 1960s of the Library College that attempted to combine librarianship and faculty teaching to produce a hybrid that would be greater than either (Shiflett 1996).

CONCLUSION

There are few options for the transformation of library buildings and the role they play on campus. Either the library—whose role is often threatened by newer campus facilities that are technology-rich and that feature collaborative learning spaces—reenvisions itself as a cohesive learning environment where an atmosphere of scholarship, collaboration, and community can be fostered, or it will increasingly be bypassed by our students as a relic of the past. If the educational environment in the library is transformed from a model that caters to the faculty and librarians to one that is student-centered and reflects contemporary learning models, however, faculty and librarians can work together to create and guide students' learning experiences within it. C. Carney Strange and James Banning observed that "the creation and maintenance of campus environments that attract, satisfy, and sustain students in the achievement of their educational goals" (2001, 74) is critical in a market-driven climate for institutions that want to focus on learning. To prosper, academic libraries must consult broadly with their constituents to ensure that they become and remain one of those environments. If the library is designed to emphasize what Charles Osburn refers to as "a place with a latent essence that is rich in the potential for experience" (2007, 82), it will succeed in maintaining its centrality on the campus.

NOTE

1. Personal correspondence, December 2006.

REFERENCES

Baker, B. 2000. "Values for the Learning Library." *Research Strategies* 17: 85–91.

Bennett, S. 2003. *Libraries Designed for Learning*. Washington, D.C.: Council on Library and Information Resources.

Bennett S. 2005. "Righting the Balance." In *Library as Place: Rethinking Roles, Rethinking Space*, ed. K. Smith, 10–24. Washington, D.C.: Council on Library and Information Resources.

Brown, M. 2005. "Learning Space Design: Theory and Practice." *EDUCAUSE Review* 40 (4): 30–38.

Carlson, S. 2005. "Thoughtful Design Keeps New Libraries Relevant." *Chronicle of Higher Education* September 5, B1–5.

Freeman, G. T. 2005. "The Library as Place." In *Library as Place: Rethinking Roles, Rethinking Space*, ed. K. Smith, 1–9. Washington, D.C.: Council on Library and Information Resources, 2.

Lippincott, J. K. 2005. "Net Generation Students and Libraries." In *Educating the Net Generation*, eds. Diana G. Oblinger and James L. Oblinger. Boulder, Col.: EDUCAUSE, 2005. http://www.educause.edu/educatingthenetgen/ (Accessed March 21, 2007.)

Morris, J. 2002. "History Meets State of the Art: 2 Case Studies." *University Business* 5 (8).

Osburn, C. B. 2007. "Regaining Place." In *Advances in Library Administration and Organization*, Vol. 24, 53–90. Amsterdam, N.Y.: Elsevier.

Perkins, Fellows & Hamilton, Architects. 1925. Educational Buildings. Chicago: Blakely Publishing.

Shiflett, Orvin Lee. 1996. *Louis Shores: Defining Educational Librarianship*. Lanham, MD: Scarecrow Press.

Simons, K., J. Young, and C. Gibson. 2000. "The Library as a Learning Place." *Research Strategies*, 17: 123–132.

Strange, C. C., and J. Banning. 2001. *Education by Design: Creating Campus Learning Environments That Work*. San Francisco: Jossey-Bass.

Sutton, L. 2000. "Imaging Learning Spaces at Wayne State University's New David Adamany Undergraduate Library." *Research Strategies* 17: 139–146.

Williams, D. E. 1996. "Reengineering Existing Buildings to Serve the Academic Community." In *The National Electronic Library*, ed. Gary Pitkin, 85–99. Westport, CT: Greenwood.

II

SERVING MILLENNIALS

2 REFLECTION AND THINKING AND ALL OF THAT STUFF: LEARNING, ENGAGEMENT, AND THE NET GENERATION

Anne-Marie Deitering

The net generation, born after 1982, is big and diverse, and is described in diverse ways: technology-obsessed, social and connected, traditional, achievement-oriented, and attention-challenged. Every new generation of students is different from their parents and grandparents; articles about the "generation gap" can be found in every era. The amount of attention paid the net gens, however, suggests that there is more going on here than generational disagreements over music or clothes. This is partially due to their numbers. Substantially larger than generation X, their immediate predecessors, they are a commercial force to be reckoned with and were bound to attract attention. Their buying power might make them interesting to marketers, but to educators it is their relationship with technology that makes them seem so different. It is impossible to think that growing up in a world where the Internet, cell phones, digital music, and Tivo have always been there has not had a major impact on how the net generation expects to learn. As this group makes their way from K-12 schools to higher education, educators at all levels are asking, "what does this mean for us?"

Some observers believe that it means nothing will, or should, ever be the same again. To these people, technology has shaped these "digital natives" so profoundly that they cannot be taught using the methods of the past. Marc Prensky, frequently described as a futurist and video game designer, is at this extreme. In October 2005, he told readers of *The Chronicle of Higher Education* that they should not expect today's students to respond to old-fashioned expectations and methods: "the things that have traditionally been done—you know reflection and thinking and all that stuff—are in some ways too slow for the future....Is there a way to do these things faster?" (Carlson 2005, 34) Librarians and educators alike must consider what this means. Can learning happen without reflection and thinking and "all that stuff?"

Before the net generation was a gleam in marketers' eyes, librarians were aware that the Internet would have a profound impact on their work. Having been told for years that the Internet would render them obsolete, twenty-first century librarians have had to walk an important line to show that they are still relevant and effective. Libraries have adapted their resources and designed new services to meet the rising expectations of a public that has become more self-sufficient in their information seeking. If today's teens and young adults truly have been so profoundly shaped by their experience with technology that they cannot learn from traditional forms of scholarship, however, libraries will have to do more than adapt.

What makes this particularly complicated is that when they are designing services and selecting resources, librarians must not only consider the needs of learners, but also those of their teachers. In this sense, librarians have always served changing clienteles: students, who are new to research and scholarly inquiry, and their teachers, whose research skills and scholarly habits have developed through years of practice. As partners in the educational mission of schools and universities, librarians sometimes have to balance the desire to give users what they want and to meet users where they are with the responsibility to provide users with the things they actually need to be successful in the classroom, and as lifelong learners.

This balance is particularly delicate when the two clienteles have different expectations for learning. Although differences between twenty-first century learners and educators are frequently discussed in the context of technology, by focusing too much on technology we can miss an important piece of the puzzle. When students and educators have fundamentally different ideas about what learning is, they will be at cross-purposes no matter how deeply technology is integrated into the learning experience. This is not to say that technology is irrelevant. The academic experiences of students born after 1982 have been profoundly affected by the presence of the Internet in their lives. The learning habits of the net generation have been shaped by the immediate availability of information and the ubiquitous presence of communication channels. Many have limited experience with sustained reflection and have learned to succeed in their school environments while multitasking and paying partial attention. It is not true, however, that educators must find ways to teach these students that allow them to succeed without thinking and reflection. This chapter examines how engaging, inquiry-based activities like student research contribute to deep learning, and how librarians can maintain the balance between giving students what they want, and making sure they have what they need to be successful learners.

THESE KIDS TODAY: WHY AREN'T THEY ENGAGED?

On June 23, 2005, the documentary *Declining by Degrees* aired on PBS stations across the United States. This film told public television audiences that higher education in America, for all intents and purposes, is broken. It made the case that students are frequently ill-prepared for the rigors of college level work, and the schools that admit them do little to ensure that they succeed. With faculty focused on research, huge, impersonal survey courses taught by harried adjunct instructors, and students pulled in several directions trying to keep up with rising tuition rates, *Declining by Degrees* suggests that higher education is coming up short in many ways.

One of the students interviewed in this documentary, Nate, illustrates yet another dimension to this picture. Nate does not struggle to maintain his 3.4 grade point average. He can identify what he needs to do to perform well enough on tests and assignments, and he very rarely exceeds that minimum. He reports studying less than an hour a day and, despite his reasonable grades, he is not learning much. On some level this bothers him; he wonders aloud, "shouldn't college be challenging?" At the same time, he never interrogates his own role in the learning process. He might not be challenged by the traditional lecture-textbook-test framework of most college classes, but he resists instructors who challenge that framework. In classes where teachers have created learning activities that require students to thoughtfully prepare in advance, he is bored; but he does not consider that his own lack of preparation might be at fault. Although classes that reward low-level thinking skills do not challenge him, his behavior indicates that, to him, recitation and memorization are simply what school is (Merrow 2006).

In the last 15 years, a lot of research has focused on the question of student engagement. It is evident that there are students at all levels who are disengaged and learning less than they should. The National Survey of Student Engagement (NSSE) shows that today's college students are reading less, writing less, and taking advantage of fewer cultural and educational opportunities than even they thought they would during their college years. Further, most college students report spending far less time preparing for their classes than their teachers think is necessary; about 20 percent of students admit they are not prepared when they come to class (Kuh 2003).

Disengagement is not just an issue for higher education. Martha McCarthy directs the high school equivalent of the NSSE. Her work shows that about half of high school seniors report spending less than three hours a week preparing for classes. At the same time, only a tiny percentage (3%) of these students say they are always unprepared when they come to class. Despite minimal out-of-class engagement with schoolwork, most high school students feel that they are meeting the expectations schools have for them, and their grades support this contention (McCarthy and Kuh 2006, 666).

Some students, like Nate, can earn good marks without being truly engaged in their learning. Others are not so fortunate and drop out of school altogether. With schools, colleges, and universities under increasing pressure to demonstrate that they are producing students ready to contribute in the workforce, this disengagement is a source of growing concern. To observers like Prensky, the answer is obvious—schools, colleges, and universities are not engaging students because they are not teaching in a way that works for the net generation.

The Breed Apart

No previous generation has brought with it the sense that they might be so different as to require an entirely new approach to learning. Even the baby boomers, with their huge numbers behind them, were feared more for the strain they would place on infrastructures than for the challenges they would make to pedagogy. Those who believe the net generation signals a crisis point for education-as-usual point to the rapid dissemination of networked information and communication technologies as the thing that shifted the paradigm. At one extreme, Prensky argues that the impact of technology on those born after 1982 has been so profound that they *"think and process information fundamentally differently* from their predecessors" (Prensky 2001, 1). Most observers do not go this far, yet they still conclude that educators must change their practice or lose these students altogether.

In *Educating the Net Generation*, Diana and James Oblinger discuss the impact of "growing up digital" on this generation's expectations for learning. Like many others, they contend that today's students expect technology to make their educational experience more convenient, delivering information to them instantaneously and allowing them to submit assignments from anywhere. These students expect to use technology to communicate with each other and to socialize. They do not always distinguish between social and academic activities, moving seamlessly from one to the other. They expect their learning experiences to be participatory, interactive, and collaborative. They favor speed, even over accuracy, when it comes to communication and to information retrieval.

Because technology is understood as the reason why the net generation is different from its predecessors, more technology is often presented as the way to connect with these students and to engage them in learning. There is good evidence that the effective use of educational technology does have positive impacts on engagement, increasing the time students spend on task and providing them with point-of-need instruction. Asking teachers to deliver information in new ways is one thing. It is something quite different to claim that these teachers must also change their expectations for student learning: "Change your teaching style. Make blogs, iPods, and video games part of your pedagogy. And learn to accept divided attention spans" (Carlson 2005, 34). It is this last point, that educators cannot expect focused attention and engagement, that brings us back to the tension discussed previously. In the fall of 2005, Marc Prensky told teachers that today's students will tune out anything taught in the old way.

> If we educators don't start coming up with some damned good curricular gameplay for our students—and soon—they'll all come to school wearing (at least virtually in their minds) the T-shirt I recently saw a kid wearing in New York city: "It's not ADD—I'm just not listening!" (Prensky 2005, 64)

The implication that net generation students will shut down and disengage if their attention is not caught and held with technology, without considering learning outcomes, content, or any other criteria, appears over and over again.

In a companion discussion to the *Chronicle* article discussed previously, librarian Richard Sweeney defends his interpretation of the following story. A professor asks a multitasking student to focus on the class lecture. The student responds that he is listening while e-mailing and challenges the professor's contention that attention is important, saying that he has an "A" in the class and that he knows what was just said. Sweeney uses this story to show how the millennials multitask and that they should not be expected to focus on one thing, even if that one thing is their teacher. More than this, he suggests that the professor should change. "To the professor it was rudeness. To the student, it was, 'Why shouldn't I do it in a way that works for me?'" Sweeney's interpretation is not without its critics. Librarian Rob Bertram suggests that to tolerate this behavior is a form of "social grade inflation." Marc Meola's critique is even stronger: "[t]he student is treating the professor as if he is another gadget or device, a means to get a grade, instead of as a human being."

It's Not Technology, It's Learning

By shifting one's perspective away from the behavior being demonstrated, and toward the learning environment that serves as the context for the story, an additional interpretation emerges. One can look at it as an indictment of the type of learning going on in many classrooms. The e-mailing student might simply be another Nate, coasting through his education by doing enough to succeed but not enough to learn. Even paying partial attention, he can identify those pieces of information he needs to repeat on a test or assessment without engaging in higher-level thinking skills like analysis or synthesis. Similarly, the professor could be like many of the instructors highlighted in *Declining by Degrees*, hoping for students who will engage in critical thinking and synthesis, but not assigning the kind of work that requires students to use those skills to succeed. When challenged in the discussion, Sweeney points to examples like academic conferences where the educators themselves frequently come and go and multitask during presentations. He never challenges the pedagogy of the lecture model, but accepts it as a given. Strikingly, his example primarily points out that one doesn't have to be part of the net generation to successfully multitask in the lecture environment. When pressed by Meola to identify ways that educators can meet students where they are while still promoting thinking and reflection, Sweeney does not give satisfying answers.

Nate's sense that college should be harder is vague and unfocused, and he does not see his own lack of engagement as part of the problem. In 2005, Holly Hassel and Jessica Lourey argued that there is both anecdotal and empirical evidence suggesting that there may be some basis to faculty complaints about students unwilling to take responsibility for their own education. They suggest that students are increasingly likely to expect good grades for minimal effort and that faculty and students have different ideas about what grades even mean: "[m]ore than ever, college instructors have reason to believe that their students are out of touch with what their grades really symbolize, why they are even in college, and what responsibilities they have as students" (Hassel and Lourey 2005, 2).

At the same time, Hassel and Lourey are clear in their contention that many common classroom practices reinforce the idea that learning, even college learning, is primarily a mechanical process of mastering and regurgitating facts. Tests that reward memorization and recitation suggest that these skills are important. Grade inflation tells students that they should expect high grades for mediocre work. Attendance policies are arbitrary when students can perform perfectly well on tests and assignments without attending. If students come to college believing that learning is mechanical, and if they can succeed in most of their classes by mechanically mastering facts, then no one should be surprised when they do not develop the higher-level thinking skills they need to engage deeply with course material.

At all levels of education, the connections between learning and engagement are clear. Students who spend significant amounts of time working on a variety of challenging, enriching activities learn more than those who do not. As George Kuh puts it, the idea behind student engagement is very simple, and something most educators already know:

> The more students study a subject, the more they learn about it. Likewise, the more students practice and get feedback on their writing, analyzing or problem solving, the more adept they become. (Kuh 2003, 25)

Engagement is equally important in K-12 classrooms. In all environments, the research shows that engaging learning activities are challenging, promote focused attention, lead to a feeling of control and responsibility, and frequently result in enjoyment and enthusiasm for learning (Shernoff et al. 2003). Knowing this, the contention that net generation students cannot be expected to focus their attention, think, or reflect is sobering.

LEARNING IS HARD

It is easy to understand students who are frustrated by disengaging lectures that do not efficiently give them the information they need to perform well on assessments and tests. "Why can't this be quicker" is a reasonable question to ask in this context. There is a great deal of evidence, however, that deep learning, the kind of learning that comes from engaging educational practices, cannot be accomplished quickly.

In *How Students Learn*, Bransford, Brown and Cocking argue that the "ultimate goal of learning is to have access to information for a wide set of purposes—that the learning will in some way transfer to other circumstances" (Bransford et al. 73). This short statement contains two fundamental points about the nature of learning. The first is that it must go beyond the mastery of facts. It is simply a given that no one could possibly master enough facts in their formal education to cover every one of the "wide set of purposes" they will encounter in their life. The second point is the concept of transfer. To learn something well enough to apply it in only one context or circumstance, like a final exam, is not to have learned it at all.

Part of effective learning, therefore, is learning how to learn. Students not only need to leave school with a body of factual knowledge, but they also need the cognitive skills that will allow them to effectively deal with new situations and new information on their own. This kind of learning is not easy, and that is why any analysis of why students are not engaged or are not successful learners must go beyond their reliance on technology. Sometimes students find learning hard, not because new information is presented to them badly, but because deep learning is hard.

Sense-Making

Deep learning challenges the learner's fundamental assumptions, a process that is never easy. There are many theories that explain how students develop and learn. Examining these in detail is beyond the scope of this chapter, but it is worth noting some overarching themes. Pascarella and Terenzini's 2005 update to *How College Affects Students* provides a useful summary of learning theory. Particularly interesting here are the cognitive-structural theories, which present learning as a series of developmental stages. Although the specific stages described by each theory differ, present in each is the primary concept that the basic cognitive structures people use to make sense of the world around them are changed by the learning process. In other words, learning can change the way the learner looks at and understands the world (Pascarella and Terenzini 2005, 33).

Pascarella and Terenzini's work focuses on the effects of college on student learning and development; sense-making as a fundamental part of learning begins long before college. Children of all ages have preconceptions and ideas about how the world works. Before they can effectively integrate new information, they must start from those preconceptions. When students do not start from what they know, they can completely fail to understand new information. In other cases they learn it temporarily, long enough to repeat it on a test or assignment, and then revert to their previous way of thinking. Bransford et al. (2000) show that helping students engage with their preconceptions is a crucial first step in helping them expand their knowledge. This explains why the research process can be so powerful for students; it is a process of finding new information that challenges their preconceptions. It also shows why learners need to be guided through the process of inquiry. Given new information that challenges what they know about a topic, students have difficulty learning from that information in a meaningful way.

Metacognition

To learn in this way, students must be aware of their own beliefs and perceptions. Even more profoundly, they must understand knowledge itself as something that is uncertain and constructed. This is not a concept that most students are comfortable with when they first get to college. According to Pascarella and Terenzini, the idea that students develop self-awareness and an understanding of themselves as participants in a learning process is a concept shared by most theories of college student learning. When they come to college, most students have a black-and-white view of what learning and knowledge is. Problems have identifiable solutions and there are two sides (one right and one wrong) to controversial issues. Knowledge is something concrete that can be transmitted and mastered. As they develop, students come to understand that some problems have multiple solutions. They learn how to build an argument and to analyze the arguments of others to advocate for particular solutions or perspectives. Knowledge is something constructed out of the best information one has available at the time. To function in this more uncertain world, reflective thinking is a necessary skill (Pascarella and Terenzini 2005, 37–38).

Metacognition, often described as "thinking about thinking," is a reflective process that allows students to understand their own thinking and to place that thinking within larger epistemological structures. Obviously, younger students will not develop the same reflective thinking skills as their counterparts in higher education, but metacognition and reflection are important to learners at all levels. Michael Martinez discusses the connections between metacognition and several important learning goals, including critical thinking and problem solving. At every stage of the learning process, successful learners can ask themselves "do I know enough to solve this problem" or "is this information good enough to support my conclusion." These questions are automatic to experienced scholars, part of the habits of mind they develop through years of scholarly inquiry. Students, however, must learn to ask them.

To ask these questions, students need to practice. They need to engage in learning activities that require metacognition, activities that require them to think critically and solve problems. Martinez notes that allowing students to interact and work together on such activities can help them develop metacognitive skills. Working alone, they may not see the need to "think about their thinking," but communicating thought processes to others is a natural part of collaborative learning (Martinez 2006). At all levels students need to learn how to learn, and they cannot do this without being self-aware and reflective about the learning process.

INFORMATION LITERACY, LEARNING, AND ENGAGEMENT

Librarians have a strong interest in promoting meaningful, engaging learning activities on their campuses. The information literacy goals presented in documents like the *ACRL Instruction Section's Information Literacy Standards for Higher Education* dovetail neatly with student learning and engagement initiatives. Meaningful learning experiences that give students the opportunity to practice metacognition, critical thinking, and problem solving frequently require strong information literacy skills. Engagement-focused initiatives that give students the opportunity to engage in authentic inquiry, problem-based learning, or collaborative research projects with faculty not only highlight the need for effective information literacy instruction but also provide students the opportunity to learn information literacy concepts and skills in a meaningful way.

Pascarella and Terenzini show that it is particularly important that students master broad, cognitive outcomes like reflective thinking and information literacy if they are going to be successful "in a society and world where factual knowledge is becoming obsolete at an accelerated rate" (Pascarella and Terenzini 2005, 114–115). These cognitive outcomes include the ability to effectively use new information, evaluate new ideas, draw appropriate conclusions from the new information they encounter, and make reasonable decisions in light of the information they have (Pascarella and Terenzini 2005, 155).

Carol Kuhlthau's (1993) research further illustrates the connection between engaging, inquiry-based activities like student research and cognitive learning outcomes. Kuhlthau's highly influential model draws heavily from constructivist educational theories that describe learning as a sense-making process based on reflective thinking. According to this model, successful researchers can analyze their own knowledge and then find, evaluate, and use information to construct a personal focus or new understanding of a complex question. The focus formulation stage is the most critical stage, or the turning point in the research process. It is not a stretch to say that students who successfully find a focus during the research process are engaged in their learning. Kuhlthau's research shows that students who do not find a focus continue to have difficulty throughout the research process and frequently report dissatisfaction with their results even when their grades are acceptable. On the other hand, students who create their own meaning are engaged in the learning process, reporting increased interest and enjoyment (Kuhlthau 1993, 113–115).

Supporting authentic learning experiences like these requires libraries to balance the needs of their two clienteles. In many ways, neither side has the complete picture. Every librarian who has worked at a reference desk has heard some version of, "I already wrote my paper, now I just need some articles for the bibliography." Students who do not expect research to be a recursive learning process want to find their articles, and to find them quickly. They will choose which articles to use by considering one question, "does it say what I want it to say?" Approached this way, research is not an engaging learning activity, but a mechanical process. There is little chance that students will engage with information in a way that forces them to challenge their own preconceptions, because they are not trying to expose themselves to new ideas.

At the same time, many librarians who have worked with faculty have been frustrated by requests for research instruction sessions that do not reflect what we know about how students learn. Research skills taught when the students don't need to do research, arbitrary requirements about the types of sources students may use, or busywork assignments that require students to "find an article" that is never analyzed or discussed are just a few examples of frustrating requests from faculty members that seem designed to keep students far away from engaging learning experiences.

STRIKING THE BALANCE

With a plethora of quality information resources easily available to students, educators can design a variety of learning activities that require authentic research and discovery. As schools look for ways to improve engagement and learning, librarians have an opportunity to promote information literacy and to demonstrate the linkages between information literacy and student learning. With this opportunity, however, comes a responsibility. Librarians need to work with faculty as equal partners, making sure that these learning experiences are authentic and based on the research skills students really need in the twenty-first century. This means helping students as they enter the world of scholarship and research, providing them with the tools and instruction they need to use information to make sense of complex problems, and recognizing that this represents a new way of thinking about information for many students. It also means helping teachers understand the information needs of the net generation.

Were the Good Old Days Really That Good?

In a recent issue of *College & Research Libraries News*, Justine Alsop expressed her concerns about the impact that technology has had on library users' capacity for sustained thought and reflection. She watches users who tend to scan books instead of reading them closely, or who are unwilling to negotiate complex databases, and she worries that something important about the academic enterprise is being lost. A few months later, Karen Munro responded to Alsop with an essay of her own. Munro agrees that librarians, students, and faculty are reading less and differently than before. She suggests, however, that a variety of forces have contributed to these changes, and that to understand the situation will require more complicated questions than "is technology making us dumber?"

It is easy to forget that 10, 20, or 50 years ago, students were not necessarily using high-level critical thinking skills when they used scholarly articles and books in their research papers and projects. When they did their own searching, they were not looking at the entire world of information. Instead, they were searching a limited, professionally selected collection. Using scholarly journal articles as the basis for their own writing was not always a conscious choice so much as it was using those sources that were the most convenient and most available.

Simply by teaching students how to find information in the analog era, teachers and librarians had to start introducing students to the idea of discourse and context, and to be successful in this environment students could not avoid thinking and reflecting on their research process. Looking for sources in a card catalog forced students to think about controlled vocabulary, broader terms, and narrower terms. Without keyword searching pulling information from a variety of disciplines and perspectives together, students had to think about their topics holistically. When the subject-searching process broke down, as it inevitably did, troubleshooting the search also forced students to think about context and discourse.

Even more important, research could not start and end with subject searching. Finding additional entry points into the discourse, like key authors, was another way of thinking about the broader context. Particularly effective undergraduate researchers knew about literature reviews. Others knew that works cited lists and bibliographies could be mined for additional sources. Even if these students did not think reflectively that these ways of finding sources were possible because of academic disciplines or the norms of scholarly communication, and even if their teachers and librarians were not telling them about these epistemological contexts, they were getting hands-on experience finding information within a disciplinary discourse structure.

Munro argues that before we can decide how to use technology well, we have to decide exactly what it is about scholarly practice that we want to preserve. In the case of student learning, libraries must continue to support student inquiry and discovery, providing spaces and resources that support authentic, engaging learning activities.

Supporting Student Inquiry and Discovery

There are some, even some librarians, who believe that if libraries would just create systems that are as easy to use as Google, then "library instruction" and even "information literacy" would no longer be necessary. Leaving aside the question of how well today's students really know how to use information technologies and search tools, this assumption is problematic because it accepts the pre-Internet perception that finding information is the hard part of doing research.

In reality, even if finding information was as automatic and seamless as the most optimistic net gen student could imagine, researching complex questions would still be hard. In a *Library Journal* "Backtalk" column, Stephen Bell interrogates the popular quip that "only librarians like to search, everyone else likes to find." As Bell points out, the more one thinks about this comment, the more clear it is that it is based on a fundamentally erroneous assumption about the role of research in learning (Bell 2005, 79). When librarians need a single fact, statistic, or answer to a question, they like to "find" as much as anyone else. Nobody likes chasing after the needle in the haystack, especially when they are not even sure if it is there.

When librarians are doing research because they want to learn about a topic, or because they think that is what their user needs to do, they treat the search process itself as a learning experience. Just because library systems are more complex than Google is not in and of itself a reason to change them. Sometimes, the process of inquiry that these systems support is itself complex. It is dangerous to assume that because Google is an option for our users, they cannot handle any complexity in information seeking. This leads to the conclusion that complex inquiry is inherently too hard for students, which is a dangerous and ultimately destructive path to follow.

This does not, however, mean embracing complexity for complexity's sake. Libraries should work to make their information retrieval tools and systems as transparent as possible. When students struggle, it should be with the concepts and ideas they encounter, not with questions like "how do I print?" At the same time, librarians need to remember that even when library systems are as transparent as they can possibly be, when library collections are as complete as they can possibly be, and when students are as well trained in searching techniques as they can possibly be, the process of academic research can still be hard. Libraries should make the tools as easy to use as possible while recognizing that part of their role is to support students through a learning process that is difficult and complex.

Context Is Key

One of the most important ways that librarians can provide this support is by helping students identify the context of the information sources they find. This means taking a broad perspective when we identify the information literacy skills students should have. Information literate students need to know more than how to find information effectively. Without a broader view that includes an understanding of how information is produced, and how it can be used to construct new knowledge, students will not necessarily use what they learn about finding information to find the sources worth learning from.

Ten years ago, Jeremy Shapiro and Shelley Hughes suggested that information literacy is a "liberal art." Considered this broadly, an information literate learner has the skills and knowledge to "think critically about the entire information enterprise and information society" (Shapiro and Hughes 1996). In a keynote address at the 2006 WILU library instruction conference, Shapiro and Hughes took the opportunity to broaden the scope of their analysis to fit the current information landscape. They suggested that their initial argument is now too narrow, in part because it failed to predict the extent to which information and communication technologies would infiltrate everyday life. In our "highly digitized" society, the information literate must be able to communicate with others in a world mediated by technology, and to manage the complexity that a constant connection to technology generates (Shapiro and Hughes 1996).

An overarching theme is the need to help students who are new to discourse and to scholarly inquiry understand context. When students participate in classroom discussions, they are obviously contributing to a community. When they engage in the research process, finding articles and generating their own ideas, they are also (although less obviously) contributing to a discourse community. Different groups of people have different norms that govern how they interact with information. These range from scholarly communication methods, to the practice of professional groups, to the communications patterns of friends and families. To participate effectively in any community, students must be able to identify its norms. Given how much research and communication students do online today, they must also learn how to identify these contexts without the visual cues that are present in the analog world.

Without context, or a way to make sense of the larger discourse, students can have a difficult time identifying which sources are worth learning from. Given an undifferentiated mass of hits in a results list, they will use "it says what I wanted it to say" as their primary criterion for evaluation. There are many ways to support students as they explore a topic, finding and understanding the context in which the information was created. Giving them the chance to practice authentic inquiry, with engaging learning experiences throughout the curriculum, is an important part of this effort.

Institutional Partnerships

It is also important to present students with these opportunities throughout the curriculum The best inquiry-based activity in the world will not have a lasting impact if students are introduced to it once, in one class, and never given the chance to practice those skills again. This means that today's librarians must advocate for authentic learning experiences on the curricular level. This can mean pursuing the one-on-one collaborations with individual teachers that librarians have been engaged in for years. It can also mean working more strategically, through campus curriculum committees and other campus-wide bodies.

In 2002, Ken Kempcke argued that librarians should learn some lessons from Sun-Tzu to make institutional partnerships more strategic and effective. He suggests that instead of serving faculty, librarians and classroom faculty need to be equal partners in the educational mission of the institution. Like Pascarella and Terenzini, he argues that cognitive outcomes that support lifelong learning, like information literacy, are crucial learning goals that should be supported by the entire institution. Ultimately, individual collaborations are not enough. To accomplish Kempcke's vision, librarians must advocate for information literacy and research skills at the institutional level; truly effective collaborations must influence the curriculum (Kempcke 2002, 541).

Librarians should not limit their collaborative partnerships to classroom teachers. With the growing research about the importance of student engagement, all kinds of campus departments must now demonstrate their impact on engagement and learning. Any engagement advocate is a potential ally for information literacy initiatives, whether they want to improve NSSE or HSSSE scores, increase retention rates, or help underrepresented groups succeed. These engagement advocates can be found in student affairs offices, residence halls, writing centers, advising centers, athletics departments, student health units, extracurricular organizations, and student government.

Balancing the Old with the New

Librarians should also stay current, identifying ways that new media and new technologies can support learning. In a 2005 book, Steven Johnson suggests that *Everything Bad Is Good for You.* Johnson's main argument centers on the consumption of popular media and challenges the common assumption that this consumption is an inherently passive, mindless activity. He argues that a variety of forces have combined to make popular media more complex, and that this complexity supports the development of problem-solving skills among those who consume it. Librarians should not embrace the idea that every new technology is useful or that every activity that captures student interest can be used to promote learning. But librarians should follow Johnson's lead and find out what students are actually doing with new technologies and media, even when their first assumption is that they are not being used for learning.

Librarians are in a position to walk a very useful line here, between one clientele of users who understand the value and importance of sustained analysis, and with another that understands the value of newer, participatory forms of media. In today's library, there is no reason to choose one over the other. Some learning activities will be supported better by the participatory nature of a blog discussion that extends students' time on task outside of the classroom. Others will require narrative approaches, sustained attention, and reflection. Today's library can provide the resources and spaces to support both.

One of the most important assumptions that librarians should interrogate is the assumption that study and learning should be a solitary, quiet activity. One does not need to buy into the idea that net gens are incapable of focused attention and study to realize that there is a great deal of pedagogical value in collaborative learning activities. Collaborative learning experiences are one of the benchmarks for student engagement identified by the NSSE. Working collaboratively and informally supports the development of metacognitive skills, and actually increases the amount of time students spend on task. In the "real world," problem solving frequently happens when groups and teams of people work together. Authentic learning activities are not always solitary. It is important to recognize that social, collaborative, and informal spaces promote student learning.

Libraries should provide a variety of workspaces, both physical and virtual, to meet the needs of students engaged in a variety of learning activities. Flexible spaces that allow students to move furniture and take control of the space for their own needs are also important. Information commons, media centers, and teen learning spaces are all examples of the kind of flexible, dynamic learning spaces needed in today's libraries. These dynamic spaces, designed to connect students with the information sources they need to learn, as well as the production software they need to communicate what they have learned, are an excellent example of how libraries can adapt their spaces to meet students' learning needs at every stage in the research process.

Recently, the learning commons has emerged as an even more dynamic space within the academic library or school media center. Learning commons are frequently supported by cross-campus partnerships and include a variety of services including tutoring, writing assistance, multimedia production, and career advising.

Similarly, virtual spaces can also be configured to allow social and informal learning. Instant messaging reference, for example, is one way libraries can show that they recognize that students use communication technologies in a variety of ways, both social and academic. Libraries can provide virtual spaces for students to add their own content to library resources. The University of Pennsylvania allows their users to assign their own metadata to library catalog entries, and to share that metadata with others (http://tags.library.upenn.edu/). The University of Minnesota supports student blogs as part of their Virtual Undergraduate Library page (http://www.lib.umn.edu/undergrad/).

CONCLUSION

There is no doubt that today's students find their first steps into the world of scholarly research and complex inquiry difficult. It is tempting to look at this group of students, the net generation, and conclude that it is their reliance on technology that makes it difficult for them to learn how to do the things that scholars have always done. It is important that librarians do not fall into this trap. Technology does make it easier for today's students to find information, but it does not make it easier for them to learn from the information they have found. In research projects at all levels of education, teachers and librarians are asking students to learn about complex topics. This requires students to be deeply, cognitively engaged in the work they are doing. It is unrealistic to expect that this kind of learning will be easy.

Teachers and librarians need to work together to provide the engaging learning activities, resources, feedback, and context that students need to succeed in these challenging endeavors. Information and communication technologies are an important tool educators can use to help students learn. By themselves, however, these technologies will not create authentic learning experiences or engaged students. The research on student learning and engagement is clear. What students do with the information they receive or find is far more important than how they receive it, but too many of today's students are not getting enough opportunities to work with information in meaningful, authentic ways. Instead of assuming today's students cannot learn from "old fashioned" practices involving reflection and thinking, librarians, teachers, and others interested in student learning should give them the chance to try.

REFERENCES

Alsop, J. 2005. "Losing Our Minds: The Impact of Technology on Reading and Reflection." *College & Research Libraries News* 66 (11): 790–791, 838.

Bell, S. 2005. "Don't Surrender Library Values." *Library Journal* 130(9): 79. Retrieved September 5, 2006, from EBSCOhost Professional Development Collection.

Bransford, J. D., A. L. Brown, and R. R. Cocking, eds. 2000. *How People Learn: Brain, Mind, Experience and School.* Washington, D.C.: National Academy Press.

Carlson, S. 2005. "The Net Generation Goes to College." *The Chronicle of Higher Education* 52 (7): A34. Retrieved September 5, 2006, from Lexis-Nexis Academic.

Carlson, S. (Moderator), and R. Sweeney (Guest). 2005. Higher Education for Multitaskers. *The Chronicle of Higher Education Live Discussions Series.* http://chronicle.com/colloquy/2005/10/millennial/ (Retrieved September 5, 2006.)

Hassel, H., and J. Lourey. 2005. "The Dea(r)th of Student Responsibility." *College Teaching* 53 (1): 2–12.

Johnson, S. 2005. *Everything Bad Is Good for You.* New York: Riverhead Books.

Kempcke, Ken. 2002. "The Art of War for Librarians: Academic Culture, Curriculum Reform, and Wisdom from Sun Tzu." *Portal: Libraries and the Academy* 2 (4) October. np.

Kuh, G. D. 2003. "What We're Learning about Student Engagement from NSSE: Benchmarks for Effective Educational Practices." *Change* 35 (2): 24–32. Retrieved September 5, 2006, from EbscoHOST Professional Development Collection.

Kuhlthau, C. C. 1993. *Seeking Meaning: A Process Approach to Library and Information Services.* Norwood, N.J.: Ablex Publishing Corporation.

Martinez, M. E. 2006. "What Is Metacognition?" *Phi Delta Kappan* 87 (9): 696–699. (Retrieved September 5, 2006, from EbscoHOST Academic Search Premier.)

McCarthy, M., and G. D. Kuh. 2006. "Are Students Ready for College? What Student Engagement Data Say." *Phi Delta Kappan* 87 (9): 664–669. (Retrieved September 5, 2006, from EbscoHOST Academic Search Premier.)

Merrow, J. 2006. "Declining by Degrees." *Carnegie Perspectives.* Carnegie Foundation for the Advancement of Teaching. http://www.carnegiefoundation.org/perspectives/ (Retrieved September 5, 2006.)

Munro, K. 2006. "Reading and Technology: The Bigger Picture." *College & Research Libraries News* 67 (5): 312–313.

Oblinger, D., and J. Oblinger 2005. *Educating the Net Generation.* Boulder, Colo.: EDUCAUSE. http://www.educause.edu/educatingthenetgen (Retrieved September 5, 2006.)

Pascarella, E. T., & Terenzini, P. T. (2005). *How College Affects Students, Volume 2: A Third Decade of Research.* San Francisco: Jossey-Bass.

Prensky, M. 2001. "Digital Natives, Digital Immigrants." *On the Horizon* 9 (5): 1–6. http://www.marcprensky.com/writing (Retrieved August 24, 2006.)

Prensky, M. 2005. "Engage Me or Enrage Me: What Today's Learners Demand." *EDUCAUSE Review* 40: 60–64. http://www.educause.edu/ir/library/pdf/ERM0553.pdf (Retrieved September 5, 2006.)

Shapiro, J. J., and S. K. Hughes 1996. "Information Literacy as a Liberal Art: Enlightenment Proposals for a New Curriculum." *Educom Review* 31 (2). Pagination varies. http://www.educause.edu/pub/er/review/reviewArticles/31231.html (Retrieved September 5, 2006.)

Shernoff, D. J., M. Csikszentmihalyi, B. Schneider, and E. S. Shernoff 2003. "Student Engagement in High School Classrooms from the Perspective of Flow Theory." *School Psychology Quarterly* 18 (2): 158–176.

3 BABY BOOMERS AND GENERATION Y IN THE PUBLIC LIBRARY: KEEPING THEM BOTH HAPPY. AN AUSTRALIAN PERSPECTIVE

Carolyn Jones

"What is scary about generational change, anyway? That's what a globalised world is all about. You can't live in the 21st century and suddenly decide you don't like change. That's not how modernity works" (Heath 2006, 177).

In Australia the social researcher Hugh MacKay (1997) has identified three generations in our community competing for services and demanding understanding of their needs. These three generations he labels as the "lucky" generation, that is those born in the 1920s, the "baby boomers" and "generation X." These three generations, argues MacKay, operate like three different societies within our culture. To this mix can now be added the generation that follows generation X—generation Y, the children of the baby boomers. Generation Y, also called the net generation, the millennials or the echo boomers, is the last generation to be born in the twentieth century. The title "echo boomer" reflects the status of this cohort as both the children of the baby boomers and the largest cohort to be born since the boomers. As the twentieth century was influenced by the baby boomers, so will the twenty-first century be shaped by generation Y.

A generation is defined not only by the span of time within which members were born but also by their shared experiences. Economic, social, and political conditions affect people of different ages in different ways. Each generation is distinguished from others by these formative events that occur during childhood and adolescence. Demographers call these events "social markers" or "generational indicators." These events not only mark the beginning or the end of a generation but also influence the beliefs and values of members of that cohort. For the baby boomer generation, social markers included the end of World War II, the arrival of television, rock and roll music, the Cold War, and the Vietnam War. For generation Y, it is widely believed that the events of September 11, 2001, and the resulting war on terror will mark both the end of their generation and define it. Other significant events that generation Y has experienced are the ever increasing influence of the Internet, cable television, globalization, and a concern for environmental issues.

These two generations share some common characteristics, but they also hold different values, attitudes, and expectations. If the aim of a library service is to be customer focused, it is timely to consider how the provision of services, resources, programs, and the marketing of these may need to evolve to adequately cater for the unique demands of both generations of library users. To achieve this aim, it is essential to first understand the characteristics of the two generations.

WHO ARE THE BABY BOOMERS?

The Australian Bureau of Statistics (1997) defines the baby boomers as the generation born between 1946 and 1961. This group also includes people born overseas who were immigrants to Australia, even if their country of origin did not itself experience a baby boom. The large numbers of baby boomers was due to several factors. Not only was Australia enjoying the end of a protracted world war and the benefits of peace, it was also enjoying great economic success with rising standards of living and shortages of skilled labor. Increases in population were seen as crucial to the continuation of that economic success, and so the naturally high birth rate at home was further enhanced by aggressive government policies encouraging high levels of immigration of young couples and families. Consequently between 1925 and 1995, the number of children in Australia more than doubled from 2.2 to 4.6 million.

Having grown up in a time of prosperity and privilege, the baby boomers have also lived with great social change. As a group they have been described as demanding, well educated, and widely traveled with a lifelong interest in learning. They are distinguished from previous generations by their impatience. "This is the generation who have become famous for their need of instant gratification: the generation who believe that whatever they want, they had better have it now" (MacKay 1997, 62). Baby boomers have also been identified as possessing a desire for convenience, technology, and novelty. Coupled with this affection for new technology the boomers have a seemingly endless thirst for information. To quote MacKay (1997, 118), "boomers will never catch up with their children when it comes to the mastery of information technology but many of them have been sufficiently dazzled by the information revolution to fall for the trap of believing that information is a new kind of god...so they consume information voraciously." They are a culturally diverse cohort, as many have been born overseas. Approximately half have professional qualifications and many express a keen interest in lifelong learning and self-development.

Baby boomers will live longer and healthier lives than their parents in part because of improved nutrition and in part because of advances in medical science. Having been the original teenage generation, the baby boomers will certainly redefine what it is to be elderly as they age.

The baby boomers have profited by living through economically prosperous times. An article in the *Sunday Age* newspaper entitled "Generation Xcluded" (cited in Heath 2006, 90) noted that more than three-quarters of baby boomers owned a home worth an average of $231,000, and they control 37 percent of national wealth. In contrast, generation X controls 19 percent of national wealth and generation Y only 1 percent.

Although generation Y is the first truly user-pays generation, they have also enjoyed far greater economic opportunities than the generation before them, generation X. Generation Y has only ever known a world of prosperity. In that regard they have a greater similarity to their baby boomer parents than to the Generation X cohort, who have experienced both unemployment and underemployment. As the boomers retire, bringing with it a skills shortage, generation Y will, like the baby boomers before them, have their pick of employment. As well, having been the beneficiaries of the material success of their boomer parents during childhood generation Y will eventually inherit their considerable wealth.

As the boomers also prefer to spend rather than save, some social commentators believe that personal investments may need to be relied on more often than in the past as a result of a tightening of access to the aged pension. (MacKay 1997).

WHO ARE GENERATION Y?

The term generation Y is used to describe those born between 1982 and 2000. According to the Australia Bureau of Statistics (2001) there are 5.15 million in this cohort representing 28 percent of the population, compared to 4.83 million generation X (26 percent of the population) and 4.75 million baby boomers (25 percent of the population). They are a socially and culturally diverse group. They are also an optimistic generation, with 80 percent reporting that they were happy with their lives (Australian Institute of Health and Welfare 2003 cited in Marriner 2003). MacKay (2000 cited in Huntley 2006) concluded that there had been a fundamental attitude shift from pessimism to optimism over the 20 years from 1980 to 2000. He reached this conclusion by comparing the attitudes of a 19-year-old in those two years, corresponding to generation X (1980) and generation Y (2000). In 1980, the average 19-year-old feared nuclear annihilation and saw their future, particularly their career prospects, as grim and uncertain. The average 19-year-old in 2000 is confident about both his/her own future and the future of the planet. Those in this group are relaxed and place a high premium on having fun. They are confident in their ability to cope with uncertainty. Having been raised in an uncertain era, they embrace change rather than fear it. What MacKay found particularly intriguing is that many of the concerns that existed in the 1980s still exist today. He concluded from this that generation Y were either more capable than previous generations in dealing with these concerns or were possibly more skillful at ignoring them.

The 2005 AustraliaSCAN survey revealed that 36 percent of 20- to 29-year-olds still live in the parental home. In 1976, only 21 percent of people in this age group lived with their parents. The main reason for this development is believed to be the deferment by generation Y of traditional markers of adulthood such as marrying, buying a house, and parenthood. This has lead to the derogatory description of generation Y as "adultescents." The fact that 40 percent of 20- to 24-year-olds are involved in tertiary study must also play a part in their reluctance to leave home. Since 1971, there has been a substantial increase in the number of Australians with a higher educational qualification. In 1971, 3 percent of the population ages 20 to 64 years held such a qualification, but by 2001 this rate had increased to 16 percent. Approximately 1 in 5, or 21 percent of people ages 25 to 29 years now hold a higher educational qualification. Of those young people studying full-time, 36 percent were also working, the majority of those (91 percent) working in part-time positions (Australian Bureau of Statistics 2001).

As this cohort generally has few financial commitments at this stage of their lives, more than 70 percent of their income is spent on entertainment, travel, and food. Like their boomer parents they are a very well-traveled generation.

Generation Y has been raised in smaller families, usually composed of one or two children. Many have grown up in single parent families. After the introduction of no-fault divorce legislation in 1975, Australia's divorce rate increased from 4.2 per 1,000 in 1971 to 18.8 per 1,000 in 1976. Since then the divorce rate has fluctuated but has always been of an upward trend (Australian Bureau of Statistics 2001). Smaller families and smaller class sizes at school resulted in a greater amount of adult attention for this generation compared to the perceived parental neglect experienced by generation X. They are possibly more indulged and protected than any previous Australian generation as a result of this trend. Some researchers, for example Huntley (2006), argue that this has resulted in generation Y being more influenced by their parents rather than the generation that came before them, generation X.

Generation Y have also been fortunate to grow up in an era where much focus has been on the rights and protection of children. Howe and Strauss (cited in Huntley 2006, 12) call this "kinderpolitics," that is, "the political trend to translate concerns about children's current and future status into aggressive public policy on everything from crime to media content to welfare payments." At the same time as this increased political interest there has been a focus on them as consumers, with the number of movies, television programs, and even clothing aimed at them increasing dramatically. They also share some common experiences with their parents when it comes to entertainment; many of the toys, crazes, movies, and television programs popular when the boomers were young have returned to be enjoyed by their children.

The education of generation Y has emphasized a collaborative, problem-solving, highly interactive style of learning. Their learning has been technology based and highly visual. To this generation computer skills are as fundamental to their education as the "three Rs" were to previous generations. Online teaching and learning is commonplace in many educational institutions. Indeed, generation Y expresses a preference for this style of learning. (Veldof and Beavers 2001; Dupuis 1999 cited in Yi 2005). As well as being the most formally educated generation of

Australians, generation Y has benefited from a plethora of stimulating extracurricular activities provided for them by their parents.

Recent research by McCrindle (2005) into generation Y in Australia has provided some useful insights into this generation. He has identified three core values of Generation Y, which he has described as a desire for relational connection, a desire for a bigger meaning in life, and the desire for guidance from a trusted mentor. Acknowledging these three core values will help explain generation Y more readily, assisting in plans to attract and retain them as library users, while also keeping the baby boomer clientele happy.

The first value identified by McCrindle, relational connection, describes a wish to be part of a community where they are liked, accepted, understood, and included. Generation Y is often accused of lacking commitment to causes or institutions, and indeed they are reluctant to commit themselves to anything long term, but they are very loyal to their friends. Friendship groups for many provide the sense of caring, acceptance, and support once provided by the nuclear family.

The second core value identified by McCrindle, the desire for a bigger meaning in life, is a consequence of their upbringing. Generation Y has seen the emotional and physical cost to their parents in working hard and are not prepared to make the same sacrifices. This has huge implications for the future employment market, as generation Y does not intend to live to work but rather to work to live. When deciding to accept a job, financial rewards are not the top priority of generation Y; rather they look for flexibility, variety, fulfillment, and recognition. Herceg (cited in Huntley 2006, 97) found that the majority of young people "talk about a way of working that is smarter rather than harder." Mental speed and the ability to multitask and absorb new information rapidly are essential in the new global workplace. Being a socially and culturally diverse cohort makes them also a tolerant one, and so generation Y is comfortable working with others of different ages, race, and gender. The provision of on-going training and education is important to them, as they recognize that as the world becomes ever more complex, knowledge based, and global in focus, it is essential to maintain their technological competitiveness. Indeed, many members of generation Y will be working in jobs that did not exist when they began school. They find that uncertainty in the workplace gives them greater opportunities and more freedom. Flexible work options such as job sharing, flexible hours, and working from home appeal to them. In fact, many generation Y start their own businesses; in 2006, there were approximately 50,000 businesses in Australia owned and operated by people under 25 years old (Sheahan cited in Taylor 2006). This flexibility in the job market has led to many time-rich but money-poor Gen Ys becoming involved in volunteering in practical ways, donating their skills rather than merely donating money.

The third core value identified by McCrindle, a desire for guidance from a trusted mentor, reflects the fact that generation Y has been heavily marketed to during their childhood and is subsequently less idealistic than previous generations. Rather than being influenced by authority figures or by facts, they are heavily influenced in their decision making by their peers. Other than their friendship groups, gen Y is most influenced by television, movies, and music. Many of the views they hold do not come from their parents or other authority figures but from a diverse range of media and other sources. Figures they admire are usually drawn from these celebrity groups rather than from the arts, sports, or politics.

Of particular importance to libraries is the fact that this generation is the first to grow up with technology from infancy. Technology has changed how generation Y lives, works, educates, entertains, and communicates with one another. Being raised in a highly digital age "has given them a new orientation in space and time...they see the world as global, connected and round the clock" (Zemke, Raines, and Filipczak 2000, 136). Before the 1980s, there were only three forms of mass communication: radio, telephone, and television; however, Australians are eager, it appears, to take up new technologies. Between 1994 and 2000, the number of homes with computers doubled, with over half of all Australian households—some 3.8 million—now owning a computer and one-third of all households—2.3 million homes—having access to the Internet. Furthermore, Australia is ranked in the top 10 users of the Internet in the world, with usage constantly increasing (Australian Bureau of Statistics 2001). In the lifetime of generation Y, the Internet, especially the World Wide Web, has become prolific for many young people, replacing newspapers and television as their primary source of information. Howe and Strauss (cited in Huntley 2006, 18) have described gen Y as "the world's first generation to grow up thinking of itself as global." The Internet has allowed those with a shared interest to become connected with each other regardless of time and distance constraints. Many activities that were once communal can now be undertaken alone, and technology can create communities that do not have, and never will have, a physical location.

Personal communications are now dominated by e-mail and text. In April 2000, when Australia gained the ability to send text messages between telephone networks, there was a 600 percent increase in text messages in six months (Macken cited in Heath 2006, 44). The popularity of texting as a means of communication continues to rise. In fact, generation Y's preference for text is resulting in the development of a new language. They also enjoy the cross-use of technology, for example, using their mobile phones to send e-mail or to take photographs. Personal computers are used not only for educational and information-seeking purposes but also for entertainment. Computers, television, and other forms of media are now interactive. If television helped to define and create the baby boomers, then technology will do the same for this generation. The Australian Lifestyles Survey of 2001 (cited in McCrindle 2005) found that, "Australian teenagers are now spending more time watching TV today compared to four years ago, up from 2 hours 16 minutes per day to 2 hours and 20 minutes, a growth of 3.6%. In addition to the growing Internet and video game use, they are now approaching 4 hours screen time per day."

Given their reliance on technology, many Generation Ys worldwide are now sharing common experiences; however, there is the potential for a great discrepancy to develop between the poorer and the more affluent members of this generation. If access to technology, particularly communication technology such as mobile telephones, e-mail, online chat rooms, and texting, is limited, then the life of a member of generation Y is also limited. Old technology or no technology means social isolation.

There are many similarities between the baby boomers and their generation Y offspring in their expectations of a library service. To quote Heath (2006, 116), "the days of compromise are gone. Customers and consumers want it all: affordability, reliability, security, simplicity, manageability, adaptability, innovation, connection." Both generations value information and are impatient to have their information needs met. The fundamental difference between the generations is the greater competence in and acceptance of technology by generation Y. If generation Y feels that their needs are not being met by libraries, then those with money, expertise, and access to technology may choose to use alternative providers for their relaxation, education, and information needs. This will also be true of the more computer-literate members of the baby boomer cohort. This will make public libraries increasingly irrelevant to their lives. Indeed for the younger, highly computer-literate members of generation Y, there is already a wealth of resources online. Mobile telephones and the Internet, for example, allow instant access to information that was once out of reach, with the additional benefits of minimal cost and inconvenience. This is an enormous challenge to libraries in an era where one can at any time in the comfort of home or the convenience of the workplace be in effect one's own librarian. If the opportunities offered by the appearance of generation Y are seized, libraries have a good chance to reposition themselves in peoples' lives. Failure to do so will leave libraries obsolete.

As discussed previously, generation Y are accustomed to using technology for their information, social, and recreational needs. They expect the immediacy of Internet communications and the ability to personalize services. In fact, "We are entering an era where everything is going digital. It's going to be the main event of our lives for decades to come. The digital age is bringing about the democratization of information, the removal of traditional barriers of time, distance and wealth, and the onset of total transparency" (Fiorina 2004 cited in Heath 2006, 43). What does this mean for public libraries? First, libraries should view their resources and services as commodities and generation Y as consumers. It makes sense to use the medium in which they already spend large amounts of time, the Internet, as the primary tool for developing strategies to serve this generation. As there is now a greater societal acceptance of technology as a means of communication and training, technology will be a powerful tool for any library as it strives to tailor services to satisfy changing needs. A library's mastery of new technologies may lead to the formation of closer alliances with other organizations that serve Generation Y and the baby boomers, possibly forming partnerships to more effectively provide services to them. The first step in this process, however, is successfully marketing library services to these target groups.

MARKETING OF LIBRARY SERVICES AND RESOURCES

The notion of effective marketing of library services is often discussed as desirable, if not essential, in this era where the Internet can provide consumers with many of the so-called traditional library services. Yet marketing is an area that many libraries do poorly, or not at all. As well, not many libraries have "cradle to grave" services to market. Singh (2004) argues that a customer-centered focus, with all library employees working toward that aim, is essential to developing the right kind of "marketing culture" in libraries. Although most library managers in his study saw the value of the Internet as a marketing tool, very few had clear objectives for their library Web sites other than informing customers of library facilities, resources, and services. Singh concluded that, "Library directors must develop and nurture an appropriate marketing culture in their libraries to understand the meaning of their brand, how to measure their brand, and, of course, how to position their brand in the "market" (2004, 97–98). This conclusion has implications for libraries in their marketing to the two generations. It is imperative that libraries seize the opportunity to market their unique features, especially to the more technologically sophisticated among the generations who have many more options available to them. If we recognize that generation Y may choose to chiefly use the library as virtual patrons, then it becomes essential for libraries to market themselves in the environment in which this group spends large amounts of their time, that is, online platforms. In addition, libraries may need to follow the lead of advertisers who have recognized the marketing potential of the Internet, e-mail, and text message and have developed campaigns that speak to generation Y's love of technology and the need to belong to friendship groups. The mass customization developed by Web marketers also appeals to generation Y who crave individuality and the personalized approach more than any preceding generation (Smith cited in Peattie 2002). If libraries can develop the concept of a brand for the functions of their libraries, this may be well received by generation Y who "believe brands symbolize something important. Brands reflect a sense of security and reliability but also excitement and glamour" (Huntley 2006, 158).

As libraries respond to the demands of the electronic age, there must be a greater emphasis on a library being "a collection of services" rather than merely a "place." By emphasizing online delivery of services and resources, libraries will increase their potential to remain relevant to the lives of young people. In 2003, approximately 80 percent of public libraries offered Web access to their library catalogue, and approximately 60 percent offered access to subscription databases (Australian Bureau of Statistics cited in Hildebrand 2003, 269). Although this is encouraging, some Australian researchers such as Hildebrand (2003) and Strempel (1997) would argue that libraries have not continued to seize the opportunities new technologies offer to provide appropriate services to their clients. Strempel (1997, 4–7) argues that, "Technology is becoming an affordable enabler which can allow us to redefine our library services, and add value to the lives of all in our community where they work and recreate, rather than see libraries as separate entities which people MUST VISIT. This integration of library services into everyday life is one way of ensuring the future of libraries. Failure to reach out to customers will lead to marginalization."

Although public libraries should market their electronic library functions more widely to both groups of users, it must be remembered that there will always be a demand for the traditional services of libraries. From the time of the development of the first Australian public library Web site in 1994, there have been varying predictions of gloom regarding the future of libraries in the face of new technologies. Despite the Internet changing the way people access and use information and the way that librarians, in particular, access, use, and present information, researchers have found that the traditional services of libraries remain popular with Australian national, state, and local government libraries, reporting 99.4 million visits in the 12-month period ending June 2000 (Australian Bureau of Statistics 2001 cited in Hildebrand 2003, 269). The ability to satisfy the needs of both face-to-face and virtual patrons will present many challenges to libraries. The following areas offer potential to satisfy the desire of generation Y for electronic delivery of public library services and would also be of interest to baby boomer patrons.

An Online Branch of the Public Library

The development of a Web site that is a unique, completely online branch of the main library is one such service that would be well received by both the baby boomers and generation Y, as it offers convenience and flexibility. This sort of public library Web site would not seek to offer those activities best suited to take place in a physical building, for example, author talks, but would, according to Hildebrand (2003, 272), "Seek to attract users by enhancing convenience. To do so, public library web sites need to be established and operated as a unique branch library rather than simply a repository for information about a physical library. With a few exceptions...a service oriented web site should enable users to do online what they would traditionally be able to do in a physical library."

Online Interactive Reference Services

In an interesting study examining the varying ways adults use both the Internet and their public library, Rodger, D'Elia, Jorgensen, and Woelfel (2000) found that use of the library and use of the Internet were inversely related to age, but that use of the library and use of the Internet were positively related to educational levels and income levels. They also found that use of the library and use of the Internet were complementary but that consumers were differentiating between the two "both in terms of how they evaluate the service characteristics of each provider and in terms of which provider they chose to use for specific purposes" (Rodger et al. 2000, 16). Regular users of both the Internet and the library rated the Internet as superior in 10 out of 16 service characteristics. These characteristics particularly related to speed and convenience. If this trend continues, the Internet will make further encroachments into traditional library fields of information provision, necessitating the modern library to further redefine its role. An Australian assessment of the most highly used Web sites on the Internet reveals them to be those providing services similar to ones traditionally offered by public libraries and that, given "the convenience of accessing competitor sites such as free advice and commercial information services, it is time for libraries to consider how they can take advantage of existing and emerging web technologies to develop web sites which become a one stop shop for delivering and accessing a wide range of library services" (Hildebrand 2003, 272).

The establishment of interactive online reference services is another area that public libraries have been slow to develop. This has allowed commercial and free competitors such as Allexperts and Liveadvice to flourish. In 2003, Hildebrand reported that only 18 percent of Australian libraries currently offer an e-mail reference service, with responses taking between 1 and 10 days. The collaborative e-mail reference project AskNow! is described by Hildebrand as superior to other e-mail reference services because the reference librarian can conduct a reference interview, increasing the likelihood of the online user receiving accurate information. None of the currently available e-mail reference services operate around the clock, however, but they are the foundation of a superior information and reference service to online users.

To attract the technologically savvy in both generations, but particularly those in generation Y, these sort of online services need to become more readily available and more widely publicized. As discussed previously, their outlook is global and they are accustomed to using technology for their information, social, and recreational needs This approach will inevitably lead to "changes to library services in the electronic era [which] emphasize electronic/remote access to library resources and services without the constraints of time and space" (Yi 2005, 50).

E-book Services

Another area that should be more actively developed by libraries is the subscribing to e-book services such as Netlibrary and Ebrary. Although a few libraries offer access to e-books within the library, none as yet make them available to online library users.

Tailored Reading Services

Although using technology is natural to this generation, they also appear to read more than the generations before them, particularly generation X. Whereas the boomers prefer to read self-help books and guides "publishers say the annual sales of children's and young adult books have quadrupled in the last ten years" (Zemke, Raines, and Filipczak 2000, 244). New technologies offer the possibility of a more tailored service in recreational reading to patrons, not only because the library catalog is available online but also because reader profiles could be created with the computer then suggesting and selecting suitable reading material.

This material could then be mailed or couriered directly to patrons. This service is currently available from the Amazon.com Internet bookshop and has proven popular.

Educating for Information Literacy

Information literacy is among the most crucial of skills for an information age, and the ability to critically evaluate information is central to this. Many generation Y members overestimate their ability to find, critically evaluate, and use suitable information sources (Manuel 2002; Brown et al. 2003 cited in Holliday and Li 2004). Many seek immediate answers to their questions, compromising the quality of their research for convenience. Carlson (2003 cited in Yi 2005, 51) calls this process "research by Googling." Many baby boomers are bewildered by the array of information available to them online. Rather than being concerned about information overload, as the baby boomers are, gen Y may be overwhelmed by too easy an access to information, which encourages them to stop searching as soon as they have found something that is somewhat suitable for their purposes. This approach leads them to believe that the research process should always be easy and encourages short-term rather than long-term learning. Many users do not understand that they need to be involved in the research process through both reading and critical thinking, two of the fundamentals of information literacy. This results in ineffective searching and produces poor quality and a lack of variety of information being obtained. Researchers, for example Davis (cited in Holliday and Li 2004), report a reduction in the scholarly content of assignments and bibliographies, as the Internet rather than the library has become the primary source of information for many students.

Holliday and Li (2004, 365) have described this situation in the following way:

> The impact of fulltext articles might change students' cognitive behaviour. Instead of having to read through books, encyclopedias and journal articles in the library, students can now download and print information from the convenience of their desktop. They no longer have to take notes and then read through them for themes and ideas, an activity central to the development of a focused research topic. Electronic articles also encourage cutting and pasting. In addition to enabling plagiarism, it might also discourage students from reading simply to become informed about a topic. Fulltext articles might make students "commit" to their final paper sources before they have a clear idea of their topic.

The familiarity and convenience of the Web may also lead young people to believe they should be completely independent in their research process, lessening their likelihood to ask for assistance from a librarian.

The public library is in a good position to offer training in information literacy both to overwhelmed boomers and overconfident gen Ys. Both generations recognize the necessity of ongoing learning. Both generations crave information that is available to them swiftly, and is accurate. In addition to instructing patrons in how to search electronic information resources other than Google, librarians are well qualified to teach Web discernment. If the library decides to take on this role, then learning should be experiential, with an emphasis on outcomes rather than teaching techniques. As generation Y likes technology, it is important that any librarians involved in training should acknowledge their preference for the Web and be positive about the uses of technology emphasizing "what the web is good for, such as exploring the major issues and opinions surrounding a topic, rather than focusing only on evaluation of web resources for credibility and accuracy" (Holliday and Li 2004, 359).

Developing New Forms of Social Capital

The concept of social capital and its important role in building successful communities have been widely discussed of late. The term *social capital*, however, is not a modern one, having been first used in 1916, and the concept itself can be traced back to early sociological theory (Winter 2000). Researchers such as Bordieu, Coleman, Putnam, and Cox define social capital as "the advantages that accrue to a society from the aggregated networks of individual trust" (Bundy 2003, 12). Those networks may be either small or large, formal or informal, and are composed of the people one knows and interacts with. As it is through interacting cooperatively with one another that social capital is generated, concepts of trust and reciprocity are fundamental in enabling people or institutions to act for their mutual benefit.

Communities with high levels of social capital work well, with better quality of life for both individuals and the community as a whole. Communities that work well are peopled with citizens who are more likely to use institutions and to become involved in activities such as volunteering and civic matters. Involvement in these roles further enhances a community's level of social capital; however, this beneficial effect is seen only if communities are inclusive of a variety of different groups (Winter 2000) rather than being exclusive.

Concern has been expressed by many commentators that social capital has been declining in the Western world over the last 30 years. In his book *Bowling Alone*, Putnam (2000) sought to find an explanation for the reluctance of modern-day Americans to become involved in formal organizations such as social clubs or sporting groups. He felt that the declining rates of participation in both informal and formal relationships with others translated into reduced opportunities to generate social capital, leading inevitably to a decline in trust and reciprocity. Several explanations for this decline have been proposed and Putnam claims that the rebuilding of social capital is the greatest challenge facing communities in this century.

The public library has an important role to play in the development and maintenance of social capital. Recent research has demonstrated a strong correlation between the quality of libraries and social capital. This endorses the view that "libraries serve as both an indicator and creator of social capital" (Preer cited in Bundy 2003, 17). How do public libraries do this? It can be argued that there are three major ways in which public libraries contribute to the generation and maintenance of social capital. First, libraries offer free community space, which is used by diverse groups of people interacting with each other in a trusted environment (University of Technology Sydney, 2000). Public libraries are the most frequently visited public institution in Australia, with more than 100 million visits a year, and they are accessible by more than 98 percent of Australians (Bundy 2003). Cox, Swinbourne, Pip, and Laing (2000) commented that public libraries are easily recognized and highly valued, even by those who are not regular patrons In this role public library space has been described as a community's village green, "a much used venue that is already providing experiences of universal sharing" (MacKay cited in Bundy 2003, 12). This experience of universal sharing translates into feelings of trust between diverse groups of library users.

The second way in which public libraries contribute to the development of social capital is in the provision of civic information, enabling people to educate themselves as to their civic rights and obligations. Becoming better informed and more involved citizens is an important element in the creation of social capital.

The third way in which public libraries contribute to social capital is through the opportunities they provide to patrons to become involved in formal networks such as book discussion groups. Many public libraries now also offer activities in conjunction with other organizations such as government agencies. When libraries do this they are said to be involved in "bridging networks." These bridging networks are viewed as crucial to the development of social capital.

Library staff play an important role in providing social contact to face-to-face users, but it would be foolish to assume that all encounters in public libraries are positive, leading to increases in social capital. Public libraries are no different from other busy institutions—sometimes understaffed or peopled with staff with neither the time nor the inclination to respond in a kindly manner toward patrons. Also some library policies may seem harsh and inflexible, resulting in patrons feeling negatively toward the library.

In the future how can a public library assist in the creation and maintenance of social capital when most of their patrons may be virtual ones? New technologies may challenge the ability of public libraries to help foster and maintain social capital in their communities, but it may not all be negative. It is possible to use communication technology to fulfill the basic human need for social contact. As discussed previously, there is potential to provide new forms of group activity, community involvement, and connectedness through communication technology. Heath (2006) argues that access to professional networks is a form of bridging social capital. Allowing systems of semiformal membership to operate, for example, by joining an e-mail list, is a means of maintaining contact between people and distributing information widely and at little cost. This will enable gen Y, with their interest in global and local issues such as environmentalism, to stay connected and informed. Public libraries may also seek to address the potential inequalities in gen Y between those who have access to communication technologies and those who do not by acting in roles such as a broker.

CONCLUSION

Public libraries have faced many challenges to their success in the past. The current challenge is to maintain a professional service for patrons who visit the library while facing an increasing generational demand for electronic delivery of services. There is enormous goodwill toward libraries in older generations, even among those who are not regular library patrons. Generation Y, however, will expect services and resources from their libraries that are better than those they can source themselves. They will not use libraries just because they are there. If the challenges presented by this generational shift are mastered, this will not only attract generation Y as users but improve library services for all patrons.

REFERENCES

Australian Bureau of Statistics. 1997. *Australian Social Trends. Population Growth: Australia's Child Population*. Canberra: ABS.

Australian Bureau of Statistics. 2001. *Census of Population and Housing: Australia's Youth*. Canberra: ABS.

Bundy, A. 2003. "Best Investment: The Modern Public Library as Social Capital." In *Proceedings of the AGM of Friends of Libraries Australia*. Altona: Friends of Libraries Australia.

Cox, E., K. Swinbourne, C. Pip, and S. Laing. 2000. *A Safe Place to Go. Libraries and Social Capital*. Sydney: Public Libraries Branch of the State Library of New South Wales.

Heath, Ryan. 2006. *Please Just F* Off It's Our Turn Now: Holding Baby Boomers to Account*. North Melbourne: Pluto Press.

Hildebrand, I. 2003. "Service Please! Rethinking Public Library Web Sites." *Library Review* 52 (6): 268–277. Viewed August 10, 2004. (Available from Emerald Fulltext.)

Holliday, W., and Q. Li. 2004. "Understanding the Millennials: Updating Our Knowledge about Students." *Reference Services Review* 32 (1). (Emerald Fulltext). http://www.emeraldinsight.com.ezlibproxy.levels.unisa.edu (Viewed May 2, 2006.)

Huntley, R. 2006. *The World According to Y: Inside the New Adult Generation*. Allen and Unwin Proprietary Ltd., Crows Nest: Queensland, Australia.

MacKay, H. 1997. *Generations. Baby Boomers, Their Parents and Their Children*. Sydney: Pan MacMillan Australia.

Marriner, C. 2003. "Generation Y not—It's Happy Days for the Young." *The Sydney Morning Herald*.

McCrindle, M. 2005. *McCrindle Research: Fast Facts*. North Parramatta: The Australian Leadership Foundation.

Peattie, S. 2002. "Using the Internet to Communicate the Sun-Safe Message to Teenagers." *Health Education* 102 (5): 210–218. (Available from Emerald Fulltext.) http://www.emeraldinsight.com/0965-4283.htm (Viewed May 2, 2006.)

Putnam, R. D. 2000. *Bowling Alone: The Collapse and Revival of American Community*. New York: Simon & Schuster.

Rodger, E. J., G. D'Elia, C. Jorgensen, and J. Woelfel. 2000. *The Impacts of the Internet on Public Library Use. An Analysis of the Current Consumer Market for Library and Internet*

Services. Buffalo: State University of New York at Buffalo: Urban Libraries Council. http://urbanlibraries.org/pdfs/finalulc.pdf (Viewed August 10, 2004.)

Singh, R. 2004. "Branding in Library and Information Context: The Role of Marketing Culture." *Information Services and Use* 24: 93–98.

Strempel, G. 1997. "Mobile Libraries and Beyond: Outreach Services of the Future." *Proceedings of the Hamilton ALIA Mobile Libraries Conference*, 1–9. Hamilton: Australian Library and Information Association.

Taylor, D. 2006. "The A to Z of Generation Y." *The Age Newspaper*. Melbourne.

University of Technology Sydney. 2000. *A Safe Place to Go: Libraries and Social Capital*. Sydney: University of Technology Sydney.

Winter, I. 2000. "Social Capital and Public Policy in Context." In I. Winter, ed. *Social Capital and Public Policy in Australia*. Melbourne: Australian Institute of Family Studies.

Yi, H. 2005. "Library Instruction Goes Online. An Inevitable Trend." *Library Review* 54 (1): 47–58.

Zemke, R., C. Raines, and B. Filipczak. 2000. *Generations at Work. Managing the Clash of Veterans, Boomers, Xers and Nexters in Your Workplace*. New York: AMACOM.

SELECTED BIBLIOGRAPHY

Australian Bureau of Statistics. 2005. *Australian Social Trends. People in Their 20s: Then and Now*. Canberra: ABS.

Gummins, R., R. Eckersley, J. Pallant, and M. Davern. 2002. *Wellbeing in Australia and the Aftermath of September 11*. Survey 3, Report 3.1, May 2002. Melbourne: Australian Centre on Quality of Life.

Jorgensen, B. 2003. "Baby Boomers, Generation X and Generation Y? Policy Implications for Defence Forces in the Modern Era." *Foresight* 5 (4): 41–49.

Lumby, C. 1999. *Gotcha: Life in a Tabloid World*. Sydney: Allen & Unwin.

MacKay, H. 2005. "Annual Manning Clark Lecture: Social Disengagement: A Breeding Ground for Fundamentalism." *A.B.C. Radio National. Big Ideas*. http://www.abc.net.au/rn/bigidea/stories/s (Viewed April 13, 2006.)

MacKay, H. 2005. "Australia and the World: The Australian Paradox." *New Matilda*. http://www.newmatilda.com/policytoolkit/policydetail.asp (Viewed April 13, 2006.)

Manual, K. 2002. "Teaching Information Literacy to Generation Y at California State University, Hayward." *Journal of Library Administration* 36 (1): 195–217.

O'Keefe, C. 2004. "The Traveling Bra Salesman's Lessons." www.shelleconomistprize.com/winners2004.html (Viewed May 31, 2006.)

Pitman, S., T. Herbert, C. Land, and C. O'Neil. 2003. *Profile of Young Australians: Facts, Figures and Issues*. Melbourne: Foundation for Young Australians.

Salt, B. 2006. Y-front: They Just Won't Wait In Line. *The Weekend Australian*. Melbourne.

Veldof, Jerilyn R., and Karen Beavers. 2001. "Going Mental: Tackling Mental Models for the Online Library Tutorial at the University of Minnesota Libraries." *Research Strategies* 18 (1): 3–20.

Wiseman, R. 2002. *Queen Bees & Wannabes*. London: Piatkus (Publishers) Ltd.

4 REACHING OUT TO GEN Y: ADAPTING LIBRARY ROLES AND POLICIES TO MEET THE INFORMATION NEEDS OF THE NEXT GENERATION

Susanne Markgren

An 18-year-old walks into her college library. She is simultaneously listening to music on her iPod, sending a text message on her cell phone, and scanning the computer area to see if she knows anyone. She plops down in a comfortable chair in front of a computer and logs on. Within a few short minutes she has checked a favorite music site for new downloads, logged onto her MySpace account to make some quick updates, and started doing research for a class assignment using Google. She is clearly comfortable with her surroundings and focused on her many tasks. She pays little attention to those around her, including the reference librarian sitting a short distance away. When her classmates arrive, they congregate around her computer table and discuss their group assignment. Surprisingly, this college freshman, who uses libraries primarily for printing papers and meeting friends, is very important to the future of libraries. Her generation, generation Y (also known as gen Y, millennials, NextGens, and net generation), represents a major shift in the expectations and information needs of library patrons. Unlike any generation before them, they will challenge traditional library roles and policies and force librarians to rethink the way they perform their jobs, and the way they market their services.

Members of gen Y are different from other generations. Because they grew up with technology, they feel comfortable with it and capable of figuring things out for themselves. It may not even occur to them that they might need assistance in finding information or in using a resource. What are librarians doing to address the needs of gen Y—a generation often described as technologically savvy, but not necessarily *information savvy*; who are quick in finding online information, but may not be adept at evaluating it, or even understanding where it comes from; a generation who cares more about immediacy than format? What can we librarians do to attract and retain gen Y as library patrons, as library advocates, and even as library employees? We can start by learning about them and their information needs and expectations, and then we can use what we know about them, especially their communication style, their connectivity, and their collaborative spirit, to make changes in our existing library roles and policies intended to engage and inform this distinct generation.

Margaret Mead, the notable American anthropologist and writer, once said, "As long as any adult thinks that he, like the parents and teachers of old, can become introspective, invoking his own youth to understand the youth before him, he is lost." This rings especially true with generation Y. Although we can try to understand them and define them, they cannot be compared to those generations who came before them.

UNDERSTANDING GEN Y

Generation Y, born in or around 1982, is the first generation to have grown up in a computerized world, as digital natives. They differ from other youth generations because they are more affluent, better educated, and more ethnically diverse; and they display positive social habits such as teamwork, achievement, and good conduct (Howe and Strauss 2000, 4). They are the largest generation next to the baby boomers, with more than 80 million members. They have been written about extensively, as experts, scholars, and others attempt to understand and define them in an effort to prepare academia, the workforce, and libraries for their inevitable invasion. Some gen Ys are already entering librarianship and working in libraries, and they will no doubt be a major force in shaping the direction of libraries and library roles for the future.

Generational characteristics are formed and shaped by a shared history and by major events that occur during formative years. Although defining an entire generation of people will, no doubt, result in sweeping generalizations and unavoidable presumptions, the one characteristic that is undeniable in gen Y is their close relationship to technology and to the online world. Members of gen Y grew up with the Internet, and they feel at ease in an online environment and quite adept at searching the Web for information; yet their online activities are by no means limited to finding information. A recent Pew memo states that, "Internet users ages 12 to 28 years old have embraced the online applications that enable communicative, creative, and social uses. Teens and gen Y (ages 18–28) are significantly more likely than older users to send and receive instant messages, play online games, create blogs, download music, and search for school information" (Fox and Madden 2006, 2). Gen Ys are considered to be extremely connected individuals who prefer experiential learning, are multitaskers, and are quite social and collaborative in nature (Abram and Luther 2004, 36). As library patrons, these attributes will help to establish their information needs and their expectations of library services and resources.

The Internet has defined the way information is stored, organized, found, and used; and librarians have responded by embracing the Internet and adapting their roles within the library as they built digital environments, acquired online materials, and instructed library users in how to find and evaluate online information. New roles and titles such as Web Librarian and Electronic Resources Librarian were created; but, for the most part, traditional services stayed the same and librarians continued in their same roles. As more and more people turn to the Web for their information and research needs, traditional library services and functions will need to change and be updated or the library itself will be in danger of losing its importance and relevancy in society.

THE CHANGING LIBRARY

In the past 10 years or so librarians have touted the virtual library and the seamless integration of technology with traditional library services and resources, but times are changing and the next generation of patrons are choosing the Web over the library. It is time for librarians to evaluate the effectiveness and usefulness of existing services and resources and to think about creating new roles and policies. A Pew Internet report found that only 9 percent of college students say they use the library for information searching more than they use the Internet; nearly three-quarters of college students said they use the Internet more than the library (Jones and Madden 2002, 3). An OCLC white paper found that 7 out of 10 college students used the library's Web site for some of their assignments, but only 1 in 5 used it for most of their assignments (OCLC 2002, 6). These students are confident in their abilities to search for and locate information, and most of them would choose a search engine, such as Google, over a library Web site to find what they need. These statistics, while not shocking, should at least make librarians wonder, "What are we doing wrong and how can we correct it?"

Let's face it, over the years librarians have created complicated and confusing environments that require users to *ask for help* to find something. The problem is, fewer and fewer of our patrons are asking us for help, and if they cannot find what they need by themselves, they feel that it isn't worth finding. This problem only escalates as library patrons become more secure in their own searching abilities and more adept at using Web resources. The more technologically savvy the user, the less he thinks he needs assistance; and if assistance is not available when and where he needs it, then chances are he will give up and go somewhere else for his information needs. Adapting services to meet patrons at their point of need is an essential requirement for today's libraries.

It is the nature of libraries to change and change often. Although libraries need to maintain their primary functions of acquiring, housing, preserving, organizing, and providing access to information resources, the continuously changing information needs of their patrons and the increasing difficulty of informing users of the library's resources and services will create enormous challenges. To remain relevant to all library users, especially to gen Y and future generations, librarians will have to keep their technology skills up-to-date, adopt new ways of providing access to resources and services, and develop new ways of communicating and interacting with library users.

CONNECTIVITY AND GEN Y

The biggest challenge for librarians is not *teaching* this generation, but *reaching* this generation. We need to reach them on their turf, on their terms, or risk losing them as patrons. Highly mobile, members of gen Y move from place to place without disconnecting from their network of friends and family. They use a variety of devices and formats to communicate and to socialize, including cell phones, laptops, personal Web sites, blogs, photo sites, games, podcasts, instant messaging, and e-mail. They are digitally literate and are able to adapt quickly to new technologies, even though their in-depth knowledge of the technology and how it actually works may be fairly superficial (Oblinger and Oblinger 2005, 5). Their expectation of technology is mainly focused on what activity they can do with it, or what service it will provide them in their daily lives. New technologies are the norm for this generation. They will learn what they need to and effortlessly adapt the technology to suit their lives. In contrast, older generations tend to be more awed by new technology, often hesitant at accepting it wholly and learning it fully, and skeptical of its value in society and the workplace.

If we build a better Web site, will they come? The library Web site is a library in itself, an environment that houses and organizes resources, a space where users can find information quickly, and a place that provides services similar to the in-person services found in the physical library. Gen Y is a generation accustomed to the simplicity and immediacy of sites like Google and the collaborative and customizable nature of sites like Amazon.com, MySpace, and Wikipedia. Library Web sites must do a better job at effectively enticing patrons, all patrons, to stay and search for information and to communicate with library staff if they need assistance. Web sites must be simple to use, use natural language, and provide links on the homepage to the most critical and most sought after resources. They should be collaborative and instructive, providing patrons with tools that will help them in their searching and tools that they can use to provide feedback. Library Web sites should fully reflect the library's mission and goals and facilitate information retrieval for all users. And perhaps most important, library Web sites should be changing regularly as information needs change, as resources and services change, as library policies and librarian roles change. "For millennials, the physical and virtual libraries must not just be intertwined, they must be inseparable. Librarians should expect millennials' digital information and communication expectations to remain forever radically different and in most cases far ahead of the baby boomers and even generation X" (Sweeney 2005, 170).

Library Web sites should adapt to the expectations and needs of gen Y and at the same time be sensitive to the needs of other generations. They can be much more than portals for resources and services; they can be spaces that encourage and promote socialization and collaboration with the use of social networking tools like wikis, blogs, RSS, and tags; and they can provide different types of content and different types of media. Members of gen Y, and increasingly all users, expect to find content quickly and easily. For a growing number of users, the content *must* be readily available online, or it will not be used. As a generation brought up with the Internet, instantaneous access to information as well as the networks for which that information is relevant is the standard (Squire and Steinkuehler 2005, 40). Libraries, in order to expand their digital content collections and remove the divide between the physical and virtual libraries, will need to rethink and revise their collection policies, find better ways to track online usage, develop new ways of marketing their online resources, and look at new platforms for information storage and retrieval.

A question we should be asking ourselves is, "How many of our policies reflect the support and maintenance of the online library?" Online reference services exist to support the virtual library and are increasingly important as more and more library patrons are visiting *only* the virtual library, never to walk through the building's doors. Library services should be convenient for all patrons, available at the point of need. As for gen Ys, "Their communities and social networks are physical, virtual, and hybrid. Personal does not always mean 'in person' to the net gen. Online conversations may be as meaningful as one that is face-to-face" (Oblinger and Oblinger 2005, 11). Policies that take into account both the in-person and the online patron are important in today's hybrid libraries. Supporting online users can be problematic for many libraries, especially when attempting to use newer technologies and relying on librarians who are not comfortable using the technology. Gen Ys use e-mail, but we also know that they use instant messaging (IM) software and interactive Web sites. Libraries should be looking at different ways to offer reference services to meet the needs of all patrons, and that might mean offering the service in multiple formats and locations. An e-services librarian in a public library said, "I don't know of a single public library that doesn't have a hard time bringing middle and high schoolers into the library, nor do I know of a single public library that wouldn't want to do a better job at providing services for this age group. So in addition to trying to bring teens into the library, let's also bring the library to the teens" (Houghton 2005, 192). She's talking about using IM as a reference service.

COLLABORATION, MARKETING, AND OUTREACH

Librarians historically have not been very clever at outreach or at advertising and marketing what they do. With search engines as the number one resource for class assignments, libraries are in danger of losing patrons and losing their importance in society and the academy. It is crucial for libraries to get involved in their communities, their schools, their institutions, and to embed themselves into the social and educational structures around them.

Members of gen Y are social beings who gravitate toward interaction and collaboration. They openly share information (some quite personal) on the Internet, without hesitation. They prefer to work and learn in teams. Group work was introduced to them at a very early age and collaboration has been encouraged and rewarded in school, at home, and in extracurricular activities. In a collaborative approach, librarians can target gen Ys for *marketing surveys*, which are quick and easy ways to acquire information and feedback; *focus groups*, which provide a forum for discussion; and *student library committees*, which provide a continual voice for student opinion and direct involvement in library decisions and change. As consumers, gen Ys are accustomed to choosing from a wide selection of products and services on a daily basis, and they expect these products and services to continuously change and improve, as this is what they have experienced throughout their lifetimes (Sweeney 2005, 167). Library services and products are no different, and continual improvements to them are expected by this generation.

Libraries can learn from the business world and attempt to market themselves, their resources, and their services more aggressively and with more style. First, we need to find out where our patrons are going for information (or research or fun), and then put ourselves there. Members of gen Y are using and creating blogs, they have personal sites (MySpace), they watch and listen to podcasts, they listen to the radio, and they use instructional software like Blackboard. These are excellent venues for informing patrons about new resources, new services, changes in library space, upcoming classes, and more. It isn't enough, anymore, to assume that all students or young people will use the library because they have to do research—librarians actually need to "attract" clientele such as a store or commercial Web site would.

Another potentially positive outcome of outreach to gen Ys is to collaborate with them in ongoing improvements of services and products. Librarians can make use of the imagination, creativity, technical skills, and imagination of this generation to best ensure that new services and resources will be responsive to their needs and to their style (Lippincott 2005, 9). By involving gen Ys in decisions on everything from Web site design, to class exercises, to the types of services, resources, and software they would like to have access to, we are reaching out to them and learning about their information needs at the same time. This is one generation who will not be afraid to offer their opinions and consequently assist in helping to redefine the purpose and function of libraries for the future.

BRIDGING THE GAP

Generational differences will come into play as more and more gen Ys enter the library workforce. They will bring new skills, enthusiasm, and undoubtedly a fondness for change. Libraries will rely on them to attract younger generations to the library and to use emerging technologies in new and unique ways. As discussed already, libraries need to adapt existing services and roles that will attract the younger generations as both patrons and employees, and offer resources and services that gen Ys and future generations will use. And, if libraries want to attract gen Y librarians into the profession, they need to find ways to bridge the generational gap by creating a collaborative, exciting, and challenging workplace for all.

One simple way to begin to bridge the gap is to maintain open communication with all members of the library staff in a variety of ways to address individual and generational communication styles—e-mail, in-person meetings, casual interactions, instant messaging, wikis, or blogs. By doing so, administrators create an atmosphere of inclusion and participation. They can request input from all staff members on new ideas and encourage the formation of management teams that include members of different generations to work on developing specific areas of the library such as reference, access services, and instruction and to work on updating existing policies and developing new policies.

When it comes to managing younger generations, both gen X and gen Y prefer a more participatory management style where their voices can be heard. "Millennials tend to see leadership as a participative process and will learn best from managers who engage participants in orientation rather than just lecturing" (Lancaster and Stillman 2002, 231). They prefer team management and the opportunity to be involved in decision making. Developing management style teams is a good way to engage older generations and help to keep them up-to-date on emerging technologies and promote discussion amongst the generations, especially when evaluating and rethinking traditional services and policies. Traditional library values and policies certainly should not be pushed aside, but used to form new services and adapted into updated policies that will help to attract and promote the library for all generations; however, librarians should attempt to think outside the box and be creative and inclusive when developing new policies. "Too often library culture reflexively condemns the new or little understood creative opportunity offering more flexibility and technological enhancement, creating an obstacle for opportunities either in technology or policy advancement" (McDonald and Thomas 2006, 6).

Training and cross-training should be emphasized when rethinking library policies. Nothing promotes the library better than a well-informed staff. Patrons do not necessarily know the difference between a librarian and a paraprofessional, nor should they need to all the time. All library staff should be well informed and trained on basic library functions, resources, and services. Cross-training staff in different functions of the library will promote better communication among library staff and provide all staff members with a stake in decision making and policy making (Stuhlman 2003, 11). Training paraprofessionals and student workers in basic reference skills, or circulation functions, promotes knowledge and learning as well as good customer service skills, and provides library staff with a sense of empowerment.

ADAPTING TO CHANGE

Creating new roles, redefining existing ones, and developing new policies will require time and commitment from all library staff members. These are significant changes that cannot be accomplished without administrative support. It is important for library administrators to realize that not only are times changing, but library patrons are changing too. Libraries need to reach out to new patrons and create new services that will attract them, on their terms and on their turf, and librarians need to engage in active learning and keep their computer skills up-to-date, or risk becoming extinct. Administrators need to develop new roles for librarians that will address the information needs of gen Y and future generations. And librarians need to know that their administrators are supportive of their efforts to promote change. It is imperative to the future of libraries to stay current and to change often. This doesn't mean that all traditional library values or functions need to be transformed; librarians just need to do a better job at regularly evaluating existing services, resources, and policies and of understanding the changing needs of library patrons—and then adapting to meet those needs.

In evaluating existing policies, library staff should be cautious of implementing, or retaining, restrictions in regards to certain types of technology, such as cell phones, instant messaging software, or gaming to name a few. By doing so we are telling a large portion of our patrons, gen Y in particular, that we do not understand them, and that we do not care what is important to them. By putting up signs that start with "NO" we are pushing patrons out the door, patrons who might feel more comfortable at the local bookstore or campus computer lab where, it may appear, they are less restricted. Rather than emphasizing the negative, we should be promoting the positive. "This is what you CAN do in the library." And, perhaps we are missing the bigger picture. Gen Ys use a multitude of software and devices to communicate, collaborate, and get information. Shouldn't libraries be promoting information sharing and collaboration? And shouldn't libraries be using existing technology, especially devices and software that our patrons use every day? The days of "shushing" are over as librarian roles get updated for a new generation of patrons.

The recent emergence of innovative librarian roles with titles like Next Gen Librarian, E-Services Librarian, Emerging Technologies Librarian, and Technology Innovation Librarian is a sign that the profession is changing and not just in response to new technologies, but actually adapting to the needs of new and potential patrons. Gen Y is going to redefine the purpose and the function of libraries and help to bring the library into the future, as long as librarians from all generations are willing to go along for the ride.

REFERENCES

Abram, Stephen, and Judy Luther. 2004. "Born with the Chip." *Library Journal* 129: (8) (May 1): 34–37.

Fox, Susannah, and Mary Madden. 2006. "Generations Online." Pew Internet & American Life Report. http://www.pewinternet.org/pdfs/PIP_Generations_Memo.pdf

Houghton, Sarah. 2005. "Instant Messaging: Quick and Dirty Reference for Teens and Others." *Public Libraries* 44: (4) (July/August): 192–193.

Howe, Neil, and William Strauss. 2000. *Millennials Rising: The Next Great Generation.* New York: Vintage.

Jones, Steve, and Mary Madden. 2002. "The Internet Goes to College: How Students Are Living in the Future with Today's Technology." Pew Internet & American Life Project. http://www.pewinternet.org/pdfs/PIP_College_Report.pdf

Lancaster, Lynne C., and David Stillman. 2002. *When Generations Collide: Who They Are. Why They Clash. How to Solve the Generational Puzzle at Work.* New York: Collins.

Lippincott, Joan K. 2005. "Net Generations Students and Libraries." In *Educating the Net Generation*, eds. Diana Oblinger and James Oblinger. EDUCAUSE. http://www.educause.edu/educatingthenetgen

McDonald, Robert H., and Chuck Thomas. 2006. "Disconnects Between Library Culture and Millennial Generation Values." *EDUCAUSE Quarterly* 29 (4): 4–6.

Mead, Margaret. BrainyQuote. http://www.brainyquote.com/quotes/quotes/m/margaretme 115939.html (Accessed February 22, 2007.)

Oblinger, Diana, and James Oblinger. 2005. "Is It Age or IT: First Steps Toward Understanding the Net Generation." In *Educating the Net Generation*, eds. Diana Oblinger and James Oblinger. EDUCAUSE. http://www.educause.edu/EducatingtheNet Generation/5989

OCLC. 2002. "How Academic Librarians Can Influence Students' Web-Based Information Choices." OCLC White Paper on the Information Habits of College Students. http://www.oclc.org/research/announcements/2002–06–24.htm

Squire, Kurt, and Constance Steinkuehler. 2005. "Meet the Gamers." *Library Journal* 130 (7): 38–41.

Stuhlman, Daniel. 2003. "Think Like a Business, Act Like a Library: Library Public Relations." *Information Outlook* 7 (9): 10–15.

Sweeney, Richard T. 2005. "Reinventing Library Buildings and Services for the Millennial Generation." *Library Administration & Management* 19 (4): 165–175.

5 DECONSTRUCTING LIBRARIANS' FASCINATION WITH GAMER CULTURE: TOWARD MAKING ACADEMIC LIBRARIES VENUES FOR QUIET CONTEMPLATION

Juris Dilevko

In the middle and late 2000s, when academic librarians talked about how best to serve members of the millennial generation, their discussions were built on the principle that, because millennials were steeped in gamer culture, academic libraries should therefore adhere more closely to a gamer-culture ethos. Richard T. Sweeney (2005, 168) summarizes this view by observing that, because millennials take for granted the "immediate gratification" that they "have encountered both with online services and their gaming experiences," they are "increasingly less tolerant of institutions that model the old paradigm, that consume more of their time in performing activities not part of their immediate goal." Library decision makers must therefore "respond with rapid, immediate new services that appeal to Millennials, and they must do so very soon" (Sweeney 2005, 175). In a telling analogy in their much-cited "Born with a Chip" article, Stephen Abram and Judy Luther (2004, 36) assert that, because millennials are "format agnostic," "nomadic," "multitasking," and "experiential," libraries must stop being institutions that are "often run by Lisa Simpsons trying to herd a crowd of Bart Simpson users." In short, it was a world in which the rambunctious and entertainment-based "Gamer Generation" (Storey 2005, 7) of Bart Simpson triumphed over the quiet studiousness of Lisa Simpson. In the eyes of these commentators, library administrators could "create libraries compelling to the next generation" (Sweeney 2005, 173) only if current librarians, most of whom were "over 50" and thus "one to two generations" removed from "a growing group of our primary users," rose to "[t]he challenge of change" embodied by an army of Bart Simpsons immersed in gamer culture (Abram and Luther 2004, 37).

The work of Abram, Luther, and Sweeney became part of the conventional wisdom of the library world in the 2000s, but it was also a troubling manifestation of librarians' tendency to blindly adopt fashionable rhetoric and erect it into unassailable professional truth. Librarians' obsession with accepting "the challenge of change" by infusing libraries with a gamer-culture ethos falls squarely within this tendency, revealing an insecure profession not confident in its underlying purpose. Lacking a philosophical core and anxious to embrace the precepts of edutainment rather than meaningful education, librarianship in the 2000s established itself as a profession content to adopt "discourse fashions" (Day 2002, 231) as it sought to occupy a central place within the ever-shifting landscape of information provision and information technology.

DERIVATIVE THINKING

From a structural perspective, the inability to formulate a set of abiding principles representative of its fundamental beliefs was not something new for librarianship. As Wayne A. Wiegand (1986, 386–387) observed, the history of librarianship has long been marked by a willingness to let "outside experts" define those objects of "cultural and intellectual authority" that librarians subsequently acquire, catalog, classify, and circulate. As a result, librarians really do not "know books"; rather, they know "how to apply the standards dictated by conventional canons that have been developed outside the profession" (Wiegand 1986, 395–396). The curricula of Library and Information Science (LIS) schools reflect this emphasis, "generally follow[ing] the dynamics of a changing environment affected by outside forces like the introduction of new technology and improved methods of administration," rarely straying "beyond the professional boundaries" demarcated by the latest advances in database management, online catalogs, automated circulation systems, and electronic reference services (Wiegand 1986, 396–397).

Just as librarians relied on outside experts to define objects of cultural and intellectual authority, they also relied on outside experts for their knowledge of management theory in the 1980s and 1990s. As Mark T. Day (2002, 282) demonstrated, "transformational discourse about organizational change in libraries has been dominated by the most popular management fashions" as represented by "management gurus" such as Peter F. Drucker, Thomas J. Peters, Michael E. Porter, and Everett M. Rogers. Taken as a whole, their ideas were the basis of a socially constructed ideology in which "heroic capitalistic entrepreneurs apply innovative technology to continuously reengineer production and create new consumer markets, thereby increasing wealth and promoting progress" (Day 2002, 235). These ideas were imported into librarianship in the 1980s and 1990s by, among others, Richard M. Doughtery, Donald E. Riggs, Thomas W. Shaughnessy, Charles R. McClure, and Robert S. Taylor. Benefiting from their influential positions within LIS, they became "implementers, interpreters, and propagators of contemporary popular management fashions" such as repositioning and reengineering; total quality management and benchmarking; and nimble, flexible, and agile organizational cultures (Day 2002, 275). They argued that, because libraries were experiencing an era of "unprecedented, discontinuous (but somehow perpetual) environmental change," libraries should undergo "radical, discontinuous (but somehow continual) organizational improvement" if they were to remain viable (Day 2002, 285). But, as librarians listened to Doughtery, Shaughnessy, and McClure, they often dismissed alternate approaches that "resist[ed] radical change and reinforc[ed] traditional institutional customs," neglecting to inquire whether "the increased adoption of business management fashions" positively affected "organizational performance" (Day 2002, 284–285).

When Abram, Luther, and Sweeney urged librarians to reinvent academic libraries for the millennial generation, they inscribed themselves within the reliance-on-outside-experts tradition identified by Wiegand and documented by Day. And, just as there were clear ideological implications to librarians' adoption of "transformational discourse about organizational change," there was also a significant ideological valence to librarians' fascination with all things millennial, especially because librarians convinced themselves that the concept of the millennial generation was coextensive with gamer culture and its primary attribute, technology-based multitasking. Thus when librarians spoke about rethinking libraries to serve the gamer generation, they were speaking in favor of an edutainment approach to learning—eye-catching yet superficial entertainment masquerading as meaningful education—that had become part of the constellation of ideas undergirding market ideology: economic rationality and unbridled consumerism that culminated in postmodern capitalism verging on social Darwinism. But in doing so, they gave short shrift to Lisa Simpson-type students who wanted to pursue "extraordinary excellence" in learning environments that were conducive to the kind of serene reflection and quiet contemplation that is the precursor of "first-rate work in one area" (Lewis 2001).

THE IDEOLOGY OF GAMER CULTURE

Even more than Neil Howe's and William Strauss's *Millennials Rising: The Next Great Generation*, Marc Prensky was one of the most prominent voices drawing attention to the rise of the gamer generation and the need to adapt social structures, especially educational processes, to its perceived needs. Establishing the frame for what would become a stereotypical portrait of millennials, he defined them as highly networked, speed-obsessed, and visually oriented individuals who, because they "like to parallel process and multi-task" and "thrive on instant gratification and frequent rewards," prefer "games to 'serious' work" (Prensky 2001b). By the time they left for college or university, they had spent more than 10,000 hours playing video games, 10,000 hours conversing on cell phones, 20,000 hours watching television, and sent more than 200,000 e-mails and text messages. On the other hand, they had spent "maybe, *at the very most,* 5,000 hours of book reading" (Prensky 2001b; original emphasis).

As a result, they had a different learning style that demanded an entirely new way of teaching. Because millennials find traditional teaching techniques such as "lectures, step-by-step logic, and 'tell-test' instruction" boring, educators must use "the very video and computer games they so enjoy" to reach them (Prensky 2001b). Video-game-based teaching thus became a moral imperative because it alone could tap into the skill-set millennials possess: parallel processing, graphics awareness, and random access (Prensky 2001b). Moreover, "legacy content," defined as "reading, writing, arithmetic, logical thinking, [and] understanding the writings and ideas of the past," should be deemphasized, with educators instead focusing on topics such as "software, hardware, robotics, nanotechnology, genomics," as well as *the ethics, politics, sociology, languages and other things that go with them*" (Prensky 2001b; original emphasis). Prensky was therefore adamant that education should be redefined in terms of edutainment. Otherwise, an entertainment-saturated millennial generation, whom he referred to as digital natives, will become frustrated and angry, refusing to comply with the educational strategies of those he disdainfully labeled as digital immigrants: teachers interested in "legacy content" and teaching methods based on lectures and logical arguments (Prensky 2001b).

In addition, Prensky was convinced that video-game-based edutainment produces the type of "highly successful" people valued by "business, the professions and the military" (Prensky 2001c). Using Stephen R. Covey's bestselling book *The Seven Habits of Highly Effective People*, Prensky described how video games develop skills associated with being proactive: beginning with the end in mind, putting first things first, thinking in a win-win paradigm, understanding the needs and motivations of fellow team players, developing synergy, and implementing a continuous-improvement mentality. Highly prized among business people, these seven skills are often seen as prerequisites for creating lean-and-mean businesses, and Prensky suggests that video games are crucial to developing this ultracompetitive and take-no-prisoners approach to business and life. "The youngest workers don't need to adapt to fit into the agile, flat, team-based organizations older executives are striving to design," he wrote, because they already fit there insofar as gamer culture has given them the skills necessary for survival in the predatory business environment (Prensky 2001a). In fact, concepts such as blogs, wikis, and real-time strategy games are simply updated versions of "cross-functional cooperation," "team-based management," and "360 feedback" (Prensky 2001a).

Others reinforced Prensky's arguments about the value of video games for business. As John C. Beck and Mitchell Wade (2004, 2) explained, because gamers have "learned to concentrate on a computer game with music playing and TV blaring in the same room" and because "many of the games are all about fighting off one foe while three others attack you at the same time," millennials are proficient in the art of "[s]witching from back-of-mind to front-of-mind" activities with ease (Beck and Wade 2004, 88–89). This ability to multitask is thus "a real asset in today's workplace" where companies need employees that can "handle more simultaneous data streams than their parents even imagined" and where "[c]utting-edge analytic tools...look[ing] a lot more like video games than office suites...help[] serious decision makers produce real progress on problems that seem impossible to analyze" (Beck and Wade 2004, 90).

Caught up by the positive attributes of gamer culture, Abram, Luther, and Sweeney imported Prensky's ideas into librarianship, starting a groundswell to redesign college and university libraries based on an edutainment philosophy.

Sweeney (2005, 172) noted that because "Millennials seamlessly weave their work and recreational activities, making no artificial distinctions," library "computers, search engines, and information resources must enable and enhance their multitasking, whenever desired." Multitasking should therefore be "built into library technologies to speed up and improve searching as well as learning," leading to scenarios in which "a group of Millennial students will work together at a table in the library" such that "several of them will have cell phones, chat with others at the table, and work on wireless laptop computers at the same time" (Sweeney 2005, 172). And because millennials approach the world from a lucid perspective, libraries should not be concerned about a sharp decline in reading; instead, they "must respond to the Millennial need for audio and visual media and monitor their reading to determine what mix will work" (Sweeney 2005, 173). Abram and Luther (2004, 35) offered similar advice: libraries should permit users to "focus differentially" because millennials want to "run several IM [instant messaging] conversations at the same time" and "listen to MP3s on a PC as well as surf the web while adding content to homework projects and assignments."

For these writers, academic libraries should become commotion- and noise-filled venues dedicated to edutainment, if not outright entertainment, where students could have access to as many simultaneous data streams as possible. But, given the connection between success in playing video games and success in the business world, making edutainment the cornerstone of future libraries was not an ideologically neutral enterprise. What linked the two was multitasking, the linchpin of early twenty-first-century business and industry. For all intents and purposes, the valorization of video-game-based multitasking became a valorization of market ideology.

POSTMODERN CAPITALISM AND MULTITASKING

An important development of the late 1990s and early 2000s was what Thomas Friedman (2006, 76–92) identified as "work flow software" (WFS), the culmination of a series of technology-based work procedures through which postmodern capitalism took economic rationality to new levels. Based on a series of standardized electronic protocols known by acronyms such as SMTP, HTML, HTTP, TCP/IP, XML, SOAP, and AJAX, WFS gave birth to an "all-world supply chain" where discrete work tasks and entire business processes were carried out 24/7/365: "once everyone's applications started to connect to everyone else's applications, work could not only flow like never before, but it could be chopped up, disaggregated, and sent to the four corners of the world as never before" (Friedman 2006, 82–86). Because this chain was "seamlessly interoperable," there was a constant rush to automate, digitize, outsource, and offshore every aspect of production (Friedman 2006, 82, 126–127). People and production facilities became easily interchangeable parts, and the efficacy of these parts was constantly evaluated by quantitative performance metrics. Employees had little choice but to multitask to keep their jobs, juggling more and more disaggregated units of work. As technology advanced, even jobs requiring specialized skills became fungible on a regular basis, creating yet more disaggregated work units that had to be multitasked by someone somewhere to meet ever-rising performance metrics (Friedman 2006, 279).

For Friedman, the fungible world was paradise—an opportunity for each person "to work a little harder and run a little faster" so as to be able "to justify your job every day with the value you create and the unique skills you contribute" (Friedman 2006, 276–277). Multitasking was not only expected, it was a means of survival. Friedman (2006, 281, 446–453) happily observed that "we are all temps now," where the state of being a "temp" was a good thing and where outsourcing was presented as something that "idealists" do to innovate. It was a world where the preferred way of doing business was outsourced "reverse auctions"—a phenomenon where, "[t]o make sure that [they are] getting the best deals on [their] parts and other supplies," large companies such as Boeing let suppliers "bid down against each other rather than bid up against each other" (Friedman 2006, 229). All this was part of the natural order of things, since "[t]here are dozens of people who are doing the same thing you are doing, and they are trying to do it better. It is like water in a tray, you shake it and it will find the path of least resistance" (qtd. in Friedman 2006, 222). As desperate competitors undercut each other in race-to-the-bottom scenarios inspired by social Darwinism, fungibility and temporariness created a "new world order" that incorporated as many people as possible into "a transnational zone of flows," where they all became what Heather Menzies (2005, 27–31) termed *standardized units* alienated from themselves, their local communities, and larger social institutions.

In short, multitasking was a key component of market ideology, and it was not long before the ethos of the "hyperworld" (Menzies 2005, 27–41) and "the cult of speed" (Honoré 2004, 3–18) infiltrated the public sector.[1] If increased reliance by the private sector on strategies such as "reverse auctions" was attributed to exigent shareholders, the specter of irate overtaxed citizens was used to justify an era of stringent accountability in the public sector (Menzies 2005, 9). Among those most affected were mid-level professionals and managers: healthcare workers, educators, and social workers. Not only did the volume and pace of their work increase, but they were also "being drawn away from the realities in front of them and into a new, almost virtual level of reality that is remote and based on abstract symbols ... to which they are increasingly held accountable" (Menzies 2005, 44). What Janice Gross Stein described as "the cult of efficiency" took over, leading to the imposition of "self-referential," impersonal, and technical performance measures devoid of "fundamental human and social values" (Menzies 2005, 9; Stein 2001). As organizations mandated stepped-up expectations in an effort to be seen as accountable, anything that impeded those goals was viewed as a "negative statistic" that had to be eliminated by a series of euphemistically named "best practices" whose underlying purpose had more to do with "cost containment" and "competitiveness" than real concern for people (Menzies 2005, 135; Stein 2001).[2] The cult of efficiency in the public sector stemmed from the same political agenda as "reverse auctions"—economic rationality as the touchstone of all decision making (Buschman 2003, 109–123).

COGNITIVE AND PSYCHOLOGICAL IMPLICATIONS OF MULTITASKING

As WFS became the structuring element of industry and the public sector, the complex reality of the contingent, messy world inhabited by contingent human beings eroded (Menzies 2005, 43). Indeed, the ability to discount "messy" human beings was the whole point of a virtual, abstract, and ultimately "anaesthetizing" hyperworld linked by WFS "because any squeeze on the people and the natural environment is out of sight and out of mind" (Menzies 2005, 43). Soon, negative consequences associated with multitasking appeared. Multitasking was not the key to success envisioned by Friedman, but rather "a formula for shoddy work, mismanaged time, rote solutions, stress and forgetfulness," not to mention "dangers of inattention" such as car crashes (Healy 2004). Consider the following examples.

- "[P]sychologists at the University of Michigan reported that when they asked subjects to perform two or more experimental tasks—solving arithmetic problems, say, at the same time they identified a series of shapes—the frontal cortex, the executive function center of the brain, had to switch constantly, toggling back and forth in a stutter that added as much as 50 percent to the time it would have taken to perform the tasks sequentially instead of simultaneously" (Henig 2004).
- "[S]cientists at Carnegie Mellon put subjects in an M.R.I. machine and asked them to listen to complicated sentences at the same time that they mentally rotated geometric shapes. The two tasks activated different parts of the brain, but each region was operating at a suboptimal level" (Henig 2004).
- "Two Harvard professors see evidence of what they call 'pseudo-attention deficit disorder'—shorter attention spans influenced by technology and the constant waves of information washing over us" (Seven 2004).
- "In a series of tests carried out by Dr. Glenn Wilson, Reader in Personality at the Institute of Psychiatry, University of London, an average worker's functioning IQ falls 10 points when distracted by ringing telephones and incoming e-mails. This drop in IQ is more than double the four-point drop seen following studies on the impact of smoking marijuana" (Hewlett-Packard 2006).

Analyzing these effects, Jordan Grafman, chief of the cognitive neuroscience section at the National Institute of Neurological Disorders and Stroke, predicted that "[k]ids that are instant messaging while doing homework, playing games online and watching TV...aren't going to do well in the long run," partly because "the brain needs rest and recovery time to consolidate thoughts and memories" and "[h]abitual multitasking may condition their brain to an overexcited state, making it difficult to focus even when they want to" (Wallis 2006). David E. Meyer, director of the Brain, Cognition and Action Laboratory at the University of Michigan, agreed: "[i]f a teenager is trying to have a conversation on an e-mail chat line while doing algebra, she'll suffer a decrease in efficiency, compared to if she just thought about algebra until she was done" (Wallis 2006). To think otherwise, he concluded, is a self-deluding "myth" because "[w]ith such complicated tasks [you] will never, ever be able to overcome the inherent limitations in the brain for processing information during multitasking" (Wallis 2006). Far from conferring advantages, multitasking left people of all ages prone to "mental antsyness" (Wallis 2006), which manifested itself as increased intolerance, sleep deprivation, chronic fatigue, attention deficits, burnout, and workaholism (Honoré 2004, 3–13, 187–215; Menzies 2005, 70–71, 79–98, 153–157).

As the notion of "instrumental efficiency" that was at the core of multitasking embedded itself in "the lived environment of daily life," individuals "trash[ed]" themselves, their personal relationships, and their way of looking at the world (Menzies 2005, 90, 115–116). Self-forgetfulness merged with forgetfulness of others. When tasks multiplied, the time that could be devoted to each of them shrunk into tiny fragments. Parents became less meaningfully engaged with their children, leading to a series of negative outcomes for family life (Honoré 2004, 246–272; Menzies 2005, 161–182). Caught up in the "culture of the glance" instead of the "culture of the gaze," students read less deeply and reflectively, eschewing critical thinking in order to download the latest "ready-made knowledge bit[]" (Menzies 2005, 189, 185).[3] Healthcare workers abandoned patient-centered care for "timed-care requirements," where attention was shifted onto "a series of tasks to be successfully completed in the most efficient way" (Menzies 2005, 128–129). Administrators and managers talked in "glib, mix-and-match sound bites," using empty "plastic words" such as "developments," "norms," and "indicators" in a "new global language of public-issue management" that could "be mobilized in an almost virtual form of public dialogue while masking the fact that very little has been communicated, explained or justified" (Menzies 2005, 210–211).[4] In a multitasking hyperworld, the social fabric gradually unraveled as "space-time compression" destroyed "face-to-face rhythms and continuities" (Menzies 2005, 23, 40, 166).

ACADEMIC LIBRARIES AND THE COMMERCIALIZATION OF EDUCATION

It was logical that the business world, with its incessant demands for economic rationality, was supportive of gamer culture and multitasking. But why did college and university libraries become strong advocates of them? One clue is provided by the tendency of their parent institutions to let market ideology intrude on both their fundamental mission and operating procedures. The result was a creeping corporatization and commercialization, eloquently documented in books such as Jennifer Washburn's *University, Inc.: The Corporate Corruption of Higher Education* and David L. Kirp's *Shakespeare, Einstein, and the Bottom Line: The Marketing of Higher Education*. For Washburn (2005, ix–x), the corporatization of education was nothing less than "a wholesale cultural shift" in which "[a]cademic administrators...refer to students as consumers and to education and research as products" and where "campuses take on the look and feel of shopping malls."

As federal and state governments drastically reduced their funding of colleges and universities beginning in the late 1970s and early 1980s, higher-education institutions confronted the "resulting fiscal squeeze" using two complementary approaches (Kirp 2003, 15; Washburn 2005, xii–xx). First, universities successfully lobbied for the Bayh-Dole Act of 1980, which allowed them to stake proprietary patent claims on discoveries made under the auspices of federally funded research and to undertake exclusive licensing arrangements with small businesses to commercialize those patents (Washburn 2005, 57–69). Research results were thus taken out of the "public domain" where they could "serve as the wellspring for future innovation and discovery" (Washburn 2005, 63). When a 1987 Executive Order extended the applicability of the Bayh-Dole Act to include businesses of all sizes, many universities, seeking to maximize their financial returns on research, entered into multimillion-dollar alliances and partnerships with industrial giants such as Novartis, Bristol-Myers, and Monsanto, which injected large sums into the budgets of science, medical, and technology departments in return for proprietary claims on research produced there (Washburn 2005, 69–72). By the middle 2000s, corporations "directly influence[d] an estimated 20 to 25 percent of university research funding overall" insofar as "much federal research support [was]...tied to corporate matching grants, cost sharing, and other cooperative research arrangements" (Washburn 2005, 71, 9). Not only did industry appropriate taxpayer-funded research for private commercial purposes, it also often defined the research agendas of entire university departments, tainted the integrity and objectivity of many individual research projects, exerted control over publishing the results of sponsored research, and attempted to deter universities from hiring or granting tenure to researchers who were critical of corporate products (Washburn 2005, 9, 1–24, 73–197). In other words, it was not just the naming rights for buildings, academic chairs, institutes, centers, and faculties that were for sale on late twentieth- and early twenty first-century campuses.

"Financial desperation" also caused colleges and universities to adopt a "customer orientation" with regard to "the care and feeding of prospective students" (Kirp 2003, 13–15). Admissions officers metamorphosed into enrollment managers whose job was to maximize enrollments in a way "not very different from boosting tourism or increasing membership in church congregations" (Kirp 2003, 16). Adhering to the strategies presented in books such as Philip Kotler's *Strategic Marketing for Educational Institutions*, they "[e]xplicitly and unapologetically" treated students as "customers" and education as a "product students consume," making sure that the "product matche[d] the demand" (Kirp 2003, 16). And because demand was often gauged by "sophisticated market research on what you need to keep an 18-year-old happy" (Leonard 2002), students became "pampered consumers" (Kirp 2003, 11). Institutions embarked on measures to enhance and "revamp[] the college experience," using disingenuous phrases such as "community building" to justify "facilities race[s]" in which multimillion-dollar recreation centers and dormitories featuring gourmet chefs, personal trainers, big-screen

TVs, therapeutic bubble-jet tubs, juice bars, cybercafés, climbing walls, and putting greens were used to instill a "student-knows-best philosophy" (Kirp 2003, 22–24). In sum, colleges and universities came to believe that their purpose was "to distract and entertain" (Leonard 2002); the notion that students were "supposed to be [intellectually] *formed* by a college education [was] dismissed as quaint" (Kirp 2003, 11; original emphasis).

The intersection of these two revenue-enhancing trends can be illustrated using the representative example of George Mason University (Fairfax County, Virginia) (GMU). Proclaiming that its new mandate was to be "networked," GMU in the late 1990s added information technology and computer science programs; spent hundreds of millions of dollars developing its biosciences, bioinformatics, and biotechnology sectors; forged strong links with "northern Virginia's booming technology industry"; imposed a "technological literacy" test; eliminated "[d]egree programs in classics, German, French, and several other humanities departments"; and built a "mall-like" student center "replete with a Taco Bell, a Cinnabun, a campus bookstore run by Barnes and Noble, and a movie theater" (Washburn 2005, 212–213). Justifying these changes, GMU's president forthrightly stated that "people with money are more likely to give you money if you have restructured and repositioned yourself, got rid of stuff that you don't need to have" because "[t]hey take a very dim view of giving you money to run an inefficient organization" (qtd. in Washburn 2005, 212–213). And because GMU students are "good consumers," the university has "a commitment to produce people who are employable in today's technology workforce" (qtd. in Washburn 2005, 213–214).

Academic priorities evolved not on the basis of "intellectual concerns," but because of "financial considerations and pure market demand" (Washburn 2005, 215–216). Highly efficient northern Virginia-based technology companies funded GMU so that GMU could conduct sponsored studies (in new or upgraded facilities) that would lead to proprietary discoveries that, once commercialized, would provide both GMU and the sponsoring companies healthy financial returns, which GMU could use to maximize enrollment by enticing consumer-students with amenities designed "to distract and entertain." These "pampered" students were then funneled into programs that were exclusively committed to employability and dependent to a large extent on the continuing good will of corporate sponsors. At the same time that they were kept busy with various types of entertainment, students became blinkered trainees preparing for employment at the Virginia-based technology companies that funded GMU and laid proprietary claims to sponsored GMU research. As other companies saw the benefits of partnerships with GMU—a ready pool of future workers already socialized into market ideology and professors eager to conduct research that matched the agendas of sponsoring companies—additional university-industry collaborations were formed, starting this cycle over. The days of attending college and university to gain an "understanding of the writings and ideas of the past"—knowledge for the sake of knowledge; knowledge for the sake of making independent judgments about timeless issues—were a distant memory. As Kirp (2003, 4) observed, "[t]he new vocabulary of customers and stakeholders, niche marketing and branding and winner-take-all" entrenched "business-like ways of thinking" such that "[e]ach department is a 'revenue center,' each student a customer, each professor an entrepreneur, each party a 'stakeholder,' and each institution a seeker after profit, whether in money capital or intellectual capital."

When librarians read articles by Abram, Luther, and Sweeney that advocated a profound reconceptualization of academic libraries, many of them became convinced that they too had to offer services that would entice and entertain millennial-generation student-consumers. After all, college and university libraries that adopted a gamer-culture-friendly philosophy were said to be far-sighted, progressive, and future-oriented. These in turn were qualities that made academic libraries attractive to potential corporate sponsors, for they indicated that libraries had "restructured and repositioned" themselves, jettisoning inefficient and tradition-bound "legacy content" and the teaching methods associated with it. Many academic librarians thus understood that the establishment of a gamer-culture ethos in their libraries was a *sine qua non* not only for gaining access to corporate funding, but also for demonstrating their libraries' commitment to their parent institutions' acceptance of market ideology. If the developments at the University of Virginia Library were an indicator of the future, an era loomed in which library budgets would be "privately endowed," where decisions about library policies and practices would be made exclusively by those making such financial contributions (Kirp 2003, 142).

But in the process of adopting a consumer-satisfaction ethos based on gamer culture, academic libraries, like their parent institutions, reified the negative characteristics of market ideology: technology-based multitasking that was inextricably linked to a hyperworld whose glossy surface sheen concealed its psychologically and emotionally destructive nature. The tenets of hyperworld philosophy became an accepted part of the mental infrastructure of students as they studied in libraries using video-game-based processes. This was greeted favorably by corporations, because video games taught the skills sought by companies and public entities that privileged "the cult of efficiency" and "the cult of speed." Edutainment designed to satisfy student-consumers became indistinguishable from workforce development. While students were being entertained by video games, they also internalized the premises of postmodern capitalism in preparation for becoming multitasking employees in Friedman's disaggregated 24/7/365 world. The colonization of librarianship by market ideology was complete.

LOST OPPORTUNITIES

In early 2006, the magazine *Information Week* ran a cover story with the startling headline "Can You Trust This Man? Gartner CEO Gene Hall and competitors insist all is right with I[nformation] T[echnology] research. A closer look suggests otherwise."[5] The story questioned the integrity of the reports published by Gartner, Forrester Research, and IDC because these research firms had a complex array of direct and indirect financial relationships with the technology vendors whose products they were evaluating (Greenemeier and McDougall 2006, 32–39). Their dual roles—on the one hand, independent observers, reviewers, and therefore shapers of a field in which competing technology vendors struggled to gain ascendancy; on the other hand, for-profit businesses dependent on the profitability of the vendors whose products they were assessing—was an invitation to concern and scrutiny.

Similar concern and scrutiny should take place about librarianship's embrace of gamer culture at the behest of Abram, Luther, and Sweeney. Was it an embrace driven by the best interests of college and university students? Or was it an embrace driven by financial considerations tied to librarians' desire to be important team players in the new commercialized world of education, where fiscal exigencies and "institutional status wars" (Kirp 2003, 263) turned colleges and universities into relentless competitors for corporate funding and entertainment-seeking student-consumers? As noted previously, librarianship has never achieved a coherent philosophy about its essential attributes, constantly relying on and importing the advice of outside experts to orient it in one direction or another. This choice of direction is largely dependent on the fashionable discourse of the moment. Just as librarians adopted a "transformational discourse about organizational change" after reading "management gurus" such as Drucker and Peters (Day 2002, 282), the rush toward reorienting libraries toward gamer-culture-inspired edutainment based on multitasking is another example of librarianship's fascination with and implicit acceptance of market ideology that may not be in the best interests of library users. Urged on by Abram, Luther, and Sweeney, libraries became more interested in creating technology-friendly edutainment environments than in drawing on their historic roots as educational institutions.

As a result, they placed less emphasis on their traditional role in furthering a rigorous liberal-arts education, where primacy was given to exploring significant cultural, economic, geographic, historical, and social issues through extensive reading and discussion of enduring literature. But even stalwart supporters of market ideology such as the former chairman of the Board of Governors of the Federal Reserve System, Alan Greenspan, decried the loss of liberal-arts education. Because "the ability to think abstractly will be increasingly important across a broad range of professions," he remarked, it is important that students realize that "the ability to think conceptually is fostered through exposure to philosophy, literature, music, art and languages" (qtd. in Washburn 2005, 214). And, although the liberal arts are valuable as "a means of increasing technical intellectual efficiency," they are even more valuable because they encourage "the appreciation of life experiences that reach beyond material well-being and, indeed, are comparable and mutually reinforcing" (qtd. in Washburn 2005, 214).

As academic libraries worked to attract millennials by offering services that would allow them to "run[] several IM [instant messaging] conversations at the same time" and "listen[] to MP3s on a PC as well as surf[] the web while adding content to homework projects and assignments" (Abram and Luther 2004, 35), they overlooked not only scientific evidence that multitasking was cognitively detrimental, but also the lessons they could have drawn from many MacArthur

Fellows, commonly referred to as "genius-grant" recipients. Befitting their status as geniuses, they provide the philosophical underpinnings for an approach to library service that was at the antipodes of the gamer-culture direction championed by Abram, Luther, and Sweeney.

Their idea was simplicity itself: the need for quiet time and a quiet place to reflect and have a "light-bulb moment" (Haberman 2005). Although the "compulsion to be wired at all times" may be pleasurable and self-aggrandizing for those multitasking on cell phones, BlackBerries, and IPods, that same compulsion prevents them from "thinking freely [and] letting their minds wander," thus missing potential "eureka moment[s]" because of their obsessive "busyness" (Haberman 2005). Majora Carter, a MacArthur Fellow in 2005, worries that young people "don't have the ability anymore to create things in their own head, to create fantasies, to create dreams for themselves" (Haberman 2005). Citing the need for "ruminative time," Jonathan Lethem, another MacArthur Fellow and author of *Motherless Brooklyn* and *The Fortress of Solitude*, observed that "[n]onconnectivity becomes a commodity, something to cherish" (Haberman 2005). Carter and Lethem intuitively sensed that it was vital not to become "lost in the multitasking blur" (Wallis 2006) if one wanted to achieve great things. David Levy, the guiding spirit of the evocatively titled "Information, Silence and Sanctuary" conference held at the University of Washington in 2004, would no doubt have agreed with them, for the conference framed the issue of cognitive overload, multitasking, and fragmented time "in terms of the environmental movement" and Rachel Carson's *Silent Spring* (Seven 2004).[6] Just as pesticides destroyed the natural environment, technology-based multitasking and fragmented time destroys "mindful presence" (Seven 2004).

THE NEED FOR CONTEMPLATION

Instead of evolving into sites for edutainment and technology-based multitasking, academic libraries should become places exclusively devoted to contemplation, "ruminative time," and "mindful presence." In so doing they would be a real alternative to ubiquitous edutainment and multitasking: a refuge devoted to meaningful education. By providing Lethem's gift of cherished nonconnectivity, they would allow individuals to think conceptually and analytically about timeless issues in the humanities, social sciences, and sciences. How best to do so?

One way is by adopting the ideas described in "The Library Arts College, where Louis Shores (1935, 112) proposed that academic libraries move in the direction of "educational librarianship" instead of "research librarianship." Whereas research librarianship is concerned merely with "the acquisition and organization of printed material *ad infinitum,* and the provision of even larger quarters for their accommodation," educational librarianship deals with both acquisition and elimination of materials (Shores 1935, 112). It is therefore of a higher order, simply because it is more selective. Shores recommends that educational libraries have a maximum of 35,000 volumes—a number beyond which they may "*never* expand" (Shores 1935, 112; original emphasis). They may buy

500 new volumes annually, but only if they weed out a comparable number. In this way, the educational library's contents "will always include the basic books, plus an ever-changing collection of ephemeral material" (Shores 1935, 113). Taken as a whole, the collection will have "abundant material to furnish a true culture to young people who want it" (Shores 1935, 113). And, because librarians will have few acquisitions and organizational tasks, they will spend most of their time as teachers. Indeed, "[t]he positions of librarian and professor will merge" such that incumbents will be "library-trained, subject-matter experts" with a wide range of knowledge (Shores 1935, 113–114). Chemistry teachers, for example, will not only be able "to supervise a general reading course in science," but will also "be able to express an intelligent opinion on James Joyce or the Herbartian influence in American education" (Shores 1935, 114).

Students will not take a hodge-podge of unrelated courses, but will follow "a carefully planned reading program" covering "man's accomplishments of the past and problems of the present" (Shores 1935, 114). Books for the reading program will be "intelligently" selected by teacher-librarians, each of whom will hold "reading periods" in their subject specialty at the library (Shores 1935, 113). Thus, "[w]hen the student reports to the history reading room for his history reading period, he finds there a history teacher thoroughly trained in library methods, who, among other things, combines the duties of the history instructor and the reference librarian" (Shores 1935, 113). Instruction follows the tutorial method, with upper-class students tutoring lower-class students under "faculty supervision, supplemented by occasional inspirational lectures, and checked by the requirement of frequent papers, tests, and a final comprehensive examination" (Shores 1935, 114). Discussion and dialogue take center stage: thorough understanding of the subject matter supersedes rote recapitulation.

This is an educational model light years away from the edutainment paradigm. Whereas edutainment represents superficiality, a frenetic "culture of the glance," and harried technology-based multitasking, Shores's "library arts college" model represents the slow accumulation of in-depth knowledge through the "culture of the gaze" and "mindful presence." Here, cherished nonconnectivity provides ideal conditions for students to think conceptually about enduring issues. Just as MacArthur Fellows found that they cannot do without "ruminative time" in order to create at a high level, members of the millennial generation need places where they can think deeply and reflectively. Otherwise, they will become examples of what a French sociologist calls "le fast thinker"—"a person who can, without skipping a beat, summon up a glib answer to any question" and not feel embarrassed about being wrong because "in the land of speed, the man with the instant response is king" (Honoré 2004, 12). It is no coincidence that businesspeople laud gamer culture, as it enables the world of "le fast thinker" and contributes to "the cult of speed" undergirding workflow software and market ideology.

If colleges, universities, and academic libraries wish to remain institutions that offer multidimensional educational opportunities of the kind mentioned by Greenspan rather than institutions providing edutainment options, they should orient themselves more toward Shores's vision than that of Abram, Luther, and Sweeney. For many academic libraries, however, it is too late. These libraries believe that technological change is always the equivalent of progress and that technology-based multitasking and video-game-based learning are key elements in attracting a generation of Bart Simpsons. Yet, to judge from United States Department of Education statistics, the future belongs not to video-game-playing Bart Simpsons, but to bookish and studious Lisa Simpsons with a strong work ethic and serious purpose who are interested in the intellectual and cultural capital offered by the educators Prensky condescendingly categorized as Digital Immigrants. As Tamar Lewin (2006, 1, 16) reports, "men, whatever their race or socioeconomic group, are less likely than women to get bachelor's degrees—and among those who do, fewer complete their degrees in four or five years." In addition, men "get worse grades than women" and "studied less and socialized more than their female classmates" (Lewin 2006, 1, 16).

Consider the case of Jen Smyers, described as "a powerhouse in her three years at American University in Washington" and as someone whose "intense motivation is not so unusual" (Lewin 2006, 1, 16). Her accomplishments are more than impressive: a dean's scholarship, internships, grades sufficiently high to make frequent appearances on the dean's list, involvement in and leadership of campus women's programs, and completion of a master's degree in the time it took her peers to earn bachelor's degrees. How has she done it? One answer is her view about video games: "That's my litmus test now: I won't date anyone who plays video games. It means they're choosing to do something that wastes their time and sucks the life out of them" (Lewin 2006, 1, 16).

Smyers's comments about video games circle back to Prensky's assertions that members of the millennial generation prefer gaming to serious work. Certainly, some do. Lewin (2006, 1, 16) describes numerous Bart Simpson-like male students who boast of spending significant amounts of time playing video games, confident that the "male entitlement thing" will see them through life (Lewin 2006, 1, 16). But a generation of Jen Smyers was moving in a different direction: serious and purposeful education based on hard work, meticulous preparation, and intensive reading. As a gamer-culture ethos geared toward Bart Simpsons became the dominant paradigm in academic libraries, these libraries turned their backs on such ideas as "ruminative time" and "mindful presence," thus preventing many millennials from undertaking a regimen of serious and purposeful study.

One way that academic libraries can help millennials become like Smyers is by adhering to the "library arts college" model. Discussing the many small towns in the Catskill Mountains in upstate New York that were deliberately destroyed—as well as the thousands of people that were physically and psychologically uprooted—so that New York City could have an endless supply of water, Melissa Holbrook Pierson (2006, 26, 35, 115–169) writes that change, no matter how much it is presented as a positive development leading to progress, is really a form of "theft." In the much smaller world of academic libraries, the changeover to a gamer-culture ethos can also be interpreted as theft. Abram, Luther, and Sweeney presented this changeover as progress, but it deprived many millennials of the foundational knowledge that permits individuals to think reflectively, conceptually, and analytically "through exposure to philosophy, literature, music, art and languages" (qtd. in Washburn 2005, 213–214). By emphasizing technology-based multitasking and gamer culture that, on the one hand, precluded the existence of "ruminative time" and "mindful presence" and, on the other, fit perfectly within the framework of market ideology, academic libraries stole from the millennial generation the possibility of gaining what Shores called "true culture."

Of course, progress cannot be stopped, except by "progress itself" (Pierson 2006, 157). As Pierson remarked, "when the spring comes four weeks too soon, when the floods come, when the trees wither, when the billion diverse creatures that weave together in ways we cannot comprehend to make the net that holds us up die, when selfishness calls the chickens home to roost, then [progress] will stop [although]...we won't be around to celebrate our triumph over ourselves at last" (Pierson 2006, 157). Before librarianship "triumphs" over itself "at last" by pursuing the fashionable discourse of the moment, academic libraries tempted to meet "the challenge of change" by adopting a gamer-culture-inspired reconceptualization that pays homage to "the cult of speed" and multitasking should, instead, look to Shores's model of the "library arts college." Shores's approach to librarianship may appear outmoded, but it can be placed within the parameters of the early twenty-first-century slow movement described by Honoré, itself an offshoot of a broadly conceived environmentalism that pays due attention to individuals' physical, psychological, and emotional well-being (Menzies 2005, 243–251; Seven 2004).

Just as there are numerous benefits to slow food and slow cities—two pillars of the slow movement—so "slow librarianship" can pave the way for the type of renaissance in learning envisioned by Harry R. Lewis, dean of Harvard College from 1995 to 2003, who urged students to "slow down" without compromising "high achievement" or their "pursuit of extraordinary excellence" (Lewis 2001). Accomplishing "first-rate work in one area," he said, is possible only if students allow themselves "some leisure time, some recreation, some time for solitude, rather than packing [their] schedule with so many activities that [they] have no time to think about why [they] are doing what [they] are doing" (Lewis 2001).[7] In many respects, Lewis's words were an indictment of the "velocitization" of life (Honoré 2004, 27–36) enabled by technology-based multitasking at the center of gamer culture. If "first-rate work in one area" can be achieved only by slowing down, then the best way that academic libraries can serve members of the millennial generation is to provide an atmosphere conducive to slow and in-depth accumulation of knowledge. Shores's "library arts college" model is a good place to begin.

NOTES

1. Much of Menzies's discussion about the hyperworld is based on David Harvey's *The Condition of Postmodernity: An Enquiry into the Origins of Cultural Change* (London: Blackwell, 1991).

2. Menzies uses Janice Gross Stein, *The Cult of Efficiency* (Toronto, Ontario: House of Anansi Press, 2001).
3. Menzies quotes David Solway, who invokes William Butler Yeats.
4. Menzies draws on the German linguist Uwe Pörksen for the phrase "plastic words."
5. Text taken from the cover of the February 6, 2006, issue of *Information Week*.
6. For more information, see http://www.ischool.washington.edu/iql/conference/pro gram.html (June 30, 2006).
7. Also mentioned in Honoré 2004, 246–248.

REFERENCES

Abram, Stephen, and Judy Luther. 2004. "Born with the Chip." *Library Journal* 129 (May 1): 34–37.

Beck, John C., and Mitchell Wade. 2004. *Got Game: How the Gamer Generation Is Reshaping Business Forever*. Boston: Harvard Business School Press.

Buschman, John E. 2003. *Dismantling the Public Sphere: Situating and Sustaining Librarianship in the Age of the New Public Philosophy*. Westport, Conn.: Libraries Unlimited.

Day, Mark T. 2002. "Discourse Fashions in Library Administration and Information Management: A Critical History and Bibliometric Analysis." *Advances in Librarianship* 26: 231–298.

Friedman, Thomas L. 2006. *The World Is Flat: A Brief History of the Twenty-first Century*. New York: Farrar, Straus and Giroux.

Greenemeier, Larry, and Paul McDougall. 2006. "Credibility of Analysts." *Information Week* 1075 (February 6): 32–39.

Haberman, Clyde. 2005. "Feet and Minds Need a Chance to Wander." *New York Times*, September 27, B1.

Harvey, David. 1991. *The Condition of Postmodernity: An Enquiry into the Origins of Cultural Change*. London: Blackwell.

Healy, Melissa. 2004. "We're All Multi-tasking, but What's the Cost?" *Los Angeles Times*, July 19, F1.

Henig, Robin Marantz. 2004. "Driving? Maybe You Shouldn't Be Reading This." *New York Times*, July 13, F5.

Hewlett-Packard Development Company, L. P. 2006. "Abuse of Technology Can Reduce UK Workers' Intelligence." Available from http://h41131.www4.hp.com/uk/en/pr/UKen22042005142004.html (Accessed June 17, 2006.)

Honoré, Carl. 2004. *In Praise of Slow: How a Worldwide Movement Is Challenging the Cult of Speed*. Toronto: Vintage Canada.

Howe, Neil, and William Strauss. 2000. *Millennials Rising: The Next Great Generation*. New York: Vintage Books.

Kirp, David L. 2003. *Shakespeare, Einstein, and the Bottom Line: The Marketing of Higher Education*. Cambridge, Mass.: Harvard University Press.

Leonard, Mary. 2002. "On Campus, Comforts Are Major Colleges Hope Perks Can Boost Enrollment." *Boston Globe*, September 3, A1.

Lewin, Tamar. 2006. "At Colleges, Women Are Leaving Men in the Dust." *New York Times*, July 9, A1, 16.

Lewis, Harry R. 2001. "Slow Down: Getting More Out of Harvard by Doing Less." Available from http://www.college.harvard.edu/deans_office/dean_lewis/slow_down.html (Accessed July 7, 2006.)

Menzies, Heather. 2005. *No Time: Stress and the Crisis of Modern Life*. Vancouver, B.C.: Douglas & McIntyre.

Pierson, Melissa Holbrook. 2006. *The Place You Love Is Gone: Progress Hits Home*. New York: W. W. Norton.

Prensky, Marc. 2001a. "Capturing the Value of 'Generation Tech' Employees." Available from http://www.strategy-business.com/press/enewsarticle/enews063004?pg=0 (Accessed June 17, 2006.)

Prensky, Marc. 2001b. "Digital Natives, Digital Immigrants." Available from http://www.marcprensky.com/writing/Prensky%20-%20Digital%20Natives,%20Digital%20Immigrants%20-%20Part1.pdf and http://www.marcprensky.com/writing/Prensky%20%20Digital%20Natives,%20Digital%20Immigrants%20-%20Part2.pdf (Accessed June 17, 2006.)

Prensky, Marc. 2001c. "The Seven Games of Highly Effective People: How Playing Computer Games Helps You Succeed in School, Work and Life." Available from http://www.marcprensky.com/writing/Prensky-The_Seven_Games-FINAL.pdf (Accessed June 17, 2006.)

Seven, Richard. 2004. "Life Interrupted: Plugged into It All, We're Stressed to Distraction." *Pacific Northwest: The Seattle Times Magazine*, November 28. Available from http://seattletimes.nwsource.com/pacificnw/2004/1128/cover.html (Accessed June 17, 2006.)

Shores, Louis. 1935. "The Library Arts College, A Possibility in 1954?" *School and Society* 41 (January 26): 110–114.

Stein, Janice Gross. 2001. *The Cult of Efficiency*. Toronto: House of Anansi Press.

Storey, Tom. 2005. "The Big Bang!" *OCLC Newsletter* 267 (January–March): 7–12.

Sweeney, Richard T. 2005. "Reinventing Library Buildings and Services for the Millennial Generation." *Library Administration & Management* 19 (Fall): 165–175.

Wallis, Claudia. 2006. "The Multitasking Generation." *Time* 167 (March 27): 48–55. Available from http://proquest.umi.com (Accessed June 17, 2006.)

Washburn, Jennifer. 2005. *University, Inc.: The Corporate Corruption of Higher Education*. New York: Basic Books.

Wiegand, Wayne A. 1986. "The Socialization of Library and Information Science Students: Reflections on a Century of Formal Education for Librarianship." *Library Trends* 34 (Winter): 383–399.

III

MILLENNIALS AND INFORMATION LITERACY

6 REMODELING THE IVORY TOWER: INFORMATION LITERACY AND THE MODERN UNIVERSITY LIBRARY

Carol C. M. Toris, Ashlee B. Clevenger, and Katina Strauch

Despite the beautiful image evoked by the literal interpretation of the phrase "ivory tower," its figurative meaning is pejorative, evoking a sense of profound separation between the academic specialists who dwell in that tower, high above and out of touch with the real world, and the rest of humanity and its concerns. And although even a figurative ivory tower can connote something both beautiful and noble—a purity of intellectual pursuit, for example—for the layperson, it traditionally has suggested knowledge that is impervious to access or understanding.

Certainly, it is the case that, for the specialist communicating among his or her peers, the need for precise terminology and the presence of a shared intellectual context may create a communication code that appears to shroud information in mystery. Moreover, the esoteric pursuit of any intellectual endeavor, when taken to the extreme, is likely to remove it from the most mundane considerations of everyday life. (This does not excuse the fact that, by failing to stay at least somewhat grounded in life-at-large, many disciplinary ivory towers at times find themselves built on shifting and uncertain sands.) Regardless of the explanations of or excuses for it, however, the apparent elitism of traditional academic life is changing; the ivory tower has been stormed by technology. Now, ascending the tower and observing the mysteries within is open to anyone with access to the Internet. With a bit of persistence, all can be revealed. In the virtual world, most intellectual endeavors are accessible to the curious Internet traveler. With a few clicks, one can get the ingredients for chicken bombe or for a suitcase bomb. One can read books, watch movies, and play games, even compete with distant strangers. One can contact others around the globe to chat, exchange documents and pictures, even peer into their homes and communicate with them in real time (given the right hardware and software). One can seek out obscure facts. And if, while reading that arcane work of scholarship, some point evades you, you can go to the author's Web page and send him or her an e-mail with your query. Newton might not respond, but one of his intellectual offspring probably will.

Defenders of the ivory tower point to the function of intellectual elitism as providing an evaluative yardstick for information. In the sciences, for example, the best information will be published in peer-reviewed journals, which will be tiered (at least in scholars' minds) according to their importance in the field. And the criteria for inclusion, although not always agreed on by those authors whose work is not accepted for inclusion, at least are clear. What is worrisome to those who would defend this function of the ivory tower is that, in the modern technological age, the wall that once separated the wheat from the chaff has begun to collapse. It is no longer easy to identify the standards by which information is gleaned or regarded, and it becomes more difficult each day. (For example, if a scholar posts unpublished research on his or her Web page, is this work not published because of some obscure but important flaw; because its content deviates from the status quo maintained by the ivory tower gatekeepers; or, alternatively, is the Internet user now simply getting this information in advance of the slow publication process?) On the other hand, the everyday concerns of the "everyman" Internet user have encouraged the development of media (e.g., Web pages and blogs) that can help to bridge the gap between the obscurities of scholarly pursuits and their appreciation and application by students and others.

Clearly, something profound has happened to the academic elitism typified by the notion of the ivory tower. Both the amount and nature of information available to the average person has changed. Indeed, with regard to their information desires and needs, the common contention is that the average person has changed. What is more, the library, especially the university library, stands at the vortex of this change. As the providers of the raw materials of many intellectual pursuits, it is the librarians who are the primary architects of the remodeling of the ivory tower of old to the new "e-tower" of modern times.

And what does academe have to say about this? When the nation seeks advice and direction in science, engineering, and medicine, it turns to its advisors—the National Academies—including the National Academy of Science, the National Academy of Engineering, The Institute of Medicine, and the National Research Council (NRC). The presidents of the Academies launched a two-year project in 2000 involving 261 U.S. doctoral/research universities to better understand the implication of information technology for the research university. Among its important observations is the following:

> The preservation of scholarly knowledge is one of the most rapidly changing functions of the university...Throughout the centuries, the intellectual focal point of the university has been its library, its collection of written works preserving the knowledge of civilization. Today, such knowledge exists in numerous forms—including almost literally in the ether, distributed in digital representations over worldwide networks—and it is not just the prerogative of the privileged few in academe but is accessible to many...The library is thus becoming less of a collection

house and more of a center for knowledge navigation, a facilitator of information retrieval and dissemination.[1]

The questions librarians have been asking and which they must continue to ask are what, exactly, has changed with regard to the library's function as a center of knowledge? What remains the same? And perhaps even more important— what should change and what should be preserved? And the purported inhabitants of the ivory towers of old—the academic researchers and university teachers— must contend with the changing landscape of information available to them, and prepare their students for these changes. Among the many ways in which librarians have responded to this challenge is to recognize that, in order to take fullest advantage of what the library (and the Internet itself) has to offer, the "end user," the consumer of information, must have a facility with a set of abilities referred to as "information literacy." In the words of our metaphor, this is the bedrock on which the "e-tower" of the future must be built. Although various insightful definitions of and perspectives on information literacy have been proposed,[2] the definition offered by the American Library Association[3] and detailed in the standards approved by the Association of College and Research Libraries (ACRL)[4] is among the most widely cited. It includes the following:

1. Determine the extent of information needed.
2. Access needed information effectively and efficiently.
3. Evaluate information and its sources critically.
4. Incorporate selected information into one's knowledge base.
5. Use information effectively to accomplish a specific purpose.
6. Understand the economic, legal, and social issues surrounding the use of information, and access and use information ethically and legally.

Acquisition of these skills by university students can best be attained if university librarians and faculty form an active partnership to meet this goal. And, while the concerns and expertise of these two groups may vary, suggestions regarding their shared responsibilities can be addressed from a consideration of two things: first, the changing features of the information contained in the collections of the modern academic library and second, some important characteristics of the users of these collections.

CHANGING FEATURES OF THE INFORMATION IN THE MODERN UNIVERSITY LIBRARY COLLECTION

Increased Access to and Amount of Information

Since the ancient Sumerian and Egyptian "House of Tablets" and "House of Books" 3000 years ago, humans have attempted to create and maintain an "ark of human knowledge" dedicated to its collection, classification, and preservation.[5] Despite its challenges, the electronic age puts us closer to this ideal than ever before. Perhaps more important, its electronic form makes it practical to consider making this storehouse of information available to everyone, all the time. The first three information literacy skills listed previously are directly affected by the increased access to information of any Internet (or modern library) user—how do I know how much information I need, how do I get to this information efficiently and effectively, and how do I evaluate the information and its sources?

The first skill, knowing how much information I need, will be specific to a knowledge base as well as to the importance of that information to the knowledge user. Searching for the dates and times of local movies will not require the same degree of thoroughness as searching for information on the latest and best cancer treatment for a loved one. The resources acceptable for a term paper will differ from those necessary to complete a dissertation. It is suggested that faculty begin by making this point eminently clear to their students; that is, although even a cursory search for information may be somewhat fruitful, it will not necessarily suffice in meeting one's informational needs.

Technological Access

Effective and efficient access to information, the second information literacy skill, is impacted and necessitated by several characteristics of the "e-tower" of information. First of all, greater access to information exists only if one has the necessary technology available for that access. Dismantling the ivory tower of old assumes that the library user will, first and foremost, have access to a computer and the Internet. When a sample of students on our campus was asked to indicate "the most important thing I would change about our library," their overwhelming concern was for the need for more computers and printers even though we have recently built a new library with full wireless access and more than double the number of computer stations as the old library. It is true that if you build it, they will come, often in much greater numbers than you anticipated! This issue of access to technology is of even greater concern if one envisions the e-tower as including all citizens, not just tuition-paying students and university employees.[6] To diminish the digital divide that might exist in the academic environment, as well as to provide full access to its online services, libraries must have a sufficient number of computers and printers available for all users. A recent survey of 101 student patrons of our campus library at the College of Charleston revealed that, although 92 percent of our students reported that they had a home computer to which they had access, 55 percent reported that they use available computers on campus at least once a day. Only 4 percent reported that they did not sometimes use computers on campus.[7]

With regard to the collection itself, it is indeed a cruel joke if we teach our students about the best databases and other sources of information, but then make many or even most of these resources inaccessible to them (at least via their University library) as soon as they graduate. According to the American Library Association, information literacy "forms the basis of lifelong learning."[8] As such, universities should consider themselves involved in the lifelong learning pursuits of their students. Allowing alumni to purchase continuing access to their university library holdings would be a start. Creating consortia of publicly funded libraries, both academic and municipal, would be even more inclusive. No matter how large or comprehensive a repository of information the Internet might be, as long as some information (like access to online journals) comes at a price, libraries will be providers of what the individual user cannot him/herself afford. Our aforementioned survey of student library patrons revealed that 78 percent reported that they had used an online database, and 87 percent reported that they had used the online library catalog. The good news of these high numbers must be tempered by the fact that these commendable search strategies (or the resources they point to) will not be available to the graduated student, as least not from the source they have become accustomed to using (namely, their university library). Fortunately, groups such as the Scholarly Publishing and Academic Resources Coalition (SPARC), an alliance of academic and research libraries developed by the Association of Research Libraries, are being formed. SPARC is focused on facilitating "the emergence of systems that capitalize on the networked environment to facilitate research...its strategies expand competition and support open access to address the high and expanding cost of scholarly journals."[9]

Technological Literacy

Technological literacy, of course, is a part of the more general issue of information literacy. Both faculty and librarians should be concerned about where and how our students/library users learn about technology. It is often assumed that just because the current generation of students has had access to technology in the form of digital games, iPods, cell phones, and Internet access, they understand the technology of the modern library equally well. This assumption is unverified, and, from our observations, untrue. Many students manage to get some use of technology, but the resources available to them are woefully underused because of their lack of complete familiarity with their features and functions. Libraries now have the new responsibility of educating users about the devices and products that allow them to access the library's collection. In our survey of student patrons at our library, 59 percent reported that they had either taken a formal library tour as part of a class or had a librarian guest lecture about library resources in at least one of their classes; 38 percent reported they had taken a college-level computer class, and 61 percent reported they had taken a course that involved in-class computer use.[10]

Searching for and Archiving Information

A recent Dilbert cartoon characterized the information explosion of our age with an apt but disturbing simile—"Information is coming at your brain like a fire hose at a teacup." The explosion of information available to the Internet—and library—user has important implications for the processes of learning, researching, and decision making. First of all, greater access to information exists only if one knows how to find what one seeks; if you can't find it, it might as well not exist. This point suggests the need for better instruction in search techniques and strategies. And, because sources for and access to information change constantly, librarians and faculty must put in place mechanisms to stay informed about such changes, as well as to communicate them to their users/students. Ninety-nine percent of our student library patron survey respondents reported that they had used an online search engine; 70 percent reported that they perform an online search at least once a day. An analysis of variance revealed that they also were statistically significantly more likely to report that they used a search engine than a database of published works when doing research for a class [$F(2,71)$ = 38.04, $p < .001$], a fact that has implications for the potential quality of their searches.[11]

Related to issues of searching is the important function of how to best archive information. Any librarian can tell you that the quantity of available—and important—information is growing exponentially faster than the space available to contain it as a printed record. If the amount of space were to remain the same, criteria for print archives would necessarily become more stringent, especially for older materials. The ability of the user to print electronic records when needed may solve some problems. In addition, developments in nanotechnology will continue to allow the proliferation of increasingly greater amounts of digitized information in more accessible formats. On the other hand, certain types of digital resources (e.g., Web sites and online databases) are more ephemeral than print media; only the print format is guaranteed to look the same tomorrow. In preparing this chapter, we were dismayed to discover that several interesting Internet sources of information mentioned in recently published works were no longer available.

In both searching for and archiving information, there is an increasing influence of market forces, from the paid advertising links of search engines to the many subject databases prepared for libraries. Indeed, one might argue that the ivory tower has now become a trade center and the intellectual gatekeepers have undergone a metamorphosis into commercial gatekeepers. This is no small issue, and both librarians and faculty, because of their expertise, must decide to play a greater role in the creation of search engines and aggregated databases. One possible solution to this need for noncommercial expert input recently was reported. Two university professors, R. David Lankes and Michael Eisenberg, have been awarded a grant from the MacArthur Foundation to create something they call the Credibility Commons Web Site. Among other things, the Web site may offer a search engine that would direct users toward Web sites already identified by skilled researchers, including reference librarians.[12]

Finally, greater access has come to mean constant access; the 24/7 library. As with so many other services (e.g., banking, online shopping), current users expect library services (especially those that are online) to be available around the clock and they report that they prefer doing research online.[13]

In summary, the greater amount and availability of access to information should increase our concerns for eliminating any digital divide among our students (and ultimately, all citizens) and for contributing to the enhanced techno-logical literacy of the library user. Moreover, we should attempt to provide ade-quate instruction and guidance regarding search techniques and attend carefully to decisions about what should be archived in print format. Finally, we should demand a greater role in information product development when appropriate and take full advantage of the release from some of the limitations of time and space that were features of libraries of the past.

Increased Variety of Information Formats

It was clear when the neighborhood was full of ivory towers just who their inhabitants were (by their academic degrees) and what they contained (peer-reviewed journal articles and the like). Although intellectual pedigrees still may be discernible, the predominance of a tier of peer-reviewed journals as the best (if not the only) source of reliable information in the academic realm has been altered. In the e-tower environment, scholars can post their data, conclusions, opinions, etc. on their Web pages without concern for peer review or publication lag; innovation and creativity can emerge from blogs and posting of all kinds. Indeed, it is a testimony to human intellect to see the vast wealth of informa-tion that has emerged on the Web with no pecuniary incentives. On the other hand, Web pages that appear professional can contain biased and/or fabricated information.

The third information literacy skill cited previously, "to evaluate information and its sources critically," always has been an important part of scholarship, but the challenges of this task have increased as the variety and forms of information have increased. For example, some of our survey respondents demonstrated con-fusion between a search engine and searching an online database. On the other hand, many information evaluation skills that have long been with us are relevant regardless of the type of content, and pose familiar questions: Who is the author of this information? What are his/her qualifications? How objective can I expect this person to be? Who published this information? For example, in today's digital environment, URL extensions of Web sites may give a hint to the nature, quality, and/or motivations of the source (edu, org, or gov versus com or net). And, just as we once were cautioned not to judge a book by its cover, one should not judge the quality of the information in a Web site by the sophistication of its Java script! Finally, when a user of the library collection has any questions about a source of information, the user should know that he or she can turn to an expert—a reference librarian (in person, or, in many cases, online)—for help. Research by Holliday and Li[14] found that students, in conducting their library research, report that they do not seek help from librarians and only occasionally seek help from professors or peers. Institutions should take steps to encourage library users to make full use of the expertise of its trained personnel.

An interesting possibility being considered for the aforementioned Credibil-ity Commons Web site is to sponsor "digital reference face-offs" wherein experts will offer competing strategies for researching answers to questions and the public will vote on what they consider to be the most effective technique. Perhaps this sport may one day become part of the Olympics (both winter and summer games, of course)! Faculty can create interest in quality searches by conducting similar "competitions" among students who are working collectively on a project. From a broader perspective, faculty must ensure that students' informational literacy is a prominent curricular goal with appropriate assessment of that goal.[15] Also, as experts in their respective fields, faculty must become more helpful to librarians in judging the quality of resources and in prioritizing them by importance to best use limited funds. In summary, both librarians and faculty must alert students and other library users of the need to apply critical thinking skills to the evaluation of information resources and to take advantage of the expertise of others in their research endeavors whenever possible.

From Information to Knowledge

The last three information literacy skills listed by the ALA have less to do with information and more to do with knowledge. As the definition of information literacy delineates, the information consumer should be able to incorporate selected information into his/her knowledge base; use information effectively to accomplish a specific purpose (the antithesis of the stereotypic "ivory tower" notion, which sometimes connotes impractical knowledge); and understand the economic, legal, and social issues surrounding the use of information, as well as access and use information ethically and legally. Not only are these skills important to meeting the generally accepted goal of higher education to create life-long learners, but, as has been pointed out, "information literacy is required by accreditation organizations, expected by employers in the workplace for organizational success, and desired by society, which needs an informed citizenry that is capable of making well-reasoned and well-founded decisions."[16] No less an expert than Bill Gates (the chairman of Microsoft) has suggested that, as intellectual property becomes increasingly important to business, employees are "morphing" into knowledge workers. He predicts that "the road ahead" will involve (in fact, already does involve) the development of software that can synthesize and manage knowledge as well as mere information, that is, to mimic how experienced professionals think and work.[17]

Incorporating and using knowledge are two activities that should represent both current and future goals of any college student. And, although very little empirical work has been done with regard to information literacy skills, some early research suggests that these skills can be highly situated and that developing the appropriate attitudes toward pursuing information literacy is likely to involve a contextualized and iterative process.[18] That is to say, students need to be challenged to apply information literacy skills in their class assignments, not just for a single required "library course," but in a variety of classes and again and again.

One of the difficulties in creating appropriate research assignments in our current digital environment is the temptation it affords students, via the availability of electronic sources, to cut and paste passages without appropriate documentation of source, that is, to cheat. Plagiarism may or may not have increased in the electronic age, but it clearly has become easier. Faculty must be more careful and explicit in their instruction and enforcement of ethical standards of scholarship. Fortunately, information technology tools have been and continue to be developed to thwart plagiarism.[19]

SOME IMPORTANT CHARACTERISTICS OF THE USERS OF THE MODERN UNIVERSITY LIBRARY COLLECTION

The primary user of the university library is, of course, the student. Today's typical undergraduate student, somewhere between the ages of 19 and 24, was born during the 1980s and is considered to be part of generation Y, which also is known as the net generation, the digital generation, or the echo boom generation. These individuals, perhaps most commonly referred to as the millennials, include anyone born between 1980 and 2001.[20] As such, they have peopled our universities since about 1998, and much has been written about their networked, interactive, multimedia-oriented culture. They now are being followed by generation Z, considered by some to be the youngest of the millennial generation. These are the true digital natives in that they have been surrounded by digital technology all of their lives. They have never known a world without URLs and personal computers.

Certain claims about this digital generation have been made, although most either remain untested or have been verified only by self-report measures. As such, when certain trends are reported, usually the best we can say is that they represent stereotypes that may or may not be accurate. Nevertheless, it is constructive to examine some of the claims that have been made about this generation and to explore what evidence, if any, supports them.

The End of Reading?

That the up-and-coming generation of students, generation Z, represents the end of the alphabet is hopefully *not* a prescient labeling process that suggests that we also have reached the end of the need for an alphabet and for reading! Crying out for empirical verification are claims that millennials are reading less than other generations[21] and that their best way to learn involves interactive and visual representations (as opposed to more traditional text-based forms),[22] especially since decisions of acquisitions librarians may be influenced by these claims. It is the case that based on 2005 ACT-tested high school graduates, only about half of our nation's ACT-tested high school students are ready for college-level reading.[23] One reason for this, suggested by Mary Little of Questia Media, Inc.,[24] is that most states define grade-level standards in reading only through the eighth grade. In other words, if students indeed are reading less and/or are unskilled readers, this may be due to factors besides technological changes. But if they are influenced to read less by the relatively greater availability of nonprint media, it may be that parents and teachers support choices in that direction by what they make available in the home and classroom. The same may be true of libraries. A student may opt to avoid reading the published synopsis, let alone the entire classic work of literature, if he or she can access and watch the movie in a fraction of the time and with much less effort. The question librarians must ask themselves is this: Are we implementing new media formats to fit the changing needs of the user (adaptation of media to the user), or is the user being changed to fit the media that are most widely and easily available (accommodation of user to media)?

The distinction between adaptation and accommodation is somewhat reminiscent of the popular information technology notions of continuity or evolutionary change versus discontinuity or revolutionary change toward an information-oriented society. In the former case, change emerges slowly and as an extension of earlier forms of media; in the latter case, change is thrust on people and social institutions, forcing them to come to grips with new functions and demands or cease to be relevant. Borgman (2000) argues that the most likely future scenario will continue to involve both types of change; people will select and use technologies that suit their existing needs, and new technologies will be propelled into the marketplace.[25] Some of these new technologies, but not all of them, will eventually find their niche. For example, the demise of paper and the emergence of the "paperless office" were predicted decades ago as a result of the emergence of the personal computer and the Internet.[26] Although the uses of paper may have changed somewhat, its importance has not diminished. Moreover, it is commonly reported that people prefer to read documents on paper rather than on screens. Borgman[27] provides an interesting analysis of why this might be the case, including such explanations as the relatively lower quality of the screen display, the ease of manipulating paper, the ability to annotate it, its greater portability, freedom from the need for a power source for access, and so on. Technological products can, and have been adapting many of their features to accommodate the preferences of users, but until and unless they can surpass whatever the underlying reason(s) are for the preference for paper, they will not completely replace it. As with this hypothesized preference for paper over electronic displays, the hypothesized (but still unverified) preference for nonprint over print media will require empirical verification and elucidation as to any underlying possible causes.

Continuous Partial Attention

An example of changes brought about by media is suggested by the term *continuous partial attention*, a label coined by Linda Stone, formerly of Apple and currently with Microsoft.[28] She uses this phrase to describe modern life and our overwhelming desire to be "connected" via e-mail, instant messaging, cell phones, and other distractions. We constantly attempt to monitor these media, and, as a result, are seldom able to give our full attention to anything. (She adroitly points out to her corporate audiences that most of them are attending to their Blackberries or cell phones or laptops even as she speaks.) Needless to say, this kind of fragmented attention is counterproductive to the intense and constant attention required by scholarly and other productive pursuits. Stone suggests that "continuous partial attention" is an adaptive (or, in our terminology, accommodative) behavior, a consequence of our attempts to keep up with the growing number of responsibilities and relationships engendered by our technologies. When we queried students on our campus about what they would improve in our library, their second most frequent suggestion (after requesting more computers and printers) was a room they could go to—with computers and Internet access—to use their cell phones (which they are not permitted to use inside the library). They wanted glorified phone booths, where they could talk on the phone while they read their e-mail (and perhaps while they researched their assignments). Should libraries try to accommodate every technological need articulated by their users or draw a line in the sand? There are no easy answers.

EASE ÜBER ALLES?

It is commonly claimed that millennials expect research to be easy, and, when they can't find what they need, they give up.[29] Weiler's[30] focus group of millennial respondents claimed that one of the highest criterion on their list of needs when seeking information was ease of use. Of secondary importance were such characteristics as trust, quality, credibility, validity, completeness, and comprehensiveness of their sources. But is this really that different from previous generations? While ease may be more common and, therefore, more expected, there is no evidence to suggest that it is any more important than it always has been. There is, of course, seductiveness to the ease with which we now can find some kind of information about anything. The fear, of course, is that we may find ourselves living in a society where the only things worth doing are those that can be done easily, where the least costly information (in terms of time and/or money) always is considered the best, and where the truth is too demanding a criterion with which to be reckoned. Some[31] have already suggested that any information that is not readily available online (for example, as a full text article) will be underused and, consequently, considered to be second-rate. On the other hand, the ability to access an original source instantly, for example, through hypertext links, might make it *more* likely that readers will use *those* sources and perform more thorough research than they might have otherwise.

In our survey of our student patrons,[32] we inquired about online research habits. According to their self-reports,

- 9 percent stop searching as soon as they've found one good source.
- 63 percent sample 10 or fewer sources and use the best of those.
- 16 percent sample more than 10 sources and use the best of those.
- 12 percent claim to examine all available resources to find the best sources.

We cannot conclude much from these data because we don't know the nature of their search inquiries, except perhaps to note that most of our respondents reported that they consider at least more than one different source most of the time. It makes sense, however, to suggest that faculty giving research assignments should encourage a willingness among their students to recognize that the best information may require additional effort. This can be accomplished by requiring, for example, not just "10 (or some other number of) references" but "10 (or some other number of) relevant references," along with instruction as to how best to evaluate what is relevant. Grades (a highly "relevant" motivator) can then be a function of the degree to which sources make the mark. If students expect all scholarly research to be easy (and it's not clear that they do), it may be because this is the expectation for which they have been prepared by their educators or, perhaps, because they have never been challenged to expect otherwise by the assignments.

The Overconfidence Effect

In the psychological literature, there is growing support for a construct called the overconfidence effect—namely, the finding that people place too much confidence in the insightfulness of their judgments, overestimating the chances that their decisions about the present are sound and that their predictions about the future will prove correct.[33] Although this is particularly the case in research that focuses on self-assessment measures, numerous studies also support the fact that confidence in one's judgment of facts is unrelated to accuracy in judgment.[34] This raises the uncomfortable possibility that library patrons or Internet users searching for information may be more confident in the utility of their search activities (and researching abilities) than they should be. There is yet little direct evidence to support this particular possibility, but one recent study did report that 144 college-level students overestimated their information literacy skills as demonstrated by actual performance test scores.[35]

A nationwide phone interview survey of 2,200 adults conducted by the Pew Internet and American Life Project on Search Engine Users in 2005 reported some interesting findings regarding Internet use, search engine use, and confidence in use:

- 84 percent of Internet users have used a search engine.
- 47 percent of searchers will use a search engine no more than once or twice a week; 30 percent of searchers will use a search engine at least once a day.
- 87 percent of searchers say that they have successful search experiences.
- 68 percent of Internet users claim that search engines are a fair and unbiased source of information; only 19 percent say they don't place trust in search engines.
- 92 percent of search engines users say that they are confident in their search abilities; of those, 52 percent say they are very confident.
- Those most confident in their searching are young, better educated, and in a higher income bracket.
- Of people 30 and under, 94 percent expressed confidence in their search abilities.[36]

Since this survey was conducted, the Pew Internet and American Life Project has continued and their latest data as of this writing, from September, 2005, indicate that the daily use of search engines continues to increase dramatically, from 30 percent of the Internet-using population in June 2004 (as cited previously) to 41 percent in September 2005.[37] These numbers represent a daily increase in users of Internet searching from 38 million to 59 million people in a little more than a year. Clearly, the use and dependence on search engines among the population at large are increasing. Are people accurately evaluating the quality of that information, or are they confidently, but mistakenly, overestimating it? Fortunately, there are many efforts underway to establish information literacy competency assessments in academia, a necessary prerequisite for determining the accuracy of one's confidence in these abilities.[38]

In summary, we must be careful that what we assume about the library user goes beyond stereotypic beliefs and reflects actual skills and preferences. We also must consider carefully the effects of the professional choices we make on our academic library users, especially our students.

CONCLUSION

While this ivory tower remodeling is occurring, and the library collection is undergoing such dramatic changes with regard to the amount, access to, and variety of information formats it contains, we may find ourselves asking: what is the changing shape of the library itself? Unlike the "e-tower" or the "ivory tower" that we have been describing here, which are merely concepts—more specifically, descriptions of conditions—the library as we know it is a place. Especially on the university campus, the library is an intellectual center, a community organized and maintained by people who are experts in accessing and assessing sources of information. It is *the* place to ask a question, seek an answer, and to learn—even with all of the construction going on both within and outside. As long as people inhabit places, the need in our society for such an important place, no matter what its ultimate intellectual architecture, is not likely to change.

NOTES

1. National Research Council of the National Academies. "Preparing for the Revolution: Information Technology and the Future of the Research University" (Washington, D.C.: The National Academies Press, 2002), 33.

2. Cf. Doyle, Christina S. *Information Literacy in an Information Society: A Concept for the Information Age* (Syracuse, N.Y.: ERIC Clearinghouse on Information Literacy, 1994).

3. American Library Association Presidential Committee on Information Literacy. "Final Report" (Chicago, Ill.: American Library Association, 1989).

4. Association of College and Research Libraries (ACRL). "Information Literacy Competency Standards for Higher Education." 2000. Available online at http://www.ala.org/ala/acrl/acrlstandards/informationliteracycompetency.htm (Accessed May 23, 2006.)

5. Kotinos Publications. "History of the Private, Royal, Imperial, Monastic, and Public Libraries." Available online at http://www.libraries.gr/nonmembers/en/history_mesopotamia_soumer.htm (Accessed May 29, 2006.)

6. For an interesting analysis of the potential "digital divide" and the important role of libraries in preventing it, see Karen Coyle. *Coyle's Information Highway Handbook: A Practical File on the New Information Order* (Chicago, Ill.: American Library Association, 1997).

7. Clevenger, A. and C. Toris. "Searching for Godot: Is the Search for Online Resources Ever Complete?" *Proceedings of the XXV Charleston Conference Issues in Book and Serial Acquisition Conference* (Westport, Conn.: Libraries Unlimited, 2006).

8. See Note 4, p. 1.

9. "The Scholarly Publishing and Academic Resources Coalition (SPARC)" Homepage. Available online at www.arl.org/sparc/ (Accessed July 20, 2006.)

10. See Note 7.

11. Ibid.

12. Kiernan, Vincent. "Researchers From Two Universities Seek Ways to Find Credible Information Online." *The Chronicle of Higher Education* 52 (2006): A44.

13. Gardner, Susan, and Susanna Eng. "What Students Want: Generation Y and the Changing Function of the Academic Library." *Portal: Libraries and the Academy* 5 (2005): 405–420.

14. Holliday, Wendy, and Quin Li. "Understanding the Millennials: Updating Our Knowledge about Students." *Reference Services Review* 32 (2004): 346–366.

15. For some examples, see McCarthy and Pusateri. "Teaching Students to Use Electronic Databases." In *Handbook of the Teaching of Psychology,* eds. W. Buskist and S. Davis, 107–111 (Malden, Mass.: Blackwell Publishing, 2006) and I. F. Rockman & Associates. *Integrating Information Literacy into the Higher Education Curriculum: Practical Models for Transformation* (San Francisco: Jossey-Bass, 2004).

16. Ibid, Rockman and Associates, p. 10.

17. Gates, Bill. "The Road Ahead." *Newsweek*, December 19, 2005, 24.

18. Smith, Janice, and Martin Oliver. 2005. "Exploring Behaviour in the Online Environment: Student Perceptions of Information Literacy." *ATL-J Research in Learning Technology* 13 (2005): 49–65.

19. Foster, Andrea. "Plagiarism-Detection Tool Creates Legal Quandary." *The Chronicle of Higher Education* 48 (2002) May 17, A37.

20. Strauss, William, and Neil Howe. *Generations: The History of America's Future* (New York: Harper Perennial, 1992), 1584–2069.

21. Sweeney, Richard T. "Reinventing Library Buildings and Services for the Millennial Generation." *Library Administration and Management* 19 (2005): 165–175.

22. Lippincott, Joan R. "Net Generation Students and Libraries." In *Educating the Net Generation*, eds. D. Oblinger, and J. I. Oblinger (Boulder, Col.: Educause, 2005).

23. "ACT News Release: Average National ACT Score Unchanged in 2005." Available online at http://www.act.org/news/releases/2005/8–17–05.html (Accessed July 12, 2006.)

24. Personal communication, 2006.

25. Borgman, Christine. L. *From Gutenberg to the Global Information Infrastructure* (Cambridge, Mass.: The MIT Press, 2000), 1–3.

26. Lancaster, F. W. *Toward Paperless Information Systems.* (San Diego: Academic Press, 1978).

27. See Note 25, pp. 94–95.

28. Levy, Stephen. "(Some) Attention Must Be Paid!" *Newsweek*, March 27, 2006, 16.

29. See Note 12.

30. Weiler, Angela. "Information Seeking Behavior in Generation Y Students: Motivation, Critical Thinking, and Learning Theory." *Journal of Academic Librarianship* 31 (2005): 46–53.

31. Odlyzko, Andrew. "The Future of Scientific Information." www.dtc.umn.edu/~odlyzko/doc/future.scientific.comm.pdf, 2000, 4.

32. See Note 7.

33. Dunning, David, Chip Heath, and Jerry M. Suls. "Flawed Self Assessment: Implications for Health, Education, and the Workplace." *Psychological Science* 5 (2004): 69–106.

34. Cf. Fischhoff, Baruch, Paul Slovic, and Sarah Lichtenstein. "Knowing with Certainty: The Appropriateness of Extreme Confidence." *Journal of Experimental Psychology: Human Perception and Performance* 3 (1977): 552–564. Also see research on eyewitness testimony by Elizabeth Loftus and her colleagues.

35. Neely, Teresa Y. *Sociological and Psychological Aspects of Information Literacy in Higher Education* (Lanham, Md.: The Scarecrow Press, Inc., 2002), 113.

36. Pew Internet & American Life Project. "Search Engine Users." 2005. Available online at http://www.pewinternet.org (Accessed November 23, 2005.)

37. Rainie, Lee. "Pew Internet & American Life Project Memo Re: Search Engine Use November, 2005." Available online at http://www.pewinternet.org/PPF/r/167/report_display.asp (Accessed November 23, 2005.)

38. In addition to the assessment works cited above, see noteworthy examples in Eisenberg, Michael B., Carrie A. Lowe, and Kathleen L. Spitzer, eds. *Information Literacy: Essential Skills for the Information Age* (Westport, Conn.: Libraries Unlimited, 2004).

7 ENHANCING LIBRARY INSTRUCTION: CREATING AND MANAGING ONLINE INTERACTIVE LIBRARY TUTORIALS FOR A WIRED GENERATION

Mark Horan, Suhasini L. Kumar, and John Napp

The University of Toledo is a public metropolitan Carnegie Doctoral/Research Extensive institution with 19,675 as total enrollment in fall 2004. The university libraries caters to the needs of a diverse group of users. The percentage of first-generation college student was 44 percent; the percentage of students with family income below $50,000 was 41 percent; and the percentage of those who receive less than the high school core[1] was 29 percent. The undergraduate population is 19,840, with 20 percent of those attending as part-time students. Ohio residents make up 91 percent of the undergraduate group, with 51 percent identifying themselves as women. Eighteen percent are over the age of 24. Fifty-one percent of first-year students under 20 years old had some remediation, either math or English, or both. Nine percent of the first-year group was over 20 years old; of those 76 percent had remedial math and/or English. Our users consist of undergraduates, distance education students, international students, and non-traditional students, some returning to school after a long break in their studies, and, of course, faculty, staff, and administrators.

The advent of new information technologies has made access to information and data more immediate, and this has made engaging in research easier and more exciting than ever both for the novice and the experienced researcher. It has also created the need to acquire new sets of skills to succeed in these endeavors. Academic librarians have recognized the importance of promoting and teaching these new skills to students and of involving the whole academic community as well. Librarians have tried to provide effective library instruction, using various approaches, to impart essential information literacy skills that will help students become aware of the need for information and effectively search for, find, evaluate, and select the appropriate information. Unfortunately, engaging new students with what is a wide range of new and often sophisticated skills and experiences cannot be achieved using a single approach and expecting a common response.

Although teaching research skills in a situation where they can be related to a particular course goal in the classroom environment with live teacher student interaction seems the most desired approach in instruction programs, it is still second best to the support at the point of need, either at the in-person, or online, reference desk (Herrington 1998, 382–384). Of course, as an approach, the latter is largely impossible under current conditions of education.

Time and again, it has been found that students do not, or cannot, always listen, or hear, and comprehend everything an instructor says in class. Some students may feel that their skills and knowledge are sufficient or better than those being presented; this might be the reason for the apathy and reluctance to participate. Library anxiety also plays a role in the silence of the classroom. Students who have had no previous experience, no current learning goals, or no full understanding of what the course or degree goals are cannot relate to the importance of the presentations, although they may recognize some of the content. Thus even students engaged by the most active learning approaches may lose whatever partial engagement had been effected (Biggs 2003, 3–5).[2] As a result, reference librarians encounter students, particularly first-year students without a strong, or any, academic background, frantically requesting help to find information on a particular topic the night before an assignment is due. At that point librarians often give the student their best lessons in information literacy. So, aside from in-class instruction, librarians must participate in the general environment of campus through faculty modeling, administrators' messages,[3] and at the reference desk, as well as through individual lessons online, and at other places where students happen to frequent. Being heavily wired is indeed helpful.

Considering this and the fact that The University of Toledo is one of the top wired universities in the United States, librarians at the University of Toledo thought it would be ideal to have an interactive tutorial that students could access from their dorms, homes, or anywhere and at anytime. This tutorial would show students not only how to find information available in our catalog and at other libraries but also help find journal articles on topics of interest using the library's research databases. Before launching our own interactive tutorial, we decided to see what other libraries faced with a similar situation were doing.

LITERATURE REVIEW

There is considerable literature on information literacy tutorials and various libraries' experiences creating and evaluating them. The literature dates back to the early days of the personal computer (PC) and continues to the present. There is also considerable literature on how to design a tutorial. This literature review looks only at articles that describe the development of tutorials and their evaluation rather than those that merely review tutorials. Most of those included general tutorials aimed at freshman and sophomores. The remaining articles discuss tutorials aimed at undergraduates in specialized areas. The databases consulted for this review were Library Literature and Information Science, Library, Information Science & Technology Abstracts, and Education Abstracts. A search of Google Scholar was also conducted.

Kochtanek (1984, 130–133) describes the development of an early disc-based tutorial. This tutorial was designed to teach searching of MEDLINE and two now-defunct medical databases. It was written in the PILOT programming language and had 14 software modules. System requirements were for an IBM PC under DOS with 128k RAM and two double-density, double-sided floppy disc drives that required a 1200 baud modem.

Moore and Abson (2002) in "Really Useful or Virtually Useless" describe how they developed and launched "an interactive, self-paced first year tutorial" named InfoQuest, at Sheffield Hallam University (SHU) in the United Kingdom. InfoQuest is termed a "virtual learning environment" by the authors. The design team at SHU used Blackboard to create five modules that show students how to search databases and the Internet, avoid the risk of plagiarism, and correctly cite their sources. The tutorial can be customized for the use of different subject groups.

Franks, Hackley, Straw, and DiRenzo (2000) at the University of Akron discuss the process of developing their Information Competency Web Tutorial. The librarians planned for several modules to teach information competencies. There would be an interactive component as well as pretest/posttest components. The development was being handled by two teams: a Web Tutorial Task Force consisting of reference and instruction librarians, and a 'Web Squad' consisting of librarians with strong technical skills in programming and Web-design. Currently the tutorial is still under development.

Colorado State University (CSU) created "The Data Game" described by Thistlewaite (2001). CSU librarians wanted a tutorial that was highly interactive and entertaining. "The Data Game" has the appearance of a television game show. There are four modules, each hosted by an animated cartoon character. The modules include information about the research process, the Online Public Access Catalog (OPAC), searching for books, article searching, and Web site evaluation.

Tricarico, Daum Tholl, and O'Malley (2001) discuss the tutorial developed by Emmanuel College in Boston. The library obtained a Library Services and Technology Act (LSTA) grant in 1998. A primary Web version of the tutorial was made, with a CD-ROM version available for use by satellite campuses. The tutorial provided instruction for searching seven electronic journals and databases. The primary audience for the tutorial was undergraduate nursing students. A nonlinear approach was taken so that students could skip to specific sections as needed. Multimedia components were used to make the experience more entertaining. Calming colors were used to create a more relaxed and stress-free environment to help adult learners.

"QuickStudy: Library Research Guide" is the name of the tutorial created by the University of Minnesota Libraries. Veldof and Beavers (2001) describe the development process. Librarians along with university Java and Web programmers developed the tutorial. Three rounds of usability testing were done with undergraduates targeted as the main audience for the tutorial.

Phillips and Kearley (2003) provide a description of the tutorial TIP (Tutorial for Information Power) that was developed at the University of Wyoming Libraries. A $5,200 grant allowed them to hire a graphic designer and programmer. TIP is used in a required general education course for freshmen as part of their first-year experience. Feedback from students and faculty has aided refinements since the initial launch. A pretest and posttest provide information about the effectiveness of TIP.

Shippensburg University of Pennsylvania Library launched their "Ship to Shore" project as a way to explore information literacy on the campus. Cook (2002) and other librarians led a pilot project to develop a library tutorial. It was decided that the tutorial should be easy to navigate. It was also felt that it should be integrated into a required course to heighten its relevance. The tutorial contains six content areas. After defining information literacy and discussing how to start doing library research, the tutorial covers Internet and database searching. The final two sections of the tutorial explore evaluating electronic resources, their ethical use, and the Modern Language Association style guide.

Solanes and Gaete (2002) discuss the Pontifical Catholic University of Chile Library's Gnosis II tutorial. This is a nursing resources tutorial in Spanish. It is accessible to on-campus students and distance learners. The Library, Information Search, Source Citation, and Information Search on Nursing are the four modules comprising the tutorial.

Donaldson (1999) reported on a tutorial for business information at Seneca College of Applied Arts and Technology in Toronto, Ontario. The tutorial is part of a required course called "Success Strategies for College." There are five modules in the tutorial. The modules go over the layout of the tutorial, information formats, research strategies, and database searching. Faculty at the college were asked to give their impressions of the tutorial; most faculty felt students were helped by the tutorial.

Bender and Rosen (1998) describe how the Research Instruction Online (RIO) information literacy tutorial was developed at the University of Arizona, Tucson. Information competencies were identified by the project team. RIO an online, interactive tutorial was created especially for freshman and sophomores. OPAC searching, database selection and searching, and Web searching are covered in separate modules. An extensive marketing campaign was implemented to introduce RIO.

Johnson and Sager (1998) discuss the tutorial created at the University of Louisville (UL) Libraries. It was developed using Authorware. The result was a 45-minute tutorial for the libraries' OPAC (Minerva). Students employed by the UL Libraries were recruited as evaluators for the tutorial. The tutorial has now become a required part of the General Education 101 (Campus Culture) classes.

Dennis and Broughton (2000) wrote about the FALCON tutorial at Bowling Green State University (BGSU), Bowling Green, Ohio. FALCON is an interactive tutorial designed to teach students how to search the BGSU OPAC. It was thought that FALCON would supplement sessions with librarians rather than replace them. A conscious decision was made to limit the length and scope of . the tutorial to keep it interesting to students. It takes 30 to 40 minutes for students to complete FALCON. The design is linear, with questions following each section. FALCON is compatible with screen reading software used by the visually impaired. Student employees and colleagues in the library were asked to evaluate the tutorial.

Fowler and Dupuis (2000) describe the development of the Texas Information Literacy Tutorial (TILT). An increasing demand for teaching library skills faced with limited staff and classroom space motivated the Information Literacy Office to create an online tutorial. TILT was created as a response to fulfill the need of a large number of students requiring library instruction and was designed "to teach a progression of skills" using basic information literacy concepts in an interactive environment. Requiring that students complete TILT before a library session helped students prepare for advanced research and turned them into active participants in classroom sessions. TILT was carefully designed for the student; it worked with various browsers and on Apple Macintosh computers (MACs) as well as PCs. There is a low-bandwidth version for distance learners with slow connections and a version with Flash features.

Bianco (2005, 3–5) summarized eight articles about what worked and what did not in online tutorials and compiled them into a list of 14 tips in an attempt to create "some best practices for tutorials." The tips suggest the content of tutorials cover conceptual as well as procedural issues. They should have a practical layout that does not hinder navigation or obscure any of the clearly stated learning objectives. In short, tutorials should be active and accessible in terms of concept flow, transmission, format, navigation, and student disability.

Grassian and Kaplowitz (2001, 190–192) list the following pros and cons of online tutorials. Just-in-time rather than just-in-case instruction, 24/7 instruction for electronic haves, possible immediate feedback, printable guide information for specific circumstances, and a high degree of flexible modularity are the pros. The cons are the lack of printable instructions for the use of live connections, which can create a switch back and forth to the tutorial for guidance; the size of modules may be too small and too many to capture interest, thereby obscuring any return for effort; and maintenance and updating can be time consuming and labor intensive.

PLANNING FOR THE TUTORIAL

After reviewing the tutorials of other academic libraries, the tutorial committee tried to identify and focus on the specific needs of our library's particular diverse clientele. These groups' needs were as varied as their levels of education and expertise in effectively searching various databases to find needed information.

We also reviewed the programs and the courses that were offered at our university so as to ascertain the academic and research needs of our students.

We met with the director of English composition to get a sense for the type of assignments teachers would give their Comp I and II students and the competencies and skills that were expected as an outcome of the use of an interactive library tutorial, because they would form a significant part of our primary users.

After having collected this information, we had a clearer understanding of our users needs. We decided to create a tutorial that would primarily serve the needs of undergraduates and also fulfill the basic information-seeking needs of most of our diverse users and planned to have it structured into short modular sections. There would be four modules (Figure 7.1):

1. Orientation
2. Library Catalogs and Searches
3. Research Databases and Searches
4. Citation

Each module would be designed to contain several sections with information and interactive tutorials related to topics addressed by that particular module.

Figure 7.1
University of Toledo Library Tutorial's Home Page Displaying Access to Four Modules

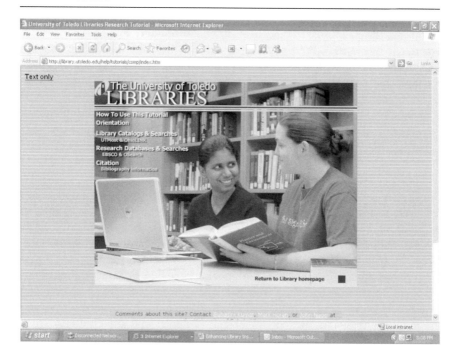

Three direct messages were emphasized aside from the procedural aspects of the modules:

1. Knowledgeable help is close at hand.
2. As a student you are already part of the academic community.
3. Everything in the tutorial is meant to help you express yourself better within that community.

At the end of each module we intended to have a self-test so that users could check their progress, as well as remember and recapitulate what they had learned in the preceding module. The interactive tutorials would be created to imitate the actual catalogs and databases with hyperlinks to other pages, which would simulate the database and catalog operation, making it at least in part interactive.

INSTRUCTIONAL DESIGNERS

We discussed our plans for the tutorial with the director of Instructional Design from the Distance Learning Department who arranged for the services of an instructional designer to help us with the tutorial. Our committee met on a weekly basis to create the overall design and text for the tutorial. We then met with the instructional designer to discuss the tutorial and what we envisioned would be the final outcome. We worked closely with the designer who presented completed parts of the modules to us and we critically examined and evaluated the modules and the designer made adjustments as we went along.

It took over a year to bring the whole tutorial together. During that time, a member of the committee left and an additional instructional designer joined us. It was nearly two years before we finally were able to present it for testing. This was largely because the designers were lent to us from the Distance Learning Department where the designers were already involved in other projects that would surge up and recede as the semesters changed; our committee members were also involved in numerous other commitments that they had to synchronize with this project.

DESIGN AND EXECUTION

The purpose of the tutorial was to provide a general overview of the relationship of service locations, library users, personnel, search techniques, and resources to academic work. We used a reading level of seventh grade in order to embrace a broad range of reading skill levels that could be expected to users of the tutorial, regardless of whether the user was in a composition course or not. We were disinclined to use a purely scholarly approach and adopted a motif of apprentice scholar; that is, the student, having become a student, has joined the academic community and the resources and knowledge presented in the tutorial would help bring them recognition from the community as members. We used a consistent theme throughout the search examples and the citations. Also, the same amorphous shape, "The Blobs," was designed as the spokespersons to

Figure 7.2
Mascot Character, "The Blob," Introduces the Navigation Pages

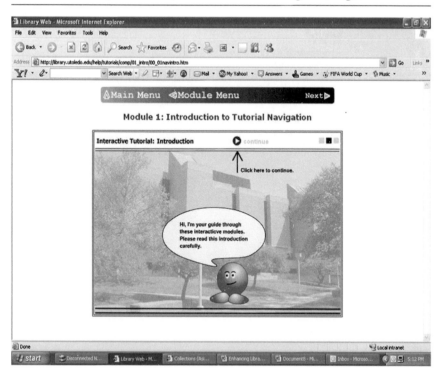

provide guidance and direction (Figures 7.2, 7.3, and 7.4). Our intent was also to introduce as much active images into the content as the designers felt could be used without slowing online use for distance learners. The distant users, while they may never see some of the places in the orientation, would at least have a visual connection with locations and services provided by the university libraries.

FOCUS GROUP

When the tutorial was almost ready, we decided to have it evaluated by students to test how well it met their needs. We applied for and received a small grant from the University of Toledo Center for Learning and Teaching to carry out a focus group test. We were interested in attracting students for the group who had had both levels of composition. After advertising on the campus-wide e-news, 12 students responded and 8 undergraduate students were eligible to participate in the focus group. These students were then divided into two groups of four each. The first group was made up of two men and two women; the second group was made up of four women. There were two juniors and the rest were seniors. Each individual was paid $25 for participation. The session was composed of a pretest,

Figure 7.3
Mascot Explains How to Read the Tutorial Pages and Its Purpose

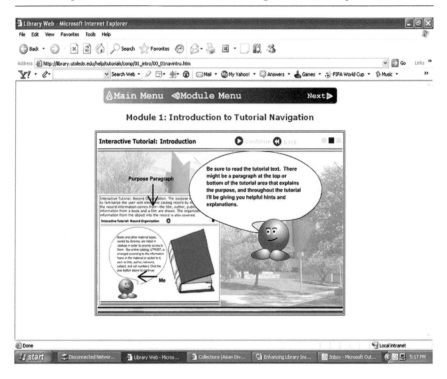

use of the tutorial, a posttest with the exactly same instrument, and a recorded discussion period. They were also given food and sodas. Each session lasted two-and-a-half hours.

The moderator for both sessions was a graduate student who had no prior experience with focus groups. He was to take care of the administrative paper-work, distribute and collect the pretest and posttest, and to instruct participants that the purpose of the focus group was to evaluate the tutorial in terms of whether or not it would be useful and appropriate for the required Composition I and Composition II courses. Then he was directed to ask a set of questions to facili-tate a discussion about the tutorial. He was to answer any questions about the tutorial by simply referring them to the authors. The sessions were both recorded and transcripts made without identifying any of the individuals using their real names.

The pretest and posttest served several purposes. One purpose of the pre-test was to stimulate memories about library use, that is, to operate as priming questions. It was also intended to elicit evidence of knowledge, experience, and basic skill level. The posttest reissued the same questions and was to measure any change that might have occurred in knowledge and affect that might be

Figure 7.4
Mascot Guides User Through Simulated Search with Artificial "Real" Link to Library's Catalog

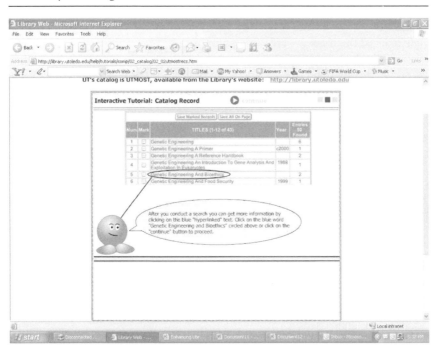

attributed to the tutorial. The discussion with the group at the end was to gather information about any undetected defects or functional or grammatical errors in the design that they may have noticed.

The initial three questions asked about experience and use related to libraries. The test included four multiple choice and one true/false question on database searching. One matching question asked the participant to match each of seven citations to their correct format. There was one library service question about interlibrary loan. The last section asked about participants' feelings of confidence in carrying out six different types of information content and format searches. One of the searches was not covered in the tutorial.

RESULTS

Seven of the participants had used between one and three libraries. One had used between four and six. All had used the library to do research and write a paper. Six also used the library for study and/or quiet space. Four used the library to socialize. All had taken Comp I and II, but for one student that seemed to have been the only writing/research experience she had had in school. Everyone else could name at least one other course in which they had done research; five could name more than four courses. One could name more than three specific topics.

In the match/citation question, one person identified all of the items correctly in both the pretest and posttest. In the posttest, three corrected their answers to all correct. Although the remaining four were not able to answer all correctly, they reduced the number of incorrect answers.

In a true/false question about keyword searching, seven of the eight got this correct both times and the last corrected himself in the posttest. Similarly in a three choice, yes/no/not sure, question about interlibrary loan, six answered this correctly both times and the last two corrected themselves after the tutorial.

In Question 4, which was to elicit an understanding of finding an article in the library holdings, two answered the question correctly both times and three corrected themselves after the tutorial. Three of the eight persisted in making errors, two by repeating the same answer.

Question 5 was meant to prime the participants to attend to index searches. Any answer other than "none of above" would have worked, although two were better answers than the remaining working answer. No one selected "none of the above" or the least efficient working answer.

Question 7, covering the definition of bibliography, was answered correctly both times by five participants; two were attracted by the distracter, "all of the above," and one answered incorrectly in the posttest. This definition, however, was not addressed in the tutorial.

The two questions that address search strategies gave a degree of indication of the level of search sophistication of the participants. Question 8 becomes ambiguous and unanswerable, as no particular database is mentioned. The answers each round remained the same; the same groups of four participants each selected the most detailed search string or "none of the above." Question 9 used a combination of truncation, nested strings, and a balancing "or" phrase, that is, gun control or (firearm* and (law* or legis* or regul*)). The other selections were either incomplete closures or illogical use of the operators or nesting. One person corrected an answer in the posttest. One person was distracted away. The issues were not addressed in the tutorial.

In the final questions, students were asked to rate their feeling of ease in finding various formats with different content on a scale of one to six, one being very easily and six as not at all. Five of the eight averaged a positive change after the tutorial, two averaged a negative change, and one registered no difference.

DISCUSSION LEADER REPORT

Group I: 10:00 AM

This group was composed of four younger (18–25 years old) and one nontraditional student. Among the participants was a self-described Web designer. Some members of this group made specific design-related comments during the discussion period.

Members of this group needed little direction, and all seemed to be computer-savvy. For the most part, their questions in the lab tended to center on understanding the reasons for the focus group, rather than on the tutorial itself. Not wanting to skew the results, I had to feign ignorance about the project.

The consensus of this group seemed to be that, with a few technical modifications, the site was ready to be launched. All members said that they left the tutorial more knowledgeable than before the tutorial, and all agreed that the content was both helpful and relevant.

Several students in this group felt strongly that the quizzes should have provided detailed explanations as to why incorrect answers were incorrect. They also seemed to agree that more use could have been made of bullet points.

Group II: 2:00 PM

This group was composed of three nontraditional students, none of whom was under the age of 35. Only one student professed any computer proficiency (this participant also self-described as having Web design experience). The other two students needed a great deal of direction in the first few minutes of the tutorial, but seemed to adapt quickly. One of the less-proficient also had English as a second language (ESL) issues, with French as her first language.

This group was very concerned about images not showing up, leading me to suspect that all three participants relied on visual cues for information. This came up in both the lab and the discussion period. All three indicated that the site seemed to need an overhaul in graphics, and that the site was not very eye-catching.

This group of three students agreed that the designers did a good job of breaking up the volume of information into smaller, more manageable chunks. They also felt that the site was easy to navigate when moving between pages.

CONCLUSIONS

The students in the focus group picked up on the key issues targeted: available help and extended resources, and greater comfort with searching for content.

The comments from the focus group were later discussed with the instructional designers who made further changes to the tutorial and linked it to the library's Web site under the library's "Help" option.

When testing the online tutorial against Bianco's (2005, 3–5) 14 tips, we found that we compare favorably with her list of best practices for online tutorials.

The online tutorial at http://library.utoledo.edu/helphome.html is now promoted to students in the library instruction classes and also to incoming instructors and teaching assistants who have found it to be a useful resource. Students will be asked to review the tutorial before they attend library instruction so as to enhance the classroom experience.

Managing and maintaining the tutorial is an ongoing task that we did not give serious thought to when we first considered creating an online interactive tutorial, but this is an important aspect of the tutorial that should have been anticipated and included in the initial plan.

Changes occur all the time in the library; we are presently all set to redesign the library and convert the main reference area to meet the information commons concept. Resource and place locations will have to be changed. In some sense, the price of tutorials is eternal vigilance. Databases are added and dropped frequently and interfaces change often, as do search engines and options. We have realized that changes will have to be made to the tutorial on an ongoing basis to keep it updated and authentic.

Will we have the help of the instructional designers to help with further changes and edits? Should we buy the software used by the designers and learn to use them ourselves? Would we be able to use them with the same expertise as the instructional designer? Where would we go for funding expensive software, especially during this time of budget cuts? All these concerns arise as we try to grapple with the reality of effectively managing and maintaining the online interactive tutorial. Recalling how creating Web pages was immensely simplified by webpage editors, we are hoping that soon we will have access to software that would simplify the whole process of creating and maintaining graphically appealing interactive tutorials that students can refer to and use from anywhere at anytime.

NOTES

1. The absence of library research from the admissions brochures or the burying of a library presence on the school Web site as a part of branding would seem to indirectly remove it as a meaningful part of the curricula or as a persona in university life. "Library as 'additional and/or optional' but not integral" seems to be the unintended message.

2. Sandra Leanne Bosacki. *The Culture of Classroom Silence* (New York: Peter Lang, 2005), 79–99, 121. Bosacki lists five kinds of silences that exert social control: hostile silence, controlling silence, resisting silence, political silence, and safe silence. She also includes another kind of silence: "Newcomers to unfamiliar situations must learn what kinds of speech acts are used; they must learn the psychological pragmatics."

3. Complete College Preparatory Core: A high school academic curriculum that includes four years each of English, math, and social studies, and at least three years of science courses that include biology, chemistry, and physics. Ohio Board of Regents. Making the Transition from High School to College in Ohio 2005: A Statewide Perspective. Columbus, OH: The Board. 2006. p. 33. http://www.regents.state.oh.us/perfrpt/2005HSindex.html (Accessed May 17, 2006.)

REFERENCES

Bender, Laura J., and Jeffrey M. Rosen. 1998. "Working Toward Scalable Instruction: Creating the RIO Tutorial at the University of Arizona Library." *Research Strategies* 16 (4): 315–325.

Bianco, Cecile. 2005. "Online Tutorials: Tips from the Literature." *Library Philosophy and Practice* 8 (Fall): 1–6. http://libr.unl.edu:2000/LPP/lppv8n1.htm (Accessed May 30, 2006.)

Biggs, John. 2003. *Teaching for Quality Learning at University: What the Student Does.* 2nd ed. Maidenhead, UK: Open University Press.

Cook, Douglas L. 2002. "Ship to Shore: An Online Information Literacy Tutorial Using BlackBoard Distance Education Software." *Journal of Library Administration* 37 (1/2): 177–187.

Dennis, Stefanie, and Kelly Broughton. 2000. "FALCON: An Interactive Library Instruction Tutorial." *Reference Services Review* 28 (1): 31–38.

Donaldson, Kelly A. 1999. "Library Research Success: Designing an Online Tutorial to Teach Information Literacy Skills to First-Year Students." *The Internet and Higher Education* 2 (4): 237–251.

Fowler, Clara S., and Elizabeth A. Dupuis. 2000. "What Have We Done? TILT's Impact on Our Instruction Program." *Reference Services Review* 28 (1): 343–348.

Franks, Jeffrey A., Robert S. Hackley, Joseph E. Straw, and Susan DiRenzo. 2000. "Developing and Interactive Web Tutorial to Teach Information Competencies: The Planning Process at the University of Akron." *Journal of Educational Media & Library Sciences* 37 (March): 235–255.

Grassian, E. S., and J. R. Kaplowitz. 2001. *Information Literacy Instruction: Theory and Practice.* New York: Neal-Schumann.

Herrington, Verlene L. 1998. "Way beyond BI, A Look at the Future." *Journal of Academic Librarianship* 24 (September): 381–386.

Johnson, Anna Marie, and Phil Sager. 1998. "Too Many Students, Too Little Time: Creating and Implementing a Self-Paced, Interactive Computer Tutorial for the Libraries' Online Catalog." *Research Strategies* 16 (4): 271–284.

Kochtanek, Thomas R. 1984. "A Computer-Based Tutorial Program for Health Care Professionals." In *1984: Challenges to an Information Society: Proceedings of the 47th ASIS Annual Meeting, Philadelphia, PA, October 21–25, 1984.* White Plains, NY: Knowledge Industry Publishing, 130–133.

Moore, Kay, and Claire Abson. 2002. "Really Useful or Virtually Useless?" *Library & Information Update* 1 (November): 34–36.

Ohio Board of Regents. 2006. *The Performance Report for Ohio's Colleges and Universities, 2005 Institutional Outcomes Measures.* Columbus, OH: The Board. http://www.regents.state.oh.us/perfrpt/PerfRpt2005/InstitutionalDetail-2005.PDF (Accessed May 17, 2006.)

Phillips, Lori, and Jamie Kearley. 2003. "TIP: Tutorial for Information Power and Campus-Wide Information Literacy." *Reference Services Review* 31 (4): 351–358.

Solanes, Elvira Saurina, and Alicia Gaete. 2002. "Gnosis II: A Library Tutorial for Undergraduate Students." *Electronic Journal of Academic and Special Librarianship* 3 (Winter): 1–9.

Thistlewaite, Polly. 2001. "The Data Game: Colorado State University's Animated Library Research Tutorial." *Colorado Libraries* 27 (Fall): 12–15.

Tricarico, Mary Ann, Susan von Daum Tholl, and Elena O'Malley. 2001. "Interactive Online Instruction for Library Research: The Small Academic Library Experience." *The Journal of Academic Librarianship* 27 (May): 220–223.

Veldof, Jerilyn, and Karen Beavers. 2001. "Going Mental: Tackling Mental Models for the Online Library Tutorial." *Research Strategies* 18: 3–20.

8 EDUCATING THE MILLENNIAL USER

Lauren Pressley

Today's younger library users are changing. These students are known as the millennials, the net generation, the echo boomers, and generation Y. This chapter will refer to these students as millennials. Neil Howe and William Strauss, authors of *Millennials Rising: The Next Great Generation,* define the beginning of the generation with those born in 1982 and suggest that this demographic has a variety of characteristics that set them apart from previous generations. Howe and Strauss point to research and anecdotes supporting that, more than former generations, millennials are employed as students, see themselves as consumers of education, want customization in all aspects of their lives, have a positive view of technology, have confidence in their abilities, learn visually, multitask, and get bored easily. Although individuals within a group may not share all the group characteristics, these traits apply in general to millennials as described in Howe and Strauss's ground-breaking book. Lee Rainie, in a recent speech to the Public Library Association, suggested that the millennial generation will continue to push learning and research towards self-directed experiences, are open to interdisciplinary work, are focused on group knowledge, and are focused on producing content (Rainie 2006, 16).

The distinct characteristics of the millennial generation that this chapter focuses on are (1) the process of teaching library instruction to a student body with an affinity for technology, who grew up in an information-rich environment, and have an interest in doing and achieving, and (2) the implications of these characteristics for learning styles. Understanding these general characteristics will help librarians realize the unique needs of this generation, thereby allowing them to create more tailored, effective library instruction.

WHO ARE THE MILLENNIALS?

Information-Rich Environment

Millennials' technological environment often includes an immersion in an information-rich environment. Millennials greatly outpace their elders in their use of the Internet for finding information about movies and television, playing online games, downloading music, reading blogs, sharing their own creations, downloading videos, and creating blogs (Rainie 2006, 8). This constant involvement with the online world has led millennials to expect continual access to information (Merritt 2002, 9). A recent Pew report illustrates their dependence on the Internet. It indicated that 73 percent of college students use the Internet more than the library; only 9 percent said they use the library more than the Internet (Rainie 2006, 3).

The Internet, however, has an entirely different organization than the library, and includes different types of information. Students searching the Internet often see parts of the whole and read sections out of context, without much need to deal with an entire Web site, journal, or book (Gardner and Eng 2005, 6). Millennials experience "knowledge fragmentation" in which they believe information should be considered equally valid, whether in context or not (Brower 2004, 7). Instruction librarians should consider how using the Internet affects what millennials believe is true, how it influences where they find information, and what information literacy means in this type of environment (Merritt 2002, 7).

In one study of millennials, all respondents said that the "huge increase in information sources that has come with the development of the Web" has not affected their ability to judge the quality of information. Ninety-three percent believed that since many people use the Internet, misinformation would be detectable, and most claimed the status of "expert at searching the Web" (Manuel 2002, 4). A recent OCLC report stated that 93 percent of respondents "agree Google provides worthwhile information." A 2000 survey of a basic information literacy course showed that 90 percent of students identified themselves as expert at searching the Web, 63 percent thought efficient research starts with the Web, and 28 percent believed that a "Central Internet Authority" checked Web sites for accuracy (Manuel 2002, 5).

This Internet experience has led students to have an "ATM attitude" toward research; they want a quick, easy, and independent experience. This expectation leads students to feel comfortable with a "compromise on quality in favor of low costs (in terms of time and effort) and convenience" (Gardner and Eng 2005, 8). Millennials also expect their education to match their experience with technology, customization, and personal assistance (Manuel 2002, 9).

Most problematic for library instructors, and useful to keep in mind, is that millennials believe themselves to have expert status in research, because they have such positive Web experiences. Because they have a lifetime of experience searching the Internet, they may overestimate their ability to search, find, and evaluate information (Manuel 2002, 4). Library instructors need to realize this as they plan class instruction and activities. Allowing students to share their expertise, as well as focusing on new skills the students may not have acquired, may allow them to continue feeling good about their research abilities while opening their mind to new types of research.

The Read/Write Web

Millennials have spent their life in an environment quite different from the generations preceding them. The Internet, as they know it, is a space where they can not only read content, but add to it as well. Knowledge containers change for them with a touch of a button. Previous generations accepted the authority of the massive *Encyclopedia Britannica* on a bookshelf. Today's generation can get "in there" and change Wikipedia to fit with their understanding of the world. Much of the technology that this generation uses is read/write. Blogs, wikis, podcasting, and social networks have become rich environments as a result of the participation of their users, largely the millennial generation.

What does this do to text and authority? In "Wreading" Tom Peters discusses the shift from expecting reference sources as products of one person's mind to the expectation that reference sources have multiple authors. Peters suggests that a similar transition is taking place on the Internet today. "Wreaders" read and write, too. They edit Wikipedia and contribute to group writing projects (Peters 2006).

Clearly students interact in an information-rich technological world. What does this mean for education as it exists today? This way of living life online has become an everyday strategy for how to live and thrive in contemporary society (Prensky 2004, 6). Perhaps because of this, Will Richardson, in *Blogs, Wikis, Podcasts, and Other Powerful Web Tools for Classrooms*, asks "How do we need to rethink our ideas of literacy when we must prepare our students to become not only readers and writers, but editors and collaborators as well" (Richardson 2006, 5)?

We need to teach students about authority while giving them credit for the skills that they have in the "wreading" world. How can instruction teach students how to critically evaluate sources as well as how to add appropriate material to public spaces on the Web? One possible extra credit activity in a credit-bearing information literacy class at Wake Forest University is to correct a Wikipedia entry. This shows the student how easy it is to change an article, how many errors exist, and how they can share their knowledge to fix errors on the Internet.

Doers and Achievers

Millennials exhibit some general personality differences that set them apart from previous generations, in addition to technology exposure. Millennial students typically display motivation, ambition, and a high level of achievement

(Gardner and Eng 2005, 3). They grew up with parents who taught them that they need to do a lot early in life to have success later. This childhood period has been called "apprentice adulthood" by some (Merritt 2002, 5). A busy childhood means students often begin college with credit hours, they expect value-added classes, and they expect that college will lead to graduate school or a job (Merritt 2002, 9). Students also expect personal support for their achievement. Millennials have parents who have done a lot for them, and they anticipate that other adults will help them through their education (Merritt 2002, 9).

The millennials' expectation that achievements have value and need to pay off with employability after they graduate means that today's education needs to focus on applicable skills that will help them meet their goals. If library instruction is tied to the "real" world, millennials will likely believe that it is important and devote energy to learning the information. Millennials want information at the point-of-need and they want information that is directly related to their project. They do not necessarily care how the library is organized and the theory of classification; they just want good information that will help them finish their homework (Costello, Lenholt, and Stryker 2004, 6). To give millennials this type of clear and pointed information, it is helpful to start instruction sessions with a clear outline of goals and an explanation of why the workshop is relevant (Kipnis and Childs 2004, 2). In library instruction it is useful to point out a real-life situation, such as the case at Johns Hopkins in which better research may have prevented a death in a scientific study, to show that good research is important, and less thorough research can have negative outcomes (Kipnis and Childs 2004, 3).

Giving students multiple options for personal assistance ties into millennials' expectations of personal support (Kipnis and Childs 2004, 7). Providing opportunities for one-on-one help during a library instruction session, advertising for personal research sessions, and making it clear that librarians are available through multiple channels helps students know that librarians will offer personal support and help them with their academic goals.

INFORMATION-SEEKING BEHAVIORS

Millennials have lived their lives in a technological world. The oldest millennials were 12 years old when Netscape came into existence. They were 16 when Google first incorporated. Twenty percent of college students first started using computers between the ages of five and eight and virtually all of today's college students began using computers before high school graduation (Rainie 2006, 2). Millennials do not see computers, cell phones, and MP3 players as technology; they see these technologies as an integral part of their lives (Merritt 2002, 6). They approach these technologies the way generation X saw cable television and how the baby boomers saw the refrigerator. Technology that has existed for someone's entire life does not seem like new technology: it is just another tool. Some millennials, though, connect with technology so much that they say technology is a key part of their identity (Manuel 2002, 4).

One reason millennials connect with technology is that their world is full of gadgets. More than half of the millennial generation live in homes with radios, CD or tape players, televisions, cable or satellite televisions, premium television channels, VCR or DVD players, video game consoles, computers, and Internet access; 46 percent have high speed Internet access (Rainie 2006, 4). Much of millennials' technology is mobile. Sixty-one percent of millennials have discmans or walkmans, 55 percent have handheld video game players, 45 percent have cell phones, 37 percent have MP3 players, 26 percent have laptops, 13 percent have handheld Internet devices, and 11 percent have personal digital assistants (PDAs) (Rainie 2006, 7). Millennials may have high exposure to technology and gadgets, but most of their use of such tools is in their personal life. They see a lot of the technology like e-mail, cell phones, text messaging, and the Internet as tools for social communication (Brower 2004, 6). This way of using technology teaches millennials to multitask. They use the phone, computer, the Internet, instant messaging, music, and television in at the same time. This level of experiences can lead to boredom when working on a task that requires just one channel (Manuel 2002, 12).

This experience has created high expectations for technology use in education. If teaching occurs in one channel, millennial students likely will become bored and uninterested. As their world is heavily shaped by technology, so they expect integrated information technology into their classrooms and educational experiences (Merritt 2002, 9). Students often have so much experience with technology that they feel more advanced than their teachers and are unimpressed with their teachers' use of technology in the classroom (Gardner and Eng 2005, 7). Students who have whizzed around their desktops may lose respect for a teacher who has trouble toggling between a PowerPoint presentation and Web sites. If students know shortcuts and see that the instructor has to take the long way to do something, they may feel that the instructor has nothing to teach them.

Library instruction has included skilled use of databases and OPACs for some time. This background has given librarians experience teaching with technology and the opportunity to polish their teaching using the Internet. This combined with millennials' expectations and experience can actually help when librarians lead library instruction for a millennial audience. Millennials may prefer library instruction, with computer components, rather than a traditional lecture. They may prefer online resources, databases, and OPACs more than traditional print sources (Manuel 2002, 4). They also see technology as a way to develop relationships, both socially and with instructors (Merritt 2002, 9). Encouraging students to e-mail, instant message, or get in touch with the librarian for further personal research sessions meets this need.

Traditional information literacy courses often move, in order, from print to the Web, which is familiar for baby boomers but may conflict with millennials' experiences. Millennials, who have primary experience with the Web, learn the importance of print materials after they have learned to value the Internet (Manuel 2002, 5). Redesigning a class to include Internet resources throughout the course, or weighted more to the beginning, can make the material seem more relevant to millennial students.

EDUCATION

With this background in millennials and their information-seeking behavior, it can be useful to consider educational theory in context of this new generation. The millennial generation's background has created a preference for holistic processing and nonlinear modes of instruction in which students would rather see the entire picture, and then learn details, concepts, and procedures (Manuel 2002, 8).

This multimedia background also has implications for reading versus seeing. Average students retain 10 percent of what they read, but 20 to 30 percent of what they see (Manuel 2002, 6). Millennial students also do much of their reading on a computer screen, which is quite different from books. When reading on the Internet, links stand out as important and draw readers away from the text they are reading (Manuel 2002, 7). Students read bits and pieces of information as they come across them, without reading for context. This bite-sized reading leads students to avoid lengthy prose, and, in fact, they may ignore lengthy text instructions (Manuel 2002, 7).

Finally, the professional literature indicates that millennial students trust their peers and prefer to work with them in the learning process. Students may prefer approaching a peer to approaching a librarian and may distrust authority figures like librarians and teachers (Gardner and Eng 2005, 9; Kipnis and Childs 2004, 6). A recent OCLC report shows that 67 percent of college students learn about electronic information sources from friends, compared to 33 percent from librarians (DeRosa et al. 2005, 38). Providing opportunities for group work and problem solving allows students to learn from others who share their values (Kipnis and Childs 2004, 6). Instructors can facilitate group activities, providing feedback and one-on-one support, and pulling teaching methods from several techniques that millennials prefer.

This section delves into the three traditional educational theory camps: behaviorism, cognitivism, and constructivism, as well as offers an introduction to a fourth, connectivism, a theory that is gaining popularity due in part to its inclusion of technology.

Behaviorism

Behaviorism is a school of thought that grew out of the research of B. F. Skinner and Pavlov's work involving salivation reflex in dogs (Grassian and Kaplowitz 2001, 35). Behaviorist educators focus the actual behaviors of students without much consideration for internal states. Behaviorists use reinforcement through rewards and punishment to encourage the behaviors they desire.

Behaviorism developed out of scientific method, focusing on cause-and-effect relationships (Grassian and Kaplowitz 2001, 35). Through the use of controlled extrinsic motivation, educators could control variables to encourage expected outcomes. Behaviorist educators know what outcomes they would like their students to achieve and reward successive movements toward those goals (Grassian and Kaplowitz 2001, 36).

Today's millennials probably have experienced behaviorist methods when they received rewards for good behaviors with gold stars or tokens in elementary school or punished with time out for bad behavior. Grading systems exist as another method of behaviorist motivation. If a student associates getting an "A" with a reward and a "C" with punishment, these letter grades act as reinforcement for good behavior—studying—and punishment for negative behavior— performing poorly on a test or not turning in assignments.

Cognitivism

Cognitivism is a newer learning theory than behaviorism and is more widely supported among educators. Cognitivism developed in response to the mechanistic view of learning of the behaviorists (Grassian and Kaplowitz 2001, 41). Instead of focusing on the actions or behaviors of an individual, cognitivism focuses on the inner processes of the learner including belief, motivation, and emotion.

Cognitivists consider how people perceive, organize, interact with, and respond to information in their environments (Grassian and Kaplowitz 2001, 41). These learning theories focus on how information is perceived, processed, remembered, or forgotten.

Cognitivist educators focus on "readiness" and "discovery" (Grassian and Kaplowitz 2001, 44–46). Readiness is the idea that some types of learning can only happen at certain life stages. Millennials have gone to school in an educational system that said their brains had not developed enough to process calculus until late high school. Their system introduced foreign language in elementary school, as much research has supported the idea that language comprehension is greater at younger ages. Discovery is the concept that learners can figure out answers on their own. Many millennial students have participated in classes where they had assignments in groups to research a topic on their own to present to the class. Some schools and instructors have developed problem-based learning models in which students work to find an answer on their own.

Constructivism

Constructivism is based on the assumption that the individual creates meaning based on his or her experiences (Jonassen et al. 2006) When learners encounter a new idea, they compare it with their understanding of the world. If it fits in, learners incorporate it into their worldview; if it does not, the learner disregards the idea.

Constructivist teachers aim to help student learn to become lifelong learners. They work with students to help them learn how to problem solve and strategize when looking for new information (Educational Broadcasting Corporation 2004). Constructivists also emphasize active process and experience. This occurs when teachers assign upper-level students research papers. Students have to use available tools such as the Internet, libraries, and conversation to develop a research process and find an answer. Open learning environments, such as research papers or science labs, offer more real-world complexities to contend with (Jonassen et al. 2006). James E. Zull, in his book on the biology of learning, says "try to understand existing networks and build on them. Nothing is new" (2002, 129). Zull explains the constructivist view that learners come to the learning opportunity with an understanding of the world and that learning builds on this previous worldview.

Connectivism

Connectivism is a relatively new learning theory championed by George Siemens. Siemens describes it as a "learning theory for the digital age" and claims it holds up where behaviorism, cognitivism, and constructivism fall short. Today's learners operate in a world that is informal, networked, and filled with technology, and this affects how people learn (Siemens 2005).

Connectivism takes into account that people want to learn actual skills; that learning is a process of connecting information from different sources; that learning can take place in a community, network, or databases; that the ability to learn or find information is more important than knowing what is currently known; and that learning may happen in a number of ways—not just classroom instruction (Siemens 2005). It adapts to a changing world by focusing on the different personal skills that are needed to learn in today's information environment and that organizational and personal learning are "integrated tasks" (Siemens 2005). Constructivism also allows that learning includes the process of knowledge creation (Siemens 2005).

Educators can use connectivist theory to guide instructional design and traditional education. Acknowledging online networks, allowing students to set out and find information on their own, and providing real-world projects with tangible outcomes give students a way to work in their natural information environment. Teachers can act as facilitators, guides, and mentors in this process.

WHAT LIBRARIANS CAN DO

Different libraries have different educational roles. University and school librarians can incorporate information about the millennial generation into their class designs. University, school, and public librarians can offer multiple channels and one-on-one instruction through instant messaging. Instruction can focus on issues of authority (as they always have) and about how students can and do alter their information environment.

Millennials are a distinct generation with several recurring characteristics that can impact library instruction. The way they approach learning and research is shaped by the environment in which they grew up (Rainie 2006, 15). Qualities that set the millennial generation apart include high exposure to technology, incredible information availability, a drive for achievement, and learning styles that include active, hands-on learning, a consumerist approach to education, and team work. Every person in the millennial generation does not exemplify all these characteristics, but it is useful for instruction librarians to have an understanding of some of the broad traits this generation shares. Librarians can then have an idea of how to adapt teaching for the newest generation and the best ways to meet the needs of their users.

REFERENCES

Beloit College. 2005. http://www.beloit.edu/~pubaff/mindset/ (Accessed July 16, 2006.)

Brower, S. 2004. "Millennials in Action: A Student-Guided Effort in Curriculum-Integration of Library Skills." *Medical Reference Services Quarterly* 23 (2): 81–88. (Accessed July 16, 2006.)

Claire Raines Associates. http://www.generationsatwork.com/ (Accessed July 16, 2006, from Generations at Work Web site.)

Costello, Barbara, Robert Lenholt, and Judson Stryker. 2004. "Using Blackboard in Library Instruction: Addressing the Learning Styles of Generation X and Y." *The Journal of Academic Librarianship* 30 (6): 452–460.

De Rosa, Cathy, et al. 2005. Perceptions of Libraries and Information Resources: A Report to the OCLC Membership. http://www.oclc.org/reports/pdfs/Percept_all.pdf (Accessed July 16, 2006.)

Educational Broadcasting Corporation. 2004. Workshop: Constructivism as a Paradigm for Teaching and Learning. http://www.thirteen.org/edonline/concept2class/constructivism/index.html (Accessed July 16, 2006.)

Gardner, Susan, and Susanna Eng. 2005. "What Students Want: Generation Y and the Changing Function of the Academic Library." *Portal: Libraries and the Academy* 5(3): 405–420. (Accessed July 16, 2006, from Project Muse.)

Grassian, Esther S., and Joan R. Kaplowitz. 2001. *Information Literacy Instruction: Theory and Practice*. New York: Neal-Schuman.

Howe, Neal, and William Strauss. 2000. *Millennials Rising: The Next Great Generation*. New York: Vintage Books.

Jonassen, David, Terry Mayes, and Ray McAleese. Manifesto for a Constructivist Approach to Technology. http://apu.gcal.ac.uk/clti/papers/TMPaper11.html (Accessed August 1, 2006.)

Kipnis, Daniel G., and Gary M. Childs. 2004. "Education Generation X and Generation Y: Teaching Tips for Librarians." *Medical Reference Services Quarterly* 23 (4): 25–33. (Accessed July 16, 2006, from Haworth Press Journals.)

Lenhart, Amanda. 2006. Testimony by Amanda Lenhart. http://www.pewInternet.org/ppt/Pew Internet Project SNS testimony—7%2007%2006—submitted.pdf (Accessed July 16, 2006.)

Manuel, Kate. 2002. "Teaching Information Literacy to Generation Y." *Journal of Library Administration* 36 (1/2): 195–217. (Accessed July 16, 2006, from Haworth Press.)

Merritt, Stephen. 2002. "Generation Y: A Perspective on America's Next Generation and Their Impact on Higher Education." *The Serials Librarian* 42 (1/2): 41–50. (Accessed July 16, 2006, from Hawthorn Press.)

MySpace. (2006). In Wikipedia [Web]. Wikimedia. http://en.wikipedia.org/wiki/Myspace (Accessed July 16, 2006.)

On Purpose Associates, 2001. Constructivism. http://www.funderstanding.com/construc tivism.cfm (Accessed July 16, 2006.)

Owen, Martin et al. 2006. Social Software and Learning. http://www.futurelab.org.uk/ research/opening_education/social_software_01.htm (Accessed July 16, 2006.)

Peters, Tom. 2006. [Weblog] Wreading. ALA TechSource. http://www.techsource.ala.org/ blog/2006/06/wreading.html (Accessed July 16, 2006.)

Prensky, Marc. 2004. The Emerging Online Life of the Digital Native: What They Do Differently Because of Technology, and How They Do It. http://www.marcprensky.com/ writing/Prensky-The_Emerging_Online_Life_of_the_Digital_Native-03.pdf (Accessed July 16, 2006.)

Rainie, Lee. 2006. Life Online: Teens and Technology and the World to Come. http:// www.pewInternet.org/ppt/Teens%20and%20technology.pdf (Accessed July 16, 2006.)

Richardson, Will. 2006. *Blogs, Wikis, Podcasts, and Other Powerful Web Tools for Classrooms.* Thousand Oaks, Calif.: Corwin Press.

Siemens, George. 2005. Connectivism: A learning theory for today's learner. http://www. connectivism.ca/about (Accessed July 16, 2006.)

Zull, James E. 2002. *The Art of Changing the Brain: Enriching the Practice of Teaching by Exploring the Biology of Learning.* Sterling, Va.: Stylus Pub.

9 ESL STUDENTS AND TECHNOLOGY IN THE COLLEGE LIBRARY

Eric E. Palo

In our rush to embrace the latest innovations to meet the perceived demands of our students, librarians should not lose sight of the fact that students really aren't all created technologically equal. Not every freshman on campus wants, needs, or perhaps understands podcasting, Real Simple Syndication (RSS) feeds or, conceivably even how to use a mouse. This is particularly true for English as a second language (ESL) students. Some are quite skilled with modern technology and others have never turned on a computer. With these wide variations in student needs and capabilities, no single statement about ESL students can be accurate for all of them; however, this will not stop me from making some generalizations and offering some advice. My intention here is to remind us to consider some of the special needs of many ESL students and to encourage academic librarians to plan to serve both the technology-savvy student and those who are new to the rapidly changing high-tech library environment we find ourselves in today.

ESL students come in two types: international (those students who are here just for the education and will be returning to their home country) and immigrant (those who have left their home country and who intend to remain permanent residents in the United States). Both groups have a wide range of technology skills and interests. Some international students are very tech-savvy; others are at a loss as to how to get what they want when they walk into a modern American library. At my college, for instance, in the same week I dealt with a student from Moldova who was a former college professor, fluent in three languages and with good research skills, and a Somali student who had never worked outside the home and couldn't read or write in her native language and may not even have seen a library before.

Even students graduating from American secondary schools may have different abilities if they come from a home where English is not the first language. Beckett and Chrisholm (2002) reported that only 18 percent of Hispanic children use a computer at home compared with 52 percent for other white children.

Combine the stress of trying to communicate in a foreign language with advanced technology and intensive computer-oriented libraries and you have a formula for creating a high anxiety student. Research has validated the obvious conclusion that students with high anxiety will avoid computer use when they can (Matsumura and Hann 2004), placing ESL students at yet one more disadvantage when facing the modern American academic library.

INTERNATIONAL STUDENTS

International students' lack of preparation for effectively using American libraries has been reported in the literature for a number of years (Onwuegbuzie, Jiao, and Daley, 1997; Kuo 2000). These students can have both limited technology skills and differing beliefs about how libraries function. Despite the international availability of the Internet, many college students from other countries are not well versed in its use. These students may also have considerable problem with English language proficiency. They might read English quite well, but have more trouble understanding spoken English or being understood by library staff. Their experience with library service in other countries will undoubtedly not have prepared them for how we do things in American libraries. One recent study (Liao, Finn, and Lu 2007) reported that about 46 percent of international graduate students at an East Coast university found that using a college online catalog was a new experience (only 16 percent of the American-born students said this was new to them). In considerably greater numbers than their American counterparts, these international graduate students said that they had limited knowledge of every category of library services listed in the study. This included what to us are such seemingly basic things as open stacks, library instruction workshops, microforms, interlibrary loans, and even self-service copy machines (new to 44 percent of the international students). All this leads to considerable library use anxiety among international students. Onwuegbuzie et al. (1997) found that these students may take more computer courses, but this did not translate into facility with library database searching. Also, Bordonaro (2006) reports that, although some studies show international students to be skilled in computer applications, there was still considerable disparity in their skills in the use of libraries. Even basic knowledge of the Internet can vary greatly within the ESL student population. In a 15-point quiz of Internet knowledge and comprehension at the University of British Columbia, Boshier, Kow, and Huang (2006) reported that native English-speaking students scored 12.5 points, Chinese-speaking students 11.22, and speakers of other languages 10.68 points. (They also reported that graduate students at East China Normal University in Shanghai knew 20 percent less about the Internet than university students in British Columbia.)

IMMIGRANT STUDENTS

With immigrant students we can expect even wider variation in library skills. Many of our colleges have ESL programs. Community education, including ESL instruction, may in fact be one of the primary missions of a local two-year college. The usual approach in these programs is to move the students as quickly as possible from non-English speakers to functional facility with the language, and they are often found attempting to use our libraries with little or no preparation. They could be a long-term resident of the United States who is merely brushing up on her/his English language skills, or a new immigrant who just set foot in this country a few weeks ago. They all deserve our support as they learn to navigate American libraries.

ESL programs on campus can help identify appropriate software and technology for the library to be aware of or to purchase to support these students. ESL students often have class-related activities that they need to continue after hours in the library. This might include participating in a chat room, accessing streaming audio or video, or using some specialized software or Web site. The library needs to be ready to support the students accessing all these resources. They may need extra instruction on how to get to the programs or perhaps on basics of computer use.

One of the first things that most immigrant students want to do is to e-mail friends and family or access news from their home country. Library staff should be able to help patrons establish and access an e-mail account. They should know how to help people do things like open attachments, scan pictures, and attach them to messages. Knowing how to find media outlets from other countries also would be useful.

Some immigrant students may know a lot about computers, but they will probably need help with how to search for information. In Greater Vancouver British Columbia, for instance, it was found that Chinese-speaking residents actually used the Internet more frequently than English-speaking residents but that their understanding of search theory and how the Internet actually works was considerably less (Boshier et al. 2006).

SPECIALIZED TECHNOLOGY

If your college has a large user population from a specific language group, or groups, it is worth investigating the purchase of a few computer keyboards for these languages. For from $20 to $60 keyboards are available for Russian, Spanish, Japanese, Chinese, French, or even Arabic languages.

There are also little-known features available for Microsoft Office programs supporting different languages. For instance, Office 2000 with MultiLanguage Pack provides special fonts, spelling, grammar, and on-screen support for the following languages: German, French, Italian, Norwegian, Japanese, Korean, Portuguese, Danish, Spanish, Swedish, Simplified Chinese, Traditional Chinese, Czech, Dutch, Turkish, Polish, Arabic, Hungarian, Russian, Finnish, Greek, Hebrew, Slovenian, Basque, Croatian, Romanian, and Slovakian. More limited, but still quite considerable support is provided for Bulgarian, Catalan, Estonian, Latvian, Lithuanian, Serbian, and Ukrainian. There is an additional program with full support for Thai, Vietnamese, and Hindi languages (Blackhall 2004).

Screen readers that were designed for people with problems reading computer screens can be useful for ESL students. They let them hear words pronounced in English as they see them in context. Some of the screen reader programs, such as *JAWS* and *IBM Homepage Reader,* are available in different languages, too.

The library should be prepared to provide basic technical support for any hardware or software that they offer. It need not be expert level, but public service staff should have basic familiarity with programs. One- or two-page handouts with key instructions are a great idea, but staff will need to be able to do one-on-one instruction and troubleshooting. If the staff aren't comfortable with the software, they will be reluctant to tell students about it, and users report that lack of technical support in the library is the biggest problem they face in using specialized software and/or hardware ("What Is the State of Adaptive Technology in Libraries Today?," 2004).

There are many Web sites libraries can bookmark that help ESL students improve their English language skills. A few examples of recommended sites include *The Internet Picture Dictionary* <www.pdictionary.com>, *Grammar Safari* at the University of Illinois Urbana-Champaign <http://www.iei.uiuc.edu/stu dent_grammarsafari.html>, *English Pronunciation/Listening* <http://international. ouc.bc.ca/pronunciation/> with brief *QuickTime* clips showing how to pronounce English sounds, and *The Tower of English* <http://towerofenglish.com/> with links to 300 other fun ESL sites.

Your library Web pages should be reviewed for clarity and ease of use. This will not only help ESL students, but will be a benefit for all users. A recent article in *Library Technology Reports* ("Computer Technology and non-English Speaking Patrons," 2004) lists several things that might be considered in Web page design including culturally appropriate colors, appropriate aesthetic elements, using inviting photographs that include a wide range of people, and clear design that facilitates ease of use. The University of Texas at Austin provides a detailed report of foreign language Web site accessibility and links to information about text-to-speech and automatic language detection software (Raizen and Lippmann 2004).

If your library offers online reference, are non-English speaking students able to use the service? In a report on his experience creating a bilingual virtual reference service at Saint John University, Lupien (2004) found that reference software like *QuestionPoint* is now available with multiple language interfaces. Remember though, you need staff with appropriate language skills to offer the service. Also, if you partner with other libraries to offer online service after hours, you need to find out if they are prepared to handle the same languages you are.

LIBRARY INSTRUCTION ISSUES

Library classes with significant numbers of ESL students should not just be repeats of traditional instruction already being offered. This might be a good opportunity to review all the library instruction efforts and apply Universal

Design for Learning (UDL) concepts. UDL proposes that you don't need different classes for students who may have physical disabilities or other barriers interfering with learning. Instead, you can redesign, or enhance, existing courses to make them more accessible for all students and for multiple learning styles. Just as the curb-cuts in sidewalks mandated by the Americans with Disabilities Act have benefited many people without obvious mobility issues, redesigning a class using UDL principles will improve instruction for people you didn't know were having difficulty, including native English-speaking students (Jenner and Culwell 2006).

In her article on language learning theory and information literacy instruction, Conteh-Morgan (2002) provides a useful checklist that can be used when preparing and delivering instruction to ESL students. It includes key factors related to social context of the instruction, communication issues, style and strategies of instruction, and the cultural context of the audience.

One thing that often is stressed for any group is that you should know your audience. Talk to ESL instructors. They can help you identify techniques that work and problem areas to avoid. Talk to your new ESL students to find out what they need. Talk to graduating ESL students to see what their experience was. Ask them what they found most helpful and what problems they encountered. And be prepared for significant differences between student groups (Helms 1995). For instance, Chinese students may have problems with the concept of wild-card searching because in Chinese, plurals are inferred from the context and not from varying word endings, whereas a Russian-speaking student may have problems with word order in Boolean searching because subject-verb-object order can be revised in Russian without changing the meaning of a sentence (DiMartino and Zoe 2000).

Making instruction relevant to the student's immediate needs is particularly important with ESL students (Kamhi-Stein and Stein 1998). Show these students how they can make practical use of what you are teaching them. Find out what their interests are or what assignments they are working on. Use these examples in your demonstration and, whenever possible, include a significant amount of hands-on practice using the techniques you teach.

The instruction will probably take longer than you expect. You should speak clearly and may have to repeat or rephrase things, avoiding jargon whenever possible. Breaking the instruction down into smaller chunks with appropriate activities interspersed is good instructional design. When using a computer in instruction you can also expect to do a lot of one-on-one work with students who aren't as proficient as others in the class. The best design would be to have a second person in the class to share this work.

CONCLUSION

Much has been said about the digital Divide, most of it about people who can afford computers and those who can't. ESL users usually fall far on the other side of the divide from our modern high-tech student. Serving them can present additional challenges that can be overcome with careful planning, some staff training, and a little bit of money. The results will make us better librarians for all users. I have never had a more grateful patron than the ESL student who I just helped learn how to do a seemingly simple task with a computer.

REFERENCES

Beckett, E. C., and I. M. Chisholm. 2002. "Integration for ESL Success: TESOL Standards, Multiple Intelligences and Technology." In *SITE 2002: Society for Information Technology & Teacher Education International Conference. Faculty Development* (601–605). Norfolk, Va.: Association for the Advancement of Computing in Education. (ERIC Document Reproduction Service No. ED472233)

Blackhall, G. 2004. "Multilanguage Features for Public Access Computers." *Feliciter* 50 (1): 24.

Bordonaro, K. 2006. "Language Learning in the Library: An Exploratory Study of ESL Students." *Journal of Academic Librarianship* 32 (5): 518–526.

Boshier, R., J. K. Kow, and Y. Huang. 2006. "How Much Do Multicultural Residents of Greater Vancouver Know about the Internet?" *Alberta Journal of Educational Research* 52 (2): 127–142.

"Computer Technology and non-English Speaking Patrons." 2004. *Library Technology Reports* 40 (3): 41–49.

Conteh-Morgan, M. 2002. "Connecting the Dots: Limited English Proficiency, Second Language Learning Theories, and Information Literacy Instruction." *Journal of Academic Librarianship* 28 (4): 191–196.

DiMartino, D., and R. L. Zoe. 2000. "International Students and the Library: New Tools, New Users, and New Instruction." In *Teaching the New Library to Today's Users: Reaching International, Minority, Senior Citizens, Gay/Lesbian, First Generation College, At-Risk, Graduate and Returning Students and Distance Learners*, eds. T. E. Jacobson, and H. C. Williams (17–43). New York: Neal-Schuman.

Helms, C. M. 1995. "Reaching Out to International Students through Bibliographic Instruction." *Reference Librarian* 51/52: 295–307.

Jenner, C., and C. Culwell. 2006. *Universal Design for Learning in Community & Technical Colleges* [Pamphlet]. Renton, Wash.: Renton Technical College. http://webs.rtc.edu/ii/DSDP%20Grant/UDL%20Manual%20final.doc (Retrieved November 27, 2006.)

Kamhi-Stein, L. D., and A. P. Stein. 1998. "Teaching Information Competency as a Third Language: A New Model for Library Instruction." *Reference & User Services Quarterly* 38 (2): 173–179.

Kuo, E. W. 2000. *English as Second Language: Program Approaches at Community Colleges*. ERIC Digest. Los Angeles: ERIC Clearinghouse for Community Colleges (ERIC Document Reproduction Service No. ED447859).

Liao, Y., M. Finn, and J. Lu. 2007. "Information-seeking Behavior of International Graduate Students vs. American Graduate Students: A User Study at Virginia Tech 2005." *College & Research Libraries* 68 (1): 5–25.

Lupien, P. 2004. "Bilingual Virtual Reference: It's Better Than Searching the Open Web." *Computers in Libraries* 24 (5): 6–8, 53–56.

Matsumura, S., and G. Hann. 2004. "Computer Anxiety and Students' Preferred Feedback Methods in EFL Writing." *The Modern Language Journal* 88: 403–415.

Onwuegbuzie, A. J., Q. G. Jiao, and C. E. Daley. 1997. *The Experiences of Non-Native English-Speaking Students in Academic Libraries in the United States*. Memphis, TN: Annual Conference of the Mid-South Educational Research Association, November. (ERIC Document Reproduction Service No. ED438815)

Raizen, E., and J. Lippmann. 2004. "Foreign Language Instructional Website Accessibility: Evaluation Report." In *Website Accessibility: Resources*. February 21. http://www.laits. utexas.edu/hebrew/personal/tts/resources.html (Retrieved December 28, 2006.)

"What Is the State of Adaptive Technology in Libraries Today?" 2004. *Library Technology Reports* 40 (3): 81–91.

IV

MANAGERIAL CONCERNS

10 CONNECTING DIVERSITY TO MANAGEMENT: FURTHER INSIGHTS

Tim Zou and La Loria Konata

Since the early 1970s, establishing a diverse workforce has been a pressing issue for libraries as a result of the drastic demographic shift in prospective clientele. A report from the National Center for Education Statistics indicates that in the states of Hawaii, New Mexico, California, Texas, Mississippi, and Louisiana, plus the District of Columbia (first tier of states), nonwhite populations in public elementary and secondary schools have become the majority. In eight other states (second tier)—Arizona, Florida, Maryland, Georgia, New York, South Carolina, Nevada, and Illinois—nonwhite students in elementary and secondary schools range from 40 to 49 percent of total population (ACE 2002) (NCES 2000–2001).

Texas, California, New Mexico, and Hawaii now have majority-minority total populations. That is, the ethnic minority population is now more than 50 percent of the total population. Not far behind are Maryland, Mississippi, Georgia, New York, and Arizona, with a minority population at approximately 40 percent (Caldwell 2005). It has also been estimated that by the year 2010, there will be more than 110 million minorities out of a total population of 309 million (Alsonso-Zaldivar 2004).

The makeup of the millennials make these numbers even more drastic. The millennials are those born between 1977 and 1994. Their age range is 12 to 29 years. After the baby boomers, this is the second largest population group, 28 percent to 26 percent, respectively. Millennials are much more racially and ethnically diverse than baby boomers or generation Xers (*The Millennials: Americans Born*

This research and resulting chapter were made possible by a 2003 ALA Diversity Research Grant. A review of the research was presented at the ALA 2004 Annual Conference in Orlando, Fla., June 26, 2004.

Figure 10.1
Percentage of Public School Students of Color, 2000–2001

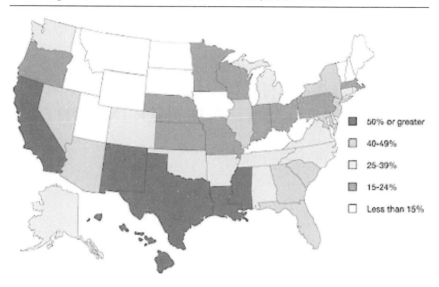

1977 to 1994, 2004, 1). In many metropolitan areas, they are the majority and will grow up being in a majority group rather than a minority group. Thirty-six percent of Americans who identify themselves as being multiracial are millennials (*Generation X: Americans Born 1965 to 1976*, 2004, 221).

Frey's (2006) analysis of the 2000 census further demonstrates this point. "A strong multi-minority presence characterizes 18 large 'melting pot' metro areas, and 27 large metro areas now have 'majority minority' child populations...In nearly one-third of the nation's largest metropolitan areas at least half of all people under age 15 are racial and ethnic minorities...Among the 27 large metro areas with 'majority-minority' child populations, there are 15 where the same can be said of their total population" (Frey 2006, 16–18). These data underline the strategic imperativeness of establishing a diverse workforce in the library profession that will reflect the needs of the diverse populations in the United States.

THE BUSINESS CASE FOR DIVERSITY MANAGEMENT

Library as a profession has been known for its homogeneity in its workforce and lagged behind many business sectors such as the service industry, the telecommunication industry, or the manufacturing industry in diversifying its workforce, although they all serve the same increasingly diverse population. There seems to be a lack of a sense of urgency for library administrators to recognize the business case of diversity other than considering it a politically right thing to do. A review of literature on diversity of the past 10 years indicates that much emphasis has been placed on recruiting and retention—that is, recruiting minorities to library schools and retaining them in the profession. Applying Thomas and Ely's (2001, 33–66) articulation of three paradigms for managing diversity, efforts in diversifying the workforce in the library profession, so far, fall mostly into the first and second paradigms but should begin to shift its focus onto a third paradigm.

The three paradigms defined by Thomas and Ely stress the connection between the shift from affirmative action to diversity management. The first paradigm, based on affirmative action, addresses the "discrimination-and-fairness" issues in business management and measures success in diversity initiatives in terms of how well a company does in recruitment and retention of minority employees. This paradigm aims to increase the number of minorities employed and correct any discrimination and unfairness in the hiring and promotion process. The second paradigm focuses on the aspects of "access-and-legitimacy" of workforce diversity. This paradigm is a necessity because we live in an increasingly multicultural society, and companies need a more demographically diverse workforce to help gain legitimacy with different ethnic groups. Companies need employees with multicultural skills to understand and serve those populations better. In this paradigm, however, minorities are sometimes pigeonholed into minority-related issues on the job. This specialization often proves fruitless because it recognizes minority employees only for their understanding of the language, the culture, and the needs of the clienteles from minority ethnic groups. This narrow application of diversity hinders advancement opportunities for the minority employees. The third paradigm includes the first and second paradigms but goes beyond those two widely accepted approaches. The third paradigm connects diversity to management and personnel development perspectives and seeks to integrate cultural backgrounds and skills as necessary strategy for organizational development in order to maintain competitiveness in an economy of globalization.

Nowadays, many business organizations view affirmative action and diversity management as two different but interconnected processes. Affirmative action is generally accepted as compliance to government mandate when a company does business with government; however, there is no direct linkage to the company's business. Diversity management, on the other hand, has direct linkage to the competitiveness and effectiveness of a company, especially in a global business environment. Philip Morris defines diversity management as necessary "management strategies and actions that effectively recognize, accept, and utilize all employees. It creates and maintains an environment where employees can contribute creative ideas, seek challenges, assume leadership, and continue to focus on meeting and exceeding business and personal objectives" (Hart 1997, 11). Since the 1990s, many business organizations have moved from strictly functionally organizational structures to cross-functional teams. Research has documented that when a cross-functional team is also demographically diverse, productive gains increase. Research has also found that companies with two or more women and two or more "minority" directors on their boards were much more likely than other companies to be named to *Fortune* magazine's "Most Admired Companies" list (Hayles and Russell 1997, 4–5). The Society for Human Resource Management (SHRM) Survey of Diversity Initiatives reports that top executives at 84 percent of Fortune 500 companies think diversity management is important. Of the non-Fortune 500 organizations surveyed, 67 percent of human resource professionals said diversity management is important to their companies' high level executives (*Women and Diversity Wow! Facts 2002*, 459). For today's business executives, diversity management has gone from being a reactive function of compliance to a proactive one of business growth.

DIVERSITY MANAGEMENT IN THE LIBRARY PROFESSION

Efforts to recruit minorities into the library profession began as early as the 1970s. Starting in the 1980s and continuing through the 1990s, several large academic libraries initiated residency programs offering scholarships and post-graduate internships for perspective minority librarians (Acree, Epps, Gilmore, and Henriques 2001, 47). In 1998, ALA began its Spectrum Initiative to recruit more minorities to the library profession by granting 50 annual scholarships to minority students enrolled in a library school graduate program. The program cost $1.3 million and included an annual leadership development institute (Acree et al. 2001, 57). Today most library administrations work closely with their parent institution and follow the affirmative action policies and regulations in their hiring and promotion processes; however, progress has been limited to the paraprofessional level.

There has been some emphasis on the third paradigm in ALA; however, additional emphasis and focus are needed in this area. The Association of Research Libraries (ARL) has developed a Leadership and Career Development Program (LCDP) that prepares members of underrepresented racial or ethnic groups who have demonstrated potential leadership ability to become more competitive in the promotion process (ARL 2004).

A review of the literature also shows that there have been many discussions on the scarcity of minorities entering the profession. Unfortunately, there are still only a handful of minorities entering library schools. In 1984/1985, the total number of minority graduates with a masters in library science (MLS) was only 6.8 percent. The minority graduate rate reached the 10 percent threshold in 1994/1995 before jumping to a historical height of 14.9 percent in 1999–2000, after which it settled back to 10.8 percent in 2000/2001. For the academic years 2002/2003 (NCES masters degrees conferred by degree-granting institutions, by sex, racial/ethnic group, and major field of study: 2002–03) and 2003/2004 (NCES masters degrees conferred by title IV institutions, by race/ethnicity, field of study, and gender: United states, academic year 2003–2004), the minority graduation rate was on the rise again at 12 percent. These gains, however, have not kept up with the increase in minority populations, as the general population rate for minorities in 1995 was 26.4 percent and has increased since then to approximately 30.8 percent (Census Bureau 2000). According to de la Pena and Lippincott (1997, 30–31), to achieve parity of minorities in the profession and in the population, there will need to be a 162 percent increase of minorities in the profession.

De la Pena and Lippincott (1997, 30–32) also identified 10 accredited programs that account for 41 percent of all minority graduates:

- University of Puerto Rico
- Clark Atlanta University
- University of Hawaii
- North Carolina Central University
- Pratt Institute
- San Jose State University
- Queens College
- University of Louisiana
- University of South Florida
- University of Michigan

Why are these schools more effective in recruiting minorities? One of the obvious reasons is the location of the school itself. Schools like Puerto Rico, Hawaii, and Clark Atlanta have a higher concentration of minorities in the general population. Note: Clark Atlanta's library school has since been closed (Albanese 2005). Is that the only reason or is there something more? In a survey by de la Pena McCook and Lippincott (1997, 30–31), schools achieving at least a 5 percent graduation rate of minorities were asked about their recruitment strategies. What they found is that minorities gravitate to schools that have:

- Faculty from ethnic minority groups
- Active multicultural participation such as diversity initiatives on campus
- Financial support in the form of scholarships
- Partnerships with specific libraries
- Targeted recruitment strategies such as advertising in ethnic papers
- Creative delivery of classes such as evening or weekend classes for those that work

In 1997, seven schools on the list are located in states that have at the very least 40 percent minorities in the population. In 2004, there were 10 schools located in these states with several of the same schools remaining on the list (Adkins and Espinal 2004, 53–54). This suggests that recruitment efforts should start or be concentrated in these areas first. Of course an increase in the number of recruitment only satisfies the first paradigm. Once minority MLS graduates are recruited to libraries around the country, we must be mindful that they do not become stuck in the second paradigm that focuses on "access-and-legitimacy." For instance, a Latino American can be trained and developed to be responsible for more than just being the Latino librarian. Recruiting Latinos merely for their bilingual capability often does not help advance Latino librarians in their early career. This tokenism approach of recruitment plus what Isabel Espinal (2003, 19–24) calls "linguistic double standards" often negatively affects the way that Latinos are perceived. Latinos

Table 10.1
Schools That Graduate Most Minorities in Library Profession

1997	2004
University of Puerto Rico	University of Puerto Rico
Clark Atlanta University	**Clark Atlanta University**
University of Hawaii	**University of Hawaii**
North Carolina Central University	**Pratt Institute**
Pratt Institute	North Carolina Central University
San Jose State University	**UCLA**
Queens College	**St. Johns University**
University of Louisiana	Queens College
University of South Florida	**CUNY**
University of Michigan	**San Jose State University**
	University of Texas, Austin
	Florida State University

Note: Schools listed in bold are located in one of the first or second tier states with a high concentration of minorities.

are often considered effective only in their interactions with Latino patrons. In other situations, "native Spanish speakers who speak English with an accent are viewed as lacking linguistic ability, whereas native English speakers who speak Spanish with an accent are considered to have linguistic breadth or diversity" (Espinal 2003, 23). The double standard, in reality, frustrates Latino librarians, especially when they are perceived to be too Latino to fit into the library as an organization.

This brings us back to the third paradigm, which seeks to integrate cultural backgrounds and skills of minorities within the organization, especially in management. Moving beyond recruitment and retention to promotion requires commitment from the library director down to the low-level manager/supervisor. A new thought process needs to take place first. To acquire this new thought process, it will also be necessary for many library directors and supervisors to engage themselves into diversity training. No longer shall we view America as a melting pot where non-Anglo-American (white) cultures assimilate and acculturate, but instead look at it as a stew pot where all the races mesh to make a delicious blend without losing their own individuality and cultural well-being. Joan Howland notes that this does not take place in corporate America nor in libraries but rather in "the concept of 'success through conformity'" (1999, 5). People usually hire those that closely resemble themselves in thought, speech, dress, etc. While once serving on a search committee, someone said that he supported a certain candidate because he felt that that person would be someone with whom he could socialize. Luckily, in this case, both candidates were white females, so the issue of diversity wasn't as big an issue as it could have been if ethnicity was a factor. But, suppose it was otherwise?

How do we reach paradigm three in libraries? Thomas and Ely's (2001, 51–54) research suggests eight preconditions that help an organization make the paradigm shift. The eight preconditions require the leaders of an organization to embrace "different perspectives and approaches to work." Another emphasis in Thomas and Ely's eight preconditions is the presence of an organizational culture that stimulates personal development, encourages openness, and values all workers. Howland (1999) suggests that libraries create an environment conducive to retention. As stated earlier, the initiative must come from the very top, the library director. It must be clear that this issue is important to the library director. Time and funds invested in diversity, in addition to cultural awareness or sensitivity training, must be continuous and should allow for open expression of ideas from all. Everyone should know that diversity is a goal of the organization, and this can be stated in an annual report, at a library-wide meeting, through internal newsletter, etc. Regardless of how the message is transmitted, it should be clear that this is an expectation or requirement of all in the organization. In addition, "an organization must have a 'relatively egalitarian, non-bureaucratic structure'" (Howland 1999, 8). Bureaucracy for the sake of bureaucracy is not acceptable. If it hinders the free flow of ideas and information, it needs to be adjusted. Everyone should feel that they are valued and respected and have an opportunity to contribute to the overall goals of the organization.

According to Musser (2001, 65–66), retention strategies fall primarily into six categories:

- Mentoring
- Networking
- Career and learning opportunities (professional development)
- Interesting work
- Good benefits
- Balance between work and home life

Mentoring is particularly important in assisting a new hire to adjust to the organizational culture. This holds true even more for minorities who may have a different communication style and other cultural differences. Mentoring relationships do not always develop naturally, so a formal program is crucial. It may also prove more difficult for minorities to find networking opportunities. In some cases, a minority may be the only minority faculty personnel. This often leads to feelings of isolation, especially when nonminority colleagues are not welcoming and receptive to a minority. So, here again, a networking program is important for minorities to make those connections.

Other strategies relate to:

- Job satisfaction
- Climate
- Residency programs
- Promotion

Howland also suggests that libraries ensure equity in regard to promotion, professional development, and success. Being valued and being promoted are two uniquely different ideas. What are some of the reasons given for minorities hitting this "glass ceiling" or "concrete wall"? Howland (1999, 8) says reasons given "are most likely based on unspoken and unexamined assumptions, values, mythologies, apparent and perceived 'differences,' and, perhaps, fear." It could also be based on stereotypes such as communication styles. The criteria for promotion, whether it is nontenure track or tenure track, in libraries are centered on "(1) performance of primary duties, (2) scholarship, and (3) service" (Howland 1999, 9). Performance of primary duties is easily measured according to the job description. Scholarship and service aren't as easily determined and can be hindered by superiors who aren't aware of diversity issues. Minorities often get stuck with many responsibilities that are not considered or credited during the evaluation process. This ranges from mentoring other minorities to serving on various committees and task forces. According to Howland (1999, 11), service to the profession, such as an appointment to a national, regional, or local committee, isn't easily attained, as this is out of the candidate's control and is decided by officers on the committee.

PURPOSE OF RESEARCH

The purpose of this research project was to track the career development path of librarians of underrepresented racial and ethnic groups in relation to their white counterparts. Although the general characteristics of the library profession demand qualifications, specific educational, and skill requirement for librarians who choose to enter this profession and want to continue to move up in the career ladder, we hypothesize that there are elements in an organizational environment that have contributed to their success in their career development and barriers that have hampered their career advancement. The personal career experience of a minority manager reflects the quality of a workplace in which a minority manager may find that he/she is challenged and allowed opportunities to continue to develop and grow, or that he/she finds him/herself in a disadvantageous situation in which opportunities for further advancement rarely exist. Some of the most methodical and comprehensive research published on tracking minority managers career patterns is described in the book, *Breaking Through: The Making of Minority Executives in Corporate America* (Thomas and Gabarro 1999). This book presents results from more than six years of research tracking the successful career experience of minority managers from three Fortune 500 companies, who have finally made it to the executive level. Although this study does not have the depth and scope of Thomas and Gabarro's, it, nonetheless, initiates the preliminary research and present results based on which further studies can be developed.

Two major concerns expressed in the business sector are: (1) with all the best intention, "many have failed to achieve a racial mix at the top levels of management"; and (2) "some have revolving doors for talented minorities, recruiting the best and brightest, only to see them leave, frustrated by their experiences" (Thomas 2001, 118). Does the movement in library professionals bear any similarity? To prove or disprove this assumption is the starting point for this research project.

This research project focused on the framework of the third paradigm outlined by Thomas and Ely (2001). At the conclusion of our research, we hoped to obtain data that may help us understand the career development patterns of minority library managers from our selected population. We also wanted to be able to present an overall assessment of their organizational environment and to identify some factors that have assisted or hampered their advancement to their current positions. By gathering career development data from the library managers in general and from the minority librarians, we hoped to present an analysis and assessment that may lead to answers of questions such as: Do managers of minority background often feel that they have hit the glass ceiling at a certain point of their career? Does it take longer time for minority managers to advance to middle or upper managerial positions? Do they feel that the threshold for their promotion is set higher than those for their white colleagues? What are some of the positive assistance that they have been given to further their success in career advancement? How many of them have had mentoring and networking relationships with senior managers from their own organization? How have these mentoring and networking efforts contributed to their career success? How many of them have participated in programs similar to ARL's Leadership and Career Development Program? Have they been aware of any programs of this type? How many of them want to become the director of a library? How many of them have achieved their career objective within the organization where they started their first post-MLS job?

DATA ABOUT MINORITY LIBRARIANS IN ARL

One major source that tracks the demographic changes in ARL is Demographic Change in Academic Librarianship (Wilder 2003). The following data are cited from the latest edition of Wilder's book and indicate that there has been very little change over the 20-year period from 1980 to 2000 even though a very slight gain in number and percentage of minority librarians is noticed (Figure 10.2).

The data presented here show that the number of minority librarians has proportionally increased, but the representation of each minority group has remained the same over the 20-year period.

Figures 10.3 and 10.4 show that although the minority population has significantly increased, that representation does not hold true for librarians. Asian Americans are the only group that is adequately presented in the profession. We have been unsuccessful in recruiting African Americans and Latinos into this profession. The Hispanic population, the largest and the fastest growth minority group (with a total of 13 percent of the populations) accounts for only 2 percent in the total number of ARL library professionals. African American population

Figure 10.2
Number and Percentage of Minorities in ARL Member Libraries,
1980, 1990, and 2000

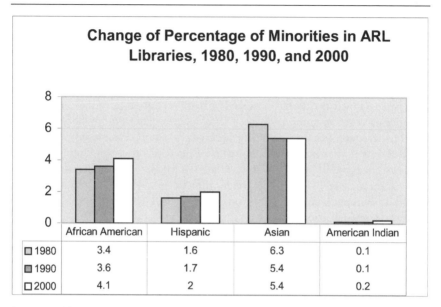

Source: Wilder, *Demographic Change in Academic Librarianship* (2003), p. 34.

Figure 10.3
Minority Librarians in ARL Libraries, 2000

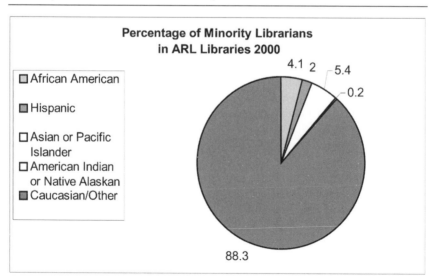

Source: Wilder, *Demographic Change in Academic Librarianship* (2003), p. 34.

Figure 10.4
Percentage of Minority Population, 2000

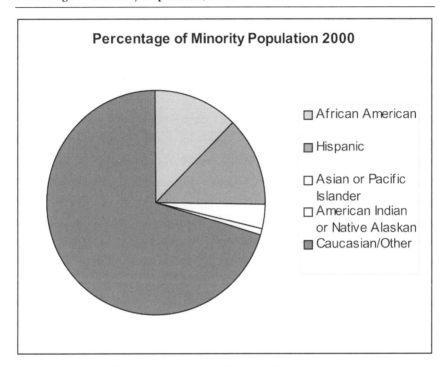

Source: U.S. Census Bureau, "Population by Race and Hispanic Origin for the United States: 2000," Overview of Race and Hispanic Origin, http://www.census.gov/prod/2001pubs/c2kbr01-1.pdf.

consisting of 12 percent of the U.S. population has seen an insignificant gain from 3.4 percent in 1980 to 4.1 percent in 2000 in the professional employment in U.S. ARL libraries.

The number of minorities in ARL member libraries also is not representative of the general minority population. Figure 10.5 shows that in the last six years, there has not been a significant gain of minorities working in libraries of ARL. The percentage of minority librarians holding managerial positions in ARL member libraries are even smaller (9.2 percent), trailing slightly the percentage of the overall representation of minority librarians in ARL population (11.7 percent).

Data were also available from the published ARL Salary Surveys about the types of managerial positions that minority librarians held. By 2002/2003, there were five ARL minority library directors and two of them were hired in 2001/2002. The number of associate directors and assistant directors, on the other hand, has decreased during this time. There were 13 minority associate directors in 2000/2001, but only 11 in 2002/2003. Likewise, the number of minority assistant directors decreased to 10 in 2002/2003, down from 14 in 2000/2001. The largest increase in minorities

Figure 10.5
Change of Minority Library Professionals in ARL Member Libraries
from Fiscal Year 2000 through 2005

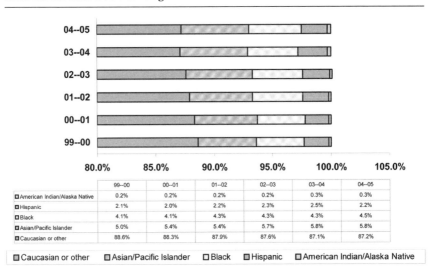

	99--00	00--01	01--02	02--03	03--04	04--05
☐ American Indian/Alaska Native	0.2%	0.2%	0.2%	0.2%	0.3%	0.3%
☐ Hispanic	2.1%	2.0%	2.2%	2.3%	2.5%	2.2%
☐ Black	4.1%	4.1%	4.3%	4.3%	4.3%	4.5%
☐ Asian/Pacific Islander	5.0%	5.4%	5.4%	5.7%	5.8%	5.8%
☐ Caucasian or other	88.6%	88.3%	87.9%	87.6%	87.1%	87.2%

☐ Caucasian or other　　☐ Asian/Pacific Islander　　☐ Black　　☐ Hispanic　　☐ American Indian/Alaska Native

Note: Compilation of *ARL Annual Salary Survey* from 2000–2001 to 2004–2005. Accessible via: http://www.arl.org/stats/salary.

is in the subcategory of "Other" under Department Head—an increase of almost 30 percent. Demographic data recently released in ARL Annual Salary Survey for 2004–2005 does not show any break from this existing pattern of distribution.

DESIGN AND METHODOLOGY

To obtain the data needed for this study, a survey instrument was designed that would allow us to gather demographic and career data that could be used as samples from our targeted populations. The target population for the first group was library managers from the ARL member libraries in the first tier of states of Hawaii, New Mexico, California, Texas, Mississippi, and Louisiana, and the District of Columbia. The focus was on these states because of the high demographic composition of minority population, which may serve as a framework for further research in the second tier of states. The qualifications for our research were that the subjects must have earned at least an MLS degree or equivalent and have already been promoted to the rank of department head, head of a departmental library, or positions above that rank such as functional director, assistant/associate dean, and assistant/associate or university librarian. (University librarians were excluded from the sample because those identified as being an ethnic minority university librarian would not

Table 10.2
Minority Managers in U.S. ARL University Libraries

	2000–2001			2001–2002			2002–2003		
	Women	Men	Total	Women	Men	Total	Women	Men	Total
Director	1	2	3	3	2	5	3	2	5
Associate Director	10	3	13	7	3	10	9	2	11
Assistant Director	7	7	14	8	5	13	6	4	10
Head, Branch	37	14	51	34	15	49	37	13	50
Department Head									
Acquisitions	7	2	9	5	2	7	6	2	8
Reference	4	1	5	5	2	7	6	1	7
Cataloging	10	1	11	9	3	12	12	3	15
Serials	2	0	2	0	0	0	0	0	0
Document/Map	5	0	5	4	0	4	5	1	6
Circulation	6	2	8	4	3	7	6	5	11
Rare Book/Manuscripts	1	1	2	3	1	4	3	2	5
Computer Systems	2	6	8	2	6	8	3	6	9
Other	39	18	57	53	18	71	55	18	73
All positions	131	57	188	137	60	197	151	59	210

Note: Compilation of ARL Annual Salary Survey from 2002–2003, 2001–2002, and 2000–2001. Accessible via: http://www.arl.org/stats/salary/

have had anonymity because there is such a small number of ethnic minority university librarians.)

The standard survey consists of two sections. The first section is intended to collect information about respondents' educational background; ethnicity; years of post-MLS experience before being promoted to the first, middle, and upper managerial position; and years of experience before being promoted to a managerial position. The second section of the survey is to poll the respondents' assessment of certain aspects of the organizational environment in their own organization. Forms designed for this survey were provided online, and selected individuals were approached via e-mail with a URL to the online survey form. A total of 200 individuals were selected to participate in this study. They were all current library professionals of ARL in the first tier of states. Libraries' Web sites were scanned by position, and names were randomly selected. Of 200 selected individuals, 52 responded, for a 26 percent response rate.

The target population for the second group was ARL LCDP participants because they are exclusively minority librarians or library managers and have been nominated and endorsed by their library administration as minority leaders or having the potential to become a leader. As mentoring, coaching, and networking have been the goals of the ARL LCDP, which is closely connected to the third paradigm of diversity, the standard survey was sent to program participants to further substantiate our finding and for comparability to the first group. An additional section was included for this group, which had six open-ended questions, to gather their personal experiences and evaluations of the LCDP. Because the program had a limited number of participants, all participants were contacted including those from the target states and all other states to assess the positive impact of the program on their career advancement. Eighty-eight past participants were approached via e-mail with a URL to the online survey form. From this group, 31 responded, for a 36 percent response rate.

SURVEY RESULTS

Profile of Survey Respondents

Profile of Group 1—ARL Managers (N = 52 respondents from the target states)

This group of 52 respondents holds various managerial positions in 18 ARL libraries, consisting of 8 associate university librarians, 28 department heads, and 10 heads of departmental/branch libraries; the remaining 6 identified themselves as other types of middle level managers. This group also has a diverse educational background ranging from 27 having an MLS or equivalent degree, 4 without MLS but advanced degree in other fields, 14 having an MLS plus an additional master degree, 2 having MLS plus a PhD, and 5 having MLS plus two or more advanced degrees. The racial representation of this group obviously does not reflect the overall distribution of the ARL Salary Report owing to the small number of respondents.

Table 10.3
Gender of Group 1

Gender	Number (Percentage)
Male	13 (25%)
Female	39 (75%)

Table 10.4
Race of Group 1

Race	Number (Percentage)
White	42 (80.8%)
Hispanic or Latino	4 (7.7%)
Black or African American	4 (7.7%)
Other	2 (3.8%)

Table 10.5
Age of Group 1

Age	Number (Percentage)
31–35	2 (3.8%)
36–40	5 (9.6%)
41–45	4 (7.7%)
46–50	14 (26.9%)
51–55	13 (25%)
56–60	12 (23.1%)
60–over	2 (3.8%)

Profile of Group 2—ARL Leadership and Career Development Program (LCDP) Participants (N = 31 ARL LCDP participants of which 19 [61 percent] hold positions from ARL libraries)

This group of 31 respondents holds various managerial positions in 31 different libraries. The types of positions and level of responsibilities are more diverse than in Group 1: one associate university librarian, eight department heads, eight heads of departmental/branch libraries, five fitting into the "other" subcategory of ARL department heads, and seven in nonmanagerial positions. The educational background of this group is more homogeneous. Twenty-five have an MLS or equivalent degree, four with MLS plus an additional masters degree, and two with an MLS plus two or more degrees. No one in this group holds a PhD.

Table 10.6
Gender of Group 2

Gender	Number (Percentage)
Male	6 (19.4%)
Female	25 (80%)

Table 10.7
Race of Group 2

Race	Number (Percentage)
Asian	5 (16.1%)
Hispanic or Latino	5 (16.1%)
Black or African American	20 (64.5%)
American Indian and Alaska Native	1 (3.2%)

Table 10.8
Age of Group 2

Age	Number (Percentage)
25–30	1 (3.2%)
31–35	3 (9.7%)
36–40	5 (16.1%)
41–45	9 (29.0%)
46–50	6 (19.4%)
51–55	7 (22.6%)

Survey Findings

As mentioned earlier, the same set of 28 questions was administered to the two groups. For the LCDP participant group, however, six open-ended questions were added asking them specifically about their personal experience with the LCDP. The standard questions were generally divided into four types: (1) career advancement information, (2) participants' ranking of eight career advancement factors in the order of importance that the respondents believe have helped them in their career advancement, (3) their perception of some aspects of the organizational environment of their libraries that contribute to or hinder the promotion of a diverse workforce, and (4) a summary of Group 2's assessment of the LCDP and some discussions of their testimonies and our findings. In other words, the data gathered from the two groups were compared to observe any similarities or significant differences and to provide possible explanations.

Career Advancement Situation

Age factor. There is a significant gap between the two groups. For Group 1, the mode is the 46–50 age range (26.9 percent). If the age of 45 is used as the dividing point, 78.8 percent of this group are older than 45. In more or less than 10 years, 51.9 percent of this group will be over the age of 60, indicating that more than 50 percent of the managerial positions may become vacant as those senior managers reach the age for retirement. The mode for Group 2 is the 41–45 age range (29 percent). If the age of 45 is used as the dividing point, 42 percent of this group are currently older than 45. In more or less than 10 years, only 22.6 percent of this group will be over 60. This result is consistent with Stanley J. Wilder's report that minority librarians in the ARL libraries were younger than their white colleagues. Considering the significant years of experience required to be qualified to fill the middle and upper managerial positions soon to be vacant by massive retirement during the next decade, there are many in Group 2 ready for competition. Our data seem to support Wilder's prediction that even without targeted recruitment efforts, "the retirement would have the effect of raising the percentage of minorities in the population as a whole" (Wilder 2003, 35). This age factor may predict that the movement of the managerial positions in ARL libraries will be intensified and thus may somehow change the general pessimistic view of advancement opportunities in the academic libraries. In one poll conducted by *Library Journal* (*A lot of satisfaction but not much room for advancement 1994*), 27 percent of librarians believe there are advancement opportunities in their current jobs versus 73 percent who do not.

Post-MLS Experience (Total years of post-MLS [or equivalent degree] experience as a librarian). The mode for Group 1 with this variable is the 21–25 year range (26.9 percent), whereas the mode for Group 2 is the 11–15 year range (41.9 percent), indicating the majority of Group 2 is still in their middle career period while more than 50 percent of Group 1 have reached their later career stage. This perspective certainly promises great opportunities for managers in their middle career who are waiting in the "bullpen" for their big chance; however, there are also 19.3 percent from Group 1 who have only 10 years or less post-MLS experience and have already advanced to the middle management level.

First Managerial Position (Years between first full-time librarian position and first managerial position). One interesting result from this survey question was the number of respondents who were promoted to their first managerial position in less than a year after they completed their MLS degree. Fourteen respondents (26.9 percent) from Group 1 were promoted to a managerial position in less than a year. For Group 2, five respondents (16.1 percent) were promoted to a managerial position in less than a year after receiving a MLS. One possible reason for such a quick jumpstart was that these librarians had already had sufficient experience working in a library as paraprofessional/staff, and the completion of a MLS qualified them for an immediate promotion. A research project (Gordon and Nesbeitt 1999, 37) confirms that a large majority (71 percent) began working as paraprofessionals or student assistants at least a year before they graduated; the typical respondent worked in a library for five years before acquiring the MLS.

Post-MLS Employers (How many different library positions have you had since your MLS degree/or equivalent?). With this variable, our intention was to examine how many job changes the respondents had to make before they gained enough experience to be selected for their current positions. The mode for Group 1 was four job changes (25 percent of the 52 respondents) with 21.2 percent of respondents saying they had changed job three times and another 23 percent of the respondents having worked six different jobs. The mode for Group 2 was three job changes (29.0 percent), as this group of minority librarians is younger and worked fewer years than members of Group 1. Twenty-three percent of this group had changed jobs twice. Forty-eight percent of Group 2, however, had changed jobs four times or more before they advanced to their current position. In comparison, 59.6 percent of the respondents from Group 1 had changed jobs four times or more. Considering that Group 2 is much younger and has fewer post-MLS years of experience than Group 1, plus the fact that the highest positions for this group (except one AUL) are department head positions, the high frequency of job change in a comparatively shorter period suggests either a high job turnover rate from the minority librarians, or the necessity of changing jobs more often in their early career to seek better opportunities for career advancement.

Years on Current Managerial Position. The mode for this variable is more than 10 years (26 percent) for Group 1, with 21.2 percent of the respondents in the four-year group and 15.4 percent in the 2 year group. The 26.9 percent who have worked on the same position for more than 10 years seem to have reached a level plateau. There are 21 percent of this group who have remained in the same position between five and nine years. We should not conclude that those managers who arrived at a plateau are not content with their situation. As a matter of fact, research also confirms that not all librarians, given an opportunity, want to move into higher-level administration. Some are willing to go as far as service department head, but not to be a library director (Gordon and Nesbeitt 1999, 39). Group 2 displays a different pattern. Excluding the 35.5 percent of respondents who did not consider themselves in a managerial position, 32.2 percent of this group are managers who have been on their current job for two to three years. Another 11 percent of the group are managers who have been on their current job for only one year or less. These data again indicate that minority managers frequently change jobs and, for whatever reasons, they are less likely to stay in one job for more than four years.

Academic Status. Librarians are working under different career tracks and thus emphasize different strategies as they move along or up their career tracks. There are mainly three types of career tracks for ARL librarians: (1) librarians with faculty status and tenure track, (2) librarians with faculty status but who are nontenure track, and (3) librarians of nonfaculty status. The distribution of the three different career tracks is identical between the two groups (Tables 10.9 and 10.10).

The tenure track and faculty status have both a positive and negative impact on retention across all upper-level positions. Some tenure track positions may

Table 10.9
Group I: Academic Status

Status	Frequency	Percent
Faculty Status/Tenure Track	14	26.9%
Faculty Status/Nontenure Track	9	17.3%
Nonfaculty Status	29	55.8%

Table 10.10
Group 2: Academic Status

Status	Frequency	Percent
Faculty Status/Tenure Track	8	25.8%
Faculty Status/Nontenure Track	7	22.6%
Nonfaculty Status	16	51.6%

Table 10.11
Two Groups' Ranking of the Eight Career Advancement Factors

Ranking	Group 1 N = 52	Group 2 N = 31
1	Worked harder	Worked harder
2	Technological proficiency	Changed jobs
3	Changed jobs	Technological proficiency
4	Service to profession	Developed mentoring network
5	Developed mentoring network	Service to profession
6	Publications	Publications
7	Seniority	Seniority
8	Additional advanced degree(s)	Additional advanced degree(s)

1 = highest/most important factor (ranking based on the means of frequencies).

require a second advanced degree and considerable publications to be qualified for tenure and promotion. For both groups, about half of the respondents hold a position of nonfaculty status. In a nonfaculty track environment, library managers may be evaluated more for their services than their scholarly activities, and depending on the type of career track they are on, their career development strategy may be set differently.

Eight Career Advancement Factors. Both groups were asked to rank the eight factors of career development according to the importance of each of the factors and the immediate impact of each of the factors on their career. Answers to those questions are based on each respondent's career experience (Table 10.11).

The ranking of the eight career factors was based on each of the respondents' career experiences and thus was more factual, but it also reflected the respondents' perception of these factors, as they were not asked to answer "Yes" or "No" to the questions. The group ranking (based on the means of frequency), however, reveals a pattern of their career advancement. The two groups ranking the eight factors are largely similar. For both groups, "Worked harder" was the variable that had the strongest impact on their career advancement. Similarly, an additional advanced degree was the lowest of the ranking to have any significant impact on their promotion, even though about 40 percent of respondents from Group 1 have at least one additional advanced degree and 19.4 percent of respondents from Group 2 have at least one additional advanced degree. Survey results seem to support an ARL survey on recruitment and retention, which concludes that the requirement of a second masters degree or a PhD had "a fairly low impact either as enhancement or barriers at all levels (including management)" (Stevens and Streatfeild 2003, 12).

Seniority, ranked #7 by both groups, has the next lowest impact as career enhancement or barrier. However, six (11.5 percent) respondents from Group 1 ranked "Seniority" as the most important factor and another five (9.6 percent) respondents ranked "Seniority" as #3. This is in contrast to the distribution of Group 2 in which 68 percent of respondents ranked "Seniority" as 7 and 8. Because the minority librarians are younger and have fewer post-MLS years of experience, they may have to concentrate on other factors such as "Change jobs" or "Technological proficiency" to get where they want to be.

The differences between the two groups lie in two factors: "Changed jobs" and "Developed mentoring network." "Change job in order to look for new challenges" is the second significant enhancement or barrier for minority librarians. The higher ranking of "Changed jobs" by Group 2 here is consistent with our early observation. Another significant difference between the two groups is their ranking of the variable of "Developed mentoring network." Group 2 ranked this variable as the fourth important factor, whereas Group 1 ranked the same variable as the fifth important factor in their career advancement. This was to suggest that "Developing a mentoring network" has been a more important enhancement or barrier for minority librarians. Both groups ranked "Technological proficiency" as one of the top three enhancements in their career advancement, but for LCDP participants, "Changing jobs" was their number two career enhancement while for white managers, "Technological proficiency" was considered more important than "Changing jobs."

Perception of Diversity Environment. Part of the survey (questions 12 to 28) polled the respondents of the two groups about their perception of organizational environment in terms of workforce diversity. Table 10.12 presents the results of the survey on those environment issues from both groups. A Likert Scale format was used to measure respondents' perception of their library's climate for diversity. These results helped to identify and highlight areas where perceptions differed between Group 1, consisting of 84 percent white library managers and 16 percent minority managers, and Group 2, which was exclusively minority librarians.

Table 10.12
Data from Two Groups: Perception of Diversity Environment

Group 1: middle and upper managers from selected ARL libraries of mixed races n = 52

Group 2: exclusively minority librarians (some middle and upper managers) from the participants of ARL LCDP n =31

12. Diversity at Staff Level	Strongly Disagree	Disagree	No opinion	Agree	Strongly agree
Group I	5.8%	26.9%	9.6%	44.2%	13.5%
Group II	22.6%	35.5%	0%	38.7%	3.2%
Average Percent	14.2%	31.2%	4.8%	41.5%	8.4%

13. Diversity at Librarian Level	Strongly Disagree	Disagree	No opinion	Agree	Strongly agree
Group 1	13.4%	50.0%	5.8%	25.0%	5.8%
Group II	35.5%	41.9%	0.0%	16.1%	6.5%
Average Percent	24.5%	46.0%	2.9%	20.6%	6.2%

14. Diversity at Middle Management Level	Strongly Disagree	Disagree	No opinion	Agree	Strongly agree
Group I	23.1%	46.2%	3.8%	23.1%	3.8%
Group II	48.4%	38.7%	3.2%	6.5%	3.2%
Average Percent	35.8%	42.5%	3.5%	14.8%	3.5%

15. Diversity at Upper Management Level	Strongly Disagree	Disagree	No opinion	Agree	Strongly agree
Group 1	30.8%	38.5%	5.8%	23.0%	1.9%
Group 2	61.3%	25.8%	6.5%	3.2%	3.2%
Average Percent	46.1%	32.2%	6.2%	13.1%	2.6%

16. Easier to Relate to Own Race	Strongly Disagree	Disagree	No opinion	Agree	Strongly agree
Group 1	23.1%	51.9%	17.3%	7.7%	0.0%
Group 2	3.2%	38.7%	25.8%	32.3%	0.0%
Average Percent	13.2%	45.3%	21.6%	20.0%	0.0%

17. Easier to Communicate with Own Race	Strongly Disagree	Disagree	No opinion	Agree	Strongly agree
Group 1	19.2%	53.9%	13.5%	11.5%	1.9%
Group 2	3.2%	35.5%	19.4%	38.7%	3.2%
Average Percent	11.2%	44.7%	16.5%	25.1%	2.6%

18. Difficult to Relate B/W Races	Strongly Disagree	Disagree	No opinion	Agree	Strongly agree
Group 1	32.7%	59.6%	7.7%	0.0%	0.0%
Group 2	12.9%	74.2%	9.7%	3.2%	0.0%
Average Percent	22.8%	66.9%	8.7%	1.6%	0.0%

19. Difficult Communication B/W Races	Strongly Disagree	Disagree %	No opinion %	Agree %	Strongly Agree %
Group 1	32.7%	57.7%	5.8%	1.9%	1.9%
Group 2	19.4%	64.5%	6.4%	9.7%	0.0%
Average Percent	26.1%	61.1%	6.1%	5.8%	1.0%

20. Recruit Diversity Workforce	Strongly Disagree	Disagree	No opinion	Agree	Strongly Agree
Group 1	1.9%	25.0%	23.1%	36.5%	13.5%
Group 2	9.7%	29.0%	16.1%	42.0%	3.2%
Average Percent	5.8%	27.0%	19.6%	39.3%	8.4%

21. Retain Diverse Workforce	Strongly Disagree	Disagree	No opinion	Agree	Strongly Agree
Group 1	1.9%	17.4%	36.5%	36.5%	7.7%

(continued)

143

Table 10.2 (continued)

	Strongly Disagree	Disagree	No opinion	Agree	Strongly Agree
Group 2	9.7%	48.3%	19.4%	22.6%	0.0%
Average Percent	5.8%	32.9%	28.0%	29.6%	3.9%
22. Has Diversity as Strategic Priority	**Strongly Disagree**	**Disagree**	**No opinion**	**Agree**	**Strongly Agree**
Group 1	1.9%	17.3%	19.3%	51.9%	9.6%
Group 2	19.4%	16.1%	16.1%	38.7%	9.7%
Average Percent	10.7%	16.7%	17.7%	45.3%	9.7%
23. Should Have Diversity as Strategic Priority	**Strongly Disagree**	**Disagree**	**No opinion**	**Agree**	**Strongly Agree**
Group 1	1.9%	5.8%	26.9%	44.2%	21.2%
Group 2	3.2%	0.0%	0.0%	71.0%	25.8%
Average Percent	2.6%	2.9%	13.5%	57.6%	23.5%
24. Has Diversity Committee	**Strongly Disagree**	**Disagree**	**No opinion**	**Agree**	**Strongly Agree**
Group 1	11.5%	34.6%	13.5%	25.0%	15.4%
Group 2	16.0%	22.6%	19.4%	35.5%	6.5%
Average Percent	13.8%	28.6%	16.5%	30.3%	11.0%
25. Diversity and Affirmative Action	**Strongly Disagree**	**Disagree**	**No opinion**	**Agree**	**Strongly Agree**
Group 1	0.0%	7.7%	11.5%	51.9%	28.9%
Group 2	0.0%	0.0%	3.2%	48.4%	48.4%
Average Percent	0.0%	3.9%	7.4%	50.2%	38.7%
26. Hiring and Promotion Should Be Color Blind	**Strongly Disagree**	**Disagree**	**No opinion**	**Agree**	**Strongly Agree**
Group 1	1.9%	7.7%	11.5%	55.8%	23.1%
Group 2	0.0%	16.1%	9.7%	38.7%	35.5%
Average Percent	1.0%	11.9%	10.6%	47.3%	29.3%
27. Hire on Existing Culture	**Strongly disagree**	**Disagree**	**No opinion**	**Agree**	**Strongly Agree**
Group 1	7.7%	28.8%	23.1%	34.6%	5.8%
Group 2	0.0%	32.3%	9.6%	45.2%	12.9%
Average Percent	3.9%	30.6%	16.4%	39.9%	9.4%
28. Encourages Hiring Diversity	**Strongly Disagree**	**Disagree**	**No opinion**	**Agree**	**Strongly Agree**
Group 1	1.9%	11.5%	11.5%	55.8%	19.3%
Group 2	3.2%	29.0%	25.8%	35.5%	6.5%
Average Percent	2.6%	20.3%	18.7%	45.7%	12.9%

Questions 12 to 15 asked respondents about their perception of diversity at staff, librarian, middle management, and upper management levels. The two groups agreed to a certain degree in their assessment of the diversity of workforce in the library. If we average the two groups, only 27 percent agreed that their library's employees are a balanced representation of the racially diverse population on campus among librarians; 18 percent agreed the same is true at the middle management level; and 16 percent agreed the same is true at the upper management level. But we noticed perception gaps between the two groups to questions 12, 14, and 15. The percentage of agreement from the minority group was statistically lower than the average percentage. As for question 12, we observed that 58 percent of respondents from Group 2 disagreed with the statement but 59 percent of respondents from Group 1 agreed with the statement.

Perception gaps were also present in questions 16 and 17, which asked about communication and empathy within and across the race. Thirty-two percent of minority respondents from Group 2 agreed that at work it is easier to relate to people from their own racial and cultural background, but only 7.7 percent of respondents from Group 1 agreed with this statement. Forty-two percent of minority respondents from Group 2 agreed that at work it is easier to communicate with people from their own cultural background, and only 13 percent of respondents from Group 1 agreed with that statement. Although some minority respondents felt it was easier to relate/communicate to people of their own cultural and racial background, few of them felt that it was difficult to relate/communicate with people from different cultural background. The perceptions of the two groups were very similar on questions 18 and 19. Both groups were positive about their library's efforts in recruiting a diverse workforce in the past five years. The perception gaps appeared again in their assessment of their own library's efforts or effectiveness in retaining a diverse workforce and encouraging managers to hire people that can bring diversity and enrichment to their organizational culture. Forty-four percent of the respondents from Group 1 agreed that their library had made strides in the past five years to retain a diverse workforce. Fifty-eight percent of the respondents from Group 2 disagreed that this was true in their library. When asked if their library has diversity as a strategic priority, only 48 percent of the respondents from Group 2 agreed. When asked if their library should have diversity as strategic priority, however, an overwhelming 97 percent of the respondents from Group 2 agreed. When asked if their library has a diversity committee or task force that addresses issues of diversity and supports the implementation of all the diversity goals, only 40 percent of the respondents from Group 1 agreed, and only 42 percent of the respondents from Group 2 believed their library has a diversity committee. Fifty-eight percent of the respondents from Group 2 believed that their library tends to hire employees that conform to their existing organizational culture compared with 40 percent from Group 1 who agreed with the same assessment. Seventy-five percent of Group 1 confirmed that their library encourages managers to hire people that can bring diversity and enrichment to the organizational culture, but only 42 percent of Group 2 agreed with the statement.

Summary of Group 2's Assessment of the LCDP

Six open-ended questions were added to the standard survey to ask about LCDP participants' experience before and after the program and their assessment of the program's impact on their career advancement. The strong, enthusiastic responses from the 31 respondents provided a valuable inside view into some of the most successful minority managers' career experience. In the following summary of their answers to these questions, one may also notice that some of their responses confirmed some of the assumptions made from early data analysis.

Question 29. What is the successful strategy you employed in your career advancement?

Most of the minority managers in their answers included one or more of the following strategies:

- Remain competent and confident at all times
- Practice flexibility and openness to change
- Change jobs
- Work harder
- Look for challenging work assignments
- Network
- Mentor
- Keep up with technology
- Increase one's skills-set

Several LCDP participants felt that because of their minority background, they had to work harder to prove that their promotion was based on their capability and competence, not just on tokenism. As one of the respondents asserted, "By giving 200 percent on the job I have proved my competence and value to the institution and become more than just an 'affirmative action hire.'" Another respondent agreed saying, "As a minority librarian, I always have to prove myself. I have to be twice as good as everyone else, because others are watching me and because I don't want to bring dishonor on my people. At various institutions where I have worked, I know there have been people who felt I did not get my job on merit alone, that it was because of my minority status—and I feel pressured to prove my worth."

Thus we can see that for minority librarians, the term *working harder* also means making greater efforts to overcome barriers that their white colleagues do not have to encounter. Research on career experiences of minorities has long identified race- and gender-based prejudice as a major barrier to a minority's professional advancement. Our respondents' comments confirmed the existence of the same organizational bias in the library profession. To disprove the rule of their inferiority, minority librarian managers had to develop some strategies to counter and overcome these barriers.

Being willing to change jobs and relocate is a strategy mentioned over and over by several respondents. Some moved because they did not feel they were treated fairly. As one respondent put it, "Work hard, be active in professional organizations and treat others as you would like to be treated; if you are being overlooked and mistreated by an employer do not be afraid to move to another job." Others had to relocate for better advancement opportunities. "[I] identified positions for which I was qualified and was willing to change locations to take them."

Most of the respondents from Group 2 were optimistic and positive about their career objectives and opportunities. While acknowledging some barriers embedded in their own organizational environment, they chose to concentrate more on self-development and expansion of critical skills and networking. Instead of waiting for opportunity to find them, they wasted no time to ready themselves for the next move. One responded, "[I] continually scanned job postings to be sure my skills were up to date and marketable. When opportunities presented themselves, I was prepared."

One respondent emphasized the importance of collaboration with colleagues and providing support to them as a way to win peers' recognition, "To take every opportunity I can for professional growth and development and to work hard to be the best I can in my job. To bring my organization the best of my skills, abilities and talents and to support everyone around me as much as I can. To seek mentors wherever I can find them."

Developing technological competence was also mentioned as a crucial strategy for furthering one's career. As information and communication technology continue to redefine our profession, a proactive strategy used by one respondent was "keeping up with technology. Looking at the big picture. Getting along with people. Looking for best practices. Following my own counsel." In addition to increasing one's skills-set, our respondents also stressed the importance of being more attuned to the political and social climate of one's library and university.

Question 30. Did you receive any minority scholarship from your library school toward your MLS degree? ALA Spectrum Initiative?

Fifty-one percent of the respondents said they did not receive any kind of minority scholarship toward their MLS education. Thirty-one percent of the respondents said they received financial support from the following programs:

- U.S. Department of Education Title II grant for Science Librarianship
- Title IIB Higher Education Minority Fellowship
- Title 9 Federal funds for Women Students
- State minority scholarship
- Full tuition scholarship from the library school
- Allowed to pay in-state tuition with a waiver that was provided to reduce the out-of-state portion of the tuition.
- Received tuition remission by working as a paraprofessional in a library
- A work-based program where an in-library internship was offered to participant that allowed release time to attend MLS classes and a job at 50 percent time with full benefit.
- University-sponsored minority fellowship
- Mary P. Key Minority Internship—a temporary but full-time postgraduate position on a two-year term.

Question 31. How were you nominated and selected for the LCDP? Did you receive support including financial support from your library administration?

Most LCDP participants were nominated by a Dean/Library Director or an immediate supervisor. Again, the vital role of the library director in the nomination process was obvious. Of the 28 respondents who answered this question, 22 received nomination or support from their library director or dean. Respondents considered being nominated by their library director an affirmation of their leadership potential, an endorsement from their own institution, and a commitment to their career development from the administration. A few respondents were self-nominated after having a former LCDP participant recommend the program to them. Many institutions granted full financial support for their LCDP participants, but those that did not offer financial support granted leave time for the participant to attend meetings. Some financial assistance was provided by ARL. In most instances, participants were not granted reduction in workload, so personal time has been used to complete the online courses.

Question 32. What was your immediate benefit from the LCDP and your relationship with your mentor?

The immediate benefit for participants has been a better understanding of their own skills and abilities, especially as it relates to leadership. Many responded that the program has helped them develop a career path for advancement. In addition, the sense of community that the program fosters has been beneficial, because participants have connected with someone sharing the same difficulties in the profession. With the program, many no longer feel alone in their struggle and now have a peer group to discuss these issues.

The mentoring relationship has been advantageous with most participants. Again those who had a committed mentor benefited the most from the relationship. One respondent described her relationship with her mentor as being terrific from the beginning, "She had made it clear to me from the outset that our relationship was a priority to her and she was committed to make it work. In fact we still get together regularly...She has been there to offer advice on everything from coping with institutional politics to which step I should take next in my career." In fact, a few of them expressed the sentiment that the relationship would continue long after the program is completed. The positive relationship with mentors has increased the self-esteem of participants and confidence in their own skills and abilities. In a few cases, participants regretted that a relationship did not develop with their mentor. For those who were unable to develop a relationship with their mentor, their response was obviously less enthusiastic than those who had a strong, committed mentor.

Question 33. Have you been given enough opportunities on your current position to gain desirable experience to get you ready for a position of higher authority than your current position?

Most of the respondents felt the need to redefine their career goals after the LCDP. Some reported that they have since then rewritten their job description with their supervisor and added more responsibilities in their job description. Some reported that they were given more opportunities to chair a committee or to attend workshops or seminars on management and leadership. None of them reported any immediate promotion. Most of them returned after LCDP to where they were and are going through the process of "priming" themselves for a higher position. A few of them felt they had little chance to get a promotion in their current organization. Still a few stated that they were worried about their opportunities with current employers. As one respondent put it, "I have had to be very proactive, however, in requesting support for various things. I do not feel I am getting enough mentoring and preparation for the next step. I worry about where my career is going as I see few opportunities for promotion here. My boss isn't planning on going anywhere, so sooner or later I will have to face the question of whether I am willing to leave my institution in order to advance." Not all participants are looking for a management position. For those who have not been granted such an opportunity, it has been a result of organizational structure or a low turnover rate. For those who aspire to seek an upward move, they wish they were given an opportunity to gain some critical management skills in the areas of personnel management, project management, and coordination that require complex responsibilities, budgeting, and higher level decision making.

Question 34. Has the LCDP effectively prepared you for a leadership position? Why or why not?

All but one responder stated that the LCDP had effectively prepared them for a leadership position. What LCDP prepared them for was the ability to think "from a leadership perspective" and what they have gained from the program was a discovery of leadership potential in themselves. One respondent thus commented: "The self-assessment aspects of the program were key to developing my professional self-confidence in ways that don't come as easily on the job." They also considered their interaction with library deans/directors and the opportunities to hear and question speakers who are nationally recognized leaders in the library profession incredibly inspiring. One person responded, "LCDP identifies and incorporates critical skills and attitudes that are necessary to being a leader." Another respondent concurred: "The experiences and learning institutes provided by the LCDP certainly gave me the organizational framework, the educational vision, and the important belief in self to prepare me for accepting leadership opportunities and challenges."

Question 35. Was the LCDP at all beneficial and would you recommend it to other ethnic minority librarians? Why or why not?

An enthusiastic YES was given by the participants with the exception of one. Many have already recommended the program to other minorities and one said that: "It was definitely beneficial, and I have and will continue to recommend to other ethnic minority librarians because we all know we need leaders, particularly leaders from diverse backgrounds who can address issues [of] equity and equality." Another participant reflects: "Many programs address management and skills, but LCDP is on a much higher philosophical level...This program provides a forum for issues specific to ethnic minorities, that may not have ever been vocalized. I have recommended LCDP to other ethnic minorities, and believe that the content would be useful to all in leadership positions regardless of ethnicity." Other reasons given reflect some of the strategies that Musser (2001) suggested for the retention of employees:

- Networking opportunities
- Self-assessment
- Mentor relationship
- Development of skills for career advancement
- Establish balanced work life
- Develop understanding of organizational culture

ANALYSIS AND SUMMARY

The scarcity of minority librarians at middle- and upper-management levels, combined with a shortage of minority library school graduates entering the librarian profession, has been well documented. Considering that many Fortune 500 companies have reached 15 to 40 percent minority representation within management levels, the 9.2 percent representation of minority managers in ARL reveal the lack of effective strategies in diversifying the ARL at the management level. Our survey results on the diversity environment show that diversity in ARL has been successful, at most, only at the paraprofessional level. Less than 20 percent of our respondents (based on two group average) agreed their library has a balanced representation of the racially diverse population at middle- and upper-management levels. Our data also show that minority respondents are less satisfied with certain aspects of the diversity environment in their library than their white colleagues. Most respondents acknowledge the existence of a strategic plan in their library, but the execution, follow through, and measurement of the plan were found to be lacking. Although efforts for recruiting minority librarians have intensified, retaining minority librarians and preparing them to advance to the next level remain as critical issues yet to be addressed. The feeling of isolation, the lack of mentoring for minority librarians in their early career, and the need for specific programs to assist them to grow within the organization have yet to be recognized by their library administration. On the other hand, minority librarians, if well prepared, will have greater opportunities to break through into the top managerial level in the ARL libraries within this decade because of the possible massive retirement of the senior library managers in the near future. Given equal opportunity for competition, minority librarians may have to work even harder to overcome unnecessary obstacles to win approval for their ability and competence because of some institutionalized bias.

From the management point of view, the goal of integration of diversity in management and leadership demands serious commitment from leadership at the top. Library directors must become personally involved in diversity initiatives. We have presented powerful testimonies from ARL LCDP participants on what a difference a library director/dean's personal commitment and support could make in legitimating this process and in affirming the true value of diversity. When a library director fails to understand his/her vital role, the diversity program tends to become stagnant. When a library director is actively involved in diversity initiatives, he/she serves as a role model for those managers who are responsible for implementing those diversity initiatives.

ARL LCDP initiative has been effective in developing leadership skills among minority librarians. It exerts external assistance and influence on library directors who want to implement effective diversity program, but has been limited by financial and personnel resources. ARL LCDP operates on a national level and attracts the most qualified minority managers or potential future managers to the program. The program offers an enabling environment for minority librarians to reinvent themselves with powerful networking and mentoring. As developing a mentorship is the most critical part of this program, only those who have successfully established, developed, and sustained their relationships with their mentor have been able to capitalize on this benefit. Those who were not well matched with their designated mentor seem to have missed a major benefit of the program. A new initiative of the ARL will start an outreach program to encourage minority undergraduates to pursue graduate library education (Offord 2004). This initiative is an important strategy to attract potential young librarians and to enlarge the pool of minority candidates for middle- and upper-management positions.

Recommendations

Based on the literature review and survey results, the authors offer these recommendations to reach Thomas and Ely's (2001) third paradigm in libraries.

1. **Recruitment.** There is still a need to increase the number of minorities in the field of librarianship. To adequately represent those "majority-minority" populations, more librarians of color will be needed. Continuation of ALA's Spectrum Initiative (*scholarship*) is mandatory, but should incorporate more aggressive measures of recruitment including establishing relationships with historically black colleges and universities (HBCUs). (first paradigm). Library schools that are not located in states that have "majority-minority" populations or the first or second tier of states with high minority populations, should either set up *distance learning programs* in those states or have an online course that actively recruits in those states. Library programs and career opportunities should be advertised in publications that are read by minorities such as *Ebony* and *Selecciones*.

2. **Retention.** Once librarians of color are in the field, it is imperative that they remain in the field. Retention efforts through mentoring, professional development opportunities, etc. should also continue. In 2004, the Institute of Museum and Library Services (IMLS) awarded more than $14 million to recruit and educate new librarians. The IMLS also awarded ALA's Office of Diversity with $928,142 (Oder 2004, 18). *Funding* of programs that focus on recruitment as well as retention of librarians of color will obviously need to continue (second paradigm).

3. **Recruitment and Retention of Minority Library Information Science (LIS) Faculty.** The profession has long been aware of the need to recruit and retain minority librarians at a level representative of the general population. More than 10 years ago, E. J. Josey stated that the recruitment of minority faculty is the "key to success" in this area. He noted that "only 11.24 percent of our total library and information science faculty are from the four [minority] groups combined...something needs to be done in terms of recruitment of minority faculty—if we truly believe in having a culturally diverse faculty" (Josey 1993, 305). This is important because "students of color expect to see their counterparts on the faculty" (Josey 1993, 306). Having minority faculty in library schools can be an effective recruitment tool. Only 19 percent of LIS faculty members are of color (Adkins and Espinal 2004, 53). To achieve this objective, minorities in the profession need encouragement and support in pursuing a PhD in librarianship. Between 1995/1996 and 2000/2001, only 13 percent of LIS programs' doctoral degrees were given to students of color (Adkins and Espinal 2004, 53). Minorities entering library school should be identified and recruited early to pursue the PhD. Distance learning and online courses should be made available for the PhD, as well as the masters.

4. **Leadership Training Programs.** "In 2003, more than 30 library leadership programs were held annually or biannually" (Mason and Wetherbee 2004, 203). Unfortunately, only three have minority librarians as a target audience: American Library Association Spectrum, Association of Research Libraries Leadership and Career Development, and University of Minnesota Training Institute for Librarians of Color. It goes without saying that the profession needs more of these programs that specifically target minority librarians. ARL's LCDP, the preeminent program, has been highly successful in preparing minorities for leadership positions. The majority of their participants hold managerial positions. Individual libraries should incorporate aspects of this program beyond mentoring that would include professional development and training in the area of management and being paired with an upper-level manager/supervisor for mentoring. Mason and Wetherbee (2004, 192), however, note that "there is no common vocabulary among library educators or professionals about what constitutes the core body of leadership skills." A clear and agreed on definition of "leadership skills," perhaps stated by ALA, is imperative. Having a clear definition of "leadership skills" provides a measuring tool that can be used in the hiring process, as well as in establishing minority-focused training programs. This fits into the first paradigm seeking fairness.

5. **Diversity Training.** Diversity training for all library personnel is a necessity and should include a better understanding of the general population dynamics that libraries are facing. It should be stressed that diversity education and training is an opportunity to learn and does not call into

question a person's ethics or morals. Library directors, deans, and managers should really buy in to this idea to better sell it to all library personnel. This training should be ongoing and not just a one-time occurrence. Mandatory updates or refresher training should be required.

6. **Measuring Diversity Progress.** Measurement is key to ensure the effectiveness and success of any diversity initiative. Without proper measurement it is difficult to convince doubters or supporters of the necessity of those programs, not to mention justifying continuing budget support. In business organizations, areas of internal measurement usually include tracking the parity of the minority employees, their turnover rates, promotion, movement of career path, complaints or grievances, compensation analysis, networking groups, organizational employees' perceptions of organizational culture and environment, leadership behavior and practice, or top management accessibility. External measurement usually examines customer satisfaction, market segments, and success in global markets. Hayles and Russell (1997, 91–95) list six key diversity areas where measurements can be applied: (1) program evaluation—to ascertain the effectiveness in achieving the objectives of the program; (2) representation—to study the population of the organization with respect to the flow of people through it; (3) workplace climate—to examine whether the quality of work life is accessible to all groups and individuals; (4) benchmarks and best practices—to model after the best practices used in leading organizations within or across industry; (5) external reorganization—measuring made by external sources in the form of reputation and ranking in terms of diversity; and (6) relating diversity to overall performance—to examine the correlation between the specific diversity activities and the desired organizational outcomes. A research library, as a suborganization of a parent organization (its university) or a member of a national organization (ALA, ARL) should align its measurements to the overall strategic objectives, as well as to the desired organizational outcomes.

7. **Change in Management Principle.** Libraries should adopt a modified form of Theory Z. Theory Z is a management principle/style that originated in Japan. It is characterized by lifelong employment, and on retirement, retirees are hired part-time (Konata 2003, 428–429). Many baby boomers will retire in the next two to four years, with many more retiring when the youngest millennials enter the workforce. To retain institutional memory, when baby boomers retire, working part-time should be an available option. This may also be attractive to baby boomers, as they are living longer than any previous generation, with many having to supplement their retirement income. These "retirees" can provide guidance for minority librarians in understanding the culture of the organization and what goals to set to establish a path to management.

8. **Bridge Generational Gap.** Generation Xers shouldn't be lost in the discussion of baby boomers and millennials. Generation Xers can help

bridge the gap between baby boomers and millennials. Although smaller in number, generations Xers provide an excellent opportunity for baby boomers to begin to make the transition. "Baby boomers haven't retired yet, but genXers are looking for their positions to be open. A big vacuum in middle- and upper-management will be created when they do retire. For self-preservation, NextGen librarians need to ask their administration if they've set up succession planning and ways to transfer the knowledge of baby boomers when they do retire. NextGen librarians will improve libraries when baby boomers are gone, but we need their knowledge of the organizations!" (Gordon 2005, 46). Baby boomers as well as generation Xers can then integrate millennials, many of whom will be ethnic minorities, within the organization.

CONCLUSION

Although there is still a need for recruiting and retaining minorities to the profession of librarianship, emphasis should also be placed on developing these librarians to become leaders in the profession. Having more minorities in the profession at all levels has become a strategic imperative. Thomas and Ely's third paradigm calls for actions leading to a desired result to ensure that an organization "become more effective in developing and advancing people of color to its upper-middle and executive levels" (Thomas and Gabarro 1999, 213). An organization with a strong commitment to diversity management and an inclusive environment could very well be the most effective tool for attracting and retaining high potential employees.

ALA's Spectrum Initiative falls into Thomas and Ely's first paradigm of increasing the number of minorities to the profession. This is a necessary step but is only the beginning. A recent trend has been to hire multilingual librarians with titles such as the Latino studies librarian or Asian studies librarian. This falls into Thomas and Ely's second paradigm of "access-and-legitimacy." In this paradigm, minorities are hired to reflect the minority population and sometimes work mainly with this population. Although this is also necessary, it is still only half the puzzle. The ultimate goal is to reach Thomas and Ely's third paradigm, which calls for diversity in management and a *complete integration of diversity* within the culture of the organization. ARL's LCDP is the preeminent program with the sole purpose of preparing minorities for leadership positions in the profession. From the 31 LCDP participants who responded to the survey, 23 are managers or supervisors.

In a fable called, "The Giraffe and the Elephant," the giraffe, a master craftsman, builds a home to his family's specifications. It had tall, yet narrow doorways with high ceilings. It was built perfect for a giraffe. One day, the giraffe sees an elephant, another master craftsman, through the window and invites him over. The elephant comes in and admires the giraffe's wood shop and is equally impressed with his work. They are so impressed with each other's work that they decide to work together on various projects. The giraffe excuses himself to take a phone call upstairs and instructs the elephant to make himself at home and get familiar with the wood shop. The elephant takes him up on this offer and begins to look around. Unfortunately, it immediately becomes clear to the elephant that the house is built to the giraffe's specifications because he realizes that he can't get through the doorway because it is too narrow. He can't make it up the stairs because the stairs can't hold his weight. The giraffe returns, and the elephant brings this to his attention. The giraffe suggests the elephant take aerobic classes to lose weight and take ballet classes to become light on his feet (Thomas and Woodruff 1999, 3–4). Obviously, this will not work and, more to the point, should not be expected. A house built to certain specifications will be comfortable only for those with that specification. By building the house to a giraffe's specifications, the giraffe made an assumption that most of us make. He assumed that he would be surrounded by those physically similar to him. Those in management cannot make that same assumption. Diversity in libraries is imperative at each level, and we must all learn to see beyond our limiting belief we have about people who may be different from us.

REFERENCES

ACE, The American Council on Education. 2002. Percentage of public school students of color, 2000–01, http://www.acenet.edu/AM/Template.cfm?Section=Search&template=/CM/HTMLDisplay.cfm&ContentID=7350 (Accessed May 1, 2006.)

Acree, E. K., S. K. Epps, Y. Gilmore, and C. Henriques. 2001. "Using Professional Development as a Retention Tool for Underrepresented Academic Librarians." *Journal of Library Administration* 33 (1/2): 45–61.

Adkins, Denice and Isabel Espinal. 2004. "The Diversity Mandate." *Library Journal* 129 (7): 52–54.

Albanese, Andrew. 2005. "Can Clark Atlanta Program Move?" *Library Journal* 130 (7): 20.

Alsonso-Zaldivar, Ricardo. 2004. "Census Predicts Higher Diversity in Next 50 Years." *Chicago Tribune*, March 18, 2004. Available from EIU Viewswire database www.viewswire.com (Accessed March 22, 2004.)

ARL, The Association of Research Libraries. 2004. About ARL's leadership and career development program. http://www.arl.org/diversity/lcdp/index.html (Accessed May 2, 2006.)

ARL, The Association of Research Libraries. 2004. *ARL Annual Salary Survey 2004–05.* Washington, D.C.: Association of Research Libraries.

ARL, The Association of Research Libraries. 2004. *ARL Annual Salary Survey 2003–04.* Washington, D.C.: Association of Research Libraries.

ARL, The Association of Research Libraries. 2003. *ARL Annual Salary Survey 2002–03.* Washington, D.C.: Association of Research Libraries.

ARL, The Association of Research Libraries. 2002. *ARL Annual Salary Survey 2001–02.* Washington, D.C.: Association of Research Libraries.

ARL, The Association of Research Libraries. 2001. *ARL Annual Salary Survey 2000–01.* Washington, D.C.: Association of Research Libraries.

Caldwell, Alicia A. 2005. Texas now a majority-minority state: Texas becomes fourth state to have non-white majority population, U.S. Census bureau reports: ABCNews. com. http://abcnews.go.com/US/wireStory?id=1027640&page=1 (Accessed March 7, 2006.)

Census Bureau. 2000. Population by race and Hispanic or Latino origin, for all ages and for 18 years and over, for the United States: 2000. http://www.census.gov/population/ cen2000/phc-t1/tab01.pdf (Accessed April 4, 2006.)

De la Pena, Kathleen, and Kate Lippincott. 1997. "Library Schools and Diversity: Who Makes the Grade? (Cover Story)." *Library Journal* 122 (7): 30–32.

Espinal, Isabel. 2003. "Wanted Latino Librarians." *Criticas* 3 (5): 19–24.

Frey, William H. March 2006. Diversity Spreads Out: Metropolitan Shifts in Hispanic, Asian, and Black Populations since 2000. Brookings Institution. http://www.brookings. edu/metro/pubs/20060307_Frey.pdf (Accessed March 7, 2006.)

Generation X: Americans Born 1965 to 1976. 2004. *The American Generations Series.* Ithaca, N.Y.: New Strategist Publications.

Gordon, Rachel Singer, 2005. "The 'Bridge' Generation." *Library Journal* 130 (19): 46.

Gordon, Rachel Singer, and Sarah Nesbeitt. 1999. "Who We Are, Where We're Going." *Library Journal* 124 (9): 36.

Hart, Margaret. 1997. *Managing Diversity for Sustained Competitiveness. Conference Board Report; no. 1195–97-ch.* New York: Conference Board.

Hayles, V. Robert, and Armida M. Russell. 1997. *The Diversity Directive: Why Some Initiatives Fail and What to Do About It.* Madison, Wis.: ASTD; London: McGraw Hill.

Howland, J. 1999. "Beyond Recruitment: Retention and Promotion Strategies to Ensure Diversity and Success." *Library Administration and Management* 13 (1): 4–14.

Josey, E. J. 1993. "The Challenges of Cultural Diversity in the Recruitment of Faculty and Students from Diverse..." *Journal of Education for Library & Information Science* 34 (4): 302.

Konata, LaLoria. 2003. "Theory Z." In *Encyclopedia of Public Administration and Public Policy,* ed. David A. Schultz, 428–429. New York: Facts On File: London.

"A Lot of Satisfaction but not Much Room for Advancement." 1994. *Library Journal* 119 (18): 48.

Mason, Florence M., and Louella V. Wetherbee. 2004. "Learning to Lead: An Analysis of Current Training Programs for Library Leadership." *Library Trends* 53 (1): 187–217.

McCook, Kathleen de la Pena, Kate Lippincott, and Bob Woodard. 1997. "Planning for a Diverse Workforce in Library and Information Science Professions." Variation: Eric reports; ED 402 948. Tampa, Fla.: University of South Florida, School of Library and Information Science, Research Group.

The Millennials: Americans Born 1977 to 1994. 2004. Edited by New Strategist editors. *American Generations Series.* Ithaca, N.Y.: New Strategist Publications.

Musser, Linda R. 2001. "Effective Retention Strategies for Diverse Employees." *Journal of Library Administration* 33 (1/2): 63.

NCES, National Center for Education Statistics. 2000–2001. *Public School Student, Staff, and Graduate Counts by State—School Year.* Washington, D.C.: U.S. Dept. of Education, Office of Educational Research and Improvement. Serial, LCCN: sn 94–28350. http://nces.ed.gov/pubs2002/2002348.pdf (Accessed April 26, 2006).

NCES, National Center for Education Statistics. 2004. Master's degrees conferred by degree-granting institutions, by sex, racial/ethnic group, and major field of study: 2002–03. http://nces.ed.gov/programs/digest/d04/tables/dt04_266.asp (Accessed April 4, 2006.)

NCES, National Center for Education Statistics. 2004. Master's degrees conferred by title iv institutions, by race/ethnicity, field of study, and gender: United states, academic year 2003–04. http://nces.ed.gov/das/library/tables_listings/show_nedrc.asp?rt=p&tableID = 2078 (Accessed April 4, 2006.)

Oder, Norman. 2004. "IMLS Gives $14.8m for Recruiting." *Library Journal* 129 (13): 18–18.

Offord, Jerome. 2004. "ARL Recruits Minority Undergraduates to Research Librarianship." *ARL Bimonthly Report* 233 (April 2004). http://www.arl.org/newsltr/233/recruit.html (Accessed April 2, 2006.)

Stevens, Jen and Rosemary Streatfeild. 2003. *Recruitment and retention.* Spec kit, 276. Washington, DC: Association of Research Libraries, Office of Leadership and Management Services.

Thomas, David. 2001. "The Truth about Mentoring Minorities: Race Matters." In *Harvard Business Review on Managing Diversity.* Boston, Mass.: Harvard Business School Publishing.

Thomas, David A., and Robin J. Ely. 2001. "Making Differences Matter: A New Paradigm for Managing Diversity." In *Harvard Business Review on Managing Diversity,* 33–66. Boston: Harvard Business School Press.

Thomas, David A. and John J. Gabarro. 1999. *Breaking Through: The Making of Minority Executives in Corporate America.* Boston: Harvard Business School Press.

Thomas, R. Roosevelt, and Marjorie I. Woodruff. 1999. *Building a House for Diversity: How a Fable about a Giraffe and an Elephant Offers New Strategies for Today's Workforce.* New York: AMACOM.

Wilder, Stanley. 2003. *Demographic Change in Academic Librarianship.* Washington, D.C.: Association of Research Libraries.

Women and Diversity: WOW! Facts 2002. 2002. Washington, D.C.: Business Women's Network.

V

COMMUNITY COLLEGE AND SCHOOL PERSPECTIVES

11 COMMUNITY COLLEGE LIBRARIES/ LEARNING RESOURCE CENTERS MEET THE GENERATION Y CHALLENGE

Michael D. Rusk

The Community College library/learning resource center (LRC) is undergoing rapid change from forces in our society at large that could well alter the entire appearance and core mission of the service once called the "heart of the college," and the "center of learning."

Changes on community college campuses related to generation Y are a part of a much larger context of sweeping cultural change brought on by revolutionary advances in networking and information technology. In the library/LRC there is a push to reinvent traditional processes and practices to accommodate new avenues of service. In this chapter we examine the impact of generation Y students on libraries/LRCs in community colleges, with attention to the overall context of technological innovation that is happening in academic libraries nationwide. Basic assumptions about materials, space, and staffing are being questioned by library administrators that have set out to keep the library/LRC a vital part of the learning process. Change has come from three directions.

First there have been changes to the overall learning environment on campus. Libraries/LRCs in the 1980s and 1990s witnessed fragmentation of their services as a result of the formation of learning laboratories, testing centers, and other specialized learning environments. Campus-wide area networks became avenues for college portals and courseware management systems. These network-based information tools have further marginalized the role of the library/LRC by placing it side by side with other campus services all contending for the student's attention. The name learning resource center has become just a label on the campus information network, not the center any longer and certainly not the heart of the college.

Next, there has been a fundamental shift to digital information. Electronic materials first appeared in the form of online access to information resources such as DIALOG, Newsbank, and others, which required only a personal computer (PC) and a modem to search and retrieve citations and abstracts. These databases grew into the aggregated resources of today with a brief existence along the way in CD-ROM format. Ebscohost, Proquest, CINAHL, and others are now attached to library/LRC Web sites accessible on the information highway to those with authorization to use them.

The way in which today's libraries/LRCs deliver information today differs from in the past. Electronic resources can now easily be made accessible college-wide and to students studying from home. They can be accessed by the student having lunch in the college cafeteria, the faculty member planning assignments from home, or the librarian teaching database skills in the classroom. Electronic information is delivered over networks "anytime/anywhere" and the librarian is a very small part of the process. Indeed, in recent years some students comment that they never visit the library during their college stay.

Finally, there has been a change in the ways in which library/LRC space is used by learners. There remains a great need on campus for well-planned study space, and the library/LRC is often the first place to which students turn when they need a place to study either alone or in small groups. Faculty are comfortable bringing their students to the library/LRC for instruction in use of materials or for class meetings using specialized resources. Comfortable study areas with appropriate lighting and some provision for privacy for both individuals or groups is a primary service offered by the library/LRC, and studies show that students don't feel that they find this comfort level elsewhere on campus.

In this chapter we examine the traits of generation Y students and the ways in which libraries/LRCs will need to adapt to the learning habits of this diverse and active group. A number of studies have been done to discern the unique characteristics of generation Y, or millennials, and speculate as to their long-term effect on society. We examine some of these studies in view of the effects of generation Y students on libraries/LRCs in community colleges. Rather than examine the entire range of services offered by a library/LRC program, we seek a few key areas in which the effects of generation Y may be felt the most strongly and in which librarians and administrators may need to emphasize when reinventing traditional library/LRC processes.

The task of this chapter is to demonstrate that changes resulting from the unique traits of generation Y students can be understood only in a larger context of institutional and cultural change resulting largely from advances in the ways in which text, images, and data are captured, stored, transmitted, and used in our culture at large. Generation Y did not invent the computer and network revolution. It has been their inheritance from previous generations, but they have found uses for information that no one had dreamed of before and promise to take technology in newer directions in the future. So what are the unique traits of generation Y and what might their effect be on community college campuses?

GENERATION Y DEFINED

A new generation came of age with the millennium and is wasting no time making their presence known on college campuses. Their impact is so compelling that librarians have had to race to keep up with the innovations adopted by generation Y in the short period in which this age group has graduated from high school and gone on to higher education or into the workforce. A number of studies have been carried out to isolate the unique traits of the "my pod" and "game" generation and one common theme seems to appear. They are extremely comfortable with technology and have high expectations for putting it to use as part of their adult lives.

For our purposes the definition of generation Y as given by Neil Howe and William Strauss in their definitive work entitled *Millennials Rising: The Next Great Generation* is useful for defining generation Y in terms that might allow some applications for library services to this unique group of users.

Called millennials, the echo generation, and a plethora of other labels, this generation of young people was born between 1982 and 2002 (Howe and Strauss 2000). They are sometimes called the Class of 2000, and they have already made a significant impact on the information world in two key areas.

First, they are deeply connected to the Internet and the rich multimedia experiences that are available in cyberspace. Participatory Web sites such as MySpace are natural draws for an age group that grew up with video games, digital cameras, and e-mail. Studies have shown that college students overwhelmingly turn first to the Internet as an information source, finding in Google, Wikipedia, and the obscure information in niche Web sites a far more convenient way to research a topic than traditional library discovery methods. The Internet is considered ubiquitous and they expect to use it fully as part of their experience in college. Libraries/LRCs have added desktop workstations to already crowded reference areas in an effort to provide adequate access to students who come to the library and go straight to the Internet.

The second early impact of generation Y has appeared in the form of "social computing." An age group that is comfortable with networked linkages between themselves and their peers has quickly developed new forms of communication that address their specific needs. From blogs to the blogosphere took only a few years as young people naturally use this form of online journal for serious information sharing. Some librarians have experimented with blogs as a way to move their service closer to their users. Early results seem positive, as any effort to move library services into the new social computing spaces used by generation Y will be a step forward. Traditional library services built around OPACs and reference desk may well need to change just to get the attention of generation Y students who would much prefer to be "on the net."

In the remainder of this chapter we use existing research and models to find traits of generation Y that may apply to their use and support of libraries. The relevancy of academic libraries to a generation raised with electronic texts and networking may depend on realizing that the library is only one of many learning spaces available to students on campus and in the community. What is the quality of the library as a learning space? What makes the library/LRC unique in an era where information is accessed anytime/anywhere? Is the library/LRC the "heart of the college" to a generation that considers the Internet authoritative and far more convenient? The answers to these questions will form a basis to reinvent libraries /LRCs for a new generation.

GENERATION Y AND LIBRARY/LRC PLANNING

The basic equation of academic library service is changing. Traditional libraries have clustered their services around a set of transactions that involve users coming to the library and somehow leaving with the information needed. Collections of books and periodicals were made accessible through the library catalog and information transactions, such as checking out books or media, photocopying periodical articles, and arranging interlibrary loans were the primary means by which libraries delivered information. Browsing the bookshelves, talking to reference staff, reserving a book, or paging through a newspaper were useful things that added to the user's experience, but the primary transaction involved "getting something" and taking it out of the library.

With the advent of electronic text, the entire transaction has changed for library patrons. The genie is now out of the bottle and a transaction is no longer required by users to access library offerings in the form of electronic databases, full-text periodical indexes, and e-books. The notion of "going to the library" is quickly passing away as information is available to authenticated users over networks in many locations on campus. Today students may be expected to make full use of networked information and will use the library if it is convenient and provides other services, such as reference assistance, that make a visit worthwhile.

Generation Y is the most studied generation in history. A great deal of research has been done to attempt to draw boundaries around the unique characteristics of generation Y, and much of this research applies to library/LRC planning. Organizations such as the Pew Internet and American Life Project and the research firm Greenberg, Quinlan, Rosner Research Inc., are among a number of groups that have gathered data on the habits, tendencies, and preferences of young Americans ages 18 through 25. These data are used by library planners to understand their younger users and reinvent libraries/LRCs to meet their unique needs.

For our purpose we look closely at the work of Stephen Abram and Judy Luther in their article "Born with the Chip" (2004). The authors listed nine fundamental differences between generation Y and their older peers in the use of information and potentially their use of libraries.

1. Format agnostic
2. Nomadic
3. Multitasking

4. Experiential
5. Collaborative
6. Integrated
7. Principled
8. Adaptive
9. Direct

Abram and Luther (2004) were able to expand on each generation Y trait and then suggested its impact on information and library use. In considering the impact of generation Y on library/LRC services in community colleges, three of Abram and Luther's fundamental differences bear closer inspection.

Nomadic

Library/LRC planners will do well to keep in mind that the younger generation of information seekers have high expectations for networked information services. Generation Y is the most "linked" age group to appear on college campuses. They are connected electronically via cell phones, instant messaging (IM) and e-mail to their parents, their friends, and their work and they expect seamless connections to instructors and campus services on a continuous basis. Pew Internet and American Life Project, 2005, studied the communication patterns of youth ages 12–17 and found that most took networking technology for granted and relied on cell phones and computers as a part of daily life.

> An overwhelming majority of all teenagers, 84%, reported owning at least one personal media device, a desktop or laptop computer, a cell phone or a Personal Digital Assistant (PDA). 44% say they have two or more devices, while 12% have three and 2% report having all four of those types of devices. (Lenhart et al. 2005, ii)

The same report found that IM has become the digital communication medium of choice for teens and that about half of those who reported using IM, roughly 32 percent of all teens surveyed, use it every day primarily to talk to their friends and to stay in touch with parents.

As community colleges move closer to a distance learning model of instructional delivery, students who are accustomed to being linked using technology will have an advantage over those who are not. The possibilities for librarians to deliver services directly to students using new network and communication technologies are endless. Even old-fashioned e-mail is being explored for its ability to interact with users. Some innovations have come about in the areas of virtual reference and delivery of streamed media to portable devices, but more will come as generation Y librarians advance strongly into the workplace and bring their personal productivity and linking devices to the library/LRC.

Multitasking

Generation Y is growing to adulthood in a busy world where complexity is natural and success is measured by how well one is able to navigate personal, educational, and work environments. Community colleges have always provided coursework for students who take classes while maintaining employment and family responsibilities. The growth of distance learning in the form of Internet-delivered courses, videoconference classes, and instructional television represent efforts by two-year institutions to provide instruction to people on the go and juggling many priorities. Instructional services that cater to the "mobile student" may well be the leading edge of planning in today's community colleges.

Libraries/LRCs have supported distance learning efforts by making electronic resources accessible via the library Web site to students studying off-campus, and recent applications of virtual reference for students have shown some success. Generation Y librarians will make their most immediate impact around the library/LRC by implementing communication schemes based on technology to reach students where they are studying. Michigan State University librarian Emily Barton has done an interesting experiment using a blog to make the reference desk information more accessible to other staff. The experiment was so successful that it led to the creation of several new blogs as staff found that newsletters, grant information, and other professional activities could be shared in this format (Barton and Wesmantel 2006).

Doing several things at once is a defining characteristic of generation Y, and librarians can anticipate greater use of electronic resources and a precipitous decline in the use of traditional print material, as these sources may be perceived as cumbersome and inconvenient. Print resources are also not accessible via a courseware management system, such as Blackboard, which makes it possible for students to access assignments, grades, and e-mail as well as search electronic resources all from the same platform. Librarians may anticipate that multitasking students will use information in the most seamless and convenient form in which it can be found in a "linked" world. This will leave most traditional print resources sitting unused on the library shelves.

Collaboration

Generation Y is adapted to group learning environments. Throughout secondary school, this age group has been encouraged to learn together and to benefit from discovery of new information originating from interaction with their peers. This is the primary reason for millennials' quick adoption of new technology. One will find something interesting and it is quickly shared with friends. New devices are understood and mastered by sharing knowledge, and interesting new features are communicated from one friend to another as quickly as they are discovered. Librarians can expect generation Y students to have an extended support group that is always "on." Instant messaging, cell phones, and e-mail make it possible to have a continuous conversation with friends throughout a busy day. Libraries/LRCs will need to search for ways to enter this world and make it comfortable and convenient for students to interact with a reference librarian on information needs as easily as they would with a friend. In this area as well, generation Y librarians will develop processes and linkages with their students that use networked communication devices to extend services and material to students whenever they choose to study.

What Generation Y Students Want

Authors Susan Gardner and Susanna Eng carried out a study in 2003 of undergraduates at the University of Southern California to determine how often students used the college library, their level of satisfaction with services and suggestions for improvement (Gardner and Eng 2005). Their findings are useful for discerning the effects of generation Y students on the changing information environment of the academic library. We consider their results in light of community college libraries/LRCs.

First it was discovered that generation Y students have great expectations both of themselves and of their higher educational experience. Howe and Strauss claim: "Millennials are the first generation since World War II to be confronted with higher academic standards than the last generation and to show early signs of meeting those standards" (Howe and Strauss 2000, 11).

Librarians can expect generation Y students to be motivated in their learning. They will likely want to do multimedia presentations for their classes and will gladly try out new databases and electronic resources as the library/LRC makes them available. Librarians will need to have some multimedia savvy to help these students and technical support will need to be readily available.

Next Gardner and Eng found that students expect a customized learning experience. At today's community college, the library/LRC is part of a campus environment that includes specialized learning labs, testing centers, computer labs, and other learning spaces. For today's students a visit to the library/LRC may be only a small part of an otherwise busy day, and they will expect to make that trip as worthwhile as possible. Gardner and Eng found that only 36 percent of their students come to the library to check out a book; the majority (61.3 percent) come to use a computer to complete an assignment. College computing resources for students must be conveniently located throughout the campus. The library/LRC may provide customized services in the form of reference assistance and technical support that will draw students in when they might otherwise choose to work from home.

Gardner and Eng also found that generation Y students are technology veterans. There may be a reason for this in an area seldom explored by library planners. Millennial students have been dubbed the "game" generation largely because they grew up with video games as one of their main preoccupations. Indeed, the experience of playing interactive videogames could frame the technology experience for millennial students in a dynamic way that is a departure from the outlook of previous generations. In their book *Got Game: How the Gamer Generation is*

Reshaping Business Forever, authors John C. Beck and Mitchell Wade explore the idea that for Generation Y "games have begun to displace the defining boomer technology television" (Beck and Wade 2004, 11). The authors further say that gaming represents a different view of problem solving itself and that failure to win is not a big deal; one can always go back to the last "save" and try again: "The basic transaction is hitting the right sequence of buttons at the right moment" (Beck and Wade 2004, 21).

Part of generation Y's inherent attachment to the Internet may have to do with its resemblance to an interactive game environment. One follows a mysterious path through the information, encountering characters and surprises and using clues to unlock secrets.

In learning experiences generation Y students demonstrate an ability to focus on immediate matters and to quickly move between tasks. These skills plus the attitude of trial and error in exploring information and technology are deeply held cognitive styles that millennials will bring to their higher education experience and will tend to use learning systems and environments that make use of this skill set and style of thinking.

The Gardner and Eng study also found that generation Y students tend to rely heavily on modes of communication that differ from previous generations. Not only do they tend to work in collaborative groups that learn by creatively pooling the ideas of those present, but generation Y students are in continuous contact with an extended peer group of friends and others that may be called on via cell phone or IM to assist with problem solving. Howe and Strauss point out that generation Y is the most racially and culturally diverse generation yet in the United States. Children from many ethnic backgrounds have grown up with each other and are far more comfortable interacting with their peers than were the baby boomers or generation X. This trait may be the single factor that enriches the communication style of generation Y students and workers. The positive implications of this diversity are immense and community colleges should be prepared to encourage in every way the spirit of cooperation and mutual understanding that this diverse generation brings to adult America.

LIBRARY/LRC AS LEARNING SPACE

Today's community colleges have well-developed learning areas across the campus. Language labs, testing centers, film editing suites, and math labs are only a few of the forms of specialized learning spaces that have been created to serve the needs of disciplines that use technology to supplement classroom lecture. In addition to learning labs, the traditional lecture classroom has been reinvented by installing video projectors, document cameras, and microcomputers so that instructors can bring the power of computer based multimedia to their lectures. Many classrooms are further enhanced with a connection to the college-wide area network for access to streamed video for use in class. The same network will connect the classroom to the Internet, allowing the rich content of hundreds of Web sites to be directly accessed by the instructor and students.

The library/LRC is part of a continuum of enriched learning spaces on campus. Connections can exist between the library/LRC and language labs on campus for the exchange of resources and technology. Often it is the library/LRC media department that provides technical support for video units, projectors, and other equipment in classrooms and labs also maintaining parts inventories and spare equipment to keep these areas running smoothly.

Generation Y students may be expected to find the learning spaces that feel best to them among a variety of options on campus. They will seek assistance in the library/LRC in making multimedia presentations that will be presented using the microcomputer and projection system in their classroom, and they may be expected to want to mix digital text and media to make electronic term papers and research projects. The library/LRC is in a unique position to provide this level of creative and information-rich learning environment.

Evaluating the Library/LRC

What factors may bring millennial students into the library/LRC? To make this evaluation we use the model developed by Stephen Kaplan and Rachel Kaplan, which they call Cognitive Determinants of Environmental Preference, to devise processes whereby the library/LRC may tailor its learning space to the unique needs and traits of today's students (Kaplan and Kaplan 1982).

Coherence

The first determinant of a learning environment concerns the ease with which the setting can be cognitively organized by those who use it. How long does it take to learn where useful resources are located? Where are natural places to study or work in small groups? The degree to which a student senses an intuitive order and a feeling of belonging is a major factor in deciding where they will spend their learning time.

Generation Y students will visit the library/LRC if it seems to be an area that is specially for them. Howe and Strauss observed that:

Not since the Progressive Era, near the dawn of the 20th century has America greeted the arrival of new generation with such a dramatic rise in adult attention to the needs of children. (Howe and Strauss 2000, 22)

Libraries/LRCs will need to think of creative arrangements of study areas so that students with laptops can easily access college systems and online resources. Assistance from librarians will be most effective if they are able to interact with the same social computing systems that students use and if librarians are ready and prepared to understand the unique role that blogs and IM play in their students lives.

Complexity

The second determinant for a learning space involves the perception that a user forms about the effectiveness of the area. Will it catch their interest? Will it be a stimulating and fascinating place to go and spend time? Is this really a place that will help me become more than I am? After all, that is the reason students come to college, and generation Y will expect to find their higher education experience interesting and perhaps even fun. This is an age group that expects a lot from themselves and will expect even more from their instructors, librarians, and others they meet in college. Studies show that this generation will not tolerate boredom for very long and can turn in many directions for amusement and diversion.

The library/LRC must be prepared to add some novelty to its range of services. It will take more than just a Starbucks café to get the attention of millennial students, and the main challenge faced by librarians today is to make learning an interesting and enjoyable experience and to make the library/LRC the first place students think of when wanting a rich learning environment that is there especially for them.

Legibility

This determinant of preference is the student's perceived ease of use. Does the library/LRC make it easy to find things that are needed? Are the service desks placed so that users can easily ask assistance? Is the library/LRC catalog easy to locate and use?

Generation Y grew up in an era that featured teen celebrities, hundreds of TV channels, and sneaker lights with replaceable batteries. It's a world where everything worth investigating has a Web site. The network is now the primary focus of user attention, and the library/LRC Web site needs to show up well against the colorful and dynamic information background that confronts millennial students. The Web site must handle authentication well, allowing students to get to the resources they need quickly and with a minimum of "signing in." It is good to remember that convenience and speed are what today's undergraduates want from information sources. Whatever resource is good enough and quickly delivered will find generation Y students using it heavily.

Mystery

The final determinant for environmental preference according to Kaplan and Kaplan is the unknown. Will this environment show me things I didn't know before? Is it a space worth exploring? Is this place worth the effort to learn, navigate, and exploit?

The challenge for community colleges has been to provide instruction on an anytime-anywhere basis. This has taken the form of providing off-campus courses delivered over cable television or, most recently, the Internet. Libraries/LRCs are able to support these courses with full-text periodical databases and other research aids to give the student at home the tools needed to carry out their courses. Virtual reference services have been implemented to provide direct assistance to students working late at night or to students on the go and not able to come to the library/LRC.

The electronic text has changed the entire way that libraries/LRCs are used in a networked world. These files are portable, sharable, and searchable in ways that traditional print resources are not. Electronic texts can be cut and pasted into another text or a multimedia presentation with a few button clicks and can be shared with a group of peers just as easily.

The "anytime-anywhere" learning delivery challenge is the place where the library/LRC needs to focus. The challenge of crafting services to students studying off-campus has become the challenge of serving the mobile user. This is the user that is fitting studies into a busy social and working day. In this area more than any other, libraries/LRCs must rise to the challenge posed by the mobile user. Here is where the mystery of the learning environment will be sensed by millennial students.

CONCLUSION: BEYOND ANYTIME/ANYWHERE

The community college library/LRC no longer holds the center stage for resources and services that it once held on campus. This fact is further complicated by the fluidity of electronic resources, which has made it possible for the "electronic library" to exist anywhere on campus where there are adequate computing resources to access it. Book and periodical collections are experiencing a decline in usage as students are more mobile today than ever and expect things like distance and platform compatibility not to be barriers in getting the information they need.

Libraries were created for services related to the traditional printed page. The electronic page, however, has a different existence and generation Y understands this in ways that previous generations fail to clearly see. Electronic resources will only grow in complexity in the future as XML, metadata, and other developments extend the uses and functionality of digital documents. A recommendation for librarians is to enlist the aid of students with trials of new electronic information products, e-books, and finding tools. The ability of millennial students to learn by trial and error will be invaluable in testing the fit of new electronic resources before they are implemented.

The anytime/anywhere goal of information delivery has been achieved by libraries/LRCs that have developed rich Web sites for accessing their electronic resources. Students can now access resources on campus, at home, or on the road and most library/LRC Web sites provide click-through linkages to the shared resources of consortia, local public libraries, and other sources. We must keep in mind, however, that generation Y students have high expectations and may well take this paradigm to a higher level. The Internet has raised the bar of ease for search and display of information and provides access to information sources such as digital data libraries that the academic library tends to avoid.

Generation Y students, librarians, and now faculty will expect information access to be absolutely transparent. Claims such as anytime/anywhere will seem outmoded, as it is assumed that there are no time or distance barriers to information that is delivered over networks. The barriers perceived by millennial students exist in the social area, and access to individuals and related information may be the next challenge. With information able to take a variety of forms from streams of pure data pouring out of sensors, to data warehouses maintained by private organizations, and even continuously changing data related to everything from airline ticket sales to financial data, the barriers to today's tech-savvy students lie in gaining access by knowing the right paths and protocols to find the information they desire. From an anytime/anywhere paradigm, generation Y students will push libraries and other information providers toward an anyone/anything access model and will find, and possibly help create, an information society that truly has no barriers.

Remember, to college students today, the Internet is an old-fashioned technology. They have their eyes on tomorrow.

REFERENCES

Abram, Stephen, and Judy Luther. 2004. "Born with the Chip." *Library Journal* 129 (8): 34–37.

Barton, Emily, and Arlene Wesmantel. 2006. "Reflogs Now: Internal Web Logs Can Rejuvenate Reference." *Library Journal* 131 (16): 28–30.

Beck, John C., and Mitchell Wade. 2004. *Got Game: How the Game Generation Is Reshaping Business Forever.* Boston, Mass.: Harvard Business School Press.

Gardner, Susan, and Suzanna Eng. 2005. "What Students Want: Generation Y and the Changing Function of the Academic Library." *Libraries and the Academy* 5 (3): 405–420.

Howe, Neil, and William Strauss. 2000. *Millennials Rising: The Next Great Generation.* New York: Vintage Books.

Kaplan, Stephen, and Rachel Kaplan. 1982. *Cognition and Environment: Functioning in an Uncertain World.* New York: Praeger.

GQR + Polimetrix Youth Monitor. 2005. *Coming of Age in America.* Greenberg, Quinlan, Rosner & Research Inc.: Washington D.C., June.

Lenhart, Amanda, Mary Madden, and Paul Hitlin. 2005. *Teens and Technology: Youth Are Leading the Transition to a Fully Wired and Mobile Nation.* Washington, D.C.: Pen Internet and American Life Project.

12 "I WANT IT ALL AND I WANT IT NOW!": THE CHANGING FACE OF SCHOOL LIBRARIES

Lesley Boon

The role of the school library and the school librarian has changed radically in the last decade. A recent article by Horton (2006) entitled "Collaboration: the virtual and real world. What muggles don't know" about letterboxing, geocoaching, and bookcrossings is apt to make one check to see if one is actually reading a journal designed for school libraries, or a sci fi magazine. Libraries have changed a great deal from the days when it was quiet as a graveyard and students were expected to read silently, speak in whispers, and take notes by hand. Access to material through the librarian, the card catalog, an encyclopedia, or printed periodical indexes is either changed or has taken on a new guise. Doing research still takes time; it's just in a different format; it tends to come in a one-stop shop instead of specialty shops. Searching for information tends be a self-help rather than sought after intervention.

Walking into a school library we are confronted with banks of computers and diminishing shelves. Students can be seen tapping away on a computer with several screens open, talking to fellow students, and listening to the latest music on their i-pods; and then there is the ubiquitous mobile phone. On screen they could be watching a movie or program for English, history, or drama, which is running off a file server somewhere in the school. They could be using an online encyclopedia, a database that includes full text journals and books that they can e-mail to themselves at home or save to their flash drives or USB sticks. They may have picked up a half-finished essay that is housed on the school intranet or be looking at the next assignment that the teacher has posted on the intranet or asking a teacher online a specific question about an assignment. They could equally be selling stuff on eBay or chatting to friends they met while overseas, making a date for Saturday night, or they could be blogging. There may even be the occasional student reading a book.

The new generation of library user wants it all and wants it now! The generation in question, some call millennials or NextGens, is made up of people born between 1982 and 2002 (Abram and Luther 2004). A growing amount of literature describes this generation.

> They are growing up connected to the world and each other; they use technologies fearlessly and seamlessly to communicate with known and unknown others and to shape their lives; they are action-oriented problem solvers and see technology as their primary tool; they define their identities by shared interests and experiences, not race, class, gender or locale; they herald creative thinking, empowerment, and, problem-solving as key qualities in the new global economies; they see themselves as competent pioneers in their personal and shared futures. Those not actually born within this generation...are inevitably and forever outsiders to the ways of being and thinking that identify the Millennials. (Henri and Asselin 2005, 3)

We need to take a long hard look at the cultural differences between the library and the library users. "There is an apparent disconnect between the culture of library organizations and that of net gen students" (Lippincott 2005). Librarians need to be aware that students can, to a degree, do their own research because everything appears to be available on screen. They seldom ask for guidance in finding material unless the culture of the school and the library staff encourages it. They consider themselves experienced drivers who do not need assistance. The 2005 Organization for Economic Co-operation and Development (OECD) study, "Are students ready for a technology-rich world," found that student's confidence in independent computer use was high. In 27 of the 32 countries, more males than females reported being confident[1] performing routine tasks. In 2001, "a Pew survey of search engines found 71% of American online teens relied mostly on internet resources for their research, and not a quarter used libraries" (Haigh 2006, 30). In most libraries, circulation numbers and reference questions have plummeted internationally.

"Different generations access information in different ways...the older generations are often undiscriminating in their use of information while teenagers and those in their twenties customize information in highly personal ways to fit in with their life goals" (Gillies 2005, 15). The net gen increasingly use search engines such as Google for information sources rather than seek the online catalogs or databases of scholarly journals (Lippincott 2005). Macinnis's (2006, 6) article about science literacy states "there are a lot of literacies out there" including basic, scientific, economic, technological, and visual to name some. "Most of them [literacies] come back to being able to think critically in an informed way."

Liu's (2005, 700) research found a screen-based reading behavior emerging from use of a digital environment. This behavior is characterized by more time spent on browsing and scanning, keyword spotting, one-time reading, nonlinear reading, and reading more selectively; less time is spent on in-depth reading and concentrated reading. There is a corresponding decrease in sustained attention. General reading ability is lower than it used to be. The Australian Council for Educational Research (ACER) (2005) found a decline in boys' mastery of basic reading comprehension, and the gap is widening between boys and girls. This has implications for how we present information. Organizing and presenting material are easier in single-sex schools where the preferred mode can be addressed. It is much more complex in coeducational schools where both groups are represented.

The library staff must consider the needs of the older user, as well as the technology-savvy student. The classroom teacher and school executive generally do not use information in the same way as students and therefore require a different approach to managing and accessing information. They would normally rely on the more traditional approaches of standard indexes, encyclopedias, and hard copy text. They may need a good deal of guidance and training in the use of the new technologies and their formats.

The role of school libraries is twofold. One is to have accessible the information both staff and students need to be able to fulfill the outcomes required by the school syllabi for that district or state and to encourage the pursuit of personal interests. The other is to provide resources and programs, both formal and informal, to develop in students a lifelong love of literature. These two roles are almost opposed to each other in regard to how a library looks and functions. On the one hand, the library should be shrinking in size as a result of remote accessibility and the virtual library. On the other hand, the collection should be expanding to allow a wider range of reading material that would be of interest to students.

"Information has gone digital...90% of the world's information resides in electronic format" (Johnson 2005, 17). "Today's libraries are much more than book depositories; they are vast information centres, offering access to, and navigation of, terabytes of articles, technical papers, patents, poetry, photographs, and more. Providing books and other catalogued material is only one aspect of the modern library's charter" (Miller 2004). It is part of the school librarian's role to package information in a format that the net gen understands. Part of information management is the gathering of relevant materials, usually online, and putting it together so that students have easy access. School librarians are creating a virtual library with the library Web page. Staff pulls together information that is both timely and relevant to student needs. Searching for this information can be federated so it is gathered together into one place.[2]

The school library can be smaller, as much information resides in virtual, not real space. Physical media have shrunk while the virtual library has expanded. Information can be accessed anywhere inside or outside the school. Ellyard (2001), however, indicates that an effective reading program requires a comprehensive book collection. If we are to maintain reading as part of what we encourage in schools and therefore school libraries, then the fiction collection must grow while the physical size of the information section can shrink as it becomes more accessible in electronic format.

"Libraries provide collections, organized information, systems that promote access, and in-person and virtual assistance to encourage students to pursue their education beyond the classroom" (Lippincott 2005, 1). She states that libraries need to be spaces not just for information gathering and storage but also for information creation and collaboration. They need to be places with access for mobile services that are increasing. Libraries need space for information gathering and storage as well and for information creation and collaboration, including library sponsored blogs and "information commons." *The ability to learn anywhere and at any time has meant rethinking how education is delivered and assessed* (Lippincott 2005, 6).

One of the problems with the plethora of information available today is that too much is available and it is difficult to find what we need. Google purports to answer this need. "We're in an era that's spoiled for choice, so we're grateful for anything that claims to discriminate or order or systematize the universe on our behalf" (Tooth 2006). The problem comes when students, or for that matter anyone searching for information, doesn't go *beyond Google; the search begin and ends at www.google.com.* "The speed with which Google has attained ubiquity is as problematic as it is intoxicating. Perhaps no innovation has been assimilated so wholly, and with so little reflection on how it may change us" (Haigh 2006, 30).

There is so much information available to students today that they must be taught to develop their own information literacy, and staff need to be made to develop their own skills so they can nurture these skills in their students. "The role of the teacher librarian is to ensure that students and teachers are information literate" (Lonsdale 2003, 9).

There are three major components to allowing students to make up their own minds; "mere gathering of information is old-fashioned and obsolete" (McKenzie 2000, 9). "Children need to be taught to think for themselves" (Johnson 2005, 16). These three components are:

1. **Prospecting.** The discovery of pertinent and reliable information, which requires the ability to navigate.
2. **Interpreting.** It is not enough to locate data and information. It needs to be translated into knowledge, insight, and understanding.
3. **Creating good new ideas.** Information literacy includes the development of new insights; good ideas make meaning from what has been prospected and interpreted (McKenzie 2000, 9).

It is the role of the teacher librarian to assist the acquisition of these literacies as part of the school program. It also the role of the teacher librarian to assist students when searching for or synthesizing information to assist where appropriate in formal or informal scenarios. The research of Ross Todd and Carol Kuhlthau has shown how much influence the teacher librarian has had on facilitating learning and particularly information literacy (Hay 2005, 4). "The data reveals that the role of the school librarian is as a dynamic agent of student learning and achievement." It also revealed that the school library serves as resource and technical agents. School libraries also offer the millennials an environment different from the classroom as it honors the learning processes preferred by millennials (Henri and Asselin 2005, 3).

The challenges facing school libraries today is the same in any other modern library. How do we serve our clientele when the face of information and how users seek it are changing so rapidly? In schools the librarian must look at the split that is occurring in the two major user groups. Teaching staff are not able to adapt and change as rapidly as the student body. Staff, particularly older staff, may have difficulty using information in changed formats mainly from print to digital. They need to know how to communicate with the net gens, or they will be discounted as a useful resource by the very students they wish to teach. Students are spending more time at home online than at school. The OECD[3] article (2005, 27) indicates that the majority of 15-year-olds have ready access to computers at home and school. A challenge for staff in school libraries and indeed public libraries is to make sure that students from backgrounds with little or no access to computers can have access and support in the library. These students will not have the sophistication and confidence of those users who have greater accessibility. Librarians can make a difference to these students by guiding them in to use computers as a powerful information tool. The main challenge for library staff facing the net gens is to prove their relevancy so that students will allow themselves to be guided in this brave new world.

NOTES

1. A high level of confidence was indicated by the answer "I can do this very well by myself."

2. A *federated search* is the simultaneous search of multiple online databases and is an emerging feature of automated, Web-based library and information retrieval systems. It is also often referred to as a portal, as opposed to simply a Web-based search engine. http://en.wikipedia.org (accessed August 29, 2007).

3. Organisation for Economic Co-operation and Development, OECD, comprises the governments of 30 democracies who work together to address economic, social, and environmental challenges of globalization. It provides a forum for discussion and comparison about new developments and concerns such as corporate governance, the information economy, and the challenges of an aging population.

REFERENCES

Abram, S., and J. Luther. 2004. "Born with the Chip." *libraryjournal.com* May 1 http://www.libraryjournal.com/article/CA411572.html (Accessed September 9, 2006.)

ACER 2005. International achievement studies: Lessons from PISA and TIMSS. Research Developments, Issue 13, Winter. http://www.acer.edu.au/publications/newsletters/resdev/rd13/RD13_PISA_TIMSS.html (Accessed July 8, 2006.)

ACT, Department of Education and Training. 2005. Emerging technologies: a framework for thinking, final report. http://www.det.act.gov.au/publicat/pdf/emergingtechnologies.pdf (Accessed May 5, 2006.)

Ellyard, P. 2001. *Ideas for the New Millennium*, 2nd ed. Melbourne: Melbourne University Press.

Gillies, M. 2005. "Educational Futures and Information." *Access* 19 (3): 15–17.

Haigh, G. 2006. "Information Idol: How Google Is Making Us Stupid." *The Monthly* 9: 29–32.

Hay, L. 2005. "School Libraries Play Major Role in Helping Students Learn." *Connections* 53 (2): 4.

Henri, J., and M. Asselin. 2005. *The Information Literate School Community 2: Issues of Leadership*. Wagga Wagga, NSW: Centre for Information Studies, CSU.

Horton, R. 2006. "Collaboration: The Virtual and the Real World. What the Muggles Don't Know." *Connections* 58 (3): 1–2.

Johnson, D. 2005. "Building Indispensability: The Virtual Librarian and Other New Roles." *Access: Australian School Library Association* 19 (4): 15–17.

Lippincott, J. 2005. Net Generation Students and Libraries. *Educause*. March/April. http://www.educause.edu/content.asp?page_id=6067&bhcp=1 (Accessed July 8, 2006.)

Liu, Ziming. 2005. Reading Behavior in the Digital Environment: Changes in Reading Behavior over the Past Ten Years. *Journal of Documentation* 61 (6): 700–712.

Lonsdale, M. 2003. *Impact of School Librarians on Student Achievement: A Review of the Research*. Melbourne: ACER.

Macinnis, P. 2006. "Science Literacy and the School Librarian." *Connections* 58 (3): 5–6.

McKenzie, J. (2000). *Beyond Technology: Questioning and the Information Literate School*. Bellingham WA: FNO Press.

Miller, T. 2004. "Federated Searching: Put It in Its Place." *libraryjournal.com* April 15 http://www.libraryjournal.com/article/CA406012.html& (Accessed May 28, 2006.)

Organization for Economic Cooperation and Development, OECD 2005. *Are students ready for a technology-rich world? What PISA studies tell us*. Program for International Student Development (PISA) http://www.pisa.oecd.org/dataoecd/28/4/35995145.pdf (Accessed July 8, 2006.)

Spence, S. 2005. "The Teacher Librarian Toolkit for an Information Literate School Community." In *The Information Literate School Community 2: Issues of Leadership*, eds. J. Henri and M. Asselin, 135–146. Wagga Wagga, NSW: Centre for Information Studies, CSU.

Tooth, G. 2006. *Google Schmoogle*. Interview of Gideon Haigh. ABC radio Australia program 8:30 AM and PM, February 16, 2006.

SELECTED BIBLIOGRAPHY

Australian Government NetAlert Limited: The Australian Government Internet Safety Advisory Body. 2006. http://www.netalert.net.au/ (Accessed June 28, 2006.)

Australian students among the highest users of computers at school and in the home: OECD report. 2006. in ACER Media Release. 25 January 2006 http://www.acer.edu.au/news/documents/PISA_ICT_240106.pdf (Accessed June 28, 2006.)

Barry, W. 1998. *Boys Reading: A School Case Study*. Melbourne: Scotch College

Chapman, W. 2004. "Learning Culture Needed for the New Millennium." *Access* 18 (2): 13–15.

Elliott, A. 2004. "Transforming Learning into Meeting the Challenge of the Digital Age." *Access: Australian School Library Association* 18 (3): 9–12.

Emerging Technologies: A Framework for Thinking. 2005. Canberra: ACT Department of Education and Training. education.au.limited

Learning for the Future: Developing Information Services for Schools. 2001. 2nd ed. Carlton South, VIC: Curriculum Corporation.

Librarians guide to Internet safety: Just some of the ways we can keep young Internet users safe in our libraries. 2005. NetAlert Limited. http://www.netalert.net.au/02083-A-Librarians-Guide-to-Internet-Safety.PDF (Accessed June 28, 2006.)

March, T. 2005. Class act portals. http://tommarch.com/writings/classact_portal_server.pdf (Accessed August 7, 2006.)

McKenzie, J. 1998. Grazing the Net. Raising a Generation of Free Range Students. September, *Phi Delta Kappan* http://fno.org/text/grazing.html (Accessed August 7, 2006.)

Twomey, M. 2003. "Dimensions for Student Learning." *Access: Australian School Library Association* 17 (2): 9–11.

Youngman, D. C. 2002. Re-shaping library service programming: new strategies for the new millennium. 23rd Annual IATUL Conference. Partnerships, Consortia, and 21st Century Library Service. Jointly held by the Linda Hall Library of Science, Engineering and Technology, and the University of Missouri Kansas City, U.S.A. June 2–6, 2002.

VI

SOME EXAMPLES

13 A TRADITIONAL LIBRARY MEETS TWENTY-FIRST CENTURY USERS

Glenda A. Thornton, Bruce Jeppesen, and George Lupone

As with so many other libraries in the late 1990s, Cleveland State University's (CSU) traditional library décor and competition from widely available online information resources were assumed to be obstacles in attracting students to use the library facility. Similar to many other libraries, gate counts were lackluster, book circulation had declined, and fewer questions were asked at the traditional reference desk. Articles such as "The Deserted Library" in the *Chronicle of Higher Education* (Carlson 2001) suggested that academic libraries were no longer critical when "everything" is online. This case study describes how CSU library has undertaken a process of continuous revitalization to attract the new generation of technologically savvy younger users while still meeting the needs of older, more traditional students and faculty.

The literature is full of examples of more affluent academic libraries that were able to adjust quickly to the changing needs of students through major renovations and implementation of the newest technologies; however, resources were not as readily available on the Cleveland State campus. Indeed administrators at CSU were questioning the future role of libraries as were many other university administrators around the country (Shill and Tonner 2003, 432–433). With digital information rapidly increasing in quantity and "freely" available, and with the realization that younger students were always "connected," the thinking seemed to be that perhaps libraries were losing their relevancy. By using available assets, partnering with other campus units, marketing services, assessing the results, and responding to user needs discovered through assessment tools such as LibQUAL+™, however, the CSU library has maintained its vitality and increased its value to the campus. Little by little, the library has been updating the facility and providing new services to all members of the CSU community.

The results? From gate count to the circulation of books, the use of every service has increased even though enrollments have not.

At CSU, resources are precious and must be used wisely. If factors did point to less need for the library and more need for other campus services, then resources should be diverted to where the need is greater. Thus the real question that needed to be answered was, "Is the CSU library no longer a vital campus resource or does it just need to adjust to meet the needs of a new generation of users?"

Articles such as the ones by Shill and Tonner (2003, 2004) confirm that this situation is not unique to Cleveland State. Considered on a broader scale then, the question is, "Is the academic library no longer the intellectual center of the campus, or will continuous updating designed to meet new user demands increase use?" Can cash-strapped universities afford these updates or do article headlines in higher education's literature such as "The Deserted Library" continue to stick in the minds of university administrators, allowing them to justify the reallocation of scarce resources? Will new roles that libraries can offer to campuses, coupled with traditional services, help universities improve student success and increase enrollments? There is significant evidence that "investments in new, enlarged, or renovated library facilities are associated with significant increases in student usage" (Shill and Tonner 2003, 433), but what about less dramatic and more affordable adjustments? Can librarians effectively document the benefits of attractive and service-orientated libraries to university administrators?

By finding ways to meet the needs of new generations of college students, assessing the results, and engaging in continuous improvements, the CSU library has begun to see increased use and improved assessment scores. It is hoped that the experiences of the CSU library in updating the facility, improving the technology, adding nonlibrary functions, improving opportunities for social networking among students, and generally listening to users will be helpful to other academic libraries, both large and small, in addressing similar issues.

BACKGROUND ON THE INSTITUTION

Cleveland State University is a relatively young institution, having been established as a state university in 1964. Its roots, however, extend much further back into Cleveland's history, as it was preceded by Fenn College, a private liberal arts institution established in 1929. Today, Cleveland State offers more than one thousand courses supporting 200 major fields of study from the bachelor's degree through the doctoral degree. Degrees are offered from six undergraduate colleges: the College of Liberal Arts and Social Sciences, the Nance College of Business Administration, the Fenn College of Engineering, The College of Education and Human Services, the College of Science, and the Maxine Goodman Levin College of Urban Affairs. The College of Continuing Education, the College of Graduate Studies and Research, and the Cleveland-Marshall College of Law complete the academic offerings. The Cleveland-Marshall College of Law traces its origins to 1897 when the Cleveland Law School was founded as the first evening law school in the state. In 1946, it merged with another evening law college, the John Marshall School of Law, and the resulting Cleveland-Marshall became part of Cleveland State University in 1969.

These colleges attract approximately 16,000 students each year, primarily from northeast Ohio, although there is also a substantial international student body. Fifty-seven percent of the students are women, 43 percent are men, and the average age is 25. Approximately 27 percent are minorities, with African Americans making up 18 percent. About one-third of the entire student body is in graduate school and the junior class is consistently larger than the freshman class.

THE CSU LIBRARY BEFORE 2000

The Facility

The use of the library facility had been problematic from its opening in 1971. As only one example, the first floor was designed to house technical services, but librarians wisely decided from the outset not to use prime first floor space for behind-the-scenes operations. Unfortunately, however, full use was never made of the first floor space after the library opened, indeed, not until 2004! Through data collection and common sense, but well before the Internet impacted library use, the most egregious functional and cosmetic issues concerning the facility had been addressed. Several floors of the library were recarpeted, but others became threadbare and malodorous after 30 years. Updating the facility became a juggling act. Without the resources for a complete makeover, some areas were improved but others languished.

Technology

The library fared much better in the early provision of technology to the campus community. From the onset, the library and computer center worked together to create state-of-the-art (for the 1960s) acquisitions and circulation systems. As a founding member of the Online Computer Library Center (OCLC), Cleveland State made extensive early use of the system not only for technical services, but also for reference. CSU was also one of the early users of Infotrac, an early member of OhioLINK, and the first university in Ohio to offer online course reserves.

Partnerships

Early partnerships helped the library implement significant innovations. For example, through cooperation with the computer center and CSU law library, the university library was able to implement NOTIS, its first integrated library system in 1989. When the information literacy movement was in its infancy, the library forged partnerships with the faculty to incorporate the principles of information literacy into the curriculum. Specifically, library/faculty groups specified that information literacy would be a component of the freshman composition course. Also, information literacy became integral to the newly developed "Introduction to University Life" course.

Customer Service

Good service was always desired, but user-driven customer service was largely an unknown concept in libraries and at Cleveland State. Staff members, primarily from the baby boom generation or earlier, seemed to set their own code of conduct, believing that simply carrying out their assigned tasks constituted satisfactory performance, without regard for friendliness or courtesy. Consequently, service quality varied from one service point to another and from individual to individual.

REVITALIZATION FOR THE NEW MILLENNIUM BEGINS

Characteristics of Today's College Student

The age of Cleveland State's student body ranges from the traditional 18-year-old college freshman to retirees who attend classes through the Project 60 program. With an average age of 25, many of the slightly older students, who are part of the gen-X cohort, expected an entirely different kind of service philosophy than that offered by the majority of the library's staff. The slightly younger students, born after 1982, are part of the net generation or millennials. They are beginning to replace the gen-Xers as the predominate age group making up the student body. These students are the ones who have been most heavily influenced by information technology before attending college, and they are the group that librarians must now entice to come to the library (Oblinger 2003, 38).

Just as institutions of higher education had begun to understand and adjust to student demands for improved customer service, they have been hit hard, once again, by the totally different expectations of the millennials. Some of the characteristics of this group are obvious to any casual observer. For example, they seem to be always connected—via cell phones or laptop personal computers (PCs). They grew up on computer games and Internet access. Clearly they are hooked on technology and are accustomed to extracting the information they need from a variety of small, wireless devices, anywhere, anytime.

According to Oblinger, millennials prefer group activity, spend more time on homework than TV, value being smart, find new technologies fascinating, feel close to their parents (one of whom is often an immigrant), and share their parents' values (2003, 38). Jason Frand (2000) offers additional insight into the "information-age mindset" of these young people. He reports that they prefer the Internet to TV because it is interactive, and they do not think of computers as technology because they are ubiquitous. They are comfortable with multitasking, prefer to learn from real-life experiences through trial and error rather than applying accumulated facts, have no tolerance for delays (services should be available 24/7), and operate as if digital information belongs to everyone.

Baby boomer librarians and library administrators have gradually begun to develop an understanding of all of these trends and how they impact library services. They have also had to learn to examine their own beliefs and values concerning how library services should be provided. With the gen-Xers, the most dramatic changes revolved around improving service philosophies. With the millennials, it appears that the greatest impact will be on how the library facility and technology evolve to meet their needs. Teaching all of these generations of students about the value of libraries continues to be a primary goal of baby boomer librarians as well as that of recent recruits to librarianship.

Use of the Library

A review of Figure 13.1 shows a little spike in visits to the CSU library from 1997 to 1998. This was probably due to the large number of PCs available in the library before the campus laptop loaner program emerged and PC ownership became so common. The spike also coincides with the remodeling of the entire fourth floor of the library, the largest study and stacks area. Because there were no other major innovations at that time and enrollment had begun to decline, this spike was probably the result of facility improvements and the installation of "the latest" technology. This spike in library use, however, is followed by another gradual decline until the library's efforts to address changing user needs began to be evident. With CSU's enrollment stagnant, it seems reasonable to attribute the

Figure 13.1
A Decade of Library Use

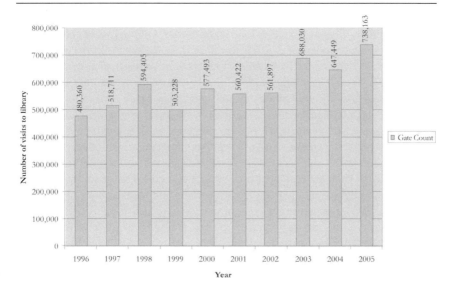

dramatic recent increase in library use to facility improvements, partnerships, and service innovations designed to meet the needs of millennials.

Facility Renovations, 1999–2005

Although late 1998 brought a new director to the university library at Cleveland State, there was very little available data to suggest to the new administration how to continue with improvements needed to attract these younger students to libraries. A facilities report prepared by Aaron Cohen Associates in 1985, although outdated, provided some still relevant data. Immediate and obvious facility issues were a leaky roof and rapidly deteriorating 1970s, orange carpet on two of the library's floors, and a botched recent carpeting installation on the main floor. The director began to petition for replacement of both; however, the university had already taken action to replace the roof by requesting capital funds from the State. This request was approved but the work was not completed until 2005. The university also found the money to replace the carpet on the first three floors of the library. That work began in the summer of 2000 and was completed in early 2001. This carpet installation presented the library with an unanticipated opportunity to make fundamental improvements to the facility.

The university's physical plant had bid the carpet and labor with the provision that the book stacks and furniture would be moved for the carpeting and then moved back into their original positions; however, this was not the vision of the library administration. The 1985 Cohen report identified the library's large, floor-to-ceiling windows, primarily on the first two floors, as major assets, and natural light is well known to be valued by students of all ages. Also, as an urban campus, one of the library administration's ongoing concerns is that all library users feel safe and secure in the building. Thus the library administration had two goals. One was to open up the views to the windows in the study areas to let in the natural light and the other was to rearrange the library stacks to create less isolated study areas. This plan required the rearrangement of the library's book stacks so that the available open study space would be immediately visible to students as they exited from the centrally located elevators. The university's initial response was that this was not possible, as it had not been provided for in the carpet bid and there was no additional money for rearranging the stacks and furniture.

The library's staff immediately went to work and presented the university's physical plant with a plan that allowed the carpeting work to begin in open spaces without the need to move anything. Stacks were then permanently moved to the newly carpeted areas, the vacated spaces were carpeted, and more stacks moved immediately to their permanent positions. As a result, open study spaces with bright, natural light were created. The financial result of this plan was a carpeting bill $10,000 less than originally estimated. The physical plant then allowed the library to use the savings to replace the tall, narrow, heavy, and unwelcoming front doors to the library with a new glass front and wide, automatic doors.

The 1985 Cohen report had identified 1,374 seats in the library; however, the report also indicated that a large variety of the seats were not "behaviorally usable." Even in 1985, it was well known that library seating needed to be friendly and comfortable, creating an environment conducive for study, for working on group projects, and for social interaction. Although all chairs have been reupholstered and the worst ones have received new seats as a result of the report, it has not been possible to replace the entire student seating; however, replacing student seating with new furniture appropriate both for use of laptops and social interaction has become an ongoing objective. In the meantime, rearranging tables and chairs in more usable configurations provided students with vastly improved group study options as well as quiet study space.

Some changes were cheap and fast to make such as painting beige walls a variety of cheerful colors and adding some green plants to counter the frequently heard comments about the dreariness of the interior. An immediate issue for the new director in 1998 was the desire to move the closed current periodicals area and the microforms collection from their remote location on the fourth floor of the library to a location on the library's first floor where the collection would be open to browsing. This move required relocating the library's instruction area to a different floor, creating more offices for reference librarians on the first floor where they could be readily available to students, and creating a semisecured space for the periodicals—renovations that were funded entirely from operating funds and technology fees. They were all completed by the summer of 2002.

A major achievement of this move was the freeing up of two large rooms big enough to house two flexible, state-of-the-art instruction facilities within the library. In one case, a very large and underused meeting room on the library's fifth floor was converted to the first instruction room. Although the room featured new technologies such as a cart of 29 laptops and SmartBoard, at first the instruction and reference librarians were somewhat unhappy with its location so far from the first floor where their offices and the reference collection were located. Initially there was concern that the laptops would be stolen and an elaborate check-out system was designed to ensure that this did not happen. Fortunately, the security of the laptops was less of a problem than anticipated. Soon afterwards, a second instruction room was created from the large, classroom-size office from which the fourth floor periodicals area had previously been managed. Both of these new instruction facilities, among the most modern and flexible on campus, were soon in demand from all segments of the campus for activities ranging from teaching, to retreats, to departmental meetings. In 2006, 628 sessions were held in the two rooms, with 9,521 individuals from the campus community in attendance. An added attraction of the fifth floor teaching room is two walls of floor-to-ceiling windows featuring a spectacular view of both Lake Erie and downtown Cleveland.

The result of just these few physical changes, based on little more than a 20-year-old report and common sense, began to have a positive effect on how the library was viewed on the campus. To begin with, it no longer smelled old! More light came into the building and the front doors were not forbidding. By observation alone and comments made to the library staff, it was clear that the campus community was appreciative of the revitalization that was occurring. Additional physical changes were still needed, but it is unlikely that facility changes alone would have been enough to bring students back into the building.

Technology, 1999–2005

In the late 1990s, CSU had one additional piece of data that provided the library with another initiative. Although many of CSU's millennial students were technically advanced, screening and testing efforts identified many others, often representing the first-generation family member to attend college, who were not. Although the CSU campus had several well-run computer labs managed by the computing center, including one in the library, none of them routinely provided instruction to students without computer skills.

Working closely with the campus office charged with overseeing first-time freshmen, the library proposed using technology fees to create a computer-learning lab with 24 workstations. Named by the student government the "Library Computer Learning Center" or LCLC, it opened in the reference area in the fall of 2000 and was the library's first step toward creating an Information/Learning Commons. What made this lab so different from the other labs on campus was that computer-savvy library employees from a number of departments provided the staffing for the lab.

The initial purpose of the LCLC was to provide free walk-in instruction in the use of *Microsoft Office* suite, e-mail, and help with Internet searching, as well as occasional free training sessions on Word and other popular software products. Almost immediately the value of the LCLC in helping students set up WebCT accounts was also firmly established. Instructors began asking permission to bring entire classes into the LCLC to establish accounts and practice using WebCT. This was the beginning of numerous faculty and staff requests to book the LCLC for occasional class meetings when they needed access to computers. While seeing the value of supporting faculty needs, librarians also realized that this was an excellent opportunity to bring students into the library and introduce them to other services. The rules for scheduling the rooms were kept simple: the faculty member had to accompany the class and the number of class sessions per semester was limited—usually not more than one.

In just a few short years, the ways in which the LCLC is used by students and faculty have rapidly evolved and use of the facility has grown. By keeping the scheduling policies somewhat flexible, the library allowed the function of the LCLC to evolve based on the needs of the campus. The LCLC began to be used routinely for bibliographic instruction; WebCT instruction; freshman advising, registration, and orientation events; taking online tests; virtual lab exercises; software demonstrations; high school student orientations; faculty and student presentations; and seminars and workshops of various kinds. The facility became so popular that a technology fee request was submitted in 2002 to more than double the size of the facility to 58 student workstations in two separate sections and to add a movable SmartBoard that could, on request, be used in either section of the LCLC. Table 13.1 illustrates the ways in which the LCLC has been

Table 13.1

LCLC Combined Events for July 1, 2005–December 31, 2005

Event Type	Sessions	Hours	Attendance
Class session (nonlibrary instruction)	95	164.3	2003
High school class	30	35.6	837
Library instruction (taught by faculty)	4	4.9	85
Library instruction (taught by librarian)	87	112.7	2152
Meeting	7	17.5	45
Other	6	20.5	175
Seminar/workshop	15	73	262
Technology/instruction	7	7.3	52
Total	251	435.8	5621

used by the library and the rest of the campus community. The data show use for the fall semester of 2005. When it is not in use for a scheduled event, the LCLC remains open as a staffed, walk-in computer lab.

At the same time that the LCLC was being developed, the library had to address another technology issue. For years, the library had supplied nearly three dozen computers, many with an attached printer, for students to use to research and print articles and electronic course reserve documents. Users would pay for printing using a Vendamat card system that the library supported. The computers that the library had placed in the reference area were older models that had previously been used by library staff. When a staff computer was replaced with a new computer, the old computer was "handed down" to the reference area. The result was a mismatched group of computers, monitors, and printers that were placed on mismatched desks and tables.

In 2000, the library, using both student technology fees and library funds, began updating the reference computer area. New computers were purchased to replace the handed-down machines, and matching computer desks and chairs were purchased. The area was expanded to its current size of 56 student workstations. The library also improved printing by implementing a Uniprint print cost recovery system and networked, high-speed printers. This new configuration also allowed the library to provide color printing as an option to students. As an added convenience to students, they could now pay for printing with funds on their ID card account, or with cash. This reference computer area has become a heavily used, popular area for students.

Expanded access to word processing, presentation, and spreadsheet software helped meet the needs of many students, but others were also seeking a place to work on multimedia projects. They wanted to scan and edit images, digitize analog video and audio sources, create animations, generate podcasts, and more. To help meet some of those needs, the library added a small number of multimedia computers, scanners, and audio/video capture and editing stations to the third floor multimedia services area. Also added was a modern languages practice and testing lab that was moved into the library from another location. Additional computers were added to run English as a second language software and for students to test a variety of educational K-12-oriented, CD-ROM-based games and software. Staff was trained to assist students with these multimedia workstations, and training workshops for students are conducted on a regular basis.

Partnerships, 1999–2005

A new collaboration and partnership developed in 1999. The university's effort to provide an adaptive technology lab to students with disabilities was floundering. Initially located in the University Center, the hours were limited and the staff charged with running the facility was not proficient with advancing technology. When the library was approached about housing this facility, the library director agreed. A room was located and a library manager was enlisted to oversee this lab. The university provided funding for the staffing and equipment for the adaptive technology lab from technology fees. An additional bonus was realized, as this facility also served the Health Science Department as both a teaching facility and a lab for interns studying adaptive technology. A partnership between the computer center, Disabilities Services, and the Health Science Department demonstrated the value of working together for the good of the campus. The success of this partnership encouraged the library to look for additional partnerships.

Customer Service, 1999–2005

Throughout the 1990s, a "culture of service" burgeoned at universities and in libraries in particular in response to the expectations of the gen-Xers. As the national competition to attract students to campuses increased, excellent customer service became one way that universities were able to differentiate themselves. At Cleveland State, however, students' perception of service was at an all-time low in the last half of the 1990s because of the debacle associated with the local implementation of the PeopleSoft administrative software. Students faced a registration system that all but collapsed, experiencing long lines, cranky overworked university staff, and numerous billing errors. As the administrative systems became stable, campus leaders recognized that customer service needed to become a priority to complement the improvement to administrative systems. Consequently, all campus job descriptions were altered to include a strong customer service component, and the human resources department hired a trainer to assist in creating a culture of customer service. Good customer service became everybody's top priority.

ASSESSING THE RESULTS, 2002–2005

Although the library administration had long been aware that many issues needed to be addressed, the financial means to make these changes, as described previously, was slow in coming. Not only was money in short supply, but some of the older baby boomer library staff members did not understand the need for the changes in services and improved customer service, as they were doing their jobs very professionally. Discrete physical changes, such as carpet replacement in 2000 and 2001, the installation of wireless technology throughout the facility, and a roof replacement in 2005 were met with immediate positive reaction by everyone, but improving customer service training and establishing a more proactive service philosophy throughout the library were more difficult and are ongoing.

Another issue facing the university was the emphasis that the North Central Association began to place on assessment. During its 2000 accreditation review, the association advised the university to put a more effective assessment process in place. The university created a new administrative structure to implement and oversee the university assessment process. Contemporaneously in the library community, the LibQUAL+™ survey of service quality added to the impetus for assessing customer service. "LibQUAL+™ is a suite of services that libraries use to solicit, track, understand, and act upon users' opinions of service quality. The program's centerpiece is a rigorously tested Web-based survey bundled with training that helps libraries assess and improve library services, change organizational culture, and market the library" (LibQUAL+™ 2007).

Customer Service

The library took full advantage of the emerging campus and national emphasis on customer service and assessment. Beginning in 2002, the LibQUAL+™ survey became the cornerstone of the library customer service assessment process as a result of unexpected poor results. The 2002 survey data showed that user perception of customer service at CSU was not as highly rated as at peer libraries. For example, in response to the LibQUAL+™ survey question concerning employees who were consistently courteous, Cleveland State users were less satisfied than users at peer institutions. Using the data, the library administration led a process to improve customer service that included the review of the data with library managers and staff. The library director polled the staff for their ideas to improve customer services. During strategic planning sessions, the library council (consisting of library managers) identified concrete actions that could lead to improved customer service. Subsequent LibQUAL+™ surveys will measure the success of these actions.

The staff initially believed that the underlying customer service issues were structural. Student workers staffed many service points and their depth of knowledge and quality of service were inconsistent. The library administration first worked with managers to address these structural issues. For example, to improve service quality, more full-time staff was assigned to the circulation desk in place of student workers. Managers also assigned their most customer-service oriented staff to service points at the busiest times to increase the impact of their excellent customer service orientation. The new head of circulation (renamed "User

Services") began to work strategic hours at the desk to set the tone for customer service. Although full-time staff covered more desk hours, student workers continued to be an important staff component. To improve their effectiveness, the library director appointed a team to revive a student worker-training program. Through the training program, student workers received continuous training in customer service. The training program has produced results. For example, in the past, student shelvers were not considered public service employees. After examining survey data, however, it became clear that shelvers might be the only staff many users encounter in the library. Shelvers are now aware that customer service is a vital component of their job and they contribute to the overall library culture of customer service.

The staff initially had been less likely to connect their own actions with library users' less-than-desirable satisfaction with customer service. Although the library administration believed that staff training could result in improved customer service, it sought an approach that would not blame the staff for the perceived level of customer service. A plan of action emerged through collaboration with the university's department of human resources on a customer services training program. The initial mandatory workshop in 2002 was entitled "Why are you yelling at me?" This initial workshop in the training series recognized the difficulties of maintaining a professional courteous demeanor while dealing with difficult users on a daily basis. The emphasis of this workshop, as with the following workshops, was to provide staff with customer service-training skills, but the first workshop placed the onus on the user. The concept began to emerge that in addition to being a decent human being, there were a consistent set of skills that staff could master to improve customer service.

The actions taken at Cleveland State to address structural and training issues are but two of many examples of the assessment methodology used for the continuous improvement of customer service. To close the assessment loop, it was desirable to re-administer the LibQUAL+™ survey to determine the effect of the actions taken as a result of the 2002 survey. The survey results from 2003 and 2005 are more positive than the results from the first survey conducted in 2002. When asked about their perception of courteous service in 2002, users rated the library a 6.73 on a 9-point scale. The users rated the library at 7.18 and 7.14, respectively, in 2003 and 2005.

In general, the 2005 LibQUAL+™ survey results were more positive than the previous two surveys. There continued to be some written responses critical of the facility and customer service. In all of the scored categories, however, the perceived service was greater than the perceived minimum desired, and by a greater margin than in the previous surveys, although the library administration had hoped for even more positive results. The written responses, however, have a much less negative tone than on the previous two surveys. In fact, there was a noticeable difference. In the first two LibQUAL+™ surveys, respondents expressed a general dissatisfaction with service. Respondents to the 2005 LibQUAL+™ were more likely to express dissatisfaction with specific individuals.

Facilities

Aside from the new carpeting and new roof that were major capital invest-ments in the first half of the new decade, it was clear that, for the foreseeable future, no other large influx of funds would be earmarked by the university for library renovations. The library staff, however, had learned the value and impact of continuous improvement through smaller, targeted facility innovations that could be managed from the operating budget and technology fee requests. With facility use steadily increasing as a result of the improvements and service innova-tions initiated by the library staff, a whole new atmosphere of achievement and pride began to emerge to drive future planning.

It was also discovered that library users might not always know what they needed until it was experienced. This situation was made clear by comparing the results of the faculty responses to the 2002, 2003, and 2005 LibQUAL+™ sur-veys. When LibQUAL+™ 2002 was administered, the facility improvement had just begun and the faculty rated "the library as place" as meeting their minimal expectations. By spring 2003, the library had moved current periodicals to its new home on the first floor and had completed the two, state-of-the-art instruc-tion rooms in addition to the LCLC. Surprisingly, on the LibQUAL+™ 2003 survey, faculty rated the library facility as exceeding their expectations. By spring of 2005, when LibQUAL+™ was next administered, although a new state-of-the-art Viewing Room was added and the LCLC was doubled in size, faculty no longer rated the library as exceeding their expectations. In fact, one respondent wrote, "The service and materials available in the library are so good that my idea of minimal service levels have increased. I wonder now how I ever got along without them" (LibQUAL+™ 2005 Respondent Comments). Thus, although it is important to ask users what they need, it must be kept in mind that library staff must also seek out inspiration from visiting other libraries, attending conferences, and reading the literature.

OTHER AREAS OF CONCERN

Three other areas of concern came up consistently in all three LibQUAL+™ surveys. Users complained about too many old books in the library, the inadequa-cies of the library's Web site, and not enough journals in print or online. With the hiring of a new library Web manager in 2005, the library's Web site was com-pletely redone and was introduced to the campus community for the start of the fall 2006 semester. Anecdotal feedback suggests that the new Web site has been well received. By the spring of 2007, when LibQUAL+™ is next administered, it is hoped that the feedback concerning the new Web site will be more positive.

It is true that CSU's book stock has not been kept as up-to-date as desired because the library materials budget has been stagnant for many years. This is a situation that has concerned the library for some time, but as yet the university has been unable to permanently improve funding. It is difficult, however, to be-lieve that an OhioLINK library could have inadequate online resources. With thousands of electronic journals purchased via the OhioLINK consortium and approximately 45 million books available for circulation throughout Ohio via OhioLINK's Central Catalog, could other impressions be affecting user's perception of available resources? This is an area that demands much more attention from the library and will be addressed in greater depth in the coming years.

OTHER ASSESSMENT TOOLS

LibQUAL+™ is a wonderful assessment tool for a library to use to assess its overall approval rating and to compare itself against its peers. It was not designed, however, to provide enough focused information to determine exactly what corrective actions are needed in all cases. Before LibQUAL+™ was available and subsequently to gain more focused insight, the CSU library turned to both targeted surveys and focus groups to guide decision making. In the fall of 1999, a survey designed to learn how the CSU community used the library and how often netted only 75 responses and rather unenthusiastic and mostly unfavorable comments. One respondent commented, "The library is a very dreary place with poor furniture," and although two responses indicated a knowledgeable library staff, nine responses indicated that librarians, staff, and student employees could be more helpful, friendly, and knowledgeable. As mentioned previously, the 2002 LibQUAL+™ results, based on 530 respondents, echoed these findings. As previously described, strong efforts to improve customer service resulted in much improved scores on the 2003 survey, but surprisingly, these scores fell slightly in 2005. Again, could improvements in service have increased user expectations about what level of service they desire? All written comments concerning service since 2002 have generally been highly complimentary, with only an occasional specific negative incident mentioned.

The 1999 survey found that help with completing research, using the library's PCs, using periodicals, and checking out books were the main activities that brought users into the facility. With many improvements in place by 2004, the library's new marketing team conducted another, similar survey in the spring of 2004, to see once again what services were being used and how often, but this time, to also learn how aware library users were of other services offered. This survey attracted 925 respondents. While completing research, using periodicals, checking out books, and using PCs continued to rank highly, so did use of the quiet study floor and use of the group study floor. Several services that the library staff had worked hard, on such as multimedia services, subject portals, and the virtual reference desk, clearly needed the benefit of greater marketing efforts.

Of equal interest to the library's administration, however, were 20 pages of comments generated by the survey. Comment after comment noted how helpful librarians and staff members had been. Unfortunately, this survey was taken just months before the library's old roof was replaced, so most of the facility comments focused on the leaks, plastic sheeting, and drip buckets that abounded on the library's fourth floor. Sprinkled throughout the comments were valuable suggestions that could be easily implemented, such as the fact that the stairwells were hard to spot, the restrooms were not clearly marked, and there was an overall need for better signage.

This survey was followed in the fall of 2004 by a series of focus groups conducted by external consultants. Three focus groups were held with graduate students and one with faculty. Graduate students were chosen for the focus group sessions, as the 2002 and 2003 LibQUAL+™ surveys identified this group as less satisfied with library services than undergraduates.

The consultants used the findings from the LibQUAL+™ surveys to ask follow-up questions concerning the collection, Web site, facility, and staff. An additional question asked how the CSU library could better serve graduate students. The questions for faculty were: How could the facility be enhanced for faculty use? How could access to resources be improved? How could librarians and faculty work together to improve information access for all students?

Both groups indicated "an opportunity exists for the library to become an even greater contributor to the education of students" because "the convenience of remote access and less physical contact is creating a need" to compensate for a perceived separation from the campus as a community (Pasadyn and Terman 2004, 1). These specific recommendations were made:

- Provide a more welcoming and comfortable physical environment that encourages group work, discussion, and serendipitous intellectual discoveries.
- Clearly define spaces for quiet study and provide strict enforcement in the quiet areas.
- Be more visible and available for instruction and support for research in the building, remotely, and through contact with academic departments to integrate the library into the whole college experience.
- Look at ways to strengthen the effectiveness of the remote users' experiences.

Using the LibQUAL results and armed with this additional data, the library administration set to work on another round of improvements—this time aimed primarily at the millennials.

THE LIBRARY AS PLACE

With customer service improvements well underway to address the gen-Xers' most pressing needs and with the most basic facility repairs completed, the library administration set about creating a more welcoming environment that would encourage not only millennials to come into the library, but all users. The library administration wanted to create a place for the entire campus community to visit for social interaction and for expanding learning.

One of the continuing issues that the CSU library faced was a lack of visibility: administrators could not easily see how many students were using the facility nor could students easily see other students using the library. The CSU library is located in a multiuse facility. Each of the first four floors of the library are the length of a city block. The entrance to the library is from the lobby of

Rhodes Tower, a campus office building that also provides access to the 19-floor tower, mostly housing faculty offices, administration, computer services, etc. The building features a series of elevators in a central core—two within the library adjacent to four more just outside of the library. The original design of the building separated library elevators and Rhodes Tower elevators by a wall of glass. Sometime in the past, this glass wall had been covered up with bulletin boards on both sides. Until 2005, however, there was nothing of interest immediately inside of the library to see.

This changed dramatically in the fall of 2005. A large area, roughly 1,300 square feet, opposite the bulletin board-covered glass wall was opened up all the way to the floor-to-ceiling windows forming the north wall of the library. Within this space, the library was able to create a beautiful "Connection Lounge" from a combination of funds from the provost, library operating budget, and technology fees (see photo 13.1). Borrowing ideas from articles such as Andrew R. Albanese's *Campus Library* (2004) and the Council on Library and Information Resources' *Library as Place: Rethinking Roles, Rethinking Space* (2005), the lounge contained colorful couches, lounge chairs with laptop arms, coffee tables wired with electricity, and small bistro tables and chairs. Wireless Internet technology had already been added throughout the building. An additional feature of the lounge is a small, popular reading library supplied by Cleveland Public Library (Thornton and Carroll 2006, 25–26). Anchored by brightly colored carpet squares and a hanging, mobile-like ceiling treatment, the Connection Lounge provides the library with an immediately visible and welcoming place for students and faculty of all ages to gather. The furniture welcomes computer users and coffee drinkers in a space that is reminiscent of their favorite coffee shop or bookstore hangout. It provides a meeting place as well as a place for social gathering or study. Almost before the final touches were added, students and older members of the campus community began to flock to the lounge. As soon as the space was completed, the bulletin boards came down from the glass wall separating the Rhodes Tower elevators from the library elevators. Faculty and administrators waiting for elevators in Rhodes Tower could now look into the library and see books and users filling up a bright and comfortable space. No longer did it seem to them that the library was deserted.

In fact, the lounge was so popular that the university president suggested that we expand it! Thus a second, almost identical lounge, opened the next spring semester. Instead of popular reading, however, the second lounge, located near the current periodicals, featured newspapers and a flat-screen TV tuned to news programs (captions only). This lounge was also immediately filled to capacity.

Coupled with these new lounges, the library updated the circulation desk, both in function and styling. Renamed User Services, the new desk finally acknowledged that this service point, immediately in front of the library's doors, is the first point of contact for most users entering the building. Instead of being faced by a "circulation desk," the more professional and friendlier looking service point encourages users to ask questions—helping to achieve the campus goal of

Photo 13.1: Borrowing from Ernest Hemingway, our Connection Lounge fulfills student desires for "a clean well lighted place" that pleases everyone.

eliminating "shuffling" students with questions from one place to another. A self-check-out machine was installed to reduce pressure on staff (concerned about holding up lines of students while answering questions) when diverted from the routine task of checking out books.

With the campus focusing on the "one-stop-shopping" concept to reduce what had come to be known as the "CSU shuffle," the library began to look for other opportunities to make similar improvements. For some time, the reference librarians had commented about students asking for help in writing term papers and citing references. This, of course, was the mission of the campus Writing Center, but it was located across campus in the far corner of another building. After reading several articles concerning collaborations between writing centers and libraries such as the one by Elmborg and Hook (2005), the library director approached the director of the writing center with the idea of moving it to a large office located on the first floor of the library. With almost no hesitation, she agreed. This opportunity solved two problems for her. The existing campus location for the Writing Center was inconvenient, and she knew that students often asked her staff how to research their topics. Little did either director realize at the time what a perfect partnership had been formed.

For the first full year (2005–2006) of operation within the library, the Writing Center reported a 26 percent increase in the number of students using the center in the fall and another 5 percent increase in the spring. Happily for librarians, the Writing Center staff escorted students needing help with research to the reference desk and the reference librarians referred students needing help with writing to the Writing Center. Writing Centers tutorial sessions increased by 17 percent during both semesters. Writing Center staff, librarians, and the English department collaborated to schedule intensive, end-of-the-semester help sessions in the LCLC for students who needed an extra boost. The director of the Writing Center has identified the following reasons for the center's success within the library:

- access to librarians
- access to library computer terminals
- conducive atmosphere (e.g., newspapers, books, periodicals)
- central location on campus
- quiet and privacy of our location, and
- ease of location for first-generation college students (M. Murray memorandum to CSU architects, Evelyn Frey, H. Holly, G. Thornton and F. Kantz, January 17, 2007).

The library's marketing efforts have also benefited from the Writing Center's support and continued delight with the location and relationship.

As a result of the success of the Writing Center's location within the library, another suggestion was made, again by the university president, to consider locating the math learning center in the library. The library director followed up immediately with the chair of the math department. The math department's situation was much more complex, as they operate a number of math support services and possibilities for collaboration are still under examination; however, one math tutoring service, again situated in a less than optimal campus location, was relocated to a visible alcove on the library's group study floor for the beginning of the fall 2006 semester. The library provided fresh paint, an office, and several new group study tables (with dry erase board Lazy Susans in the middle). With some advertisement by the math department and the library, the math tutoring center was operational. At this point, it is difficult to determine whether the new location will improve the numbers of students seeking help, but the area's supervisor reported that "the space was a hit with those who used it" and she thanked us for adding the service to the "library family" (C. Phillips-Bey e-mail to G. Thornton, December 14, 2006).

In the case of both of these partnerships, the library was able to provide space with minimal expense. Staff members had to be willing to relocate to different offices to accommodate these new services without the need for renovations. The entire library staff, however, soon understood the benefit of accommodating these nonlibrary functions. It quickly became clear that locating these critical functions within the library was extremely beneficial to students and also beneficial to the library. As technologically sophisticated as many of the millennials are today, large academic libraries are still intimidating to the uninitiated. Finding ways of bringing these younger students into the facility where they can experience a friendly and welcoming atmosphere is critical to the future of libraries in today's virtual information environment.

The math tutoring service fit so well into the library's fourth floor because it had already been turned into a group study floor once it was realized that millennials wanted and needed spaces to work together. Previously, these students were mixed together throughout the library with other individuals seeking quiet study spaces. The result was that no one was happy. Millennial students, socializing or working on group projects, or doing both at the same time, simply began to go elsewhere. The library administration understood the need to provide places for group study, but all of the original group study rooms had been diverted to other purposes.

By observing how the various study areas were being used, it became obvious that the furniture on the library's second floor was more conducive to individual study and that the furniture on the fourth floor was more conducive to group study. Thus a decision was made to designate the second floor as a deep, quiet, study zone with no cell phone conversations. Because of the ubiquitous use of cell phones, the nosier users gradually began to gather on the fourth floor, which had no designation. Then one day, a librarian reported having observed a group of math students working problems on a small, movable blackboard that had been moved into a corner of the library to get it out of the way. It immediately became clear to the library administration that the entire floor could be designated as a group study floor. Student workers, including many of the student shelvers working on that floor, were asked how the administration could enhance the area for group study and projects. Students suggested adding more pencil sharpeners, scratch paper, electrical outlets, dictionaries, and study tables with dry erase boards. They also suggested more attention to the photocopiers located on the floor, better directions for students trying to find materials, and more aggressive advertising to attract students to the space. After all, the reputation of the library as a place where quiet is required is still deeply ingrained in the culture.

Learning to see a library facility with new eyes is quite a difficult task, but one that has paid off for Cleveland State. Although few funds have been available for major renovations, many improvements have been made to the facility. This requires the ability to continuously question whether every space in the library can be used more efficiently. This practice of continuous evaluation uncovered another opportunity.

For many years a valuable collection of music monuments was housed in a lovely 37' × 20' room with two glass walls (one exterior wall facing Lake Erie) and two doors. This room is conveniently located in the multimedia services area (a staffed service point) on the same floor where the rest of the music collection is available on open stacks. These valuable materials had been locked up for years and, as might be expected, were rarely used. Because many of these materials were originally from countries behind the Iron Curtain, at one time they would have been difficult to replace if stolen. Fortunately, that time has passed, but the concern remained that the music department might still regard them as too valuable to put on open stacks. A meeting with the chair of the music department and the faculty liaison to the library resulted in a mutual decision that the materials could be moved to the open stacks and the room put to better use.

Again, by observation and reporting back on student inquires, the library administration realized that students needed places to practice group and/or Power-Point presentations. What better location for a student practice room than inside multimedia services, where a multimedia lab was located along with skilled library staff?

Once again, the primary cost of making this facility available to students was the cost of a move that the library could manage with existing staff. Next, paint and retrieving some nice furniture that had been put in storage helped flesh out the amenities. Although the library submitted a technology fee request in the fall of 2006 to divide the room in two, purchase and install permanent projectors on the ceilings (of the two rooms, once divided), and add some additional technology, this request has yet to be funded. In the meantime, a spare SmartBoard, lectern, overhead projector, and PC were located and "stored" in the room. This space became available late in 2006 and has only begun to be advertised. As soon as the space was usable, however, the library staff began to schedule it as an alternative meeting room, and word-of-mouth advertising brought many serious users almost immediately. As the university formalizes a "speaking-across-the-curriculum" option within the general education requirement, this room(s) will no doubt be heavily scheduled.

DESIGN FOR THE FUTURE

Each improvement and update of the CSU library facilities, services, and technologies have been directed at a larger, long-term goal. Many years ago, that goal was to create an information commons area in the library. This area would provide everything students and faculty required to get connected to the research resources they needed. Computers were configured for users to find and collect information, and staff was trained to help them navigate a growing array of electronic and paper resources. The library's Web site was redesigned to assist users in finding appropriate materials. An interactive interlibrary loan computer system was implemented to make requesting resources more efficient and user-driven. These changes were, and continue to be, important in serving the needs of the campus community. The library soon saw, however, that the information commons concept fell short of supplying what students needed in an educational environment that was increasingly focusing on student learning styles more appropriate for millennials. So the CSU library has continued to evolve toward what many other libraries have labeled the "learning commons."

The learning commons model builds on what had been established under the information commons model. With improvements to services and facilities connecting users with resources already established, the library sought to provide better support to students by actively helping them use the materials they found. The creation of the LCLC was an important early step toward providing students with more than a means of obtaining information. With *Microsoft Office* installed, this facility became a place where library staff could help students use library materials to write papers and complete assignments. As student demand increased, the library installed *Microsoft Office* and other popular applications on all of the computers in the reference area so that students now have access to more than 100 computers on which they can do research and complete assignments. To support these users, library staff and student workers actively move throughout the LCLC and reference areas, assisting students completing their work. These librarians and staff members are cross-trained so that they can help users with research, using computers, printing, and so on. Bringing the Writing Center staff into the library has also added an important resource to help students produce effective, higher quality work.

As described previously, to create an atmosphere more conducive to student learning, the library implemented many facility improvement initiatives to create more attractive spaces for student-faculty and student-student interaction. The library also relaxed its policy on food and drink in the library, allowing students to take advantage of a small café and vending machines in Rhodes Tower lobby, just outside the library entrance and then feel free to come into the library to relax and work.

As the CSU Library continues to seek new partnerships, develop services and support systems, and update spaces and technology to meet the needs of its users, the learning commons will continue to gain momentum on campus.

CONCLUSION

Although receiving a large sum of money to renovate a large portion of the library would certainly be desirable, the reality has been that the CSU Library has had to reinvent itself in small steps over a long period of time. With only moderate university support, stagnant or shrinking budgets, and increasing operating and materials costs, the library made improvements through small requests for one-time money. Of interest, however, is that this slow approach toward building an information commons turned into building a learning commons as the learning preferences of the millennials became known and has also yielded a number of unexpected benefits.

Too often, large projects implemented with one-time money are difficult to sustain because ongoing maintenance and support are not accounted for in the original funds. By proceeding slowly with smaller projects over a number of years, the CSU library was able to integrate ongoing support costs into each annual budget.

This approach has allowed the library to regularly assess each small phase of the revitalization process as it was completed. Ongoing feedback from users helped the library make adjustments to completed phases and be flexible in planning subsequent phases. Because new computer technology had been implemented over a period of time, the library did not run into the problem of having to replace all of the computers in the building at the same time. Replacement schedules could be staggered, and fresh technology could be added every year, showing the library's commitment to staying up-to-date and responsive to users' technology requirements. The library then, rather than being locked into a single, major overhaul of the facility, technology, and its services, was able to be more nimble, making adjustments to plans as student and faculty needs changed from year to year.

Gradual implementation of new services and facilities has also allowed CSU library administration to make necessary personnel changes at a manageable pace. These personnel changes included providing extra training, reorganizing some departments, updating job descriptions and/or classifications, and redefining vacancies before filling positions.

The question remains: Have libraries, including the CSU library, done enough, fast enough, to change university administrators' minds about the future of academic library services? The verdict is still out, but if the headline in the June 9, 2006, issue of the *Chronicle of Higher Education* stating "Facilities Play a Key Role in Students' Enrollment Decisions" is any indication, libraries are anything but passé. According to this article (based on a report by Cain and Reynolds), students look first for institutions with facilities that support their major and then next at the library. According to the *Chronicle* summary, 3 of 10 students rejected an institution if it did not have a facility they thought important and for 53.6 percent of those surveyed, the number two facility was the library!

Hopeful signs at the CSU Library indicate that Cain and Reynolds's findings are more accurate than those reported in the 2001 "The Deserted Library" article. At CSU, more and more students have begun to use the facility for a wide variety of purposes. Coupled with this increased activity, the library administration is actively looking for ways to report the effect of this activity on enrollment and student success. The increasing university reliance on assessment techniques to determine outcomes give librarians many opportunities to prove their value to the campus. Most important, however, is what students think.

REFERENCES

Aaron Cohen Associates. 1985. "Preliminary Report on Cleveland State University Library." (March) 1–45. Cleveland State University Library, photocopy.

Albanese, Andrew Richard. 2004. "Campus Library." *Library Journal* 129 (April 15): 30–33.

Cain, David A., and Gary L. Reynolds. 2006. "The Impact of Facilities on Recruitment and Retention of Students." *Facilities Manager* 22 (2): 54–60.

Carlson, Scott. 2001. "The Deserted Library." *The Chronicle of Higher Education* (November). 10 pages. http://chronicle.com/weekly/v48/i12/12a03501.htm (Accessed February 7, 2007.)

Cleveland State University Library Survey Results. 1999. (October) 1–34. Cleveland State University Library, printed copy.

Cleveland State University Library User Survey Results. 2004. (July 13). Cleveland State University Library, printed copy.

Cleveland State University Library Facility Survey Results. 2006. (May 8) 1–7. Cleveland State University Library, printed copy.

Council on Library and Information Resources. 2005. *Library as Place: Rethinking Roles, Rethinking Space*. Washington, D.C. (February).

Elmborg, James K., and Sheril Hook. 2005. *Centers for Learning: Writing Centers and Libraries in Collaboration*. Chicago: Association of College and Research Libraries.

Frand, Jason L. 2000. "The Information-Age Mindset: Changes in Students and Implications for Higher Education." *EDUCAUSE Review* 35 (5) (September/October): 15–24.

June, Audrey Williams. 2006. "Facilities Play a Key Role in Students' Enrollment Decisions, Study Finds." *The Chronicle of Higher Education* 52 (40): A27.

LibQUAL+™. 2007. Association of Research Libraries. http://www.libqual.org/ (Accessed February 7, 2007.)

LibQUAL+™ Respondent Comments. 2005. Association of Research Libraries. http://www.libqual.org/Manage/Results/Comments/index.cfm (Accessed February 7, 2007—password protected.)

Oblinger, Diana. 2003. "Boomers & Gen-Xers Millennials: Understanding the New Students." *EDUCAUSE Review* 38 (4) (July/August): 37–47.

Pasadyn, Terri, and Elaine Terman. 2004. Cleveland State University Library Focus Group Reports. (November): 1–17. Cleveland State University Library, printed copy.

Shill, Harold B., and Shawn Tonner. 2003. "Creating a Better Place: Physical Improvements in Academic Libraries, 1995–2002." *College & Research Libraries* 64 (6): 431–466.

Shill, Harold B., and Shawn Tonner. 2004. "Does the Building Still Matter? Usage Patterns in New, Expanded, and Renovated Libraries, 1995–2002." *College & Research Libraries* 65 (2): 123–150.

Thornton, Glenda A., and Holly Carroll. 2006. "The Race for Readers: A Public Library and an Academic Library Team Up to Entice College Students to Read Books." *American Libraries* 37 (9) (October): 24–26.

SELECTED BIBLIOGRAPHY

Cain, David A., and Gary L. Reynolds. 2006. *The Impact of Facilities on Recruitment and Retention of Students: Final Report*. Virginia: APPA.

Wood, Elizabeth J., Rush Miller, and Amy Knapp. 2007. *Beyond Survival: Managing Academic Libraries in Transition*. Westport, CT: London: Libraries Unlimited.

14 PLANNING AN INFORMATION COMMONS: OUR EXPERIENCES AT THE UNIVERSITY OF TOLEDO'S CARLSON LIBRARY

John C. Phillips and Brian A. Hickam

With the increasing role of electronic resources in college and university libraries and the ability of students and faculty members to access many library resources remotely, academic libraries, including our University of Toledo's Carlson Library, have experienced declining numbers of walk-in patrons. Our library's administrators and faculty members sought solutions to reverse those waning numbers. One of our solutions was to redesign the interior of the building to make it more aesthetically attractive, comfortable, functional, and conducive to collaborative learning. The goal was to provide, among other things, a student-centered learning environment in which students could conduct research and compose papers, collaborate in groups at computer workstations, get answers, assistance, and referrals at a combined Information Technology/Library Reference help desk, access multimedia production tools, attend cultural events in a multipurpose auditorium, and eat snacks at a café. We wanted to remodel our library and create an Information Commons (IC). Dr. John Gaboury, dean of University Libraries, proclaimed, "It's where we'll blend technology, an enriched learning environment and a leisure study environment" (Dr. John Gaboury, *UT News* August 21, 2006, 2).

We recognized the need to rebrand our library and many of its services and resources along with these physical renovations. Given the ways today's learners access information, as well as their learning styles and preferences, we recognized the importance of changing:

1. **Our logo** (which for decades has been an oceanographic geophysical earth globe—one of only four that currently exist in the United States—but, admittedly, is outdated);

2. **Our brand name** (we will have an "Information Commons" within our "library." Our marketing campaign will include "The Information Commons at Carlson Library");
3. **Our image** (as a resource and service) and **our product** (namely, our reference desk and computer workstations);
4. Our marketing strategy and our advertising;
5. And, perhaps most important, **our partnerships** and **affiliations.**

University Libraries have partnered with the university's Office of Information Technology (IT) to remodel each department's products and image into a combined endeavor: The Information Commons at Carlson Library. Additional offices, such as our university's Writing Center and Distance and eLearning, will have operations within the IC. Because administrators at an increasing number of colleges and universities will decide to advocate for and create Information Commons, we thought it would be useful to share what we have learned and to recommend a list of steps and considerations when planning such an undertaking. It is our hope that others will learn and profit from our experiences.

THE NEED TO REBRAND YOUR LIBRARY

As OCLC's 2006 report *Perceptions of Libraries and Information Resources* makes clear, rebranding our libraries is essential as today's young learners do not understand the role of their academic library or that of the librarians working at the Reference/Information desk. Perhaps more important, the current generation of college students, unlike older generations, learns differently. They want more multimedia resources, flexibility, and peer collaboration. We recognized that our students' images of the library are often highly influenced by their classroom instructors. A successful renovation and marketing campaign should also improve our teaching colleagues' understandings of the library. The IC, then, would be an important tool in conveying how librarians and information technologists and their respective resources can assist with professors' research and curricular needs and their students' information literacy and technology needs. The IC would be central to our success at repositioning the main library as the heart of the campus.

By "Information Commons" we are using the first of two connotations defined by Joan M. Reitz in her *Online Dictionary for Library and Information Science*:

1. A new type of technology-enhanced collaborative facility on college and university campuses that integrates library and computer application services (information, technology, and learning) in a single floor plan, often equipped with a wireless network and, in some cases, equipment for multimedia production. Most ICs are designed to support librarians engaged in assisting individual students and in teaching research skills to groups, teaching assistants helping individuals and groups of students with class assignments, and individual students and groups independently

accessing information in print and online. Some ICs are open 24/7. Syn-
onymous with integrated learning center.

2. In a broader sense, the free flow of information and ideas as a public good,
   as distinct from the for-profit marketing of information as a commodity
   by the corporate mass media, the publishing industry, and other market
   driven enterprises (http://lu.com/odlis/) (2004)

An IC differs from the traditional academic library model by acknowledging
changes in user needs and expectations and by creating an environment that
supports the research process from beginning to end (Cowgill, Beam, and Wess
2001). Beagle (1999) notes that for several years a new model for service delivery
in academic libraries has been emerging and is most often referred to as the Information Commons. The first known Information Commons in the United States
was at the University of Iowa in 1992. Some institutions have chosen to refer to
their new library model as a Learning Commons.

The IC in academic libraries is a growing, international trend, as evidenced
by ICs at The Chinese University of Hong Kong, The University of Auckland,
and University of the Sunshine Coast, to name but three. As the IC movement continues, it will become increasingly important for institutions to join
in. The models of academic libraries and IT departments are changing. Their
exterior architectures and interior designs are being modified; their models
of service are being altered; and their roles and images are being advanced.
Warnken (2004, 322) states that "[as] the new information technologies have
become critical to students and faculty, there is mounting pressure to change
library services." To successfully compete for students, faculty, and staff members, every college and university that can afford to should move to keep up
with these changes. Imagine a prospective student and her parents taking tours
of two universities in order to select the one to attend. One university has
modernized its library into an IC and appears to be more student-centered;
the other has not. The two schools are otherwise the same. Even if this family
was not familiar with the IC trend, its decision on the better, more attractive
college to choose might be influenced by such a notable difference. Therefore
like many other academic libraries before us, the University of Toledo decided
to adopt the IC concept for our library based on the successes of others.

EXPLORING THE INFORMATION COMMONS CONCEPT

The IC model offers a one-stop shopping mode of research and learning
that promises to boost the number of library users. Accounts from institutions
with recently constructed ICs show that this new library model is extremely
popular with students. For example, reference librarians at Emory University,
whose IC opened in 1997, have commented that the quality of their service
has improved overall. They have noticed that the way the library is used has
changed in significant ways because of the extensive access to technology. Halbert (1999) points out that because of the IC at Emory, many patrons use the

library more frequently and for longer periods. He observed that students used to gather information at the library and then check it out to take away with them. "Now," according to Halbert (1999, 90), "they can write papers, tabulate data, design Web pages, and collaborate in groups using computers, all without leaving the library." Such enhanced functionality is planned for Carlson Library's IC. With upgraded service points; instruction rooms; and improved furniture, carpeting, lighting, and HVAC, the library will become the central player in the university's campaign to become increasingly student-centered. By positioning Carlson Library's renovation alongside other student-centered initiatives that comprise the University's "Master Plan," we have been successful at convincing our campus administration to prioritize its planning, funding, and construction. In fact, according to Joseph Sawasky, the University's Chief Information Officer, "[The IC is] slated to be the first facility completed under the original master plan, which is quite a testament to the administration's belief in a student-centered institution" (Nowak 2006).

The Office of Information Technology and University Libraries together will oversee the operations of the IC. IT will be able to close the computer lab in our Student Union and the lab located in the library's basement, making the first floor of main library the campus's largest computer room. The reference stacks, reference help desk, circulation desk, reserve materials area, and the new books display will remain on the first floor. We believe that our library will remain recognizable as a library, and we will be gaining patron options, not losing any. In this day of online surfing and reference assistance, via e-mail, telephone, or chat, we believe that print is still a viable format and that many students, faculty, and staff members prefer in-person assistance for certain information needs. With the anticipated improved and increased traffic, we are confident that our reference librarians will be better positioned to serve our campus community.

Even though the term *Information Commons* is a buzzword with positive connotations, we realized that our campaign for campus and community buy-in and support would also need to incorporate the terms *learning spaces* and *learning environments*, which more closely align themselves with the concept of student-centeredness. Although it is true that the whole campus of a college or university has always been a learning environment, the current trend is to optimize specific areas of the campus. Creating learning spaces within libraries and within residence and academic halls has become a component of the trend toward a better integration of student-centeredness. Librarians and other educators have recognized how pedagogical needs have changed fundamentally and that we must strive to better meet the requirements of today's and tomorrow's learners.

THE CHANGING NEEDS FOR SPACE

Most universities' "traditional" computer labs do not provide sufficient spaces for books, journals, class notes, and other materials students use as they write their papers. In general, these labs are not inside or near the main library. Most "traditional" reference desks and the computers surrounding them have had their drawbacks, too. The printed resources are usually in a separate location from the computers that allow word processing. The tables, carrels, and workstations of most reference areas are not conducive to collaborative work, either among students or between faculty members and students. For these reasons, most traditional computer labs and libraries do not make it convenient for students to meet the demands of their classes.

Like many other libraries, our reference area computers are restricted to research database and Internet searching. It has been clear in recent years that our students using the reference area desired software applications such as *Microsoft Word*. Many of our professors are placing *PowerPoint* and *Excel* items in their courses' *WebCT* components and on the library's e-reserves. It remains a challenge to assist students with accessing these resources and then directing them to the computer lab in our basement to view and print them.

Students view the old model as impractical. Those who want to use resources physically located at the library, such as the reference encyclopedias or journals that are not full-text online, need to leave the computer lab where they were typing their papers to make special trips to the library. As renovation has increased the number of computers in the reference area from 30 to nearly 220, the argument for restricting the priority of use of these work stations to research use only no longer remains valid. Students have also wanted flexibility in their use of software. We have not provided all of the various programs and plug-ins that our patrons desire (for both entertainment and academic uses). IT has not allowed unauthorized downloads or changes to any computer for obvious reasons. More flexibility is now possible. Software such as Faronics's *Deep Freeze* allows patrons to download freely without changing the desired computer settings. By storing a patron's session in random access memory, this program allows patron-initiated downloads because it reboots and restores the computer's hard drive to a set state. At present, it requires a few hours of computer lab downtime to run its programs. Although this time frame would not be compatible with a network that is 24/7, we will continue to monitor our options.

Today's students also want more multimedia options. They want to be able to scan their own items; manipulate sounds, images, and videos screen casting; print and photocopy in color; and have content pushed to their iPods. They want multimedia rooms with plotters and high-end Macintoshes where they can produce high-quality results. Increased numbers of software applications and two multimedia production rooms in the IC will allow for centralized research, collaboration, composition, and learning.

DEVELOPING SUPPORT FOR THE INFORMATION COMMONS

The Carlson Library IC is a $3.7 million project that was two years in the planning. The idea for creating an Information Commons at The University of Toledo began with our Dean of University Libraries and Academic Support, Dr. John Gaboury. He shared his ideas with the University's CIO, who heads the department of information technology, hoping to foster an alliance.

Once they agreed to become partners, they held informal discussions with the provost and vice-provosts about the need for an IC and the possibility of allocating funds for it. With an agreement that the project held merit and that appropriate funding would be given, official discussions about a proposed IC commenced at a meeting of the University Facilities Planning Council. The dean of libraries and CIO co-presented an argument for the first major renovations to Carlson Library since its opening in 1973. The council's support of the IC was a prerequisite to the dean and CIO introducing the concept to the university's board of trustees, faculty senate, and student government. Convincing the campus community of the need for this project and moving it forward would require buy-in and support from all three groups. A motion to support the IC concept was passed by the university's facilities planning council without dissent.

After his success at the provost's office, the library dean brought the matter to the library faculty. Initially, we were excited about the renovations, but there were concerns that an IC would simply convert the library into one big computer lab, eliminating print resources such as encyclopedias, indexes, and journals. To ensure that this major initiative would be as library-faculty-driven as possible, the dean proposed that the library faculty compose a vision statement which would serve to guide the project from beginning to end. We librarians understood that a transition into an IC necessitated our partnering with other groups, and we did not want to lose our voice in the process. We consider ourselves to be the experts at what the library's role on campus should be.

The vision statement in the form of a white paper was written by a task force that included a cross section of library faculty members. Citing the University Libraries' Mission Statement, the task force emphasized the library's role and continued relevance in the Internet Age. Our mission states that:

> To fulfill our role in The University of Toledo's mission, the University Libraries promote the learning and research activities of the University through our collections and services including access to information resources worldwide. To facilitate the exchange of ideas, the Libraries also serve as the University's cultural and intellectual commons.

The partnership between University Libraries and IT is a definite opportunity to advance the missions of both entities. The IT/Libraries partnership is more than the sum of its parts. We foresee better funding and recognition for our contributions than we would receive were we to remain separate. The white paper noted that the Information Commons will emphasize the library's role as the heart of the university, where learning, discovery, and engagement are integrated to enable students to achieve their highest potential.

This paper has been shared with the Information Commons Planning Committee, the University Facilities Planning Council, and the architecture firm. (Information and Research Commons White Paper, January 2005).

Our successes continued. The Finance Committee of the University's Board of Trustees approved funding the project through debt financing. While many of the university's faculty members had questions about what the project entailed and why it was deemed a priority, a majority of the committee voted to approve the funding. Success with the Student Government Association regarding the funding was uncertain. Many of the students the dean and CIO would be speaking with to approve funding would graduate before completion of the project. Their positive vote would signify their agreement that the project would be good for all students, particularly future students. Fortunately, University of Toledo students have noticed that their university is striving to become more student-centered in many different areas. They understood, perhaps more than others, that the renovations to the library would be tailored to and beneficial to students. Citing the UT Board of Trustees' minutes, the Student Government Association, by a vote of 23 to 0, passed a Student Facilities Fee for Capital Projects (a resolution calling for a fee of no more than $100 per semester per full-time student allocated to two projects—the Information Commons and renovations to the University's Memorial Field House—and having a term of no more than 30 years) (http://utsg.utoledo.edu/index.asp) (2006).

PARTNERING FOR SUCCESS WITH OTHERS ON CAMPUS

The white paper included a broad definition of the IC and emphasized the significance of a balanced partnership between various entities on campus. These partnerships would include University Libraries, Distance and eLearning, the student body, Office of Facilities Planning, Information Technology, the Writing Center, the Learning Enhancement Center (LEC), and the Center for Teaching & Learning (CTL). Our Writing Center works with current UT undergraduate and graduate students and faculty and staff on a variety of writing projects. The LEC provides tutoring, supplemental instruction, and related workshops to students, and the CTL promotes excellence in teaching. Dean Gaboury noted that "It's not an isolated turf project; we're creating something to benefit the entire University" (*UT News* August 21, 2006).

Dean Gaboury has stressed the importance of partnering with others in planning the Information Campus: "We're using the next generation of design and technology to address the needs of the 21st century. To determine those needs, project planners focused on consensus building" (Nowak 2006). To build on student support, the IC Planning Committee asked some students their opinions and wishes for a remodeled library. More students' opinions were sought later by the IC Planning Committee as floor plans developed.

Since IT and University Libraries are the two principle players in the formation of most IC models, it is highly recommended that library administrators partner with their IT colleagues at the earliest planning stages. We also recommend getting student opinions and buy-in during the initial stages, as documentation of their views may assist with solicitations to the board of trustees and faculty senate and because student fees may be a necessary component of the funding.

THE IC PLANNING COMMITTEE

To bring his idea to fruition, the library dean created an IC Planning Committee comprised of representatives from all of the partners involved. The committee was formed to provide leadership and direction to the project, to learn from the experiences of two other universities that have successful ICs, and to assist in selecting an architecture firm. The committee consisted of 12 members representing the Center for Teaching and Learning, various departments of IT (University Networks, College Computing, and Administrative Computing), Distance and eLearning, student government, and the faculty and staff of Carlson Library. We highly recommend including a representative from the student government on the planning committee. In addition to providing a student's perspective, this person can report developments to their peers on a regular basis. As a result, we received strong support and positive media coverage for the project from campus student newspapers.

The IC Planning Committee concentrated on, among other things, integrating IT's services into our library, meeting the needs of library and IT personnel in the new model, selecting which physical changes would be necessary, and interviewing architecture firms. Other universities have had their committees also investigate learning styles. One institution had a separate committee solely dedicated to creating a report on learning. We relied on the expertise of our Information Literacy Librarians, the professional literature, and personal experiences for this aspect of the planning. Choice may depend on staff size and institutional culture. The committee identified minimum standards for space and service needs for patron and staff areas in the design of the IC. Interviews and informal focus groups with students gave committee members valuable feedback on suggested changes to the interior design, resources, and services students wanted in their remodeled library.

The IC Planning Committee derived a number of key objectives from the white paper:

- **Place-making:** [The Information Commons will be] "a place for students, faculty and staff to go for both research support and technology assistance. The Information Commons will be the heart of the University, where learning, discovery and engagement are integrated to enable students to achieve their highest potential."
- **Student-focused:** [The IC will] "address the needs of the 21st century student and support the university's strategic goal of being a student-centered university that provides state of the art educational technology."
- **Enhancing the library's collaborative role:** "The Information Commons will be a partnership between various entities on campus including Information Technology, the Writing Center, the Learning Enhancement Center, Distance and eLearning, and the University Libraries."

Committee members provided feedback on a regular basis to various campus groups and constituencies about plans for the IC. Open lines of communication for suggestions from library faculty and staff were created to improve the project's outcomes and to lessen the anxieties associated with the changes. A phased construction approach would be used so that the library and its resources would be accessible during construction and services would not be interrupted.

CHOOSING AN ARCHITECT AND THE FEASIBILITY STUDY

A consultant was hired to provide the IC Planning Committee with a feasibility study. This study outlined a realistic strategy to bring this project from concept to completion, and developed a conceptual design approach that would create the objective physical environment within budgetary expectations. The insight from this report was combined with our internal analyses of space and workflow needs to assist our search for the appropriate architecture firm to head the project. Our status as a state university required us to advertise nationally. We received 32 bids from firms located throughout the eastern half of the United States. The library dean, CIO, and head of facilities planning narrowed the pool of applications down to eight, at which time the IC Planning Committee was asked to evaluate each remaining application in order to select the top six firms for on-campus interviews.

The six firms were interviewed in two days. Each was given 1 hour to present and 20 minutes for questions and answers. Nearly every firm had sent someone to our campus ahead of time to take photographs and scope out the interior and exterior of the library. This was in addition to a tour that the dean and head of IT gave to all six firms as a group three weeks before the interviews. The presentations of some firms incorporated videos, others poster-sized drawings. Interestingly, two firms presented plans that exceeded our budgetary guidelines. Assuming that the university would raise and allocate two to three times as much money as provided, they presented grandiose architectural renderings that included skylights to the library's basement and cosmetic improvements to the building's exterior and the bridge over the river that leads to our library. The president of one firm informed the library dean that the project's budget concerned him. Each architectural firm had been given the project's budget up front and had been told what changes we wanted the money to cover. We informed each firm that we would prioritize these changes if funding did not allow for all of them. Two firms neglected to bring their interior designers along. Those firms whose project team included interior designers were better prepared to answer questions from the library's IC planning committee. Each planning committee member ranked his/her choices at the completion of the interviews. After discussing the rankings as a group, all committee members reranked their choices and a composite ranking was compiled. BHDP Architecture firm from Cincinnati, Ohio was selected to build our IC. They will collaborate with Motz Consulting Engineers. They were selected because we were impressed by their experience with creating ICs, working within budgetary expectations, and demonstrating a realistic strategy to bring such a project from concept to completion.

SITE VISITS AND FEEDBACK

Two site visits conducted before the architect interviews proved to be exceedingly worthwhile. Our colleagues at two other Midwestern universities lived up to the librarian reputation of being helpful and giving. We highly recommend taking the opportunity to learn from others. As most schools with ICs will have made their own site visits, you will be gaining collective knowledge on students' wishes, interior design options, learning styles, furniture choices, color schemes, etc. Many schools are several years into their IC experiences, allowing them to comment on what they have learned since their grand openings and what they would do differently. We learned some valuable information from them and offer to assist others with their planning process.

Both universities we visited had also converted existing space. One university sent the committee a fact sheet, a *PowerPoint* presentation, funding and vision information, and a project organizational chart. It had converted 25,000 square feet of space into an IC. Each on-site visit provided us with, among other things, a better understanding of arrangements of furniture and workstations, demands placed on workstations, wireless specifications, and telecommunications wiring systems. At one of the sites, our task force was invited to attend meetings with the reference and interlibrary loan departments, assistant deans, and technology personnel. They tailored their agendas to topics that would be of interest to us. We recommend that site-visit crews take along cameras and video recorders. On our group's return, we realized that the photos and videos we had taken made conveying our findings and recommendations to the other members of the committee and to administrators, colleagues, and students all the easier. At one of our sites, we were introduced to computer workstation configurations that encircle support posts and provide space for up to six desktop PCs. Every floor of our building contains 72 square support columns 20 inches wide. Thanks to a site visit, our concerns over being limited by these "barriers" were dismissed. "Support columns that used to be dead spaces, spaces to navigate around, are now bases for computer stations. The stations are circular, with plenty of elbow room for backpacks and laptops. More than 120 computer stations and 100 laptop stations will dot the commons" (Nowak 2006, 2).

We were reminded during our site visits to other universities that library administrators should ensure their ability to work closely with the architects. Librarians understand best how their libraries function and the features they desire. We learned from one of our site hosts, where such a relationship was not initially set up, that the architects had neglected to include adequate space for printers. With close collaboration, such errors can be avoided. BHDP has worked closely with each group at our library, from circulation to reference and others, to learn firsthand from them their wishes, needs, and desires.

ANXIETY BROUGHT BY CHANGE

The University of Toledo has recently merged with the former Medical University of Ohio (now known as UT's Health Science Campus). The president of the Medical University of Ohio became president of the combined universities. In one of his letters to the campus community, he briefly discussed transitions, saying that they can be exciting but also breed apprehension. Similarly, before news of the institutional merger broke, many of our library's faculty and staff members expressed apprehension about the IC's extensive changes. The offices of faculty and staff will be moving from the first floor, which has lots of windows, to the lower level, which has none. Even though the library's faculty and staff members were optimistic about the forthcoming improvements to our library's interior and image, some were not looking forward to the transition. One essential element to getting buy-in was the promise of full-spectrum natural lighting in the lower level. Environment influences morale, and maintaining high staff morale contributes to a highly productive workforce.

With the dean's approval, two members of the IC Planning Committee, one staff member and one faculty member, both of whom had attended the site visits, spent time with each of Carlson Library's 13 units or departments (government documents, cataloging, interlibrary loan, etc.). It was felt that the faculty and staff members who were not directly involved in the planning decisions for the IC would benefit from informal dialogues that included an explanation of what an IC is, discussions of the committee's ideas and decisions, the expected timeline of moves and construction, lessons the task force learned at each site visit and, most important, an opportunity for questions, concerns, and suggestions. In addition to alleviating most people's uneasiness, the two committee members received valuable recommendations that they took back to the planning group. For instance, the staff members whose offices are nearest the public restrooms were the first to point out that the walls would need to be insulated to muffle the sounds of flushing toilets. The architects likely would have caught this need on their own, but it was a helpful insight, as this location will house our new instruction rooms. Gaining a sense of appreciation and involvement with groups being affected by the IC project has assisted the dean and CIO in fast-tracking our IC.

DESIGN CONSIDERATIONS

The first floor of our six-floor library will be dedicated to the IC. Approximately 40,000 square feet of this floor will be renovated. Most faculty and staff offices will be moved to the lower level. These renovations will result in the downsizing of the reference collection and the relocation of print indexes, microforms, audiovisuals, and current periodicals to other floors. A project involving weeding the reference collection was partly completed when the IC was proposed. The number of volumes needed to be relocated, however, was greatly increased with the plans for the IC.

The IC will be open 24 hours per day, Monday through Thursday, with the ultimate goal of extending the number of days to seven. All service areas are designed to be visible and serve as focal points throughout the IC. The color palette will be expanded to create an exciting visual environment, as color-specific patterns will be used to guide patrons through the space and to the various service points. Most of the open floor space will be used for computer workstations and study tables. Three new group study rooms will be added. All study carrels, however, will be relocated to the upper floors. Twenty lounge seats near the front entrance between the circulation and reference desks and near a new books display will act as both a reception and a reading area.

While maintaining wide, open aisles and clear lines of sight, we will maximize the number of computer workstations and study tables. Circular, modular tables around the support columns will be the focal feature of the IC. Each table will accommodate six desktop computers or PCs. Some stations at these circular tables will be intentionally left open to allow students to decide that space's function, whether that be laptop use or textbook studying. With column-centric round tables, six perforated metal screens will be used to divide each table into six areas, not unlike spokes in a wheel. These screens will not come to the edge of the table and will be low enough to allow small groups to occupy two areas and work side-by-side. Printers will occupy a few of these desk spaces. PC workstations will be placed on five semicircular tables adjacent to perimeter walls. Twenty-six smaller, rectangular tables, each of which can comfortably accommodate four patrons, will serve as the IC's primary study areas. Twelve more study spaces will be at two extended tables located along the back corner walls. There will be two individual study tables in separate nooks between a stairwell and the west perimeter wall, which will be coveted for their privacy and ample window exposure.

Some successful IC include tables that are "C"-shaped, oval-shaped, and tear drop- or "artist palette"-shaped, where each table is set apart. Many of these ICs make use of cloth visual barriers to divide workstations. These lightweight barriers do not muffle sound, but they do provide a sense of privacy. Long rows, "L" shapes, and various other elongated configurations using rectangular tables are also popular. Two recommendations for such designs are (1) to use narrow tables that accommodate only a single row of PCs from left to right in order to maximize student workspace, and (2) have every other monitor face the opposite direction to create a sense of privacy for patrons.

Various styles of lightweight lounge furniture will be located throughout the space to give a more collaborative and relaxing environment and to avoid the appearance of a large computer lab. Adequate lighting, including natural lighting mounted on the ceiling and task lighting at certain workstations, will provide a more pleasing atmosphere. In planning the design of our IC, we also learned about how other libraries planned their ICs by reading the professional literature. For example, when the Miller Nichols Library at the University of Missouri-Kansas City planned its IC, one of the planners was Jeanette Nichols, who was "a strong advocate for space that is less institutional and more welcoming and comfortable for students and faculty" (Miller Nichols Library 2006, 4). Nichols and other members of the planning committee (2006, 4) also "wanted a room that would accommodate a variety of learning and study styles. More and more students are collaborating, working in small groups on projects, presentations, and papers." Our IC planning committee wanted the same thing for Carlson Library. A successful

IC provides areas where students are able to work and study together not only with desktop computers and laptops but also with print resources.

The first-floor IC will integrate information technology, computer workstations, multimedia production, laptop computer loans, and writing and tutoring services with conventional library services such as circulation, course reserves, reference, and interlibrary loan. According to UT's CIO, students will benefit from our integrated help desk: "At the desk, librarians and technologists will be sitting elbow to elbow, so if one gets a question on another's services, they can respond using expertise from both disciplines" (Nowak, *UT News*, August 21, 2006, 2). Other areas associated with the IC will include state-of-the-art classrooms, group study rooms, and multimedia production areas that offer the most up-to-date software and hardware. Our site visits, however, taught us that the latest, more expensive technology is not always what students desire. One of our site visit hosts informed us of the popularity of their "old-fashioned" white boards and markers in their multimedia section. This is not to say that *Smart Boards* would not be the best choice in another section or for another library. Some libraries are electing to offer dual monitors at some workstations. These monitors can display the same screen or allow for different windows and applications to be running. Some institutions have elected to provide two or three Webcams for general use; others restrict theirs to the distance learning and multimedia areas.

One of our main goals for creating an IC has been to foster more group-oriented learning and more active learning at our library. Improved designs to instruction rooms, functionally designed tables and chairs that are moveable, additional software options, and added support at our help desks will help us reach this goal. We want as much of an open space floor plan as possible so that learners can interact and collaborate with one another. The Joint Information Systems Committee (JISC) (2006) notes that, "learners have been shown to benefit academically from social interaction with their peers." The arrangement of furniture and space encourages learning through dialogue, problem-solving, and information sharing. Open floor plans also provide individualized learning environments. We have learned from our site visits and the literature that students want open spaces and open views. The use of glass in permanent and movable walls fulfills students' desires to "see and be seen" and administrators' desire for everyone, especially prospective students and donors, to see "learning in action." As such, the back walls of all of our instruction rooms, both the new rooms and the renovated ones, will be glass. Adjustable blinds will allow for privacy.

THE IC CONCOURSE

Toledo, Ohio is known as the "Glass City." In August 2006, The Toledo Museum of Art opened its newest addition, a $30 million Glass Pavilion. Who better to comment on the aesthetics and functions of glass walls than the museum's director and the pavilion's architects? Glass will also be the prominent feature of the library's concourse, which connects the building's two main entrances. This large hallway is a major thoroughfare connecting the north and south sides of campus. The existing concourse is dimly lit, dominated by dark brick walls, and, measuring 47-yards long, is uninspiring. Curved glass concourse walls, improved lighting, inviting seating areas, and information kiosks at both ends will engage and impress visitors while allowing spaces to be divided. Any effort to reposition the library as the heart of the campus should include a resplendent entrance. Don Bacigalupi, in his welcoming remarks about The Glass Pavilion, notes that a glass wall's "transparency encourages visitors to connect objects and activities across boundaries" (*The Toledo Blade*, 2006, Section T, 3). We hope for the same with our IC. Kazuyo Sejima and Ryue Nishizawa, the architects who designed Toledo's Glass Pavilion, note that "transparency can add many layers of impressions—you can see a lot of different things at the same time. Glass can show diversity, not only through transparency but also through reflection and refraction" (*The Toledo Blade*, 2006, Section T, 4).

Because the concourse is the library's first point of contact with faculty, students, and visitors, it presents the library's first impression. The CIO's vision to further capture the attention and interest of passersby is to have our IT/Reference help desk jut out into the concourse. One-third of the desk will be crosscut by the glass wall. This will allow for convenient service to our patrons in need of laptop, tablet, and desktop assistance. We hope that the IC's characteristic spirit is one of excitement about learning and that the transparency of the walls and the highly visible help desk will motivate passersby to come inside the IC and library.

Located within the library building and across the concourse from the library's entrance are the Writing Center and Center for Teaching & Learning. As they play important roles, both have been popular departments. Although they have been loosely affiliated with Carlson Library because they are directly across the concourse from our interior entrance, for all practical purposes they have not been integrated with the library in any meaningful way. Librarians regularly refer patrons to these service points, but they have not had formal ties to either area. With the IC model, these offices will become unified extensions of the library's operations.

THE IC'S MAIN HELP DESK

The reference/IT help desk will be enlarged and redesigned. It will accommodate two IT colleagues and two reference librarians at the busiest times. The old desk was for two librarians to comfortably work with patrons. Because the reference/IT help desk will have four attendants on duty during peak hours, it was designed for growth. The help desk will be transformed from its former rectangular shape to an oval design. It was felt that this would be more aesthetically attractive and would allow each point of the help desk to appear approachable for service. The biggest change, of course, will be the much more prominent and visible location.

The head of IT convinced the library to choose a cross-cut help desk. He made a compelling case for a tech service window that is open to the concourse. It was at a meeting halfway through the planning that the reference department representative on the IC Planning Committee fully appreciated the fact that the new help desk would belong equally to the IT department. They would not merely be joining the librarians at the desk. They, too, had design and location choices that would best serve their functions and ours. Earlier, most of the librarians had wanted the desk to be located entirely within the library. A service window open to the concourse will allow us to more effectively market all of our services. The concourse is a high traffic area, as it connects the residence halls, fraternity houses, and athletics buildings on the south side of campus to our Student Union and the north side of campus. Such convenience exemplifies our new approach to service at the help desk and throughout the library. Some cross-training will be conducted between IT workers and reference librarians, but neither group is expected to become proficient at the others' knowledge, talents, or skills. Each group should understand and respect the roles and strengths of their partners at the desk.

DOWNSIZING THE REFERENCE COLLECTION

A large portion of the library's first floor once housed the reference collection, including many print indexes and abstracts. When the dean of libraries inquired whether the reference collection could be downsized by about half, subject specialists were tasked with weeding the collection in their specialties. If, for example, an electronic copy of a reference title or an equivalent electronic resource were available, we removed the print version from the reference collection. The print copy was placed in the general collection for circulation, or sent to a remote storage site, where it too could circulate or not, or it was discarded. In the process of evaluating the reference collection, each librarian recommended a time framework for retaining a title in the reference collection and how it should be disposed of once it was either superseded by a current copy or replaced with another title. During this process, each subject specialist developed criteria for a written collection development policy. These will ultimately make up a comprehensive written collection development policy for the entire reference collection.

If the main reasons for transforming the traditional academic library into an IC were that resources are migrating from print to online formats and more patrons were accessing these library resources from outside the library, the question arises as to what to do with hardcopy reference materials. Moving the periodical indexes from the reference area to the same floor as the periodicals was an easy choice. Most of these subscriptions had been cancelled in light of online counterparts. We did not want to withdraw these indexes, as a significant number of faculty members still use them. Decisions regarding the rest of the reference encyclopedias, dictionaries, handbooks, and so on were not as clear. Subject specialists evaluated each title individually.

We were able to downsize the reference collection by nearly 50 percent. The majority of books were relocated to the circulation collection. A small number went to the depository and a few titles were withdrawn. It was recommended that all of the reference books that have been suggested by subject librarians for re-classification should be placed on a specially designated "transitional" shelf. This allows others, other librarians and teaching colleagues, to offer their opinions. Some titles were returned to the reference collection as a result of this process. Contrary to initial concerns, downsizing the reference stacks by more than 50 percent was rather painless. We will also be able to downsize our ready reference area, as the main reference collection in the IC will be significantly closer to the reference desk.

REPURPOSED CLASSROOM AND ANTEROOM

A former large classroom on the second floor of the library will be converted to a colloquium series and special functions room. Although this room is not part of the IC budget, the library dean is looking for a donor to fund this project. Designed as a multipurpose, multitask auditorium for larger classes and other activities, the room will accommodate up to 85 persons in its tiered seating and will be flexible enough to host teleconferencing, musical performances, guest lectures, and community functions. The refurbished room will include new lighting and furniture. The area currently used for photocopiers located just outside the room will become an ante room for light refreshments or registration functions during special events. This repurposed events room and the IC will be used as a recruiting tool for the university to attract students and faculty in a competitive market. The library will be responsible for scheduling this room. Library-related activities will take precedence over nonlibrary functions. There is little doubt that the auditorium will be an asset to the marketing of our IC and library.

CYBER CAFÉ LOUNGE

Plans call for a cyber café lounge, sometimes referred to as a learning café, where students will experience a mix of refreshments, social activities, and information technology. We expect the café to foster a relaxing and friendly atmosphere where conversation and social interaction are seen as essential parts of the learning process. A mixture of several computer clusters in the café will encourage collaboration. JISC (2006, 5) cites the Learning Café at Glasgow Caledonian University as a success story: "[It] was an early experiment in the use of space to support problem-based learning and group work. The café opened four years ago, and its success as a learning space is clear from student evaluations." Learning cafés have proven themselves successful at many institutions, and have shown fears about IT-based informal learning environments to be baseless. Moreover, the Learning Café at Glasgow Caledonian has proven to be a financial success. Its profits are used to cover the IC's maintenance costs. Our learning café will be an "after hours" facility because of the vending license agreement with our campus food service company. We are collaborating with Starbucks to operate the Cyber Café.

MAINTENANCE COSTS, FUNDRAISING, AND NAMING OPPORTUNITIES

As with most projects, securing ongoing operational funding will be a neces-sity. In 2006, most IT departments continued to argue that they will need to replace their hardware every four years. Software upgrades are also an ongoing cost, with many institutions choosing to update theirs weekly. Software acquisi-tions and deletions will continue to take place throughout each year as new prod-ucts are available and new needs are realized. Purchasing quality floor coverings and furniture surfaces will provide for longevity. Occasional replacements may be necessary because of projected high use. Dean Gaboury plans to work with potential donors for naming rights to the IC as a whole but also to individual rooms, including multimedia rooms, instruction rooms, and the repurposed room.

MARKETING THE IC BEFORE AND AFTER THE RIBBON CUTTING

Logo

As part of the changes brought about by the recent merger of The Univer-sity of Toledo with the Medical University of Ohio, the new president has involved the campus community in selecting a new logo for the university. We recently updated the university's logo, mission, and core values statements. Building on these achievements, work will commence to design a logo for the new IC. We will tie the new branding to that of the university, with the goal that the logo will be effective and well marketed. We plan to conduct a media blitz in the university's alumni magazine, the student newspapers, faculty and staff newspaper, the local city papers, and local radio and television stations.

Image

We are still in the planning stages for final touches such as artwork to adorn the walls and concourse of the IC. In a recent visit to another IC, one of the planning committee members was intrigued by the use of macro-photography images of modern technology. The art currently displayed at Carlson Library is primarily classic art prints such as Da Vinci and Monet. These are beautiful works that will be retained, but many feel that additional art needs will reflect and sym-bolize the spirit of the IC's new technologies. If additional art reflecting modern technology is obtained, it will be combined with more traditional art already found in the library, thereby enhancing the image of our IC as a modern learning environment.

Tours

Special library tours are planned for faculty members, student groups, admin-istrators, and individuals. These tours will be led by representatives of both IT and the library. We will especially work with the Offices of Residence Life and Admissions. In an effort to market the IC and the changes to the library's and IT's services and resources, we plan to offer tailored tours to our Office of Residence Life. We want to make certain that the coordinators and the guides of the campus tours for prospective students and newly hired faculty and staff are both kept in the loop and made to feel as though they are integral parts of the library. Dean Gaboury proudly proclaims, "It's truly developed for students, adopted by students, supported by students. It'll be an additional recruiting tool for both students and faculty, and it shows what's possible when we put aside personal space to come together for the benefit of the University and the students" (Nowak, August 21, 2006, 2). Investing in the modernization of the campus will continue to be a major component of successful recruitment for faculty and staff during the competition anticipated in the near future.

CONCLUSION

Unless ample space is available, it is recommended that construction of the IC be planned in phases. UT's project will have three phases so that library operations are not interrupted. One of the top goals of most institutions that create an IC is to encourage faculty members to incorporate multimedia resources into their courses. ICs can be used by librarians and centers for teaching excellence to encourage faculty to teach in more imaginative ways. Colleges and universities will always vary in size, organizational structure, and funding. Advanced software may or may not be offered (e.g., *Minitab* for statistics and *AutoCAD* for design and drafting). Schools that have chosen to offer such resources have also had to decide whether to offer tech support or to refer such queries to others. It may make sense, for example, to offer advanced, subject-specific applications but refer patrons to a departmental graduate assistant or the IT attendant in the appropriate computer lab. Similarly, it may be decided to hire graduate students or others who are skilled at assisting others with multimedia tools.

REFERENCES

Beagle, Donald. 1999. "Conceptualizing an Information Commons." *The Journal of Academic Librarianship* 25: 82–89.

BHDP Architecture. 2006. *The University of Toledo Carlson Library Information Commons Feasibility Study.* Cincinnati: BHDP Architecture.

Cowgill, Allison, Joan Beam, and Lindsey Wess. 2001. "Implementing an Information Commons in a University Library." *The Journal of Academic Librarianship* 27: 432–439.

Halbert, Martin. 1999. "Lessons from the Information Commons Frontier." *The Journal of Academic Librarianship* 25: 90–91.

Information and Research Commons White Paper, January 2005.

JISC (Joint Information Systems Committee). 2006. "Designing Spaces for Effective Learning: A Guide to 21st Century Learning Space Design." http://www.jisc.ac.uk/index.cfm?name=eli_learningspaces (2006) (http://lu.com/odlis/) (2004) (http://utsg.utoledo.edu/index.asp) (2006) http://www.umkc.edu/lib/MNL/About/info-commons.htm (2006).

Miller Nichols Library Information Commons. July 21, 2006. University of Missouri-Kansas City. http://www.umkc.edu/lib/MNL/About/info-commons.htm.

Nowak, C. (2006, August 21). "Extreme Makeover Set to Transform Carlson Library." *UT News*, 3–4.

"Toledo Museum of Art Glass Pavilion: A Work of Art." (2006, August 20). *The Toledo Blade*, T3–4.

Warnken, Paula. 2004. "New Technologies and Constant Change: Managing the Process." *The Journal of Academic Librarianship* 30: 322–327.

SELECTED BIBLIOGRAPHY

Cook, David A., and J. Alan. 2006. "Validity of Index of Learning Styles Scores: Multitrait–Multimethod Comparison with Three Cognitive/Learning Style Instruments." *Medical Education* 40: 900–907.

Dallis, Diane, and Carolyn Walters. 2006. "Reference Services in the Commons Environment." *Reference Services Review* 34: 248–260.

EDUCAUSE Review. Boulder, CO. http://www.educause.edu/pub/er (Each issue has something of value on teaching and learning.)

Gust, Kara J., and Clifford H. Haka. 2006. "Bringing Users Back to the Library: A Case History." *New Library World* 107: 141–148.

Malenfant, Chuck. 2006. "The Information Commons as a Collaborative Workspace." *Reference Services Review* 34: 279–286.

Mayer, Richard E., ed. 2005. *The Cambridge Handbook of Multimedia Learning.* New York: Cambridge University Press.

Spencer, Mary Ellen. 2006. "Evolving a New Model: The Information Commons." *Reference Services Review* 34: 242–247.

15 RENEWING THE TECH-FORWARD LIBRARY: INFORMATION COMMONS DEVELOPMENT AT THE UNIVERSITY LIBRARY OF INDIANA UNIVERSITY PURDUE UNIVERSITY INDIANAPOLIS

Rachel Applegate and David Lewis

Indiana University Purdue University Indianapolis (IUPUI) is an urban research university that combines academic programs from Indiana and Purdue universities. It has a largely nonresidential student population of nearly 30,000, who commute to the downtown campus from around the metropolitan area of about one-and-a-half million people in central Indiana. IUPUI came into existence in 1969 with the combination of Purdue and Indiana programs in the state capital of Indianapolis and has strong professional programs in law, business, library science, and especially in the health sciences.

The University Library is largest of five libraries on the IUPUI campus and supports the majority of the academic programs.[1] The University Library building opened in the summer of 1993. The plan was to offer a rich technological environment, and at the time it succeeded in being one of the most technologically sophisticated libraries in the country. It was one of the first academic libraries to provide a large number of computer workstations—it opened with more than 100 public workstations and now has more than 350. The University Library also was one of the first libraries to offer both library resources and other software such as word processing, spreadsheets, and presentation software on the same workstations. It was one of the first libraries to use a Web-based interface to offer access to its resources, doing so in the spring of 1994 when Mosaic was still in alpha release, and developed one of the first electronic reserve systems. The University Library, with the support of the campus, has viewed its path to excellence as being based on technology, not on the strength of paper collections.

At the time the library opened, most of the computer workstations were located in rows in open areas within the stack areas. The idea was that users would want to work with both computer and paper resources. These workstations were designed for individual users and were on custom-built, immovable tables installed at the time of construction. There were about 40 group study rooms, but computers were not provided in these rooms. During the next 10 years a variety of small modifications were made to the library that increased the number of computer workstations, but in each case the workstations were for individual use and the furniture used was simple computer tables.

The University Library had a significant amount of technology, but it began to become clear that additional space for group work was required. The library's existing configuration of computer workstations was not conducive for the increasing numbers of students working in groups. Not only were the tables difficult for more than one person to work at, but the groups naturally tended to create noise, which disrupted other users. Until 2005, all of the computer workstations were more or less the same, and it was becoming more apparent that one size did not fit all and that the library needed to create a variety of spaces for different sorts of use. The first steps were to declare two of the computer-row areas as "quiet" and to place some computers in the group study rooms. Both measures helped, but it was clear that more space for groups was required.

At this time some prime space opened up when the paper reference collection was weeded and reduced in size by about 40 percent. In addition, the current periodicals collection was consolidated and, because of the decrease in the number of paper periodicals received, was reduced in size by about half. This provided an opportunity to explore some alternative approaches to study space in the library. The library decided to focus on group workspaces and to use an exploratory approach to develop a pilot information/academic commons area.

Because the library had been built with a flexible cable management system and the flooring slab was cored, this in combination with an open design, made a pilot academic commons area installation relatively problem free. After the initial power and date cabling had been done, the furniture was installed in two days. The final power and data connections were then completed and the computer equipment was installed.

Much was at stake in this redesign: cost, including funds from the campus and from donors; services, including any necessary retraining of service personnel including reference librarians and computer support technicians; and the place of the library in the activities of students and other library users. The library determined on an evidence-based approach to guide review of the pilot. This incorporated several questions and data streams:

- Explore who library patrons are and what they do, using
  - Library-patron surveys
  - Informal interviews and casual observations
- Provide pilot options to see what patrons prefer
- Ask patrons what they want
  - Computer-station surveys
  - Standardized interviews

- Find out what they choose
  - Web-cam observations

The further development of the Commons area would be guided by these data sources, by professional expertise, and with an eye to the future. Every librarian who selects a book is predicting its future life: the library staff that designs a library area must also envision its future.

WHO ARE THE LIBRARY'S PATRON'S? WHAT DO THEY DO?

Since 1997 the library has systematically examined its patrons by means of an observation/interview, conducted in April of each year with all patrons leaving either of the two exits to the library. A trained interviewer (a library staff member or library science graduate student) observes demographic items, then inquires about activities the person has engaged in during that day's visit to the library. A notable feature of the data collection is that it provides users with a lengthy list of possible activities. Pretesting and instrument development (by a professor of marketing at a neighboring university) showed that patrons are far more likely to report several different activities when given a list to choose from than they are when simply asked to name "some."[2]

The most notable finding is the extent to which patrons use a library for "nonlibrary" purposes. That is, many activities that the UL patrons did in the library did not need library-specific resources and services. The most common uses, mentioned by more than 40 percent of respondents, were to use the computer to access the Internet for class, to check e-mail, and to print. The growing use of the Internet for class reflected a broadening use of a course management system (OnCourse) on campus: this category increased from 37 percent in 1999 to 55 percent in 2003, the largest increase in any category of use.

Other than the category of "conducted research for class" at 40 percent (2003) and "conducted research/other academic" (21 percent, 2003), no other usage requiring library resources or services was more than 20 percent. On the other hand, activities taking advantage of the library as place were very common: 49 percent used the library to study alone, 16 percent simply to relax (2003). There was an increase in the numbers selecting "studied in a group" from 14 percent in 1999 to 17 percent in 2003.

Taken overall, these users want to use this space labeled library to study; to use computers to do school work, surf, or e-mail; to do research about a quarter of the time; and about every tenth visit, to ask a librarian for assistance.

This depicts the library as a space for user activities; library services and information resources directly connect to only part of those activities. This finding is a reflection of previous thought and research about the role of a library in the life of its user (versus the user in the life of the library—Zweizig[3]). Seen one way, it seems to diminish the importance of the library—the library is "just" a lounge and computer lab that happens to be lined with books.

This would be an incorrect and limiting perspective. If the library is "just" a study space, or a meeting place, or a place to work with a group, or even a place to take a break, there is nothing wrong with that. If users need a study space, or a place to meet, or to work in a group—then to meet that need is, well, to meet a need. The word "just" should be deleted, in which case the research tells us that the physical library is a valued place and space, for a variety of activities.

During spring of 2005, two informal sources of information were added to supplement the yearly survey and the general impressions that librarians had of how students were using the library. Informal interviews were conducted with students in the various computer clusters. These interviews confirmed that many students were being assigned group work projects. This activity received rather dramatic physical confirmation when, night after night, cleaning crews needed to relocate chairs that had been adapted into ad hoc group study areas. Student needs—reflected in their behaviors—were changing, and it was time to explore how to meet those needs.

PROVIDE PILOT OPTIONS

At this time, there was an extensive formal (journal articles) and informal (Internet sites, conferences) literature on the design and development of information commons. Not much, at this point, specifically addressed group work, but the concept of group work space had received a good deal of attention in office workspace design. The tech companies of the 1990s and nontech companies that wanted to match their entrepreneurial and creative atmosphere emphasized a collaborative, nonhierarchical workplace, with a correspondingly open office layout and flexible furnishings.[4] This was reflected in the initial Commons design choices.

The first phase of the Commons project began with about 3,000 square feet. In this phase the design team wanted to create imaginative flexible spaces for group work, which led to looking at using office landscape furniture. The librarians knew that they did not really understand what kinds of space and furniture would be the best, so they consciously decided to be exploratory and to try as many things as they could. They also expected to study the results so that this work could be used to guide future developments.

Librarians also knew that they did not have office design expertise required for the project. Therefore the first step in the project was to find a design firm to work on the project. After soliciting proposals from the local business furniture firms, the library selected RJE Business Interiors, who agreed to provide design and installation services at no cost and to involve their primary furniture provider—Knoll—in the project.

To fund the project the Library looked for external support and the library's community board took the Commons project on as the major focus for its fundraising activities. The project team began the design process with several events that involved RJE, Knoll, library staff, students, members of the library's community board, and others from the community whom they hoped to convince to contribute to the project. The results of these sessions were taken into the design process managed by RJE. As noted previously, this first phase of the project was seen as exploratory and so planners purposely tried to include as many configurations of furniture as possible.

At the same time as the furniture layouts were being designed, the library's technology support unit worked on a variety of computer configurations intended to support group work. These included large screen monitors and computers with dual monitors, dual keyboards, and dual mice.

The result of the design of the pilot area was 17 workstations on a variety of furniture. One of the findings of the design process was the desire, expressed by students, to work around tables. Most of the workstations incorporated tables in various configurations; in several of the workstations the furniture was movable, and several movable marker boards were included in the space.

As can be seen in Figure 15.1, the pilot area had several differing configurations. The front section (at the top of the figure) was the only one that used "tall" chairs, on the upper/outer side of a partition. There was a counter along the partition (see photo 15.1); on the other side were noncomputer seats.

Going further in (down the figure), along the left side of the figure are wall-facing areas, at normal chair height (photo 15.2), with two floating tables.

The middle area along the right side of the photo consists of two distinct sections divided by the partition that runs down the spine. On the right (outer) area, "tall" chairs are arranged in D-table group formations (photo 15.3). On the inner side are normal desk-level D-tables (photo 15.4). On both sides, these supposedly group areas were primarily occupied by individuals, and groups first chose the more open tables along the wall (left of the figure); in fact, the photo shows far more seats than were ever actually in use.

Figure 15.1
Floorplan #1

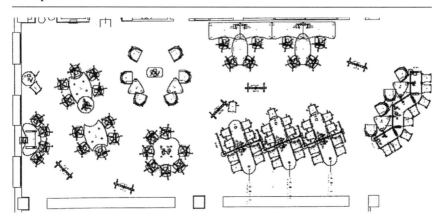

Photo 15.1: IUPUI University Library Academic Commons Pilot Area: Counter-high Area

Photo 15.2: IUPUI University Library Academic Commons Pilot Area: Wall Work Stations

Returning to the overall diagram (figure 15.1), although the squarish table just below (just past) the wall shows seven seats, interviewees found that it was a comfortable fit for two people.

The "batwing" table near the bottom (furthest in) and shown slightly separated was an interesting and flexible configuration: the "wings" were moveable

Photo 15.3: IUPUI University Library Academic Commons
Pilot Area: Exterior Counter, High D-Tables

Photo 15.4: IUPUI University Library Academic Commons
Pilot Area: Interior Desk, Level D-Tables

while the computer monitors were mounted from the central pillar. It was only in
the busiest times that it accommodated one large group, as intended (photo 15.5).
A few individual stations were scattered throughout. Along the wall, with the
squarish table, and in the batwing table, multiple keyboards (and sometimes dual
monitors) for one computer were provided.

Photo 15.5: IUPUI University Library Academic Commons Pilot Area: Large Group Tables

ASK PATRONS WHAT THEY WANT—FIND OUT WHAT THEY CHOOSE

During 2005, with this pilot area further information-gathering was developed. The largest source was a survey administered to library computer users. This was mounted on all library computers, on the opening Microsoft Internet Explorer page, at randomly selected one- or two-hour intervals, covering morning, afternoon, and evening time periods of weekdays and weekends, for the last six weeks of the semester, and the last two weeks of the spring semester. Although students had the option of exiting the survey, more than 200 surveys were returned each semester, and nearly 30 percent of students made extensive comments, indicating a quite high level of interest in providing input.

This survey was supplemented by a small number of interviews of users and nonusers of the pilot commons area involving a structured format that did not randomly select participants. Finally, a series of observations were made using in-place security Webcams.

The survey, interview, and observation findings mutually reinforced each other. The following findings are those with the strongest convergent evidence.

Convenience matters. The most frequent reason for selecting seating was "convenience" followed by "only computer available." The reference/Commons area is on the main (second) floor of the library; the most-used area of the Commons was the "tall chair" area, the first seats visible from the outside.

People like space to spread out. The "fixed" group wall stations, with D-tables jutting out from the partition (with tall or short chairs) were much more popular

232

with individuals than with groups, who gravitated to the interior wall or to the larger rectangular or circular tables. The D-tables proved too cramped to be the first choice for groups, although they did fill up later in the semester.

People appreciate quietness and privacy—and the ability to make noise themselves without disturbing others. This was seen in answers to the survey's open-ended questions and in interviews. When asked in the survey where they would prefer to do group work, by far the most popular answer was group study rooms, the most private option available. The new Academic Commons area essentially tied with "elsewhere on campus."

For Group Work Respondent Will Use

		Percent
Group study room	208	52%
Elsewhere on campus	74	19%
Academic Commons area	68	17%
Other	38	10%
Rehearsal room	10	3%
Total	398	

While there was generally a low level of knowledge about the Commons (about 1.5 on a scale of 1 = nothing and 4 = a lot), the survey itself educated participants. Most predicted they would use it in the future, although they were definitely more enthusiastic with respect to individual work than for group work.

Will Use Academic Commons

	Individuals		Groups	
Never	49	12%	118	30%
Once	79	20%	118	30%
Several times	160	40%	112	28%
Many times	113	28%	50	13%
Total	401		398	
At least once	352	88%	280	70%

Services are of limited interest. There are few ways in which reference services appear in the observations (once), surveys (six respondents), and interviews (two respondents). Computer services were even less visible: only one survey respondent said proximity to a computer consultant was a reason for sitting at that particular computer. On the other hand, librarian assistance was cited by nearly 90 respondents as a potential reason to choose the Commons area (in the future). Nevertheless, it is the facilities, rather than the services, that are the most important draw for the Academic Commons.

This Would Be an Important Reason to Choose the Academic Commons Area

	Number	Percent of Total
Reference services	89	19%
Computer consultants	74	16%
Group work facilities	182	40%

BUILD-OUT OF FULL ACADEMIC COMMONS

In the fall of 2006, a wider implementation of the Academic Commons is scheduled to open. Located within the main floor service area, formerly housing the information/reference desk, the print reference collection, computer stations and study tables, the new Commons consists of 12 "pods" or stations. Lessons learned from the pilot informed their design.

The most important feature is a sense of *privacy*. In seven of the pods, 49-inch high partitions run along the spines, have perpendicular sections at the ends, and sometimes jut out from the middle of sections. These create roomlike spaces. In surveys, the largest number of respondents students selected group study rooms, well above Commons spaces, as their choice for a space in which to work as a group. Although a room reservation system has removed some of the anxiety associated with finding a room, the University Library cannot create more "hard" rooms, but it can configure Commons space to give patrons a roomlike space.

Both *spaciousness* and *flexibility* are enhanced with larger tables and a flexible approach to seating. Observations of the pilot area revealed that supposedly three-person D-shaped tables were more often occupied by individuals. Where chairs appeared in rows, the most common occupancy pattern was "person-stuff-person-stuff"; that is, chairs were used as holding places for backpacks, coats, and other items. Middle seats in the Commons and in the regular computer areas elsewhere were not occupied until all ends were full.

In the new areas, most D-tables were lengthened from 50 inches to 72 inches, and "counter-tops" along partition walls were added. These are too narrow to work on but are the right size to place backpacks, drinks, and books. Several of the larger, more rectangular tables have floating additions: oval tables on casters. These can be repositioned as the group size changes.

In all, the seating provides for more efficient and more flexible use of the seats and computer workstations. Most areas have single computers with a space that is ample for one person, but allows two more to join on movable chairs and using movable tables. A few larger stations will accommodate two to three people working individually (with space in between them) and up to six to eight in a group.

In short, "single-person" areas were enlarged a bit, so that all of them would be used, rather than every other one. Group areas were enlarged significantly to both accommodate groups more realistically than the somewhat cramped areas in the pilot implementation and allow users to work individually during less busy times.

Small-scale *amenities* add to functionality. Power outlets at waist or desk level are liberally provided in every work area and at ends of partitions (by soft chairs). Students interviewees mentioned the need for power outlets for their laptops; often a group will have several members with their own laptops (wireless connectivity began in 2000 and by 2006 extended throughout public areas).

Most partitions have whiteboard, with a translucent section at the top. There are additional whiteboard movable partitions—walls on wheels—that both help create more private spaces and allow for brainstorming activities. There are deliberately clear sightlines (including the translucent higher panels) to the printer stations: individuals working alone need to keep an eye on their belongings as they pick up printouts.

Figures 15.2 and 15.3 show other examples. Figure 15.2 shows an area that will provide more spacious individual stations (when those seated face forward into the partitions) while allowing for additional group members (at the "floating" oval tables) during peak periods. Figure 15.3 shows two group areas. The D table is significantly larger than the pilot D tables, and on the other side of the partition, the area with the squarish table also includes a countertop along the partition for student backpacks. The partitions give each area privacy and provide whiteboard space.

Overall placement of the pods within the "reference area" reflects both building practicalities and the advantages of the original library design. The reference stacks remain in place; in fact there are no electrical conduits in the floor of that area. Instead, the new pods replace simple "library" wooden tables and chairs. "Cores" of wiring are not entirely flexible within this nonstack area, but the possible connection sites are sufficiently ample to allow for an airy, open design, with many pods turned at angles to break up a too-square format, and small nonwired tables are scattered throughout. The area has outside walls along two sides, which have large windows for abundant natural light.

Surveys and observations showed a significant increase in group use of Academic Commons areas during the last half of the fall semester. Libraries need to consider "surge" capacity, and with this in mind, the new space will accommodate both individuals (earlier in the semester) as well as a large number of large groups later. Rows of individual computers remain in the front parts of the reference area to satisfy individual needs.

A final advantage to a pod design lies in *fundraising*. The pods are distinct and of different sizes. In the pilot phase, several local companies sponsored particular areas, which was noted with small "flags" on poles rising from partitions. These "naming rights" are subtle but still convey a message: as the development officer put it, "Students will say, 'Meet at the Smith & Jones pod.'"

Figure 15.2
Floorplan #2

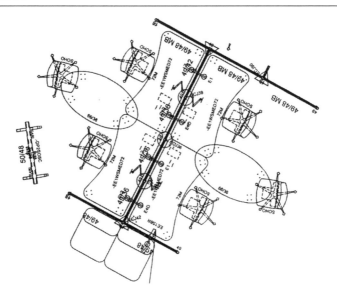

Figure 15.3
Floorplan #3

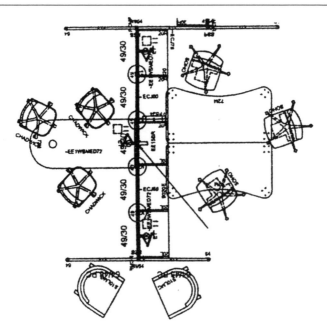

There is one disadvantage to outside funding. Among academic library professionals, at this stage, the word "information commons" has a definite meaning and connotation. The word *commons* derives from the British academic model of a "faculty commons" or "seniors commons," an area where scholars or students could gather to collaborate socially or academically. Nonacademics do not appear to share this familiarity. To them, at this point, "Information Commons" sounds new and exciting: it highlights "information," which they do indeed see as a "library" thing, and "Commons" currently connects to some digital initiatives such as the "Creative Commons." What is new and exciting to them, however, can seem "old" or "the usual" to librarians.

The IUPUI University Library looks forward to serving more student needs in the future: providing tutoring, writing, and presentation assistance, all features noted as desirable in survey responses. For this more flexible conception of the space, the term *Academic Commons* is more descriptive and desirable. It seems, however, that it does not resonate with outside companies—potential funders—the way "Information Commons" does.

The original design and concept of the University Library from its opening to today remain intact. The building's wiring and structure provide relatively open floor plans that result in opportunities for great flexibility and creativity in creating spaces. The technology-forward philosophy serves the learning needs of the campus as professors incorporate information, technology, and group processes into their assignments. The needs, characteristics, and desires of the library's patrons are part of the design process, producing a library renewed to effectively serve its community.

NOTES

1. The other four libraries are in the schools of dentistry, law, medicine, and the Herron School of Art.

2. Stamatoplos, Anthony, and Robert Mackoy. "Assessment of User Response to IUPUI University Library: 1999–2003 Studies, Report to David Lewis of IUPUI University." Indiana University Purdue University Indianapolis, 2003. IDeA: http://hdl.handle.net/1805/415

3. Zweizig, Douglas. "With Our Eye on the User: Needed Research for Information and Referral in the Public Library." *Drexel Library Quarterly* 12 (1976): 48–58.

4. At a research level, see: Peterson, Tim O., and Jon W. Beard. "Workspace Technology's Impact on Individual Privacy and Team Interaction." *Team Performance Management* 10.7–8 (2004): 163–172; a representative example in the popular business press is Mack, Linda. "Uncommon Spaces: Tech Employers Are Setting the Workplace Pace with Nontraditional Offices That Are Striking Yet Functional. Now Other Companies Are Applying Their Ideas to Recruit and Retain Employees and Boost Productivity." *Star-Tribune* (Minneapolis) Feb. 26, 2006, D1 (Lexis-Nexis).

VII

HOPE FOR THE FUTURE

16 WHAT'S OLD IS NEW AGAIN: LIBRARY SERVICES AND THE MILLENNIAL STUDENT

Jamie Seeholzer, Frank J. Bove, and Delmus E. Williams

Thirty years ago, librarians were discussing how to develop the service potential of the academic library by offering a more proactive service program that more closely met the needs of our clientele. We knew then, as we know now, that the library is an acquired taste and an important one if students are to get the most from their education and prepare themselves to continue gaining information throughout their lives. But things have changed. In the 1970s, the library was still the primary concentration of information on campus, and, although some students could get through college without coming into the building, relying entirely on textbooks, most were obliged to use the library whether or not it presented a friendly, well-organized, and intuitive information system. But the Internet has changed all that, and we are now faced with a clientele that has alternatives and that is well versed in using those alternatives. All of a sudden, academic libraries are being asked to compete for the attention of students, and we as leaders of these organizations can no longer postpone efforts to bring our libraries in line with the needs of our clientele. We have always valued good service, but the information structure in which we lived made providing that level of service difficult. Now we have technology that can make possible the kinds of services we have envisioned at a cost that we can afford.

This chapter describes the current challenges in developing library services for the millennial student and how we might address those challenges without compromising the service ideal that we have eschewed for decades now. It defines the evolving needs of millennial students, the technologies they use, and how those technologies affect the way they seek, gather, and evaluate information. It addresses the information-seeking habits of the net generation and the assumptions they bring to the library. Are these habits and assumptions substantially different from those embodied by previous generations of library users? Has technology fundamentally changed the information users' need and how they find, evaluate, and use that information? And what do librarians have to do to ensure that our users get the information they need and integrate information gleaned from various sources to meet their needs? How do we and those to whom the library reports create, promote, and sustain library services that meet both the real and perceived needs of the millennial student at a time and place that is useful and at a price that we can afford?

It is clear that the recent influx in technology over the past two decades has changed the way users seek information and the role that librarians have traditionally played as gatekeepers to information. Today, more than ever before, information is literally available at our fingertips. The current generation has developed and grown up with easy access to computers and other technologies, and nothing about them are perceived to be either strange or daunting. They have often been exposed to card catalogs or paper index with their arcane organization and less likely than their elders to be overwhelmed with the massive amounts of information that is available. At the same time, however, they may be less likely to have the patience that older users were forced to show in using paper sources and may not be as inclined to ask for help to guide them in their evaluation of resources. At the same time academic libraries are being asked to serve more older students and faculty who learned to use and organize resources at a different time and in different ways than do newly minted high school graduates and are often from older generations who were trained to use material in different ways from both students and their professional colleagues. But while style and the mechanisms for information seeking may have changed, the core values have not and neither have the eventual product that students and scholars are expected to produce. The Internet, for better or worse, is the leviathan created by the baby boomers that seemed all but mystical 20 years ago. But our students have never known a world without it, and have since found cell phones that keep them connected, blackberries and text messages that keep them tuned to the world, iPods that can allow them to hear or see what they want when they want to see it and free them from constraints of place and time. The time spent doing the mechanics associated with learning has been reduced dramatically over the past generation, and the need to be anywhere or to limit studies to any time has disappeared. We want things instantly, and this generation has found out how to make that happen.

Many librarians have accepted this situation and have considered ways of doing business to fit this paradigm. Tools like Google have certainly helped skew the playing field. Many libraries are attempting to "Googlize" their resources into powerful, simplistic search mechanisms that do not require outside assistance. This development has both positive and negative ramifications. Easy search tools are indeed a blessing, but they certainly do not address all information needs. But information comes in strange aggregations, and simple tools can make it difficult to search for that information successfully or might produce so much information that is tangentially related to the topic at hand that it is impossible to peruse.

Google has simplified the search syntax and method, but many times it only creates smaller haystacks in which to search for the needle.

Steven Bell has challenged our profession to maintain its standards and not surrender library values so easily. In his view, we must resist the temptation that eschews education in favor of simple user interfaces. As educators, we cannot and should not avoid complexity. Librarians still have an obligation to create wise information users. Bell (2005, 79) says:

> The trick is to devise methods to create wise information consumers who can decide for themselves when a simple or more complex option will return the best possible results. If our profession works collaboratively with educators, instructional technologists, information technologists, and the information industry, we can retain our core values while adapting to an increasingly complex and chaotic information landscape.

For us to meet Bell's challenge, we must understand the population we serve, accepting the fact that simple answers can be answered simply, but that we must also stand ready to address the more convoluted. The standard for library service has always been to provide "enough" information to meet patron needs, neither too much nor too little, and we must avoid the temptation to present to our users "one size fits all" solutions to queries.

Let us begin by taking a close look at the present generation, the millennial generation, and the way they address information. As a group, millennials are comfortable operating in this new technological climate, although there is a lot of variation in their skill sets and their access to technology. As a result, the service provider must learn to evaluate both the resources available ubiquitously to our clients and the technologies themselves so that we can address their needs. We must help them make their equipment work, work collaboratively with them to access information, and then as necessary assist our users in critically evaluating the information that is so much at their fingertips. This can be done on the phone, through chat services, e-mail, or in person, and assistance must reflect the fact that our clients can access the information needed as easily at 2 A.M. as they do at 2 P.M.

THE MILLENNIAL GENERATION

The millennial generation has been described by such varying names as generation Y, the net generation, the echo boom generation, the Nintendo generation, the boomlet, digital generation, and the nexters. It is made up of people born anywhere from 1977 to 1983 and sometimes capped off at the year 2000, although it sometimes extends without any cutoff date. The millennial generation is at present 80 million strong and constitutes the largest generation, beating out the baby boomers who included 77 million people at their peak.

The millennial generation is made up of technology-savvy, connected young people who value collaboration, immediate results, and interactive experiences. This generation is more optimistic, digitally literate, confident, and diverse than were their elders. Millennials are "well informed and media savvy…display a strong work ethic and have grown up understanding the new digital economy. They are comfortable with changes brought about by the new technology and e-commerce" (Alch 2000a, 42). They have "grown up in a world where they enjoy access to nearly everything a person could need or want 24/7/365" (Lindstrom 2005, 11–12). Millennials also are "more ambitious and optimistic than generation Xers, are the most ethnically diverse (35 percent are nonwhite), and favor different values and learning styles than did their predecessors. They are the largest child generation in American history, currently making up 34 percent of the country's population" (Gardner and Eng 2005, 405).

The millennial generation differs from its predecessors in a number of ways. First, the millennials have "displayed more responsibility by holding part-time jobs in high school and college. They have not been given hand outs or over-indulged to the same extent as were the baby busters" (Alch 2000b, 26). Second, the culture of millennials has a more global orientation, and their concept of the family unit is more varied, reflecting societal changes that have taken place directly before and during their life time. The millennial generation has "come to regard constant and turbulent change as normal" (Alch 2000b). It addresses global and social justice issues pragmatically and expects society to view their opinions about these issues seriously. This next generation is characterized as preferring, "teamwork, experiential activities, and the use of technology" as opposed to competition among peers and its members are often referred to as "digital natives, referring to the fact that they have grown up with technology as opposed to digital immigrants who did not" (Kvavik 2005, 7.1). Millennials are also different from other generations in terms of their childhood. Millennials were, "on average, part of the smallest families in history, which meant they received more parental time and resources. The notion that they are *special* has been with them since birth, and with this notion comes a sense of entitlement. College students today expect the same kind of attention their parents gave them" (Gardner and Eng 2005, 408).

The characteristics of the millennial generation should be taken into account as we modify or design services or buildings to meet their needs. Our core value as a profession has always been a desire to understand our clients and their expectations and requirements Given the heightened expectations of this group of people and their perspective as to what is appropriate, it is critical that we determine how they like to learn and what kinds of services, collections, and space will most effectively address their needs. The unique characteristics of millennials will impact how academic materials are delivered to them, how library space is structured, and how services will have to be tailored to keep the millennial generation visiting the library.

PREFERRED FORMATS/MATERIALS

As noted earlier, millennials are digital natives who have been raised in a time when computers are not considered *technology* but just one more aspect of their daily lives. This means that these students may prefer that their educational and research materials be offered in specific formats and delivered in different ways with different expectations than previous generations. As a group, millennial students expect access to materials that can be located easily and delivered quickly at no cost. In the classroom, it is expected that educational experiences will be delivered with the most sophisticated technology available; however, this is often not the case as several studies have shown.

As a generation, millennials are defined as being impatient and expecting instant gratification, and this affects how they prefer materials to be delivered to them (Sweeney 2005, 167). They are concerned with the "ease of use, reliability, accuracy, currency, availability, and cost" as well as "trust, quality, credibility, validity, completeness, and comprehensiveness" of the information sources they locate for research needs (Weiler 2004, 50). These information criteria are often described as the three Fs: students want to find what they need *first*, *fastest*, and in *full* text (MacWhinnie 2003, 245).

Millennials prefer materials that are easy to find and retrieve. They will often go first to the Internet to locate materials when conducting research. Millennials choose the Internet, seemingly because it is relatively easy to find some information on a subject (Weiler 2004, 50) and prefer "global searching of Google to more sophisticated but more time-consuming searching provided by the library" (Lippincott 2005, 13.3). They also "find library-sponsored resources difficult to figure out on their own" (Lippincott 2005, 13.2) and are not inclined to ask for help. They are seldom "exposed to or interested in formal instruction in information literacy, [and] they prefer to use the simplistic but responsive Google" (Lippincott 2005, 13.2). Millennials might be more open to instruction on using library resources if they understood that it would in the long run save them time and improve the quality of the results achieved.

Library searches were considered too time consuming because students must make "separate searches of the online catalog and every database of potential interest, after first identifying which databases might be relevant" (Lippincott 2005, 13.3). Libraries are quickly remedying this disconnect between the user needs and their offerings by joining up with Google Scholar, Ebsco, and other indexes and resource providers. OCLC is working with Google to create a program where information from peer-reviewed journals, books, theses, and other academic resources can be searched through Google Scholar. This service would be revolutionary and desirable for both academic libraries and millennials because it connects students directly with resources where they are already trying to look for them (Lippincott 2005, 13.4).

Despite some perceptions that millennials are unsociable and would rather conduct all research solely online, researchers have found that students still prefer face-to-face communication. Students said they preferred to talk to people first when investigating a topic they know little about rather than going straight to a book. Although some millennials prefer to find information on their own, many students, "expressed the preference to discuss information needs with a *real person* rather than find all of the needed information on their own" (Weiler 2004, 50).

Millennial students are also concerned with finding academic resources fast. A trend in the research skills of millennials is their preference for quickness over accuracy. Research conducted at the University of Idaho found that "issues of time and levels of difficulty in obtaining information" were of more importance to millennials than issues of accuracy in found information (Weiler 2004, 50). Millennials have a real problem with putting in the time necessary to find quality sources for their academic research needs. Researchers have concluded that unless there is an "intrinsic or extrinsic motivation of some kind, or the research is of crucial importance to them on a personal or professional basis, students have to 'need' to obtain high-quality information resources" (Weiler 2004, 50). This idea that users do not always need all of the information that could be made available is not new, but it is emphasized in these discussions. Millennials also prefer full-text delivery of materials rather than hunting down print resources at the library, although as often as not, they will print those resources out and read them on paper just as the earlier generation photocopied text. Many millennial generation students prefer electronic formats and electronic delivery of materials necessary for class readings and research that can be available 24/7 anyplace they happen to be. Academic libraries provide access to electronic journals for research and also often set up electronic reserve systems to facilitate easier access to class materials (Lippincott 2005, 13.1). Millennial students may also rely on electronic delivery for obtaining lecture notes, PowerPoint slides, lectures captured on audio and video, electronic reserves and for submitting class assignments (MacWhinnie 2003, 243).

Millennials are having some difficulties with the resources they find using the "3Fs" of fast, full-text, and first. The most common obstacle is the *infoglut* or the overabundance of materials retrieved from unsophisticated searching on the Internet through Google, what we once referred to as *noise* caused by having the information we need buried in a mass of information that we do not. Other problems for millennials conducting Internet research were the questionable validity of Internet materials and the difficulty presented in determining where Web sites originate (Weiler 2004, 50). Another trend in the information-seeking habits of millennials is their lack of critical thinking when determining the reliability of some Internet sources. Professors teaching millennials find that often the source of the information will outweigh the value of the information itself, which takes away the need to "think critically to verify information" (Weiler 2004, 50); this causes a problem in educating students about reliable resources.

Aside from the formats millennials prefer, studies also reported surprising findings about the preference for technology use in the classroom. A study conducted at approximately 12 universities in the Midwest had surprising results with regard to millennials and their preferred mode of educational delivery. Researchers expected to find millennial students demanding more use of technology in teaching and learning in the classroom and a corresponding need for faculty to increase their use of technology in the classroom. Instead, researchers found that millennial students do not overwhelmingly prefer advanced technology in the classroom and that at times such technology can be a hindrance to the educational process (Kvavik 2005, 7.8).

Researchers also expected students to have superior Internet technology skills but actually found many students who picked up skills as they moved through their undergraduate education. Researchers found "a significant need for further training in the use of information technology in support of learning and problem-solving skills" (Kvavik 2005, 7.17). Researchers further found that "students appear to be slower developing adequate skills in using information technology in support of academic activities, which limits technology's current value to the institution" (Kvavik 2005, 7.17). The investment made by colleges and universities in advanced technology may be slow in coming as both teachers and students learn to use this media effectively (Kvavik 2005, 7.17). Although millennial students are comfortable with technology, the use of this technology supplements, rather than replaces, expanding the options of teachers and students.

Instruction for millennials has focused on the rise in digital forms of education and instruction with emphasis (and fear) placed on distance learning and other digital modes of changing the educational interaction between teachers and students. Although some of this concern is rooted in fact, concern about the digital competence of millennials has somewhat tentative roots. Although millennials are comfortable with technology, some studies have shown that the use of technology for educational use might be overemphasized. Studies have shown that although undergraduates "reported a positive impact of the Internet on their academic experience, a closer read of the data reveals that IT usage beyond e-mail remains relatively low. For example, only 6 percent of students reported taking an online course for credit, and only half of the students in this group reported that the course was worthwhile" (Ramaley and Zia 2005, 8).

SERVICES/INSTRUCTION

Academic libraries need to alter both the way materials are delivered and the accompanying services offerings if they expect to meet the demands of millennials. These students expect customization, they are technology veterans, and they regularly use new communication modes (Gardner and Eng 2005, 406). All of these things affect how services must be created, how they are delivered, and how they will be used. To meet the changing expectations of our clients, libraries need to find a way to "use systems and technology to market personalized, customized, anywhere, anytime, digital multimedia, [and] interactive information services" (Sweeney 2005, 174). Millennials prefer digital networked services and libraries will have to merge library services with the Internet to address their preference (Sweeney 2005, 170). Contemporary students expect "flexibility, geographic independence, speed of response, time shifting, interactivity, multitasking, and time saving" (Sweeney 2005, 170) from library services, and librarians will have to incorporate each in its programs to retain their loyalty.

Digital and remote services are a highlight of the changes that will need to be made to meet the service demands of millennials. Millennials have "grown up expecting instant access with immediate feedback" (Sweeney 2005, 168) and this has, in turn, become the expected level of service. Libraries have attempted to answer this need for instant gratification and time saving by offering services online such as remote access to online journals, databases, e-books, and remote reference assistance (Sweeney 2005, 168). Services offered by the library electronically will have to be tailored to the characteristics of the millennial generation including their "propensity to work late hours and use a variety of technologies, including laptops and cell phones" (Lippincott 2005, 13.6). Because millennials perceive their learning as mobile and use these remote library services, libraries will need to have "an infrastructure that facilitates remote usage of their resources" (Gardner and Eng 2005, 414). Academic libraries can provide quality remote services through wireless networks that use password protection or Internet protocol address authentication, but it is crucial that such infrastructure works properly, that service and problem solving is available to students at all hours, and that problems are addressed quickly because millennials have high expectations for technology in college and will not tolerate disruptions of service (Gardner and Eng 2005, 414). They also expect "convenient, one-stop shopping when it comes to research," and this can be addressed by using portals on the library homepage (Gardner and Eng 2005, 415). A portal is a "network service that brings together content from diverse resources, including the library catalogue, on-line subscription reference material, e-journals and learning and teaching material" and presents these materials to the user in a single interface (Gardner and Eng 2005, 415–416).

The availability of face-to-face library services is also required to meet the service of this generation of users. Millennials demand access to information 24 hours a day, 7 days a week and use the library at all hours of the night. Twenty years ago, students wanted this level of accessibility but it was not available. Now it is. Academic libraries will need to have "facilities accessible at all times in order to adequately support student education" and to "continue as the primary hub of learning on campus" (Gardner and Eng 2005, 416). The 24/7 accessibility of the library addresses the impatience of millennials and the need for instant gratification. This accessibility is good for education, for it allows students more time to assimilate and comprehend information because it takes less time to find and retrieve it. But it means that libraries have to change because "successful library hours and service availability must be based on millennial needs, not the convenience of library staff" (Sweeney 2005, 168). Creative approaches must be developed to extend library hours and to offer chat reference and related services when students are awake and working.

Another aspect of services for millennials is the incorporation of collaborative and multitasking services. These students frequently engage in collaborative searching and learning because it can often result in the same or better results in less time. Services can be created and new tools adopted to allow for collaborative searching to be improved, but it must be remembered that millennials will not "use tools, even automated ones such as collaborative search engines, for long unless they are effective" (Sweeney 2005, 171). Millennials are also known for being multitaskers. The millennial generation has the ability and the preference to "seamlessly weave their work and recreational activities, making no artificial distinctions" and "computers, search engines, and information resources must enable and enhance their multitasking, whenever desired" (Sweeney 2005, 172). For libraries, this means that collaborative technology and multitasking must be built into library services to "speed up and improve searching as well as learning" (Sweeney 2005, 172).

This desire for improved technologies can be taken too far in academic libraries. The current use of remote reference via online chat is one example where overly sophisticated technologies result in less use by millennials. Some chat services for reference that offer the ability for librarians to push Web pages at the user or even e-mail a transcript of the chat to the user are often unnecessarily complicated. Millennials prefer the more intuitive design of some of the simpler instant messenger services that they have been using for years. These instant messenger programs are more readily used by millennials and they have a greater level of comfort with these applications. Libraries who integrate these programs can expect to see a rise in the use of remote reference services (Gardner and Eng 2005, 415).

Instructional services for millennials will also have to be tailored to meet the different learning styles of this generation of students. Millennials are often known as "gamers" based on their interest in video and computer games, and aspects of their gaming have entered into the way some millennials address information resources. Gaming implies that "you can learn by making mistakes, and there are no long-term penalties for doing so" and that "gaming gives quick feedback and requires a lot of analytical thinking" (Sweeney 2005, 170). Many of the attributes of millennial game behaviors "can be converted into skills for searching, discovering, and gaining knowledge," which is the essence of most instructional services at academic libraries (Sweeney 2005, 170). Games also promote "various types of information literacy, develop information seeking habits and production practices (like writing), and require good, old-fashioned research skills" (Squire and Steinkuehler 2005, 38). Because of the prevalence of the gaming culture in the millennial generation, libraries and their vendors will "have to build gaming characteristics into their systems to be successful with this generation" (Sweeney 2005, 171).

Another characteristic of millennials that will affect how library services are delivered is their learning preference, which leans toward experiential learning through trial and error. Libraries can format services to this learning style by refocusing educational experiences at the library. Millennials expect a "focus on learning rather than teaching. They will expect their educational opportunities to be based upon assessed knowledge, competency, and skill, not time spent on tasks as quantified in credit hours. They want their education to be more experiential, fun, collaborative, and game-like" (Sweeney 2005, 172). For librarians offering bibliographic instruction services, this means altering the way they present instruction by perhaps "changing from pure lecture to incorporate hands-on activities [that] will help to hold student interest and increase information retention" (Weiler 2004, 51). This teaching style is often referred to as "active learning" and can be used further in bibliographic instruction by incorporating "examples which students can relate to and asking students to develop their own examples" and will create "meaning between students' life experience and the material which we want them to be learning" (McGlynn 2005, 13). The goal of this learning-centered approach is to empower students and to help them build on and organize both what they already know and the additional information they acquire (McGlynn 2005, 13).

The prevalence of multimedia technologies in the classroom has specific implications for academic librarians. With the rise in usage of different technologies and multimedia devices in educational use and research, librarians will have to be trained in these technologies, or academic libraries will need people on staff and available to assist students with learning and using these tools. This *blending* of skills means that library staff will need to be trained in skills including "instructional design, instructional and information technology as well as those of traditional librarianship" (Sweeney 2005, 174). Products such as PowerPoint, Adobe Photoshop, and Web site authoring tools are in greater use in college classrooms, and librarians will need to know how to both use and teach others to use these more sophisticated multimedia tools.

Sophisticated multimedia tools are on the rise in use in academic libraries, but students still need more traditional help from librarians when it comes to researching. Because millennials expect access to information in a wide variety of formats, including print, electronic, and multimedia, they will require research assistance from librarians in using these resources (MacWhinnie 2003, 242–243). Students will require the "expertise of an information specialist to make the most of the resources available and find the information they need, and the librarian's role will become increasingly essential as students seek guidance in navigating through the many layers of electronic information resources" (MacWhinnie 2003, 242–243).

Although other library services may change and evolve, students will probably always rely on librarians for "assistance with research strategies, managing large amounts of information in diverse formats, and evaluating and selecting appropriate information" (MacWhinnie 2003, 243). Also, with the use of Internet resources, students have expressed difficulty in evaluating Web sources for their reliability and validity. Students need to develop these skills, which means librarians will "have to play a larger role in instructing students and providing assistance in this new joint information and technology environment" (MacWhinnie 2003, 245).

SPACE

Aside from the different formats and services that are preferred, library spaces are also changing to accommodate the learning styles and preferences of millennials. The library can become a unique center on campus as it listens to the needs of millennials and can have a new understanding in the university setting not only as a physical facility, but also a place that brings together, "content, access, enduring collections, and services" (Lippincott 2005, 13.1). If libraries do not listen to the needs of millennial generation students, the library as the academic center of campus will diminish and a disconnect will occur between this generation and libraries.

The trend in academic libraries is toward the Information Commons approach to service that features a physical space that "incorporates many workstations equipped with software supporting a variety of uses, offers workspace for individuals and groups, provides comfortable furniture, and has staff that can support activities related to access to information and use of technology to develop new products" (Lippincott 2005, 13.11). This organizational structure communicates a welcoming attitude to millennials because it is the opposite of "old-style formal reference rooms where students were expected to sit on straight wooden chairs and work individually and silently without accessing technology. Instead, these spaces project a comfortable, relaxed environment, a celebration of technology, and an invitation to communicate" (Lippincott 2005, 13.11). A typical Information Commons provides a central location where "access to technology and reference service is combined. Computer workstations are grouped together with a help desk, and print reference resources nearby. Students can use work stations to access the OPAC, search the Internet and electronic databases, and use productivity software to prepare assignments with print resources, technical help, and professional research assistance readily available" (MacWhinnie 2003, 244). They also provide access to tutors, writing labs, assistance in producing media and in preparing presentations, and other elements of the academic program that were not previously associated with the library.

The Information Commons movement in libraries has some great advantages for millennials including that "students can start the research process; locate, evaluate, and select the information they need; get research or technical assistance; and complete assignments from one location. This integrated access to information and technology, combined with the availability of multimedia tools and staff assistance, eliminates the need for students to go to different locations to prepare assignments or to get help" (MacWhinnie 2003, 244).

With the rise in cooperative learning at the college level and group study behaviors, the library as place remains relevant. Libraries have always provided study space, but they are now including more group study areas that have "technology for access to both physical collections and electronic resources, as well as productivity software that allows students to work together to complete shared assignments" (MacWhinnie 2003, 242). Millennials have a preference for different kinds of space in a library. They want "different types of space at different times for different purposes," and these purposes can include quiet spaces and spaces for "noisy interaction, group work, performances, study, socializing, and so on" (Sweeney 2005, 174). Indeed, libraries now have "classrooms, conference centers, group-study areas, high-end multimedia equipment, computers outfitted with advanced software, and areas designated for lessons in information literacy, along with the stacks of books" (Carlson 2005, 6).

Library space must be altered to meet the needs of millennials and to grow older gracefully. Library space must be "designed to easily, cheaply, and quickly convert to new functions even those requiring convenient storage, power, and technology" (Sweeney 2005, 174). Other things that libraries need to keep in mind as they renovate their buildings are the comfort of the building as perceived by millennials. Among the concerns listed by millennials are "the quality of natural lighting, the quality of work spaces, the quality of the heating and air-conditioning system, and the overall ambiance of the building" (Carlson 2005, 6). Also, access to computers and the Internet, as well as "the number of data ports, the quality of the telecommunication system, and the quality of the public-access workstations," were also important to millennials (Carlson 2005, 6–7).

In addition to all of the technological and academic resources that can be found in today's academic libraries, the library is increasingly becoming a social space for millennials. The fear that libraries will be done away with in some digital, virtual future is unfounded. Millennials, like every other generation, "need and still demand social and public spaces. Everybody has to be somewhere" (Sweeney 2005, 174). As part of this social need, academic libraries are incorporating noneducational services in the form of cafes and lounge areas. Aside from the convenience offered by these cafes and coffee spots, there is the argument that as the library becomes a more social space, the "strong customary association between food and socially shaped activities" (Gardner and Eng 2005, 416) will maintain at the library. The goal for the library is to continue to be the "great intellectual and cultural center of the academic community" and serve as the "academic counterpart to the student center" (Carlson 2005, 6). The academic library may also foster a sense of community on a college campus through the use of an Information Commons layout. A library can promote this sense of community by "providing comfortable spaces for informal gatherings of students," as seen with the coffee bars, and provide an "atmosphere in which social and academic interests can easily intersect." Such spaces "encourage students to continue conversations on topics of academic interest" (Lippincott 2005, 13.11). The library as a social spot for millennials has even changed the measurement of the success of an academic library. Some libraries have abandoned "circulation statistics, which are falling at some institutions, as the measure of success they show administrators and trustees. Instead, they cite library attendance" (Carlson 2005, 6).

CONCLUSION

Much has been written about the possible disappearance of the library as a place with the rise in digital communications and portable access; fortunately, this scenario appears to be unlikely. Print resources are not dead and still need to be housed in a quality library facility, and students still need a place to go to study and socialize. But if the library is to remain the place of choice for study and for students to gather in an academic setting, librarians must understand the changing view of its clientele. The millennial generation is a vibrant, large, and fascinating generation of young people with unique expectations of what service, access, and space encompass. The students from this generation have shown little interest in adapting their learning styles to those supported by traditional organizations like the library, so we must adapt our programs to meet their needs. Just as in the past, the job is to change as we need to change, maintaining our commitment to serve and to educate, but altering our delivery systems and space dynamically as needs change. In the view of Lynn Brindley (2006, 490–494), this means we must redefine the library as we have done constantly over the years. She suggests that, to meet this challenge, it is critical that we:

- Know our users and keep close to them (and to our lost users and nonusers) by constantly trying to understand what they want.
- Rethink the physical spaces of the library and create a "desirable draw."
- Integrate marketing in our organization and in the way we approach strategy and service development.
- Open up legacy print collections to digital channels and reveal them through digitization.
- Increase our efficiency and improve productivity through streamlining and cooperation.
- Invest more in innovation and digital activities.
- Develop our people, recruit and retain people who understand this new world, and ensure that we have the right mix of skills to meet the needs of a changing clientele.

When all is said, it is useful to hark back to Brindley who reiterates the words of the founders of the British Library in 1753. Their aim was to have within it the world's knowledge "preserved therein for public use, to all posterity for all studious and curious persons" (as cited in Brindley 2006, 495). Providing all the information users want and need in a comfortable, supportive place available at their convenience remains our goal for serving millennials and others. Once again we find that what is old has become new again, even if that place moves from a physical space to a virtual one.

REFERENCES

Alch, Mark L. 2000a. "The Echo-Boom Generation." *Futurist* 34: 42–46.

Alch, Mark L. 2000b. "Get Ready for the Net Generation." *USA Today Magazine* 129: 26–28.

Bell, Steven. 2005. "Don't Surrender Library Values." *Library Journal* 130 (May): 79.

Brindley, Lynne. 2006. "Redefining the Library." *Library Hi Tech* 24: 484–495.

Carlson, Scott. 2005. "Thoughtful Design Keeps Libraries Relevant." *Chronicle of Higher Education* 52 (6) (September 30, 2005): B1–B5.

Gardner, Susan, and Susanna Eng. 2005. "What Students Want: Generation Y and the Changing Function of the Academic Library." *portal: Libraries and the Academy* 5 (July): 405–420.

Kvavik, Robert B. 2005. "Convenience, Communications, and Control: How Students Use Technology." In *Educating the Net Generation,* eds. D. G. Oblinger and J. L. Oblinger. Boulder: Educause.

Lindstrom, Annie. 2005. "The Kids Are Alright." *Tellabs Emerge* (Fall): 11–12.

Lippincott, Joan K. 2005. "Net Generation Students and Libraries." In *Educating the Net Generation*, eds. D. G. Oblinger and J. L. Oblinger. Boulder: Educause.

MacWhinnie, Lauries A. 2003. "The Information Commons: The Academic Library of the Future." *portal: Libraries and the Academy* 3 (April): 241–257.

McGlynn, Angela P. 2005. "Teaching Millennials, Our Newest Cultural Cohort." *Education Digest* 71 (December): 12–16.

Ramaley, Judith, and Lee Zia. 2005. "The Real Versus the Possible: Closing the Gaps in Engagement and Learning." In *Educating the Net Generation*, eds. D. G. Oblinger and J. L. Oblinger. Boulder: Educause.

Squire, Kurt, and Constance Steinkuehler. 2005. "Meet the Gamers." *Library Journal* 130 (April): 38–41.

Sweeney, Richard T. 2005. "Reinventing Library Buildings and Services for the Millennial Generation." *Library Administration and Management* 19: 165–175.

Weiler, Angela. 2005. "Information-Seeking Behavior in Generation Y Students: Motivation, Critical Thinking, and Learning Theory." *The Journal of Academic Librarianship* 31: 46–53.

VIII

BIBLIOGRAPHIC ESSAYS

17 EVALUATION AND SELECTION OF NEW FORMAT MATERIALS: ELECTRONIC RESOURCES

Bethany Latham and Jodi Poe

THE CHALLENGE OF E-RESOURCES AS A NEW FORMAT

To meet patron information needs effectively, libraries have always had to be flexible in the types of materials they collect and thus have had to adapt to the challenges in library management presented by new format materials. It was microfilm in the 1930s, audiovisual materials in the post–World War II era, CD-ROMs in the 1980s, and DVDs in the 1990s (Nisonger 2003, 232). Perhaps more complicated than the emergence of any of these formats is the current new format challenge before librarians: electronic resources.

Electronic resource is a deceptively simple and generic term that can encompass anything from an aggregated database to a Web-based pathfinder, and the sheer multitude of electronic resources currently available to libraries makes their evaluation, selection, and management difficult. Accordingly, electronic resources and the issues they engender are salient and frequently visited topics in the current literature of library and information science. As Sadeh and Ellingsen (2005) have noted, electronic resources differ from print in the way they are acquired, accessed, and licensed. With so many electronic resource choices available, the only way for librarians to guarantee that their budgets are being allocated wisely while acquiring the e-resources their patrons need is by developing an evaluation model. This model can be used to determine which resources are most appropriate to be added to a particular library's collection. Building this model is a thorny proposition, and although there are some general criteria that should be considered in the creation of any evaluation model, individual specifications will differ by type of resource and by the needs of the library and its user population. This chapter examines evaluation and selection criteria for the four different types of e-resources that most often challenge librarians: Web sites, e-books, e-journals, and databases.

WEB SITES

It is beyond the scope of this chapter to address the debate on whether it is the province of librarians to attempt to classify or catalog Web sites. For those who do, it is accepted that because of the massive amount of information on the Internet, some form of evaluation and selection must be used to provide access to useful sites without overwhelming the user, the electronic resources staff, and the library catalog. The same is true for libraries who select subject-specific Web sites and link to them through other library resources such as the library's Web site.

Two major criteria are almost universally accepted for evaluating Web sites: authority and content. Librarians have traditionally performed the service of pointing users to authoritative sources, and this is of paramount importance when it comes to the Internet, because of the multitude of available unverified and incorrect information and because most users lack the skills to assess the credibility of Internet content. There is also the element of bias or agenda, which often undermines the authority of Web sites. Wikipedia (http://www.wikipedia. org/), a popular online encyclopedia, and other similar sources provide a good example. Information found in these Internet sources is often cited as fact when, in actuality, anyone with Internet access can write and post an article to these sources, making the lack of authority almost complete. Recent news stories have also addressed the bias aspect of these types of sources, some of which have bordered on libel. This is not to say that these sources are useless, only that users must be aware of the issues that can be engendered by their lack of authority.

The content criterion of Web site evaluation can include the Web site's accuracy and authority, but also encompasses elements such as the distinctiveness of the information provided and how useful this information is to the intended user audience. With so many Web sites out there, if the information is not unique (i.e., can be easily found through other library e-resources), then there is no reason to provide access to a duplicate source.

In addition to the criteria of authority and content, there are several others that are often used by libraries to select their Web site resources. These criteria include currency, usability, aesthetics, design, and searching capabilities. The first of these, currency, can encompass two separate aspects: the currency of the information itself and how often the Web site is updated. Although the information on a Web site may be current, if the site is not updated regularly, broken and misdirected links can seriously decrease its value and quickly frustrate users. Web site usability is a frequently visited topic in the literature and it is extremely important to user satisfaction. A Web site can contain unique, current information that is exactly what the user needs, but if the user has so much trouble navigating the site that he/she cannot access it, it is useless. Some librarians (Collins 1996) have even put forth the "three-click rule" for Web sites, namely that it should not take more than three clicks to get to useful information, as users quickly tire of looking and give up.

Although one shouldn't judge a book by its cover, librarians are less black and white when it comes to judging Web sites by the way they look. Much of aesthetics is subjective, but there are still some nominal guidelines. If the text of a site is in a trendy yet unreadable electric blue font on a black background, users are unlikely to look at much of it. Other aesthetic issues can arise when site designers add so many bells and whistles that users find them distracting rather than appealing. In the quest for ever "cooler" aesthetics and interactivity, Web designers are constantly pushing, and oftentimes exceeding, the connection speed and software capabilities of the average user. It is neither feasible nor desirable for Web designers to design for the lowest common denominator; however, librarians must take their users' software and connection speed limitations into account, not only when designing their own library Web sites, but also in the Web sites to which they provide access.

The importance of the last criterion, searching capabilities, depends largely on the type of content on a Web site and the way in which it is arranged. Many Web sites that lack comprehensive search features still score high in usability because they are arranged in a manner that facilitates successful browsing. Web sites serving as portals to databases or housing repositories of digital content (e.g., Documenting the American South, http://docsouth.unc.edu/), however, must have adequate searching capabilities or the user will never be able to get to the information he/she is seeking.

E-BOOKS

When the concept of electronic books (e-books) was first introduced, it was not well received. Most voiced the same objection: Why would I want to curl up in bed with a computer when I can curl up in bed with the actual book? This sentiment is just one example of why e-books were initially unpopular; however, e-books have been making a comeback and in a big way. This comeback can be directly related to the emergence of technical or reference materials in electronic formats that do not require an e-book reader device. Many publishers feel that these types of technical and reference books are readily convertible to the electronic venue. This sentiment is shared by John Ambrose, vice president and general manager for Books24×7. Mr. Ambrose stated that "when his company moved to the online reference model back in 1999, its approach—placing reference books in an online database, rather than using an ebook reading device— was a revolutionary idea" (Miller, 2005, 32).

The emergence and growing acceptance of e-books have given libraries yet another method of providing users with needed information. It has also made the decision process a little more difficult. There are a number of e-books and e-book packages that are available to libraries. Companies such as eReader and Knovel have introduced models that allow libraries to purchase individual titles that are accessible through the company site; other companies such as Gale allow libraries to purchase individual titles accessible through the company site or a group of titles that are accessible through a database. Still other products, such as OCLC's NetLibrary, provide sets of preselected, grouped titles, which are often available as subject-based sets.

Does a library select individual titles or purchase entire sets of titles? Or do they select a combination of each? Libraries have different opinions about which delivery method is best. Also, many libraries that are consortium members choose to purchase through the consortium for the obvious boost in buying power and pricing benefits; however, this adds consideration of the needs of the other libraries in the consortium to the equation. Whichever method is selected, the different options mean different evaluation techniques.

For a number of years, titles have been produced in print and electronic formats. This gives the library an option as to which version would be best for their users. When selecting individual titles, librarians must evaluate the electronic version with the same criteria used for the print version. First, the library must decide if the title fits within their scope and if it agrees with their collection development policies. Moreover, the normal collection development evaluation techniques also apply: quality of the content, ability to meet a need of the curriculum, relevancy, accuracy, authority, availability in other and/or better sources, and price. These are some of the most common evaluation guidelines, but there are many more. Libraries often have specific guidelines for their collection as well.

What if the library is investigating a package or set? What evaluation techniques would be used in this case? The answer may not be simple. Dumping an e-book package into a library's catalog engenders a host of issues from the technical services end: de-duping with print copies already in the catalog, authority validation, and inserting gathering features are just a few of the major ones. Also, as with most resources, librarians can apply similar evaluation techniques and guidelines, but electronic resources must also have additional guidelines. One such criterion relates to content. The content of an e-book should be the same as the content of a print book, if there is a print equivalent. For example, illustrations, charts, tables, and so on that appear in the print version should be included in the electronic version. If these elements are not included, the book's content is not equivalent.

In addition, when reviewing e-book packages or sets, the library must consider the major element of the package—the interface. The interface must be evaluated based on ease of navigation, user friendliness, need for additional equipment or software, availability of help (tutorials, help screens, or e-mail assistance options), searching capabilities, and printing options. As with any resource, if a library patron finds it difficult to use, they simply won't use it. E-books are no different. In fact, this resource, like e-journals and databases, must be extremely easy to use for the patron to accept it. There are some packages, such as eReader (http://www.ereader.com/), that require special reader software that the patron must download in order to read the book. In addition to required software, some vendors require a specific version of freely available software such as Adobe

Acrobat Reader. This can cause problems and confusion on the patron's end, so these types of issues should be evaluated in addition to the content.

The next major concern is printing options. E-books should allow printing, but how a vendor/publisher allows this varies. Unfortunately, there are no standards with this option. Some vendors allow printing with no limitations; others will limit the number of pages that can be printed during one access period. Most of the limits in place are there to protect copyright; however, printing options and limits should be evaluated to determine if they are appropriate.

Searching capability is a key element in the area of electronic resources. The searching options and capabilities should be reviewed to determine whether there are any problems and/or limitations. For example, does the search feature cover all of the words in the book, including captions, citations, and footnotes, or is the search limited to the text of the book (i.e., the meat of the chapter, excluding the words in the captions for illustrations, citations, and footnotes)? Another element to review is whether the search feature is limited to only the page in view. This would be a severe limitation of the search feature, but could be an option the vendor/publisher feels is important. These options must be evaluated to determine whether they are practical and appropriate.

One of the last elements that should be addressed is access. Will these e-book resources be accessed with a username and password or Internet protocol (IP) authenticated? Which method would be easier for the patrons? Which method does the vendor/publisher allow? How many users may simultaneously access the e-book? If there is a simultaneous user requirement, how does the patron know about it? Does the vendor/publisher require the user to create an account and "check out" the e-book for a specified period? All of these questions should be considered during the evaluation process; however, there is another part of access that must be addressed as well: permanent rights. This key component for libraries is whether or not the library can keep access to an e-book forever or is only allowed access to the material for a period of time (subscription year or until the service is cancelled). One way some vendors handle permanent rights with regard to e-books and other e-resources such as journal content is to charge "maintenance" fees. A library purchases specified e-content up front, but then must pay a yearly platform maintenance fee to be able to continue using the e-book vendor's or aggregator's interface to access the content already purchased. This is an important element that must be considered, especially during times of unsteady budgets and rising costs of these resources.

The rising cost of resources brings up another issue that must be evaluated: price. Is the price of this e-book or package appropriate? Is this same information available in another resource for less money? If this resource doubles or triples in price next year, will it still be necessary for the collection? Librarians must weigh the price of an e-book or e-book package against its potential advantage or benefit to the collection to determine its ultimate value. One way librarians determine this value, justify purchases, and decide what to drop is by examining the usage of e-book or other electronic resource collections. Readily available usage statistics from vendors and aggregators are essential to this element of evaluation, so if a vendor does not provide usage statistics, this is yet another element librarians must consider.

E-JOURNALS AND DATABASES

More and more publishers are creating an electronic counterpart to the print version of their journals. Whether this version is freely available, available for an additional cost, or available solely in electronic format differs. In the beginning, libraries were often offered the electronic version free of charge with their print subscription. As most libraries are discovering, many publishers no longer operate with this model. The electronic versions that were once "freely available with print subscription" are now becoming "for an extra cost" versions. In addition, similar to e-books, electronic journals (e-journals) are gaining popularity and they are available individually and in packages. So, what do libraries do? Do they subscribe to the print version and forget the electronic version? Do they subscribe to the print and tack on an additional cost for the electronic version? Do they subscribe to the electronic-only version? Which is better, individual titles or package deals? Individual libraries across the planet are facing these decisions. To make the correct decisions, evaluation is necessary.

The evaluation process is easy for those titles to which a library already has a print subscription. One would believe that if the library subscribes to the title, it must have already been evaluated. So the question becomes: do we want to add the electronic version? If the answer is yes, the e-journal must be evaluated. The normal collection development evaluation techniques (quality of the content: would it meet a need of the curriculum? relevancy; authority: is the same information available in other and/or better sources? and finally, price) would apply; however, most of these elements have already been addressed. Thus librarians must look further and investigate deeper. This search and evaluation must cover the platform or interface. Is navigation easy? Is there a search feature and, if so, is it effective? Does the publisher provide exact content—illustrations, charts, diagrams, etc.? If images and graphics are included in the electronic version, are they of good quality? Is the current issue available electronically at the same time or earlier than the print version? Are all of the issues that are delivered in print available electronically? Is the content available in PDF (Portable Document Format) or HTML (Hypertext Markup Language) formats? What are the access options (i.e., username and password, IP authentication)? What features does the publisher provide: printing, saving, emailing, etc.? Does the publisher require specific or special software to read the material? All of these questions must be addressed to evaluate the appropriateness of the electronic version and whether it is worth the extra subscription charge for access.

What if a library is contemplating subscribing to a new e-journal? Again, librarians must evaluate the electronic version according to the same criteria that is used for the print version. Once the basic guidelines have been evaluated, the librarians must then review the platform or interface. The evaluation procedures follow the same guidelines as stated previously; however, the librarian must pay particular attention to these elements, as the library users will have access only to an electronic version. When reviewing the platform or interface for e-journals, libraries must consider the major elements described in the e-books section. The interface must be evaluated based on ease of navigation, user friendliness, need for additional equipment or software, availability of help (tutorials, help screens, or e-mail assistance options), and searching capabilities.

Also as with e-books, printing options are a major concern. Some publishers will include PDF files for the content, whereas others will include simple text for the content. Both of these delivery methods are easy to print; however, some publishers also provide a print option that will reformat the text so that it "fits" better on a piece of paper. This clean copy is extremely helpful to the user and the library, as library users are heavy printers.

Again, searching capabilities are paramount, perhaps even more so than for e-books owing to the sheer amount and variation of the content. Does the publisher allow users to search all of the available issues or is this feature limited to single issues? Does the publisher provide limiters that will assist the user in getting to the exact content they need? Also, a major element that must be addressed is archives. Does the library obtain archival rights to the content, or does the subscription allow access only to the current year? How far back do the back files go? If the library cancels the subscription, does it lose access to the years for which there was a subscription? Is there a platform maintenance fee? Some vendors also use "rolling" subscription periods. For instance, the library may have access to a journal from 2001–2006 this year, but from 2002–2007 next year. In essence, these rolling subscriptions limit the library's archival access. If a library subscribes to a print journal and has to cancel it years later, the issues received during the subscription period stay in the library. This is not necessarily true with electronic versions and should be taken into consideration.

Libraries often deal with their e-journals as part of databases provided by aggregators. These databases afford a large number of resources within one platform, which can help libraries get more bang for their buck. Librarians, however, cannot just look at a database as a way to provide a large amount of resources to their users. Each database must be evaluated as well, because they each have their own platforms, searching capabilities, etc. The same criteria discussed previously for the e-journals themselves apply, but there are even more options to consider with a database.

One of the major issues that arises is that of the embargo. Most journal publishers willingly sell the rights to aggregators to include their journals within an aggregator's database; however, to make money from print sales, the journal publisher often will not allow current issues of their publications to be included. For instance, a quarterly publication may have an embargo of one year, meaning that no issues from the current year are available through a particular database. In considering this issue, libraries should determine how many of the titles in a database have embargoes and the average length of the embargo. If the demand is mostly for the current issues of the journal and it is embargoed, then the usefulness of the database would be significantly reduced.

Libraries must also weigh aggregated databases against the resources they already have. What is the percentage of duplication between the product being considered and the databases the library currently has in its collection? What percentage of the database's content is unique? Serials Solutions and other e-journal/database management products can help libraries keep track of what content is available in which database, thereby avoiding excessive overlap.

The interface is usually a database aggregator's major selling point, and as such must be evaluated. Ease of navigation, design, layout of materials, and additional features should all be examined and considered. Some of the initial questions to ask about the interface are: Is it easy to use? Is it easy to navigate? Will users find access intuitive or will they need instruction and support before they can retrieve information effectively? Are there any crucial features missing that should be included (especially features that are routinely offered by other vendors)? Does the publisher require specific or special software to read the material? Is online help available? All of these questions must be addressed to evaluate the functionality of the interface. If the interface is not user friendly, a library must weigh the time and effort it will take to train the users against the content. Librarians should also look to see if another database can provide the same or comparable content with a better interface.

The searching options and capabilities should be reviewed to determine if there are any problems and/or limitations. For example, is there a search feature, or is the user required to scroll through mass amounts of information? Does the publisher provide limiters that will assist the user in getting to the exact content they need? What are these limiters (e.g., journal title, date)? Are there any strange "features" when searching, such as when entering a phrase, the database automatically adds "and" between each word or a requirement to enter words of phrase is separate boxes for the search to be correctly processed? What is the response time for searching?

Finally, librarians need to evaluate the "bells and whistles" that a vendor provides. Are the vendor's printing, saving, and e-mailing options intuitive and easy to use? Does the vendor allow for the creation of individual profiles? Are the users allowed to create search alerts that can be saved for extended periods of time? Is there a bibliography creation option that will allow the users to mark items in the database and export them in a specified citation style? Does this citation generation actually work correctly? All of these special options (some of which are becoming standard options) are nice; however, librarians must decide if they are necessary and appropriate.

CONCLUSION

Obviously, the questions used for evaluation in this chapter are not the only questions to ask. They are, however, samples of what can be used to start the evaluation process. Web sites, e-books, e-journals, and databases are resources that continue to evolve, and the evaluation process used to address their selection and management must evolve also. Because of unique user populations, each library will have a slightly different evaluation model, but the questions provided at the end of this chapter can be used as a starting point for developing that model. It is also important to remember that the evaluation process does not end when a resource is subscribed to, purchased, or cataloged. Evaluation is an ongoing challenge that is vital to ensuring that a library's e-resources collection remains effectual and meets the needs of the library's user population.

General Evaluation Questions

1. **Content.** What is the content of this resource? Is there full text? If so, is it mostly HTML for full text coverage or PDF? Is the content appropriate for your library users? Is there adequate coverage? Is there a large amount of duplication? What percentage of the content is unique?
2. **Functionality.** Is the interface or platform functional? Is it easy to use? Is it easy to navigate? Will users find access intuitive or will they need instruction and support to retrieve information effectively? Are there any crucial features missing that you think should be included (especially features that are routinely offered by other vendors)?
3. **Access.** How is the database accessible? Is a username and password required, or can the database be IP authenticated? Does it load quickly? Is the search response time adequate? Is the database unavailable at peak times for maintenance?
4. **Archival Issues.** What materials are archived? What rights does the library have to the archives, even after cancellation? Is there an extra charge for archiving?

REFERENCES

Collins, Boyd R. 1996. "Beyond Cruising: Reviewing." *Library Journal* 121: 122–124.
Miller, Ron. 2005. "Ebooks Worm Their Way into the Reference Market." *EContent* 28 (7/8): 30–34.
Nisonger, Thomas E. 2003. *Evaluation of Library Collections, Access, and Electronic Resources: A Literature Guide and Annotated Bibliography.* Westport, CT: Libraries Unlimited.
Sadeh, Tamar, and Mark Ellingsen. 2005. "Electronic Resource Management Systems: The Need and the Realization." *New Library World* 106 (1212/1213): 208–218.

18 LIBRARIES AND THE MILLENNIALS: CHANGING PRIORITIES

Marilyn Stempeck, Rashelle Karp, and Susan Naylor

By 2012, all millennials will be voting adults who will profoundly affect the world. These "digital natives" who are described by Abram and Luther (2004, 34) as being "born with the chip" expect to choose from many alternatives, using every available electronic device or channel. They want flexibility in school, work, working environments, and their social lives, and they want immediate gratification resulting in an expectation that services will be available online at any time they choose to access them. They are collaborative and multitasking; prefer to learn experientially rather than through traditional seat-time in front of a lecturer, and seem less likely to engage in literary reading (Sweeney 2005; Cleyle 2004). In fact, a National Endowment for the Arts survey indicated that the rate of decline for reading in young adults between the ages of 18 and 24 during the 20 years between 1982 and 2002 was 28 percent (Hill 2004). This lack of attachment to traditional reading is reinforced by other characteristics of millennials, who "see little difference in credibility or entertainment value between print and media formats...and see little value in choosing to limit formats at the outset of an exploration or navigation when Google results include encyclopedia entries, articles, web sites, blogs discussion threads, and PDF documents" (Abram and Luther 2004, 35).

The multitasking environment in which the millennials are most comfortable will necessitate attention to all aspects of librarianship. Although recent literature describes changes throughout the profession, some areas are more prominent in terms of the quantity of literature that can be found, as well as the level of change that is indicated. Areas that seem to be most affected include patrons' increasing use of online distance education at all levels of education, increased needs for patrons to master more complex information literacy skills, a more global focus on accountability through outcomes assessment (Rubin 2005; Osborne and Hutchinson 2004), creation of virtual libraries that duplicate the best aspects of physical libraries, changes in the areas of collection development and collection management, mounting concerns about preservation, extensive changes in library organizational and staffing patterns, and changes in the processes of scholarly communication.

ONLINE DISTANCE EDUCATION

According to the Sloan Consortium, distance education has entered the mainstream of higher education, with 65 percent of schools offering graduate courses online, 63 percent of schools offering undergraduate courses online, and 44 percent offering entire masters programs online (Allen and Seaman 2005). Distance education is also entering the mainstream of elementary and secondary education. In a survey of more than 15,000 public school districts in the United States, The National Center for Educational Statistics (2002) found that during the 2002–2003 school year, a little over one-third had enrolled students in distance education classes for a total of 328,000 enrollments dispersed among high schools (38 percent of which offered distance education classes), elementary/ secondary schools (20 percent of which offered distance education classes), middle or junior high schools (4 percent of which offered distance education classes), and elementary schools (1 percent of which offered distance education classes). As of 2005–2006, 22 states had established at least one virtual school, with about 19 percent of public schools offering their own distance-learning programs for students (Swanson 2006). With subjects ranging from the social sciences (23 percent), English (19 percent), math (15 percent), science (12 percent), and foreign languages (12 percent) "some educators predict that distance education will be available in every school district in the United States within the next decade (Patton 2006).

The benefits of online distance education include decreased costs; increased control for students in terms of style, pace, and schedule (Rowlands 2003); provision of a wider array of resources; schedule flexibility; and anonymity for those students whose levels of ability (both physical and intellectual) may have disenfranchised them from the traditional school setting. It has been predicted that even though brick and mortar schools "bring so much to the table of educational effectiveness, they will either adapt their philosophies and methodologies to the use of this emerging tool, or lose their place as the premier vehicle for teaching America's youth" (Snyder 2005).

Distance education through online technology has brought about new challenges for librarians, not the least of which is the need to create an electronic community for student interaction (Mellon and Kester 2004) that duplicates the sense of community and informal conversation that grows when students are learning together in a physical place. The concept of a communication scaffold is described by Nicholson (2005) as a way to facilitate a sense of community among faculty, staff, and students who attend classes over the Web. Although

Nicholson focuses on the need for a sense of community among distance education library school students, he identifies global needs to duplicate the various physical communities in which students and faculty interact (course, peer group, school or department, university) to grow a lasting sense of community. A communication scaffold uses technologies such as discussion boards, instant messenger (IM), chat rooms, synchronous broadcasts, and virtual poster sessions to facilitate communication and also to counter bias by employers against online degree programs, many of whom perceive that such programs are not as valid as traditional programs because students don't socially interact with peers, and because students don't interact with professors in real time (Glover 2005; Kim and Kusack 2005).

Recent literature also talks about the concept of an information commons that integrates "in design and function the library's (1) spaces, (2) informational resources, (3) technological resources, (4) production resources, and (5) support services in such a fashion that patrons experience a seamless environment for contemplating, planning, researching, and bringing to finished product their academic, intellectual and...personal work" (Bailey and Tierney 2002).

The Distance Learning Section Guidelines (2004) state that "the instilling of lifelong learning skills through general bibliographic and information literacy instruction in academic libraries is a primary outcome of higher education. Such preparation and measurement of its outcomes are of equal necessity for the distance learning community and those on the traditional campus." This poses yet another challenge brought about by online distance education: the increasing need to educate students that not all online information is equal (Keller 2004). In the online education environment, students often "turn directly to a search engine for information—bypassing both their teachers and local libraries. While they may find an excess of information, they have a significant burden in assessing that information. In online education, available search engines are a double-edged sword." Although they are a resource for students to find information quickly, "they frequently deliver results that are inadequate or off-the-mark. [And], an innocent search can send a student to an inappropriate site" (Davis 2005). The challenge of helping users to become information literate becomes even more difficult when demands for 24/7 access to virtual libraries and instructional services through the internet are a part of the mix (Gandhi 2003).

Public libraries are also drawn into the challenges posed by online education because a "student enrolled in a distance education course may not have computer and/or internet access at home, and therefore, might rely heavily on the library to provide access" (Sittler 2005). All libraries feel the pressures of online education as they are forced to provide a wider array of resources and programs via heavier use of shared electronic licensing (Shelton 2003; Pival and Johnson 2004), and as they are forced to create infrastructures that integrate online distance education services into the library, as opposed to treating online distance education as an add-on (Kavulya 2004).

INFORMATION LITERACY

It is increasingly critical that librarians be proactive in helping end-users to become knowledgeable about all of their options for information while, at the same time, teaching them how to be "wise information consumers who can decide for themselves when a simple [for example, Google] or more complex [for example, the library's OPAC] option will return the best results" (Bell 2005). The methods and standards may be different for various types of libraries, but the end result is similar.

Standards for Higher Education

The Middle States Commission on Higher Education (2002), based on the Association for College and Research Libraries "Information Literacy Competency Standards for Higher Education" (2003, 32) defines information literacy as "an intellectual framework for identifying, finding, understanding, evaluating and using information. It includes determining the nature and extent of needed information; accessing information effectively and efficiently; evaluating critical information and its sources; incorporating selected information in the learner's knowledge base and value system; using information effectively to accomplish a specific purpose; understanding the economic, legal and social issues surrounding the use of information and information technology; and observing laws, regulations, and institutional policies related to the access and use of information."

In the academic arena, methods for teaching information literacy include one-credit courses that are general or embedded within a departmental curriculum, specific information assignments that teach information literacy within the context of a particular discipline, self-directed learning activities such as tutorials, and library home-pages that link to useful information sources (Assessment Planning Committee 1997–1998). "Characteristics of Programs of Information Literacy" (Association of College and Research Libraries 2003) enumerate elements of exemplary information literacy programs for undergraduate students at four- and two-year institutions. These include a mission statement for the information literacy program, goals and objectives that are consistent for the institution, assigned leadership for the program, articulation and integration into academic programs, collaboration among library and nonlibrary staff, and assessment of program performance and student outcomes.

Standards for School Libraries

For school libraries, the American Association of School Librarians (AASL) "Information Literacy Standards for Student Learning" (American Association of School Librarians 1998) are similar to the standards for college and university libraries. The AASL standards define information literacy within three categories: students' abilities to access information efficiently and effectively, students' abilities to evaluate information critically and competently, and students' abilities to use information accurately and creatively.

Standards for Public Libraries

In public libraries, Pye and Yates (2003) stress that information literacy is critical because "a flashy Web site with a stunning array of virtual activities and links is still meaningless to users who lack the skills to navigate the site effectively." Some use information literacy as an umbrella term that includes the concept of technology literacy, and others identify technology literacy as a skill that must be separated from information literacy because many users may have good research skills, but they lack the technology literacy to access to finding tools appropriately (Balas 2006). Some librarians encourage cooperative activities among schools, colleges, and public libraries to teach users basic library research skills through in-person workshops and online tutorials that are targeted to different age groups and levels of education. Other librarians believe that teaching information literacy is more suitable in the schools, with public libraries focusing more appropriately on the reading habits of children and young adults (Dotan and Getz 2005). Information literacy for school and public library patrons has been characterized as a "prerequisite for participative citizenship...required for the production of new knowledge, on which the future economic success of all countries depends, and...needed to address global problems which challenge the planet and the survival of civilizations" (Australian Library and Information Association, quoted in Spelman 2004). In some schools, information literacy also includes the ability to access information from primary resources that are most often online, thus allowing elementary and secondary students to "construct" their learning as they learn how to find and use primary sources (Bloom and Stout 2005).

Critical Literacy and Censorship

Regardless of where information literacy is taught, critical literacy, or the ability to distinguish between appropriate and inappropriate content, is at the root of the ongoing debate about Internet filtering or, as some would define it, censorship. Some librarians stress that any Internet filtering is a dangerous threat to democracy (Wang 2003) and that libraries must resist efforts to restrict civil rights and the dissemination of information by being nonpartisan providers of "people's interest in the sociopolitical issues and information needed to address the coming crises of the twenty-first century" (Baldwin 2006). Others take a more moderate view as they discuss Internet filtering in terms of needs to educate minors so that they can make informed decisions about accessing inappropriate Web sites (Jensen 2004), or as they stress the reality that in public libraries, intellectual freedom must be balanced by the interests and beliefs of the members of the community, whose taxes support the library (Wilhite 2006; Walters 2006). On the other side of the Internet filtering debate are those librarians who strongly defend Internet filters for computers that may be accessed by minors (Colaric 2003). Even those who accept the reality that filtering may be necessary, however, caution that "when libraries restrict children to filtered internet access, it may imply a contract with parents that their children will not be able to access certain objectionable material on the internet" (Munroe 2006). Librarians are urged to ensure that end-users know that filtering is not perfect, and that a filtered Internet station may still connect users to inappropriate sites. The debate about filtering even enters the academic arena, as academic librarians stress that although intellectual freedom in an academic arena prohibits filtering, threats to confidentiality for users extend the filtering debate from filtering what gets used on the Internet to filtering records of use so that patron confidentiality can be maintained (Cain 2006).

A final component of information literacy, especially because of increasing use of electronic resources, is the need to educate consumers more widely about copyright and plagiarism restrictions. It is no longer sufficient to educate consumers about the need to attribute content appropriately; it is now necessary to educate consumers about the content of electronic resource licensing agreements. For example, some licensing agreements prohibit e-mailing articles or parts of articles to someone other than the original research. Other licensing agreements limit use to a reasonable standard that vaguely defines "excessive" downloading or printing of articles. Putting forth a good faith effort to inform end-users of these licensing parameters (Emery 2005) is becoming increasingly difficult for libraries, because there can often be different licensing restrictions for each article or book that is accessed by a patron, depending on the company from which access to the resource has been purchased, and often depending on whether or not the license provides access to domestic or foreign language electronic resources from another country (Llona, Craft, and Yokota-Carter 2004).

ASSESSMENT

Growing concerns about student learning and the outcomes of library services are fueled by a global focus on accountability. Although "libraries traditionally collect data about staff activities...[such as] how many books circulate [and] how many programs are presented" (Clay 2006), the millennial world necessitates that librarians move beyond these standard input measures to outcome measures that demonstrate how the use of libraries has impacted the user (Rubin 2006). Recent literature on libraries seems to focus on the assessment of student learning outcomes in the areas of information literacy and use of online library resources and services.

Information Literacy

Assessing library end-users' levels of information literacy, both before and after library instruction, has become paramount in this century as funding authorities link financial support with demonstrated learning outcomes. Various methods of assessment include traditional evaluations used in academic and school libraries such as essay examinations, short answer examinations, practical assignments involving information problem-solving exercises, and research worksheets. Less traditional evaluations might include student-created pathfinders, research journals, research portfolios, information literacy diaries, annotated bibliographies with information about search strategies, documented speeches (Assessment Planning Committee 1996; Distance Learning Section 2004), reflective journaling (Farmer 2004), and data analysis of archives generated by electronic course-ware products (Farmer 2005).

Use of Online Library Services

Assessments of online library resources and services now go beyond traditional satisfaction surveys and suggestion boxes that measure overall satisfaction with libraries and library services. Online library resources and services are "not ends in themselves; rather they are enabling technologies for digital asset management ... electronic publishing, teaching and learning, and other activities. Accordingly, digital libraries need to be evaluated in the context of specific applications" (Borgman, Søolvberg, and Kovács, quoted in Jeng 2005), and attributes that are related to the concept of usability. Recent literature defines usability as a multidimensional construct with attributes that include "learnability, efficiency, memorability, low error rate or easy recovery" and both short-term and long-term user satisfaction (Jeng 2005). The literature also describes multiple evaluation techniques that include questionnaires, interviews, focus groups, review of digital transaction logs (Jeng 2005), e-mail surveys (Peterson 2005), and review of reference e-mail and chat transcripts (Lee 2004).

Formal assessments of online resources and services reinforce the need to design these assessments so that they "focus on the special information needs and behaviors" of different user communities. For example, in one study of college students and college librarians, it was found that although college librarians believed that online services such as e-mail reference and online request forms were very important, these services had never been used by more than 70 percent of the college students (Xia 2003).

Use statistics are also important as the value of specific online resources is measured. Although most vendors of online resources provide database use statistics, these are problematic because of the lack of standards regarding what constitutes use, and lack of standards regarding the ways in which use should be measured (Webster 2006).

VIRTUAL LIBRARIES

In addition to the considerable costs of sustaining a virtual library whose electronic infrastructure is constantly in flux (Makondo and Katuu 2004) and whose Web pages must be constantly updated (Northrup, Cherry, and Darby 2004), other issues are formidable in the age of the millennial user. Recent literature describes needs for maintaining a personal touch through face-to-face communications with librarians (Pierce 2006), even if most services can be made available online, as well as needs to continue directing patrons to print resources when these are more efficient, or when no electronic counterpart exists.

Personal Touch

When Janes (2005) says that "we have crossed the Rubicon...[to a place where] in all but the most specialized of settings, you can't have a library or be a librarian without the internet," he heralds an age where traditional library organization, especially the catalog, is outmoded and ineffective because traditional library organization meets librarians' needs but not users' needs. "Only librarians like to search. Everyone else likes to find" (Tennant 2004). When a library is substantially virtual, however, the need to advocate for libraries by informing the public about the existence of these invisible resources is critical (Maness 2005; Williams 2006; Thiessen 2006). A recent OCLC study reinforces the need to promote online library resources in its finding that "users are not aware of the electronic resources libraries make freely available" (OCLC 2005, ix).

It is also critical that libraries not lose their personal touch and that phones be answered by a live person to temper their virtual existence with the personal attention that has always been a hallmark and niche of librarianship (Wilson 2005). As Crawford (2004) reminds readers: "Libraries should integrate new technologies into an ongoing continuum of collection and services but recognize that most users are less devoted to constant technological change than they are to the heart of libraries—good people offering effective access to varied, worthwhile collections."

The Destination Library

Many library patrons rarely, if ever, visit the physical library; however, they often visit the virtual library. Recent literature refers to a "Destination Library," which needs to be as easy to use as its more traditional physical counterpart (Sarling 2003, 2005), and which ensures that patrons use the power of printed resources when these are more appropriate (Crawford 2004). Librarians in the virtual environment have been referred to as "nonpartisan bridge builders," advocating understanding of new media and formats, while at the same time "respecting and continuing to employ the inheritance and values of the old" (Berry 2005, 10). In a less glorified description of the librarian's role in a world where "crossing the boundary between atoms and bits" (Kruger 2005) makes it "so easy for people to enter a virtual library that they don't even realize they have entered a site created by librarians...it falls to librarians to be the bearers of bad news—that the information isn't necessarily free, full-text, or online, and that the user will have to come into the library go to the stacks, pull a book off the shelf, use the copier and pay for the copy. Librarians are still left to explain why they can't provide everything online" (Ennis 2005). Librarians are still left to an existence as both "technofiles and bibliophiles" (Kohl 2004).

Balancing the Computer and the Person

In discussing the use of online reference services, Maxwell (2004) points out that "technical mysticism—the myth that technology equals progress," is missing one basic element: people. Maxwell asks whether a service that must be highly promoted is one that is actually wanted by the users. And she concludes that much of what libraries put online only helps librarians, but not library consumers. Breeding (2003) refers to this phenomenon as "bloat-ware" or "feature creep," where highly functional technologies are so overly complex that they exceed the ability of people to use them (Jack 2003). Other literature discusses problems with technology when it doesn't work the way it should, especially during virtual reference transactions (Hirko and Ross 2004). Some librarians have identified a new generation of virtual reference services, where reference training needs to change from a focus on "technology, procedures, and basic online communication tactics" to a more appropriate focus on the quality of a reference interaction, engaging the end-user, ascertaining if the end-user comprehended the results of the exchange, and using constructivist teaching techniques for library instruction (Westbrook 2006).

COLLECTION DEVELOPMENT AND COLLECTION MANAGEMENT

The millennial age has affected collection development processes in dramatic ways. Not only have internal processes and procedures been changed, but the entire perspective of the profession has also changed. Recent literature focuses on three major areas of concern: access and ownership, electronic resource management, and better integration of discipline-specific applications into automated finding tools.

Access and Ownership

The insistence that libraries should mirror today's 24/7 communications over the Web (Roberts 2005) has led to a greater dependence on electronic resources that are available even when the physical library is closed. This has changed the profession's perspective on collections from a focus on tangible collection *development*, where resources are owned by the library and borrowed by patrons, to the more intangible concept of collection *management*, where libraries purchase or provide access to resources that are owned by others. Not only are these new resources owned by others, they can be simultaneously used by many people; their creators can update, change or remove access at any time; and their users can create a physical or electronic copy of the resource without alerting the creators (Irwin 2004). In a somewhat simplistic analogy, libraries used to engage in an internal process of purchasing, cataloging, and classifying for perpetuity or until a physical resource might be withdrawn; physically marking an item so that it might be found; and then tracking physical loans. Except for the few electronic resources that can be purchased outright, these activities have evolved into complex, multilayered processes of leasing; providing what is often temporary cataloging and classifying of resources that may or may not be available next year or even the next day; virtually marking so that adherence to a licensing agreement can be tracked; and then virtually tracking use so that substantial outlays of money can be evaluated against continuing licensing payments (Hunter 2005; Cole 2005).

Electronic resources must be managed and cataloged with techniques different than those used for hard copy resources (Leysen and Boydston 2005; Dendrinos 2005; Sadeh and Ellingsen 2005; Brenner, Larsen, and Weston 2006), especially because of the complexity of licensing agreements for electronic resources, the need for library systems to become compatible with external systems such as Google and Amazon (Dietz and Grant 2005), the necessity to implement external authentication authorities, user demands that electronic resources be integrated with courseware systems and corporate portals (Breeding 2005a), and needs to organize these massive virtual collections so that they can be browsed and linked effectively (Cloonan and Dove 2005).

Electronic Resource Management

An entire industry has grown up around the management of electronic resources that includes e-journal management commercial software embedded into software provided by subscription companies, locally developed software, stand-alone products and processes (Banush, Kurth, and Pajerek 2005), and products that are part of a library's integrated library software system (Fong and Wicht 2005; Pace 2004; Breeding 2005b). Unfortunately, it is only recently that add-ons to manage electronic resources have begun to be produced as integral parts of a library's entire integrated library system (Breeding 2004b) or as methods by which libraries can become as simple to use as the integrated searches on Google or Amazon (Breeding 2004b; Lee 2006). Not surprisingly, the trend toward more integration within a library's automated system has grown beyond the library. Recent literature discusses the potential for libraries to be integrated into even larger automated systems as channels or portlets within a university, institutional,or government portal. The portal provides a single point of access to a wide variety of content and services (Jackson 2005; Brown 2005), and the library is just a small part of the entire package.

Courseware

Equally important in the world of electronic resource management is the ability to insert links to library resources directly into course management systems (OCLC E-Learning Task Force 2007; Buehler 2004) to provide "seamless linking of course web sites and libraries" (Rieger, Horrie, and Revels 2004). "As course management systems and software (courseware) are increasingly being used to enhance traditional...courses...library resources are noticeably missing from this venue. Libraries risk being bypassed by this technology and losing relevance to students and faculty if they do not establish their presence in courseware...If...libraries do not find a means by which to establish their presence in courseware...commercial information distributors, who have already gained a foothold in some courseware environments, may successfully eclipse the library as the primary information provider" and teacher of information literacy skills (Shank and Dewald 2003).

PRESERVATION

Although the advantages of electronic resources are lauded because of their flexibility and fast retrievability (Bhatnagar 2006), librarians are also cautioned to be wary of too much digitization. Concerns about losing knowledge because electronic resources are so efficient at preserving information, as well as concerns about the stability of electronic journals and the digital format itself, are most prominent in current literature.

Knowledge Management

As Gorman (2003) points out, "Computers are very, very good at transmitting information, but they're poor at the transmission and use of recorded knowledge. Loss of information is unfortunate, but it's not a catastrophe. Loss of recorded knowledge—that is a catastrophe. In the printed book we have a technology that is wonderful for transmitting both information and knowledge that cannot be duplicated by digitization." Gorman's cautions are, at least in part, demonstrated by the experiences of the Amateur Athletic Foundation (AAF) of Los Angeles Sport Library, where decisions about what to digitize were based on the items most often requested by patrons, rather than on needs to make everything instantly accessible. In the case of the AAF, a digitization project focused on publications from the Olympic Games that met the needs of a specific clientele (Wilson 2003). Much of the recorded knowledge was preserved digitally, but knowledge that was the least requested was not digitized to keep costs manageable.

When making decisions about what to digitize, librarians are warned that community interest in a special collection is "not just a set of items that have some commonality that binds them together. Rather, community interest focuses on cultural and intellectual heritage, which can only be preserved through provision of information as well as the framework of knowledge in which it resides" (Noremore 2003; Connaway, O'Neill, and Prabha 2006). The concept of "knowledge management" attempts to resolve these issues through the creation of automated systems that "allow people to share what they know and then reuse the know how of others" rather than just providing access to information resources (Ghosh and Jambekar 2003, 3). Knowledge management has been particularly promoted as one method for making government information more easily accessible and usable (Prokopiadou, Papatheodorous, and Moschopoulos 2004). Librarians are also urged to resist the temptation to isolate themselves from "society's total communication structures." Instead, they are encouraged to become information critics who understand "how knowledge and documents are socially organized, because this social organization structures and influences the possibilities of knowledge organization systems...within a larger social and textual context...that constitutes the functionality of knowledge organization systems" (Andersen 2005).

Online versus Print

Related to issues of preservation is the decision of whether to purchase an online journal and at the same time discontinue the print subscription, and whether to purchase online books in lieu of, or in addition to, printed books. Walters (2004) provides six online journal criteria that should be used to make such decisions. The first three criteria include consideration of how complete the online resource is (e.g., complete content, page images), the reliability of access to the resource (e.g., stable URLs, speed), and whether the online version appears at the same time or earlier than the printed version. The second three criteria focus on how sustainable the online journal will be. Specific criteria in the area of sustainability include (1) a library license that provides for "permanent library retention of the content purchased during the license period," (2) a large enough library consortium so that the library has enough clout to "ensure that the content provider adheres to the legal provisions for long-term use," and (3) a demonstrated commitment by the journal provider to the "long-term provision of each journal included" in a collection of journals. Of particular concern in current literature is the provision of journals in perpetuity (Stemper and Barribeau 2006). The criteria for decisions about e-books are similar to those for journals, but issues of printing and saving options become more prominent (Coleman 2004).

Archives

It is tempting to replace print archives with digital archives because of obvious benefits that include random access, full-text searching, decreased storage costs, and increased availability to multiple users regardless of their physical location (Bernstein 2005). Preservationists, however, caution librarians to be careful as they digitize archives. Citing the fragile nature of digital formats, the high rate of technological obsolescence for media formats, and copyright issues, many preservationists stress that decisions about digital archiving must be made carefully and collaboratively among multiple agencies so that the integrity of the archives is not compromised (Hunter 2006; LeFurgy 2005). Adding to the complexity of digital archiving are needs to begin archiving scholarly content such as communications and research reports that were originally produced in digital format for immediate use with little consideration to their long-term preservation (Smith 2005), and needs to archive Web content (Masanes 2005). Dale (2005) summarizes the issues related to digitized archiving in terms of the need to develop a framework for digital preservation that takes into consideration: "(1) content (the stuff), (2) fixity (it does not change), (3) reference (how to access), (4) provenance (integrity and the chain of custody), and (5) context."

Another issue related to digital archives is the need to standardize access protocols so that the information is more readily accessible to consumers across national and geographic borders. Since 2001, the Open Archives Initiative Protocol for Metadata Harvesting has been gaining popularity as a means to provide access to diverse e-print archives through a common protocol that allows others to add value to the data in the archives, and to repackage the data to meet specific community and user needs (Shreeves, Haning, and Hagedorn 2005).

STAFFING OF LIBRARIES

Lancaster (2003) writes about a "generational collision" between traditionalist librarians, baby boomer librarians, and millennial librarians. Where the traditionalist wears heels and pantyhose to speak at a convention, the baby boomer wears a pantsuit and no stockings, and the millennial wears a short skirt and flip-flops. Lancaster and Stillman (2002) discuss the differing values of four generations that were shaped by their experiences. Traditionalists are described as hard-working, fiscally conservative, respectful of leaders, and loyal, preferring an environment where information comes from the top. Older boomers are described as individualistic, idealistic, optimistic, and competitive. Younger boomers are described as skeptical and most likely to leave their job for another, or retire early. Millennials are described as diversity-aware, entrepreneurial, comfortable with change, collaborative, realistic, and willing to leave a job if their needs aren't being met. Gordon (2004a) adds to the list of millennial characteristics that they are easily alienated and discouraged by an unwelcoming profession dominated by experienced traditionalists and boomers. The challenge for individual libraries is to accommodate multiple generations in the workplace (Osif 2003; Gordon 2004b), while at the same time: (1) preserving the values and expertise of the traditionalists, one-quarter of whom will reach the age of 65 by 2009 (Miller 2004; Curran 2003); (2) providing technology professional development for the boomers (Huwe 2005), whose experience and historical memory are critical (Curran 2003); (3) keeping millennial workers in whom the library has invested much time and energy to train; and (4) encouraging new recruits into the profession by demonstrating respect for millennial patrons (Adkins and Hussey 2005), providing internship experiences for this diverse population (Mack and Keally 2004; Bright and Chaudhuri 2005), and engaging boards of trustees in hiring processes so that salaries will be high enough to attract new librarians (Miller 2004). This includes the ability to "bridge categories [that will help millennials]...build solidly on...professional foundations while also forming...institutions' technological future" (Gordon 2005).

Another equally challenging frontier for librarians serving the millennial generation is the need restructure library staffing so that "just in time" services can be provided. "Just in time" services include the provision of answers to traditional questions about information as well as questions about the technologies that provide, organize, and manipulate information. "Hierarchical—pyramid-like-organizations are no longer effective. Flatter—indeed, web-like-organizations and self-directed work groups allow for more flexibility and more opportunities for communications, both within and beyond traditional library boundaries" (Warnken 2004). The flat organizational structure also provides opportunity for self-directed management teams (Lubans 2006) that are cross-trained (Olivas and McCurley 2006) to manage the operations of a library, an organizational structure that has shown positive results at The Ohio State University Libraries (Bradigan and Powell 2004). In addition to flattening the organizational structure of libraries, recent literature suggests that human resources must be reallocated and refocused so that departments and teams reflect changing library priorities and realities. For example, a study of staff workloads and responsibilities at the University of Texas Southwestern Medical Center Library found that "a preponderant amount of time was still spent on print-related activities that were no longer considered to be library priorities" (Higa, Bunnett, and Maina 2005). In addition to preparing for changes related to technology and changing end-users, recent literature also discusses "succession planning," through which "training, coaching, special assignments, and other developmental opportunities [are provided] so that staff members are ready to move into" management positions and specialty areas when vacancies occur (Singer, Goodrich, and Goldberg 2004). Because change is always stressful and is often viewed in terms of its impact on individuals, recent literature recommends a perspective on change that takes "the focus away from the individual staff member and the job as [he or she] knew it," and refocuses staff perspectives on patron outcomes (Hayes and Sullivan 2003).

Atkinson (2004) suggests that the future of libraries may well depend on librarians' abilities to take a more proactive role in the dissemination of scholarly information by integrating previously separate departments and functions (acquisitions, interlibrary loan, publishing, network design, telecommunications) into a "unified system of scholarly information delivery." Atkinson reminds readers that the major impediments to electronic publishing are economic, and that librarians must take a more active role to appropriately join the economic and technical aspects of publishing so that the greater good is met—providing scholarly information "to all who need it for educational and research purposes." This restructuring of library organization and function will also require new definitions of the roles of professionals and paraprofessionals in libraries. "Tasks once seen as exclusively professional are now being shared with, or assigned to, paraprofessionals, and there is a growing emphasis on paraprofessionals as managers, especially of day-to-day operations...Jobs held by a growing number of paraprofessionals...require sophisticated judgment calls, supervision, and complex operations" (Osa 2003).

As perplexing as the millennials are to the older librarians who are hiring them, the job descriptions in recruitment advertisements are also perplexing for millennial job-seekers, especially with regard to the requisite technological skills that are generally part of a job advertisement. It has become difficult for job-seekers to decipher which technological skills are most important to the hiring agency because often the "administrators seeking new...personnel may have an impression of what competencies they need but lack the proper technological terminology to describe those skills with precision" (Exner 2004). For example, Exner (2004) provides a list of broad skills categories that can be interpreted differently, depending on the relative importance of each for a specific job. Exner's categories include: (1) administrative and interdisciplinary skills such as evaluation of electronic resources, programming experience, and negotiation of licensing agreements; (2) digital libraries, metadata, and archiving skills such as digital rights management, scanning and imaging, and digitization processes; (3) instruction in the electronic classroom; (4) technical support and networking skills such as PC support and using data communications protocols; and (5) Web authoring skills such as HTML authoring, form creation, database design, and Web usability testing. He contends that using these broad categories in job advertisements is confusing to potential recruits, because the jargon does not adequately describe the exact skills that are necessary for the job. As electronic resources have become a larger part of library collections, however, the job of a new librarian has become more diverse. For example, libraries have experienced increasing difficulties recruiting catalogers who are prepared to "function in a world in which the organization of information includes not just the creation of the same kind of cataloging data we have been supplying for decades, but now also includes the creation, application, integration, and harvesting of various kinds of metadata" (Hill 2005).

Other librarians discuss new dimensions of technostress, which include loss of personal identity because reference services are no longer provided face-to-face; unrealistic expectations by patrons who believe that face-to-face reference should be available 24/7, as is virtual reference; and concerns about patron confidentiality and privacy in a data-rich environment where transcripts, e-mail logs, Weblogs, and circulation information are readily, but not necessarily rightly, available (Van Fleet and Wallace 2003).

Some librarians caution that the profession may be losing because "our organizations have been focusing on putting collections or other content up on the Internet—a 'build it and they will come' or, even a 'if you build it they will leave,' mentality." But these projects have not become integral parts of the business we are in (Barnett 2004)—stewardship of the intellectual and cultural heritages of the world (Marcum 2003).

CHANGES IN SCHOLARLY COMMUNICATION

The generation that has grown up with technology is profoundly changing the world of scholarship. A previous focus on scholarly *publication* is evolving into a new focus on electronic scholarly *communication* that is largely "outside of any of the vehicles and systems for scholarly publishing. These are individual efforts...that are haphazardly produced outside of well-established systems of publication and preservation and dissemination." Librarians and institutions in the millennial world are urged to proactively make investments in institutional repositories for scholarly communication, and in "trying to help people think through the structure of information in these settings" (Lynch 2003). As well, librarians are encouraged to create systems of open access "with the intention of making scholarly literature freely available to other scholars in order to facilitate scholarly communication and enhance scholarly research" (Ojala 2005). Current works identify a crisis in scholarly communication caused by spiraling costs for scholarly journals (Crawford 2005) and discuss open access as a way to bypass the traditional publishing systems by having authors "publish their scholarly work electronically without copyright constraints other than attribution" (George 2005) and by having authors hold their own copyright, rather than surrendering their copyright to publishers (Yiotis 2005). Some herald open access as a way to encourage research productivity and scholarly innovation, but others are more skeptical about such a wholesale change in way that scholarly communication is disseminated as they note that authors may not support open access because of a perceived lack of rigor for journals that are published in this manner (Schwartz 2005; Schmidt, Sennyey, and Carstens 2005).

CONCLUSION

"It's about the user, stupid" (Tennant 2005). Perhaps Tennant's blunt statement sums up the millennial generation, and indeed, the millennium. Librarians in the millennium no longer have the luxury of immersing themselves in the institution and its internal processes. Everything must be examined in terms of the end-user, and as end-users change with each generation (about every 20 years), the institutions and profession of librarianship must also change. Constant and vigilant outcomes assessment, the results of which are used to inform substantive change, will ensure that libraries and librarians remain relevant in a world where relevance to real-world applications has become paramount.

REFERENCES

Abram, S., and J. Luther. 2004. "Born with the Chip." *Library Journal* 129 (8): 34–37. (Retrieved February 2, 2006, from Wilson Web database.)

Adkins, D., and L. K. Hussey. 2005. "Unintentional Recruiting for Diversity." *Public Libraries* 44 (4): 229–33. (Retrieved August 17, 2006, from Wilson Web database.)

Allen, E., and J. Seaman. 2005. *Growing by Degrees: Online Education in the United States, 2005*. Wellesley, Mass.: Sloan-C.

American Association of School Librarians and the Association for Educational Communication and Technology. 1998. *Information Literacy Standards for Student Learning: Standards and Indicators*. Chicago, Ill.: American Library Association. (Reprinted from

Information Power: Building Partnerships for Learning, 2nd ed., by the American Library Association, 1998, Chicago, Ill: American Library Association.)

Andersen, J. 2005. "Information Criticism: Where Is It?" *Progressive Librarian* 25: 12–22.

Assessment Planning Committee and Indiana University Bloomington Libraries. (1997–1998). *An Assessment Plan for Information Literacy.* Bloomington, Indiana: The trustees of Indiana University. http://www.indiana.edu (Retrieved June 30, 2006.)

Association of College and Research Libraries. 2003. Characteristics of Programs of Information Literacy That Illustrate Best Practices: A Guideline. American Library Association. <http://www.ala.org> (Retrieved June 30, 2006.)

Association of College and Research Libraries. 2003. Information Literacy Competency Standards for Higher Education. American Library Association. <http://www.ala.org> (Retrieved June 30, 2006.)

Association of College and Research Libraries/Distance Learning Section/Guidelines Committee. 2004. "Guidelines for Distance Learning Library Services." *College & Research Libraries News* 65 (10): 604–611. (Retrieved June 26, 2006, from Wilson Web database.)

Atkinson, R. 2004. "The Acquisitions Librarian as Change Agent in the Transition to the Electronic Library." *Library Resources and Technical Services* 48 (3): 216–26. (Retrieved June 30, 2006, from Library and information science, Wilson Web database.)

Bailey, R., and B. Tierney. 2002. "Information Commons Redux: Concept, Evolution, and Transcending The Tragedy of the Commons." *The Journal of Academic Librarianship* 28 (5): 277–286. (Retrieved on July 5, 2006, from Wilson Web database.)

Balas, J. L. 2006. "Information Literacy and Technology: They Work Best When They Work Together." *Computers in Libraries* 26 (5): 26–29. (Retrieved on August 17, 2006, from Wilson Web database.)

Baldwin, M. 2006. "Librarians as Knowledge Provocateurs." *Public Libraries* 45 (2): 11–14. (Retrieved on August 17, 2006, from Wilson Web database.)

Banush, D., M. Kurth, and J. Pajerek. 2005. "Rehabilitating Killer Serials: An Automated Strategy for Maintaining E-Journal Metadata." *Library Resources & Technical Services* 49 (3): 190–203.

Barnett, Bill. 2004. On My Mind: Commentary on Web-Wise. *First Monday (Online)* 9(5). <http://www.firstmonday.dk> (Retrieved on June 26, 2006.)

Bell, S. 2005. "Don't Surrender Library Values." *Library Journal (1976),* 130 (9): 79.

Bernstein, J. 2005. "When not Re-Formatting Is The Function: The Electronic Records Archives." *EContent* 28 (11): 10. (Retrieved June 26, 2006, from Wilson Web database.)

Berry, J. N. 2005. "The Librarian's New Role." *Library Journal (1976)* 130 (16): 10. (Retrieved June 26, 2006.)

Bhatnagar, A. 2006. "Digitization in Academic Libraries." *Information Studies* 12 (1): 35–54. (Retrieved June 26, 2006, from Wilson Web database.)

Bloom, N., and C. Stout. 2005. Using Digitized Primary Source Materials in the Classroom: A Colorado Case Study. http://firstmonday.org *First Monday (Online)* 10(6). (Retrieved June 26, 2006.)

Bradigan, P. C., and A. Powell. 2004. "The Reference and Information Services Team: An Alternative Model for Managing Reference Services." *Reference and User Services Quarterly* 44 (2): 143–148. (Retrieved June 26, 2006, from Wilson Web database.)

Breeding, M. 2004a. "The Challenge of Integration." *Computers in Libraries* 24 (3): 40–42. (Retrieved June 26, 2006, from Wilson Web database.)

Breeding, M. 2005b. "Gradual Evolution." *Library Journal (1976)* 130 (6): 42–48, 50, 52, 54, 56. (Retrieved June 26, 2006, from Wilson Web database.)

Breeding, M. 2005a. "Looking Toward the Future of Library Technology." *Computers in Libraries* 25 (5): 39–41. (Retrieved June 26, 2006, from Wilson Web database.)

Breeding, M. 2004b. "Migration Down Innovation Up: Automated Marketplace 2004." *Library Journal (1976)* 129 (6): 46–50, 52, 54, 56–58. (Retrieved June 26, 2006, from Wilson Web database.)

Breeding, M. 2003. "The Right Technology: No Tech, Low-Tech, Or High-Tech?" *Computers in Libraries* 23 (9): 28–29.

Brenner, M., T. Larsen, and C. Weston. 2006. "Digital Collection Management Through the Library Catalog." *Information Technology and Libraries* 25 (2): 65–77. (Retrieved August 17, 2006, from Wilson Web database.)

Bright, K., and J. Chaudhuri. 2005. "Seeding the Vision: Designing a Minority Librarian Residency Program, Part 2." *The Southeastern Librarian* 53 (3): 6–10. (Retrieved August 17, 2006, from Wilson Web database.)

Brown, C. T. 2005. "Portals to the World: A Library of Congress Guide to Web Resources on International Topics." *Journal of Library Administration,* 43 (1/2): 37–56. Retrieved August 17, 2006, from Wilson Web database.

Buehler, M. A. 2004. "Where Is the Library in Course Management Software?" *Journal of Library Administration* 41 (1/2): 75–84. (Retrieved June 26, 2006, from Wilson Web database.)

Cain, C. C. 2006. "Intellectual Freedom in Academic Libraries." *Louisiana Libraries* 68 (3): 29–30. (Retrieved August 17, 2006, from Wilson Web database.)

Clay, E. S. 2006. "Beyond Numbers." *Library Journal (1976)* Net Connect 8–10. (Retrieved August 17, 2006, from Wilson Web database.)

Cleyle, S. 2004. "Generation Y: Helping Change the Way Library System Offices Do Their Work." *Feliciter* 50 (5): 178–179. (Retrieved February 17, 2006, from Wilson Web database.)

Cloonan, M. V., and J. G. Dove. 2005. "Ranganathan Online." *Library Journal (1976)* 130(6): 58–60. (Retrieved August 17, 2006, from Wilson Web database.)

Colaric, S. 2003. "Children, Public Libraries, and the Internet: Is It Censorship or Good Service?" *North Carolina Libraries (Online)* 61(1). (Retrieved June 26, 2006, from Wilson Web database.)

Cole, L. 2005. "A Journey into E-Resource Administration Hell." *The Serials Librarian* 49(1/2): 141–54. (Retrieved August 17, 2006, from Wilson Web database.)

Coleman, G. 2004. "E-Books and Academics: An Ongoing Experiment." *Feliciter* 4. (Retrieved August 17, 2006, from Wilson Web database.)

Connaway, L. S., E. T. O'Neill, and C. Prabha. 2006. "Last Copies: What's at Risk?" *College & Research Libraries,* 67(4): 370–379. (Retrieved August 17, 2006, from Wilson Web database.)

Crawford, W. 2004. "The Dangers of Uniformity." *American Libraries* 35(9): 64. (Retrieved August 17, 2006, from Wilson Web database.)

Crawford, W. 2005. "Open Access and Survivable Libraries." *EContent* 28(6): 42. (Retrieved June 26, 2006, from Wilson Web database.)

Crawford, W. 2004. "What Happened to Technological Fixes?" *American Libraries,* 35(6): 88. (Retrieved June 26, 2006, from Wilson Web database.)

Curran, W. M. 2003. "Succession: The Next Ones at Bat." *College & Research Libraries* 64(2): 134–140. (Retrieved June 26, 2006, from Wilson Web database.)

Dale, T. 2005. "E-Gads! E-Gone! Put Digital Preservation on Your Radar." *AIM E-Doc Magazine* 19(4): 64. (Retrieved June 26, 2006, from Wilson Web database.)

Davis, E. 2005. "Virtual Research and the Online School." *Colorado Libraries* 31(3): 14. (Retrieved June 26, 2006, from Wilson Web database.)

Dendrinos, M. 2005. "From the Physical Reality to the Virtual Reality in the Library Environment." *Library Philosophy and Practice* 7 (2) (Retrieved June 26, 2006, from Wilson Web Database).

Dietz, R., and C. Grant. 2005. "The Disintegrating World of Library Automation." *Library Journal (1976)* 130 (11): 38–40. (Retrieved June 26, 2006, from WilsonWeb database.)

Distance Learning Section Guidelines Committee. June, 2004. Guidelines for Distance Learning Library Services. *College & Research Libraries News* 64 (10): 604–611.

Dotan, G., and I. Getz. 2005. "Library Directors' Perceptions of the Desirable LIS Education for Library Service to School Children." *Journal of Education for Library and Information Science* 46(1): 59–76. (Retrieved June 26, 2006, from Wilson Web database.)

Emery, J. 2005. "Is Our Best Good Enough? Educating End-Users about Licensing Terms." *Journal of Library Administration* 42(3/4): 27–39. (Retrieved June 26, 2006, from Wilson Web database.)

Ennis, L. A. 2005. "The Evolution of Technostress." *Computers in Libraries* 25(8): 10–12. (Retrieved June 26, 2006, from Wilson Web database.)

Exner, N. 2004. "An Informal Examination of Technological Skills in Library Jobs." *North Carolina Libraries (Online)* 62(2): 84–90. (Retrieved June 26, 2006, from Wilson Web database.)

Farmer, L.S.J. 2004. "Narrative Inquiry as Assessment Tool: A Case Study." *Journal of Education for Library and Information Science* 45(4), 340–351. Retrieved June 26, 2006, from Wilson Web database.

Farmer, L.S.J. 2005. "Using Technology to Facilitate Assessment of Library Education." *Teacher Librarian* 32(3): 12–15. (Retrieved June 26, 2006, from Wilson Web database.)

Flagg, G. 2005. "Library and Information Technology Association National Forum: Showing the Way in San Jose." *American Libraries* 36(10): 34–35. (Retrieved June 26, 2006, from Wilson Web database.)

Fong, Y. S., and H. Wicht. 2005. "Software for Managing Licenses and Compliance." *Journal of Library Administration* 42(3/4): 143–161.

Gandhi, S. 2003. "Academic Librarians and Distance Education: Challenges and Opportunities." *Reference & User Services Quarterly* 43(2): 138–154. (Retrieved June 26, 2006, from Wilson Web database.)

George, P. 2005. "The Future Gate to Scholarly Legal Information." *AALL Spectrum,* 9(6): insert 1–4. (Retrieved June 26, 2006, from Wilson Web database.)

Ghosh, M., and A. Jambekar. 2003. "DESIDOC." *Bulletin of Information Technology* 23 (5): 3–11. (Retrieved June 26, 2006, from Wilson Web database.)

Glover, K. 2005. "Don't Discredit My Online Degree." *Library Journal (1976)* 130(17): 39. (Retrieved June 26, 2006, from Wilson Web database.)

Gordon, R. S. 2005. "The Bridge Generation." *Library Journal* 130(19): 46. (Retrieved June 26, 2006, from Wilson Web database.)

Gordon, R. S. 2004 a. "Let's Use the Technology We Live." *Library Journal (1976)* 129 (3). (Retrieved February 17, 2006, from Wilson Web database.)

Gordon, R. S. 2004 b. "In Our Own Words." *Library Journal (1976)* 129 (19): 38. (Retrieved February 17, 2006, from Wilson Web database.)

Gorman, M. 2003. "For Libraries, Digitization Is a Factor, Not the Future." *Logos* 14(2): 66–68. (Retrieved February 17, 2006, from Wilson Web database.)

Hayes, J., and M. Sullivan. 2003. "Mapping the Process: Engaging Staff in Work Redesign." *Library Administration & Management* 17(2): 87–93. (Retrieved June 26, 2006, from Wilson Web database.)

Higa, M. L., B. Bunnett, and B. Maina. 2005. *College & Research Libraries* 66(1): 41–58. (Retrieved June 26, 2006, from Wilson Web database.)

Hill, J. S. 2005. *Library Resources & Technical Services* 49(1): 14–18. (Retrieved June 26, 2006, from Wilson Web database.)

Hill, Kelly. 2004. *Reading at Risk: A Survey of Literary Reading in America*. (Rep. No. 46). Ontario: National Endowment for the Arts. http://www.arts.gov (Retrieved on June 26, 2006,.).

Hirko, B., and M. B. Ross. 2004. *Virtual Reference Training: The Complete Guide to Providing Anytime, Anywhere Answers*. Chicago: American Library Association.

Hunter, I. 2006. "Access Management: Challenging Orthodoxies." *PNLA Quarterly*, 70(2): 7–9. (Retrieved June 26, 2006, from Wilson Web database.)

Hunter, I. 2005. "Access Management: Challenging Orthodoxies." *Journal of Library Administration* 42 (2): 57–70. (Retrieved June 26, 2006, from Wilson Web database.)

Huwe, T. K. 2005. "Running to Stand Still." *Computers in Libraries* 25(8): 34–36. (Retrieved June 26, 2006, from Wilson Web database.)

Irwin, R. D. 2004. "Emerging Issues in Library Web Collections." *LIBRES* 14(1): 1. (Retrieved June 26, 2006, from Wilson Web database.)

Jack, L. 2003. "Making the Most of Technology: Meeting Library Needs with Technology." *Arkansas Libraries* 60(1): 12–13. (Retrieved June 26, 2006, from Wilson Web database.)

Jackson, M. E. 2005. "Looking Ahead: The Future of Portals." *Journal of Library Administration* 73(1/2): 205–220. (Retrieved June 26, 2006, from Wilson Web database.)

Janes, J. 2005. "From the Other Side of the Rubicon." *American Libraries* 36(10): 62. (Retrieved June 26, 2006, from Wilson Web database.)

Jeng, J. 2005. "What Is Usability in the Context of the Digital Library and How Can It Be Measured?" *Information Technology and Libraries* 24(2): 47–56. (Retrieved June 26, 2006, from Wilson Web database.)

Jensen, M. 2004. "Internet Filtering and Its Effects on Intellectual Freedom." *PNLA Quarterly* 68(4): 13–15. (Retrieved June 26, 2006, from Wilson Web database.)

Kavulya, J. M. 2004. "Challenges in the Provision of Library Services for Distance Education: A Case Study of Selected Universities in Kenya." *African Journal of Library, Archives & Information Science* 14(1): 15–28. (Retrieved June 26, 2006, from Wilson Web database.)

Keller, K. 2004. "Distance Education: It's Here to Stay." *Nebraska Library Association Quarterly* 35(4): 14–17. (Retrieved June 26, 2006, from Wilson Web database.)

Kim, H. J., and J. M. Kusack. 2005. "Distance Education and the New MLS: The Employer's Perspective." *Journal of Education for Library and Information Science* 46(1): 36–52. (Retrieved June 26, 2006, from Wilson Web database.)

Kohl, D. F. 2004. "From the Editor ... The Paperless Society ... Not Quite Yet." *The Journal of Academic Librarianship* 30(3): 177–178. (Retrieved June 26, 2006, from Wilson Web database.)

Kruger, H. 2005. "I, Librarian." *Information Technology and Libraries* 24(3): 123–129. (Retrieved June 26, 2006, from Wilson Web database.)

Lancaster, L., and D. Stillman. 2002. *When Generations Collide*. New York: Harper Business.

Lancaster, L. C. 2003. "The Click and Clash of Generations." *Library Journal (1976)* 128(17): 36–39. (Retrieved June 26, 2006, from Wilson Web database.)

Lee, D. 2006. "Checking out the Competition: Marketing Lessons from Google." *Library Administration & Management* 20(2): 94–95. (Retrieved August 17, 2006, from Wilson Web database.)

Lee, I. J. 2004. "Do Virtual Reference Librarians Dream of Digital Reference Questions? A Qualitative and Quantitative Analysis of Email and Chat Reference." *Australian Academic and Research Libraries* 35(2): 95–110. (Retrieved August 17, 2006, from Wilson Web database.)

LeFurgy, William. 2005. "Building Preservation Partnerships: The Library of Congress National Digital Information Infrastructure and Preservation Program." *Library Trends* 54(1): 163–172. (Retrieved August 17, 2006, from Wilson Web database.)

Leysen, J. M., and J.M.K. Boydston. 2005. "Supply and Demand for Catalogers: Present and Future." *Library and Technical Services* 49(4): 250–265. (Retrieved June 26, 2006, from Wilson Web database.)

Llona, E., E. Craft, K. Yokota-Carter, and David Pham. 2004. "Providing Access to Foreign Language Electronic Resources." *Information Technology and Libraries* 23(3): 119–122.

Lubans, J. Jr. 2006. Balaam's Ass: Toward Proactive Leadership in Libraries. *Library Administration and Management* 20(1): 30–33. (Retrieved June 26, 2006, from Wilson Web database.)

Lynch, C. 2003. "Digital Library Opportunities." *The Journal of Academic Librarianship* 29(5): 286–289. (Retrieved June 26, 2006, from Wilson Web database.)

Mack, T., and J. Keally. 2004. "Seeding the Vision: Designing a Minority Librarian Residency Program." *The Southeastern Librarian* 52(1): 4–8. (Retrieved June 26, 2006, from Wilson Web database.)

Makondo, F. N., and S. Katuu. 2004. "An Assessment of the Sustainability of Information Technology at the University of Zambia Library." *African Journal of Library, Archives and Information Science* 14(2): 109–123. (Retrieved June 26, 2006, from Wilson Web database.)

Maness, J. 2005. "The Users Are All Here, But Where Is the Library?" *Colorado Libraries* 31(3): 19–20. (Retrieved June 26, 2006, from Wilson Web database.)

Marcum, D. 2003. "Requirements for the Future Digital Library." *The Journal of Academic Librarianship* 29(5): 276–279. (Retrieved June 26, 2006, from Wilson Web database.)

Masanes, J. 2005. "Web Archiving Methods and Approaches: A Comparative Study." *Library Trends* 54(1): 72–90. (Retrieved June 26, 2006, from Wilson Web database.)

Maxwell, N. K. 2004. "The Seven Deadly Sins of Library Technology." *American Libraries* 35(8): 40–42. (Retrieved June 26, 2006, from Wilson Web database.)

McGrath, R. V. 2005. "Biblio Tech: Things You Need to Know." *Public Libraries* 44(3): 126. (Retrieved June 26, 2006, from Wilson Web database.)

Mclean, N., H. Sander, P. Albanese, B. F. Baker, D. Cohen, L. Dempsey, L., et al., eds. 2003. *OCLC E-learning Task Force*. Dublin, Ohio: OCLC Online Computer Library Center, Inc.

Mellon, C., and D. D. Kester. 2004. "Online Library Education Programs: Implications for Rural Students." *Journal of Education for Library and Information Science* 45(3): 210–220. (Retrieved June 26, 2006, from Wilson Web database.)

Middle States Commission on Higher Education. 2002. *Eligibility Requirements and Standards for Accreditation. Characteristics of Excellence in Higher Education*. Philadelphia, Pa.: Middle States Commission on Higher Education.

Miller, E. G. 2004. "Retirement Tsunami Looms over Distracted Director/Board Teams." *Public Libraries* 43(2): 77–78. (Retrieved June 26, 2006, from Wilson Web database.)

Munroe, M. H. 2006). "To Filter or Not to Filter, That Is the Question." *Illinois Library Association Reporter* 24(1): 38–39. (Retrieved August 17, 2006, from Wilson Web database.)

National Center for Education Statistics. 2002. "Distance Education Courses for Public Elementary and Secondary School Students: 2002. Fast Response Survey System." http://www.nces.ed.gov (Retrieved July 3, 2006.)

Nicholson, S. 2005. "A Framework for Technology Selection in a Web-based Distance Education Environment. Supporting Community Building through Richer Interaction Opportunities." *Journal of Education for Library and Information Science* 46(3): 217–233. (Retrieved June 30, 2006, from Wilson Web database.)

Noremore, L. 2003. "Studying Special Collections and the Web: An Analysis of Practice." *First Monday (Online)* 8(10): 1. (Retrieved June 26, 2006, from Wilson Web database.)

Northrup, L., E. Cherry, and D. Darby. 2004. "Using Server-Side Include Commands for Subject Web-Page Management: An Alternative to Database-Driven Technologies for the Smaller Academic Library." *Information Technology and Libraries* 23(4): 192–197. (Retrieved June 26, 2006, from Wilson Web database.)

Ojala, M. 2005. "Open Access: Open Sesame or Opening Pandora's Box?" *EContent* 28(6): 30–32, 34–35. (Retrieved June 26, 2006, from Wilson Web database.)

Olivas, A., and H. McCurley. 2006. "Working across Divisional Lines: How One Large University Library Cross-Trains and Works as a Whole." *Library Administration & Management* 20(2): 81–84. (Retrieved August 17, 2006, from Wilson Web database.)

Online Computer Library Center E-learning Task Force. 2007. *E-learning and Libraries: A New White Paper.* Dublin, OH: OCLC.

Online Computer Library Center. 2005. Membership Report. *Perceptions of Libraries and Information Resources.* Dublin, OH: OCLC.

Osa, Justina O. 2003. "The Dual Nature of Staffing in the Education Library: Management Issues and Solutions." *Education Libraries* 26(2): 19–29. (Retrieved June 26, 2006, from Wilson Web database.)

Osborne, D., and P. Hutchinson. 2004. *The Price of Government: Getting the Results We Need in an Age of Permanent Fiscal Crisis.* New York: Basic Books.

Osif, B. A. 2003. "Generations in the Workplace." *Library Administration & Management* 17(4): 200–204. (Retrieved February 2, 2006, from Wilson Web database.)

Pace, A. K. 2004. "Technically Speaking." *American Libraries* 35(7): 68–70. (Retrieved June 26, 2006, from Wilson Web database.)

Patton, C. 2006. "Faster, Cheaper, Better." *District Administration: The Magazine for K-12 Education Leaders*, 6. http://www.districtadministration.com. (Retrieved July 3, 2006.)

Peterson, E. 2005. "Evaluation of Digital Libraries Using Snowball Sampling." *First Monday (Online)* 10(5): 1. (Retrieved June 26, 2006, from Wilson Web database.)

Pierce, J. B. 2006. "Where Reference Librarians Do Rove." *American Libraries* 37(2): 39. (Retrieved August 17, 2006, from Wilson Web database.)

Pival, P. R., and K. Johnson. 2004. "Tri-Institutional Library Support: A Lesson in Forced Collaboration." *Journal of Library Administration* 41(3/4): 345–354. (Retrieved June 26, 2006, from Wilson Web database.)

Prokopiadou, G., C. Papatheodorous, and D. Moshopoulos. 2004. "Integrating Knowledge Management Tools for Government Information." *Government Information Quarterly* 21(2): 170–198. (Retrieved June 26, 2006, from Wilson Web database.)

Pye, M. and S. Yates. 2003. "Putting the User First in Virtual Information Services." *Public Libraries* 42(6): 383–387. (Retrieved June 26, 2006, from Wilson Web database.)

Rieger, O. Y., A. K. Horrie, and I. Revels. 2004. "Linking Course Web Sites to Library Collections and Services." *Journal of Academic Librarianship* 30(3): 205–211. (Retrieved June 26, 2006, from Wilson Web database.)

Roberts, G. 2005. "Small Libraries, Big Technology." *Computers in Libraries* 25(3): 24–26. (Retrieved June 26, 2006, from Wilson Web database.)

Rowlands, J. 2003. "A Field Guide to E-Learning. *Multimedia Information and Technology* 29(4): 125–126. (Retrieved June 26, 2006, from Wilson Web database.)

Rubin, R. J. 2006. *Demonstrating Results: Using Outcome Measurement in Your Library*. Chicago: American Library Association.

Sadeh, T., and M. Ellingsen. 2005. "Electronic Resource Management Symptoms: The Need and the Realization." *New Library World* 106: 1212–1213, 208–218. (Retrieved June 26, 2006, from Wilson Web database.)

Sarling, J. 2003. SWIFT: How Collaboration Using the Internet Helped Build This State-wide Resource-Sharing Program. *Colorado Libraries* 29 (1): 37–38 (Retrieved June 26, 2006, from Wilson Web database).

Schmidt, K. D., P. Sennyey, and T. V. Carstens. 2005. "New Roles for a Changing Environment: Implications of Open Access for Libraries." *College & Research Libraries* 66(5): 407–416. (Retrieved June 26, 2006, from Wilson Web database.)

Schwartz, C. A. 2005. "Reassessing Prospects for the Open Access Movement." *College & Research Libraries* 66(6): 488–495. (Retrieved June 26, 2006, from Wilson Web database.)

Shank, J. D., and N. H. Dewald. 2003. "Establishing Our Presence in Courseware: Adding Library Services to the Virtual Classroom." *Information Technology and Libraries* 22(1): 38–43. (Retrieved June 26, 2006, from Wilson Web database.)

Shelton, C. 2003. "Best Practices in Cooperative Collection Development: A Report Prepared by The Center For Research Libraries Working Group on Best Practices in Cooperative Collection Development." *Collection Management* 28(3): 191–222. (Retrieved June 26, 2006, from Wilson Web database.)

Shreeves, S. L., T. G. Haning, and K. Hagedorn. 2005. "Current Developments and Future Trends for the OAI Protocol for Metadata Harvesting." *Library Trends* 53(4): 576–589. (Retrieved June 26, 2006, from Wilson Web database.)

Singer, P. G., Jeanne Goodrich, and L. Goldberg. 2004. "Your Library's Future." *Library Journal (1976)*, 129(17), 38–40. Retrieved June 26, 2006, from Wilson Web database.

Sittler, R. L. 2005. "Distance Education and Computer-Based Services: The Opportunities and Challenges for Small Academic Libraries." *Bookmobile and Outreach Services* 8(1): 23–35. (Retrieved June 26, 2006, from Wilson Web database.)

Smith, M. 2005. "Exploring Variety in Digital Collections and the Implications for Digital Preservation." *Library Trends* 54(1): 6–15. (Retrieved June 26, 2006, from Wilson Web database.)

Snyder, T. 2005. "Online Learning and Its Potential Effect on School Library Services and Methodology." *Colorado Libraries* 31(3): 10–12. (Retrieved June 26, 2006, from Wilson Web database.)

Spelman, A. 2004. "In Visible Light: Illuminating Partnerships across Libraries to Facilitate Lifelong Learning for Young People." *Australasian Public Libraries and Information Services* 17(1): 4–26. (Retrieved June 26, 2006, from Wilson Web database.)

Stemper, J., and S. Barribeau. 2006. "Perpetual Access to Electronic Journals: A Survey of One Academic Research Library's Licenses." *Library Resources & Technical Services* 50(2): 91–109. (Retrieved August 17, 2006, from Wilson Web database.)

Swanson, C. 2006. "Tracking U.S. Trends." *Technology Counts '06: The Information Edge* 25(35): 50–53. http://www.edweek.org. (Retrieved July 3, 2006.)

Sweeny, R. T. 2005. "Reinventing Library Buildings and Services for the Millennial Generation." *Library Administration & Management* 19(4): 165–175. (Retrieved February 17, 2006, from Wilson Web database.)

Tennant, R. 2004. "Five Easy Pieces." *Library Journal (1976)* 129(19): 25. (Retrieved June 26, 2006, from Wilson Web database.)

Tennant, R. 2005. "What I Wish I Had Known." *Library Journal (1976)*, 130(19): 30. (Retrieved June 26, 2006, from Wilson Web database.)

Thiessen, J. 2006. "Too Busy for Advocacy? How College Libraries Can Break the Non-Advocacy Cycle." *Feliciter* 52(3): 99–101. (Retrieved August 17, 2006, from Wilson Web database.)

Van Fleet, C., and D. P. Wallace. 2003. "Virtual Libraries—Real Threats: Technostress and Virtual Reference." *Reference & User Services Quarterly* 42(3): 188–191. (Retrieved June 26, 2006, from Wilson Web database.)

Walters, D. L. 2006. "An Unintended Service." *Public Libraries* 45(2): 6, 27. (Retrieved August 17, 2006, from Wilson Web database.)

Walters, W. H. 2004. "Criteria for Replacing Print Journals with Online Journal Resources: The Importance of Sustainable Access Notes on Operations." *Library Resources & Technical Services* 48(4): 300–304. (Retrieved June 26, 2006, from Wilson Web database.)

Wang, C. 2003. "Internet Censorship in the United States: Stumbling Blocks to the Information Age." *IFLA Journal* 29(3): 213–221. (Retrieved June 26, 2006, from Wilson Web database.)

Warnken, P. 2004. "New Technologies and Constant Change: Managing the Process." *The Journal of Academic Librarianship* 30(4): 322–327. (Retrieved August 17, 2006, from Wilson Web database.)

Webster, P. 2006. "Bit by Bit." *Library Journal (1976)*, Net Connect 16–17. (Retrieved August 17, 2006, from Wilson Web database.)

Wei, X. 2003. "Digital Library Services: Perceptions and Expectations of User Communities and Librarians in a New Zealand Academic Library." *Australian Academic & Research Libraries* 34(1): 56–70. (Retrieved June 26, 2006, from Wilson Web database.)

Westbrook, L. 2006. "Virtual Reference Training: The Second Generation." *College & Research Libraries* 67(3): 249–259. (Retrieved August 17, 2006, from Wilson Web database.)

Wilhite M. Dr. 2006. "Intellectual Freedom Issues in Public Libraries." *Louisiana Libraries* 68(3): 22–25. (Retrieved August 17, 2006, from Wilson Web database.)

Williams, L. 2006. "Making "E" Visible." *Library Journal (1976)* 131(11): 40–43. (Retrieved August 17, 2006, from Wilson Web database.)

Wilson, W. R. 2005. "Automation of Library Processes/Aims and Objectives." *Illinois Library Association Reporter* 23(1): 10–11. (Retrieved August 17, 2006, from Wilson Web database.)

Wilson, W. 2003. "Building and Managing a Digital Collection in a Small Library {computer file}." *North Carolina Libraries (Online)* 61(3): 88–97. (Retrieved June 26, 2006, from Wilson Web database.)

Xia, W. March, 2003. "Digital Library Services: Perceptions and Expectations of User Communities and Librarians in a New Zealand Academic Library." *Australian Academic and Research Libraries*. 34 (1), 56–70.

Yiotis, K. 2005. "The Open Access Initiative: A New Paradigm for Scholarly Communications." *Information Technology and Libraries* 24(4): 157–162. (Retrieved June 26, 2006, from Wilson Web database.)

INDEX

INDEX

ABOUT THE EDITORS AND CONTRIBUTORS

RACHEL APPLEGATE teaches at Indiana University's School of Library and Information Science. She received her MLS from the University of North Carolina and a doctorate from the University of Wisconsin. She spent 18 years at the College of St. Scholastica in Minnesota as reference librarian, library director, and college administrator.

LESLEY BOON is currently director of Information Services at Emanuel School, a Jewish day school in Sydney, Australia, catering for students from preschool to year 12. Previously she was teacher-librarian at Trinity Grammar School, a large private boy's school. She has taught in lots of places and scenarios, one of the most interesting was an all aboriginal school on the New South Wales/ Queensland border. She has a master of arts (Information Science) from the University of Technology Sydney (UTS). Her interests are information literacy, literature for boys, library design and gifted students. She is the author of "Designing Library Space for Children and Adolescents" in *Planning the Modern Public Library Building* edited by McCabe and Kennedy (Libraries Unlimited, 2003). In 2006, she presented a paper at the International Association of School Librarianship, IASL, conference in Lisbon, Portugal on "Engaging readers through choice: Encouraging a life long love of reading." She is currently studying for her Certificate of Gifted Education COGE, through the University of NSW.

FRANK J. BOVE is assistant professor of bibliography and electronic resources librarian at The University of Akron University Libraries. He received his MLIS from Kent State University. His research focuses on E-Resource Access and Management Services (ERAMS) and information ethics.

ASHLEY B. CLEVENGER lives in Boston, MA where she is working toward an MA in Organizational and Corporate Communication at Emerson College. She is currently a Marketing Coordinator for Addison-Wesley, an imprint of Pearson Arts and Sciences.

ANNE-MARIE DEITERING is the undergraduate services librarian at Oregon State University (OSU) Libraries. She earned her MLS. from Emporia State University in 2003. She sits on OSU's Student Success and University Assessment Councils. Deitering speaks and writes frequently about the intersections between student engagement, information literacy, and the participatory Web.

JURIS DILEVKO is an associate professor at the Faculty of Information Studies, University of Toronto. He has published in, among others, *College and Research Libraries*, *Journal of Academic Librarianship*, *Library & Information Science Research*, *Library Collections, Acquisitions and Technical Services*, and *Library Quarterly*.

BRIAN A. HICKAM is an assistant professor with the University of Toledo's Carlson Library. He is the librarian for the College of Health Science and Human Service and the University Libraries' liaison to University of Toledo Athletics. His research interests include investigations into the ways that learning styles and multimedia affect information literacy.

MARK HORAN is associate professor, Coordinator of College Libraries, at The University of Toledo Libraries, Toledo, Ohio.

BRUCE JEPPESEN is the assistant director of the Cleveland State University Library Systems & Instructional Media Services.

CAROLYN JONES holds a masters degree from the University of South Australia, Magill. She is currently employed as a research assistant at that institution and also works voluntarily at her local library.

RASHELLE KARP is associate academic vice president, Clarion University of Pennsylvania. Dr. Karp has worked as an academic library dean, a children's librarian, and a special librarian, in addition to teaching at Clarion University in the department of library science. Dr. Karp has published extensively in the fields of collection development, special librarianship, public librarianship, student retention, and disabilities services.

JAMES R. KENNEDY is university librarian at Buena Vista University (Storm Lake, Iowa). He has both academic and public library experience. Active in the Library Administration and Management Association, he has served as chairperson or member of several American Library Association Building and Equipment Section committees. With his wife, Mary-Elinor, he is an active library consultant and contributor to professional publications.

LA LORIA KONATA is the political science and policy studies liaison librarian at Georgia State University Library. She holds a MLS degree from Clark Atlanta University and a masters of public administration degree from Georgia State University.

SUHASINI L. KUMAR is associate professor, coordinator of information and research services, University Libraries, The University of Toledo, Toledo, Ohio.

BETHANY LATHAM is an assistant professor and the electronic resources/documents librarian at Jacksonville State University's Houston Cole Library in Jacksonville, Alabama.

DAVID LEWIS holds a bachelor's degree in history form Carleton College, a MLS from Columbia, and two certificates of advanced study in librarianship, one from Columbia University and one from the University of Chicago. He has worked as a librarian at SUNY Farmingdale, Hamilton College, Franklin and Marshall College, Columbia University, University of Connecticut. He came to Indiana University Purdue University Indianapolis in 1993 as the head of public services and has been the dean of the university library since 2000. He has written on reference services, management of libraries, and scholarly communication.

GEORGE LUPONE is associate director at Cleveland State University Library. He has extensive experience in the management and renovation of library facilities. Another area of focus has been assessment of library services, facilities, and instruction. He has served as a consultant in both areas.

SUSANNE MARKGREN is the systems/electronic resources librarian at Purchase College, SUNY. She has worked in libraries for more than 11 years, in many different roles. She earned her MLIS from the University of Texas at Austin in 1999. She co-writes a career column for *Info Career Trends*, reviews resources for both *CHOICE* and *Library Journal*, and has published articles in *Library Administration & Management*, *College & Research Libraries News*, and *Medical Reference Services Quarterly*.

GERARD B. McCABE, retired director of libraries at Clarion University of Pennsylvania, is a principal of MSB Consultants specializing in library buildings. He is author of *Planning for a New Generation of Public Library Buildings* (Greenwood 2000) and co-editor of *Planning the Modern Public Library Building* (Libraries Unlimited 2003).

JOHN NAPP is assistant professor and engineering librarian, University Libraries, The University of Toledo, Ohio.

SUSAN NAYLOR is a graduate student in the library science master's degree program at Clarion University of Pennsylvania. She has a masters of education, with a specialization in school libraries from Mansfield University of Pennsylvania, and is former librarian for the New York State Office Fire Prevention and Control Training Academy.

ERIC E. PALO is library director at Renton Technical College, Renton, Washington, the site of half of all their library workshops for ESL students. He has also held supervisory positions in academic libraries in Kansas and North Carolina.

JOHN C. PHILLIPS is associate professor and map librarian at the University of Toledo's Carlson Library. He is library liaison to the department of sociology and anthropology and the department of geography and planning. His research interests include the digitization of maps in libraries for access and preservation, the history of cartography, and social demography.

JODI POE is an assistant professor and the electronic resources manager/distance education librarian at Jacksonville State University's Houston Cole Library in Jacksonville, Alabama.

LAUREN PRESSLEY is Instructional Design Librarian at Wake Forest University. She co-teaches a one-credit hour information literacy course each semester. She is received her MLIS degree at the University of North Carolina-Greensboro where her work in library instruction and media literacy laid the foundation for her chapter.

MICHAEL D. RUSK is dean of Learning Resources Center and college librarian, Tulsa Community College. A former member of the Editorial Board for *Community & Junior College Libraries*, he has written a number of articles for it and other journals. Most recently, he is the author of "Organizational Structure of Library/ Learning Resource Centers" in *It's All about Student Learning, Managing Community and Other College Libraries in the 21st Century* (Libraries Unlimited, 2006).

JAMIE SEEHOLZER earned her MLIS from Kent State University in 2006. She served for one year as an instruction librarian at Kent State University in Ohio.

MARILYN STEMPECK is assistant professor/database management librarian at Clarion University of Pennsylvania. Ms. Stempeck holds a MEd and MSLS from Clarion University and a BS in library education from Mansfield University of Pennsylvania.

HENRY STEWART has been dean, University Libraries, Troy University, Troy, AL since 1996. He has served previously as director, William Allen White Library, Emporia State University, Emporia, KS, associate dean, Old Dominion University Library, Norfolk, VA, and assistant professor, Graduate Library School, University of Alabama. He has served in various capacities on committees for ALA, KLA, VLA and ALLA. He has published in the area of library management.

BERNADETTE ROBERTS STORCK is a principal of MSB Consultants specializing in library buildings. She serves as parliamentarian for the Florida Library Association. Before retirement, she was library administrator for the Pinellas Public Library Cooperative, and previously, manager, Community Resource Centers (branch libraries) for Tampa Hillsborough Public Library.

KATINA STRAUCH is the head librarian, Collection Development at the College of Charleston (SC). She received her bachelor's degree in economics and her MLS from the University of North Carolina-Chapel Hill. Strauch is the founder of the annual Charleston Conference (1980), Against the Grain (1989), The Charleston Report (1996), and The Charleston Advisor (1999). In 2005, she was appointed to the Institute of Museum and Library Services Board (IMLS).

GLENDA A. THORNTON is the Cleveland State University library director and has more than 30 years of professional library service. Before coming to Cleveland State University, Dr. Thornton served as interim dean/director at Auraria Library, University of Colorado at Denver, where she was previously associate director for library services. She has also held professional positions in Texas and Arkansas. She serves on the Library Advisory Council for OhioLINK, is active in American Library Association and Association of College and Research Libraries. She received her doctorate from the University of North Texas and her MLS from the University of Oklahoma. She is the reviews editor for *Technical Service Quarterly* and has authored and co-authored a number of articles on improving library facilities and operations, technical services, and collection management topics that have been published in *Library Trends, American Libraries, Technical Services Quarterly, Serials Review, Reference Librarian*, and *Library Acquisitions: Practice and Theory*. Dr. Thornton has also been named in *Who's Who in America, Who's Who of American Women, International Who's Who of Professional and Business Women*, and is a former editor of *Collection Management*.

CAROL C. M. TORIS, is an associate professor in psychology at the College of Charleston, where she has taught courses in social psychology and the psychology of language, including associated research laboratories, since 1981. Her research interests focus on language use and nonverbal behavior, especially the functions of hand movements and gestures. She holds a doctoral degree from the University of Virginia.

LISA VARDAMAN is education reference librarian at Troy University, Alabama. Active in professional associations, she has presented papers on a wide range of topics at conferences. She is a doctoral candidate at the University of Alabama.

DELMUS E. WILLIAMS is a professor of bibliography at the University of Akron, with more than 30 years of experience serving in library leadership. He holds a PhD from the School of Library Science at the University of North Carolina and an MSLS from the University of Kentucky. He was also the director of libraries at the University of Alabama in Huntsville for six years and has taught for LIS programs at Wisconsin, Kent State, Alabama, and the University of North Carolina-Greensboro (UNCG). Williams has written and spoken on a wide array of topics relating to academic library management and change.

TIM ZOU is currently head of Access Services at the University of Arkansas Library. He graduated from the School of Library and Information Science, University of Illinois, Urbana-Champaign, with a master of science degree in 1993 and earned a PhD in theater history from University of Illinois, Urbana-Champaign in 1994.